# Tatsuki Fujimoto

I love *Joyurei*
(Don't Look Up)!

Tatsuki Fujimoto won Honorable Mention in the
November 2013 Shueisha Crown Newcomers' Awards for
his debut one-shot story *Love Is Blind*. His first series,
*Fire Punch*, ran for eight volumes. *Chainsaw Man* began
serialization in 2019 in *Weekly Shonen Jump*.

# 7

**SHONEN JUMP Manga Edition**

## Story & Art **TATSUKI FUJIMOTO**

Translation/AMANDA HALEY
Touch-Up Art & Lettering/JAMES GAUBATZ
Design/JULIAN [JR] ROBINSON
Editor/ALEXIS KIRSCH

CHAINSAW MAN © 2018 by Tatsuki Fujimoto
All rights reserved.
First published in Japan in 2018 by SHUEISHA Inc., Tokyo.
English translation rights arranged by SHUEISHA Inc.

The stories, characters and incidents mentioned in this publication are
entirely fictional.

Printed in the U.S.A.

Published by VIZ Media, LLC
P.O. Box 77010
San Francisco, CA 94107

10 9 8 7 6 5 4 3 2 1
First printing, October 2021

**PARENTAL ADVISORY**
CHAINSAW MAN is rated T+ for Older Teen
and is recommended for ages 16 and up.
This volume contains violence and gore.

# CHAINSAW MAN

# 7

**In a Dream**

## Tatsuki Fujimoto

# CHARACTERS

## Denji

A young man-slash-Chainsaw Devil who carries his partner Pochita inside him. He's always true to his desires. Likes Makima, the first person to ever treat him like a human being.

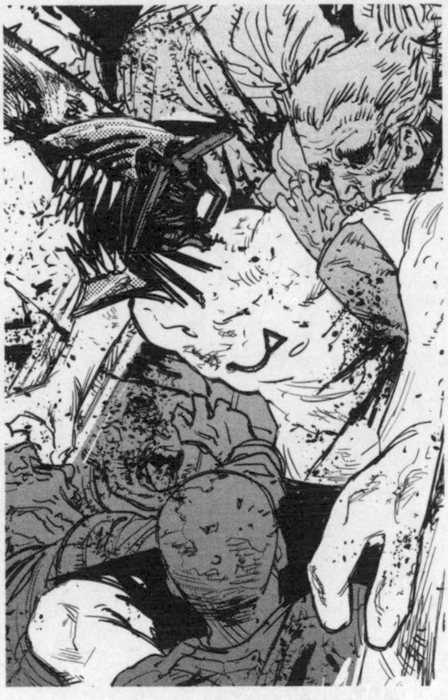

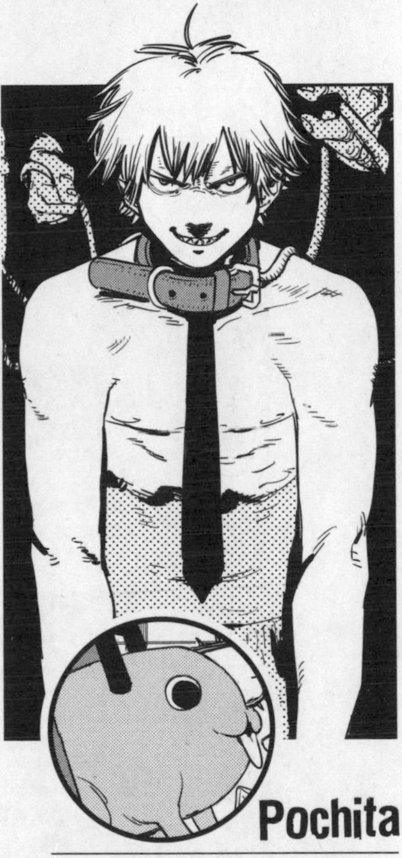

## Pochita

Chainsaw Devil. Gave up his heart to Denji, becoming part of his body.

## Makima

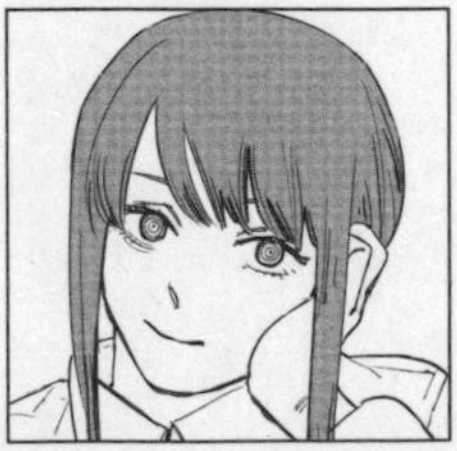

The mysterious woman in charge of Public Safety Devil Extermination Special Division 4. Can smell devil scents.

## Aki Hayakawa

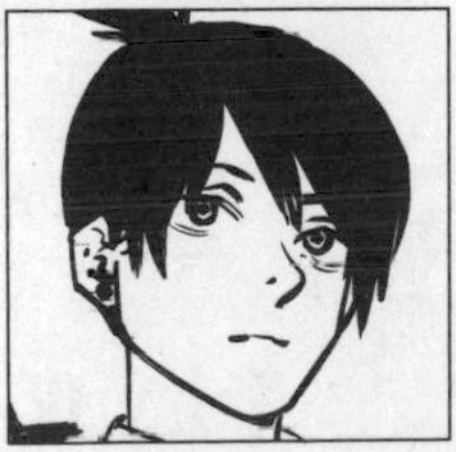

Makima's loyal subordinate and Denji's senior at Public Safety by three years. Devil Contracts: Future Devil, Curse Devil.

## Kobeni Higashiyama

A timid new recruit. Though mentally frail, her boss Himeno thinks she has talent. One of nine sisters.

## Power

Blood Devil Fiend. Egotistical and prone to going out of control. Her cat Meowy is her only friend.

## Beam (Shark Fiend)

Special Division 4 agent. Can swim through any surface such as walls and the ground. Can also take devil form for short periods of time.

## Angel Devil

Though not hostile to humans, anyone who touches this devil directly will have their life span siphoned off. Special Division 4 agent.

## Violence Fiend

Special Division 4 agent. Usually forced to wear a poison mask that restrains him, because he's just that strong.

## Kishibe

A man with extraordinary fighting ability who belongs to the Special Division. The strongest Devil Hunter. Denji and Power's teacher.

# STORY

Denji is a young man who hunts devils with his pet devil-dog Pochita. To pay off his debts, Denji is forced to live in extreme poverty and worked like a dog, only to be betrayed and killed on the job without ever getting to live a decent life. But Pochita, at the cost of the pooch's own life, brings Denji back—as Chainsaw Man! After Denji buzzes through all their attackers, he's taken in by the mysterious Makima, and begins a new life as a Public Safety Devil Hunter.

Denji is shaken by the mysterious Reze's unexpected plea for him to quit Public Safety and run far away with her. Too bad his new lady friend turns out to have been an ally of the Gun Devil all along—the Bomb Devil—and not only is she

after his heart in the literal sense, she's ready to bomb as many Devil Hunters as it takes to get to him!! As if that wasn't enough, the Typhoon Devil arrives to back Bomb up, turning the fight into a giant monster battle that embroils the entire town!!

Denji ends the brutal battle by dragging Reze down with him on a night ocean dive. Even after fighting her, Denji still likes her—and proposes they both run away together. She disappears without answering. Denji waits for Reze at their café, but before she can make it there, she dies at the hands of Makima and the Angel Devil...

# CONTENTS

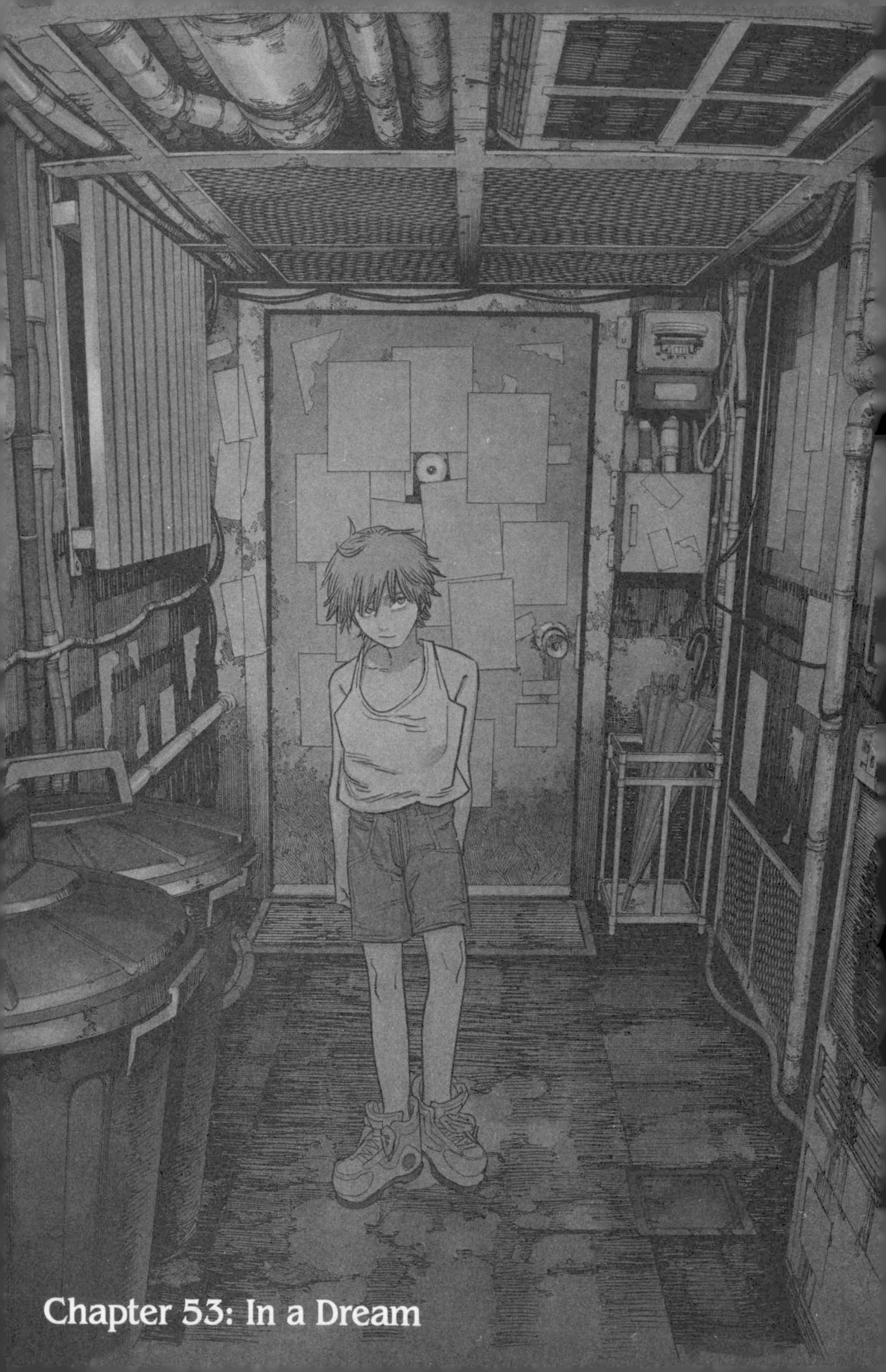
Chapter 53: In a Dream

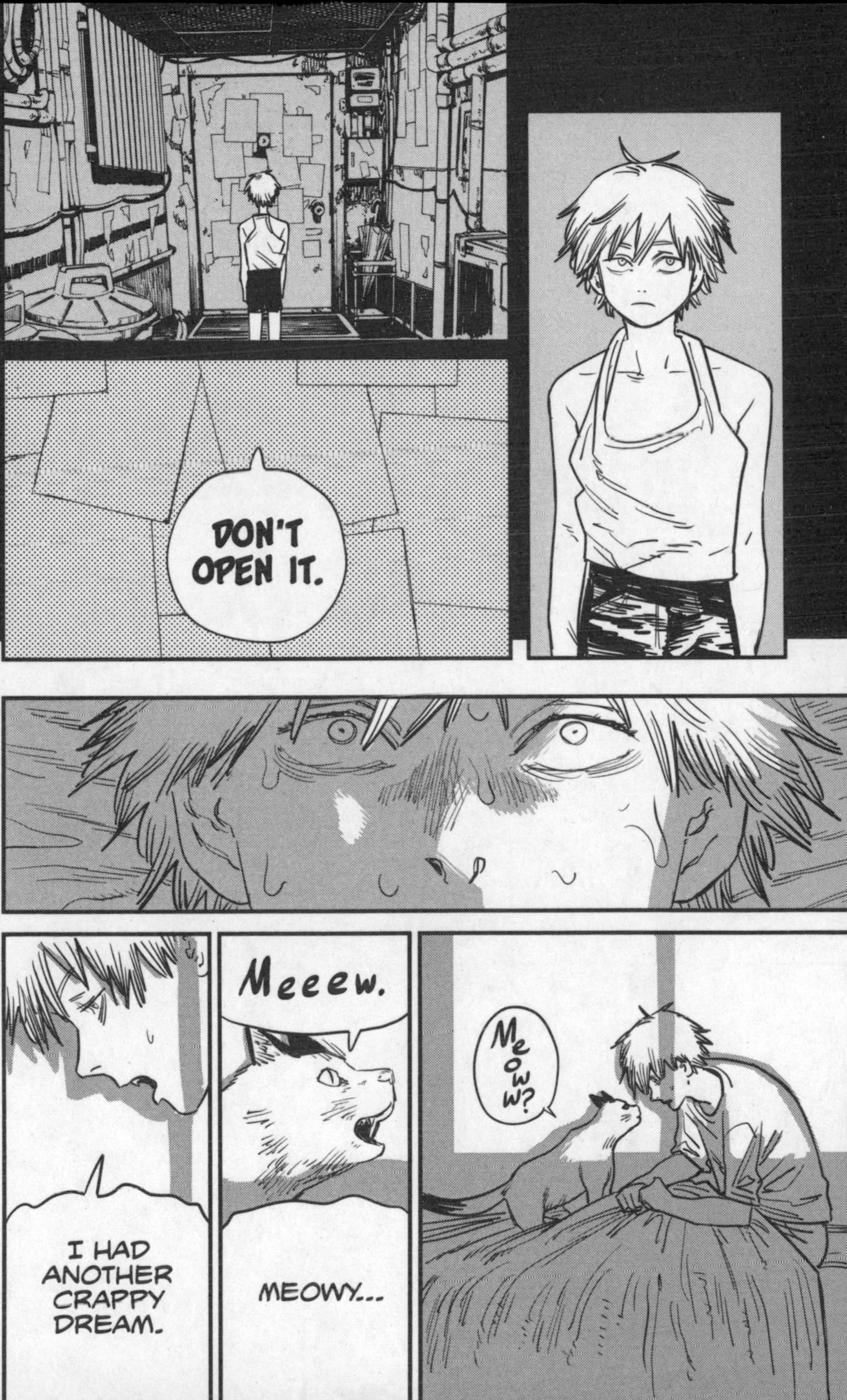
DON'T OPEN IT.
Meoww?
Meeew.
MEOWY...
I HAD ANOTHER CRAPPY DREAM.

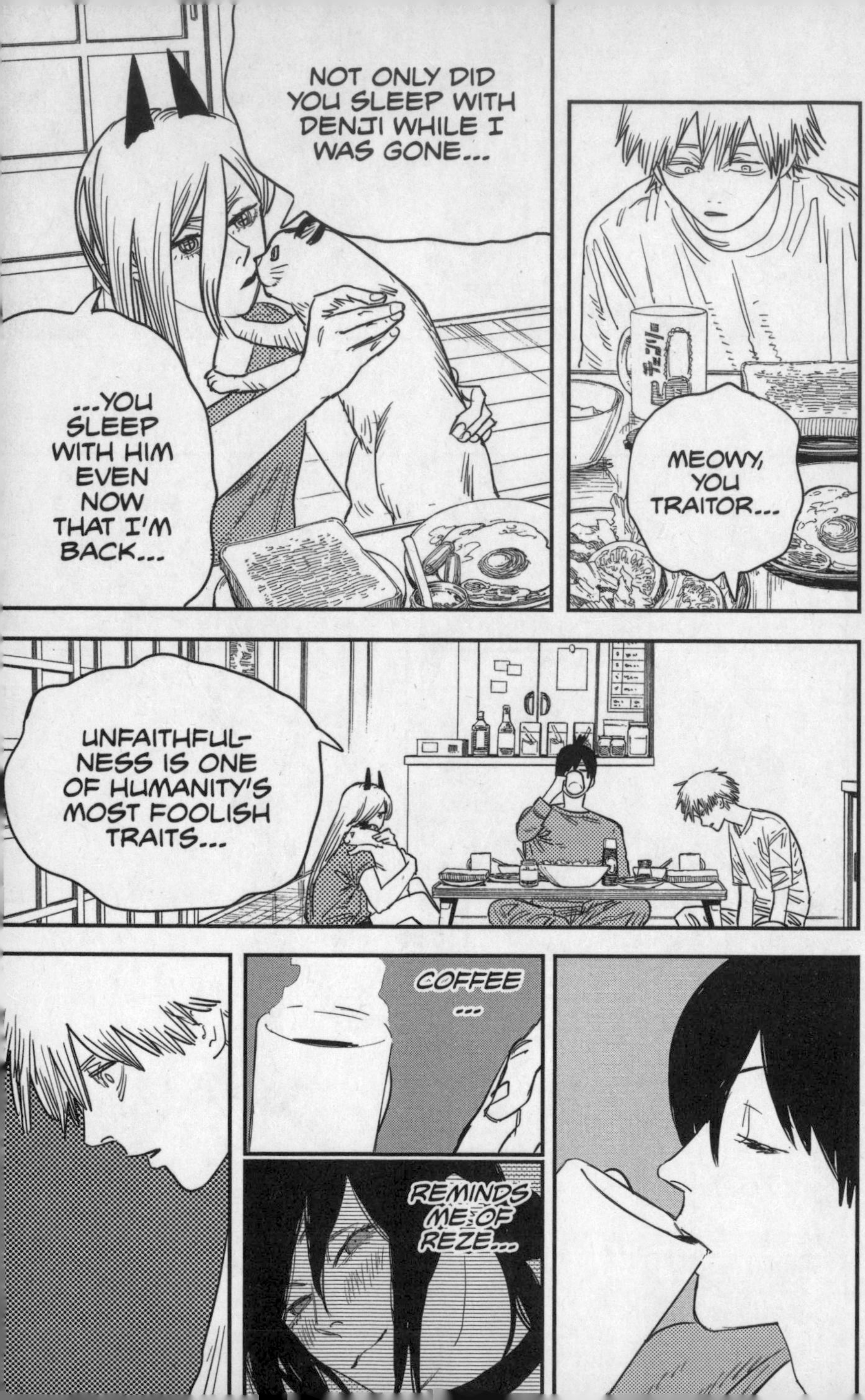
MEOWY, YOU TRAITOR...
NOT ONLY DID YOU SLEEP WITH DENJI WHILE I WAS GONE...
...YOU SLEEP WITH HIM EVEN NOW THAT I'M BACK...
UNFAITHFULNESS IS ONE OF HUMANITY'S MOST FOOLISH TRAITS...
COFFEE...
REMINDS ME OF REZE...

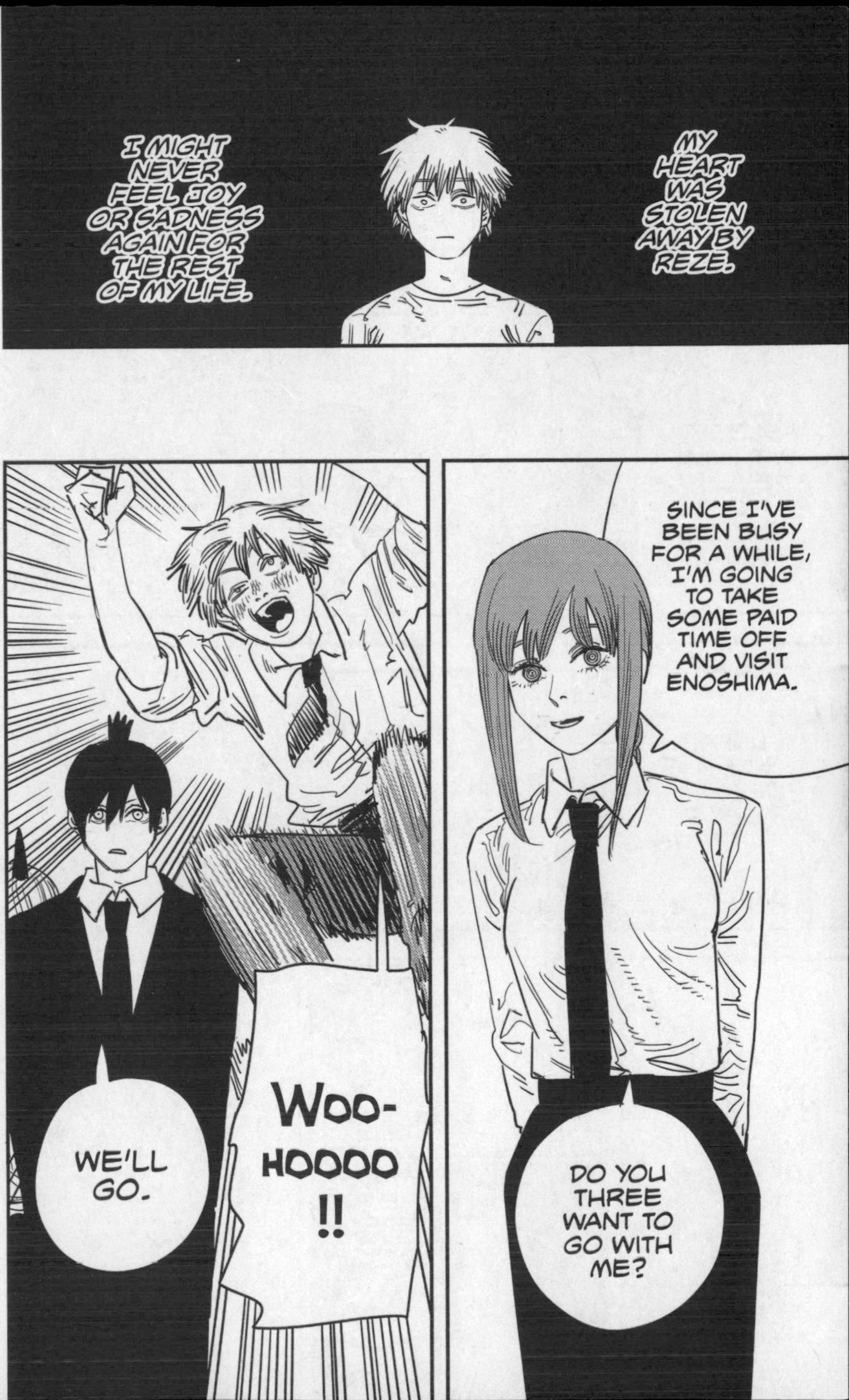
MY HEART WAS STOLEN AWAY BY REZE.
I MIGHT NEVER FEEL JOY OR SADNESS AGAIN FOR THE REST OF MY LIFE.
SINCE I'VE BEEN BUSY FOR A WHILE, I'M GOING TO TAKE SOME PAID TIME OFF AND VISIT ENOSHIMA.
DO YOU THREE WANT TO GO WITH ME?
WOO-HOOOOO!!
WE'LL GO.

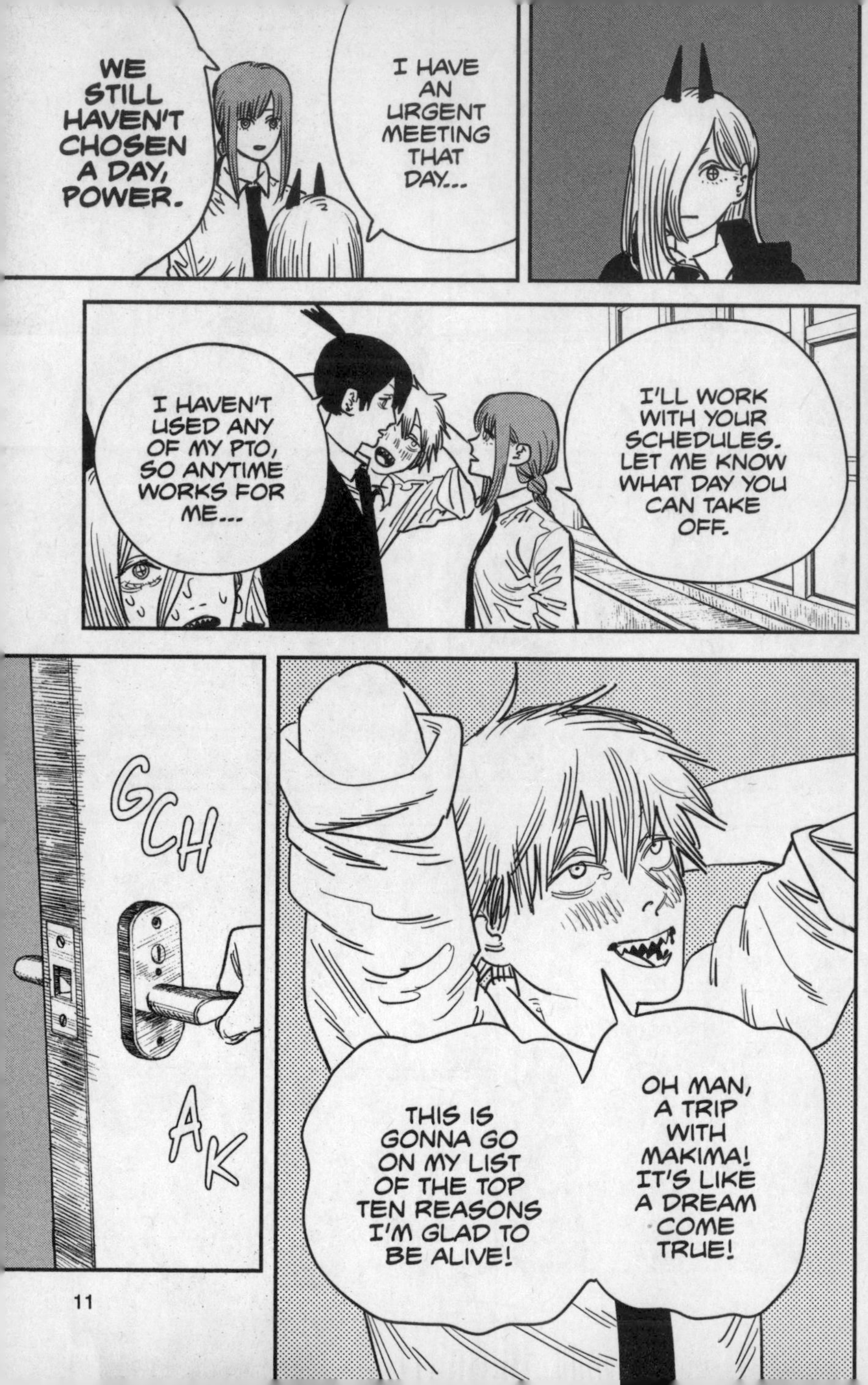
I HAVE AN URGENT MEETING THAT DAY...
WE STILL HAVEN'T CHOSEN A DAY, POWER.
I'LL WORK WITH YOUR SCHEDULES. LET ME KNOW WHAT DAY YOU CAN TAKE OFF.
I HAVEN'T USED ANY OF MY PTO, SO ANYTIME WORKS FOR ME...
OH MAN, A TRIP WITH MAKIMA! IT'S LIKE A DREAM COME TRUE!
THIS IS GONNA GO ON MY LIST OF THE TOP TEN REASONS I'M GLAD TO BE ALIVE!
GCH
AK

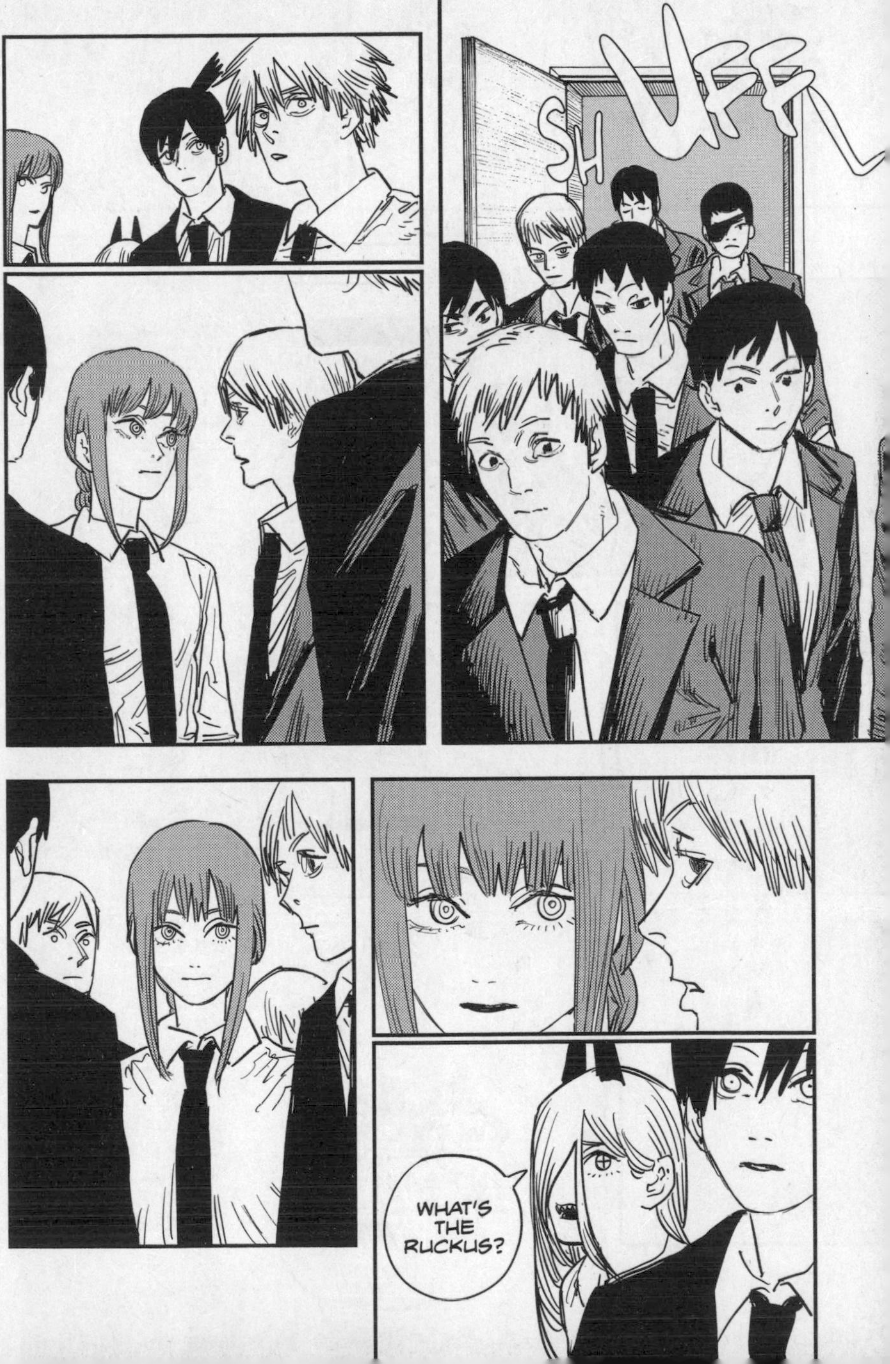
SHUFFL
WHAT'S THE RUCKUS?

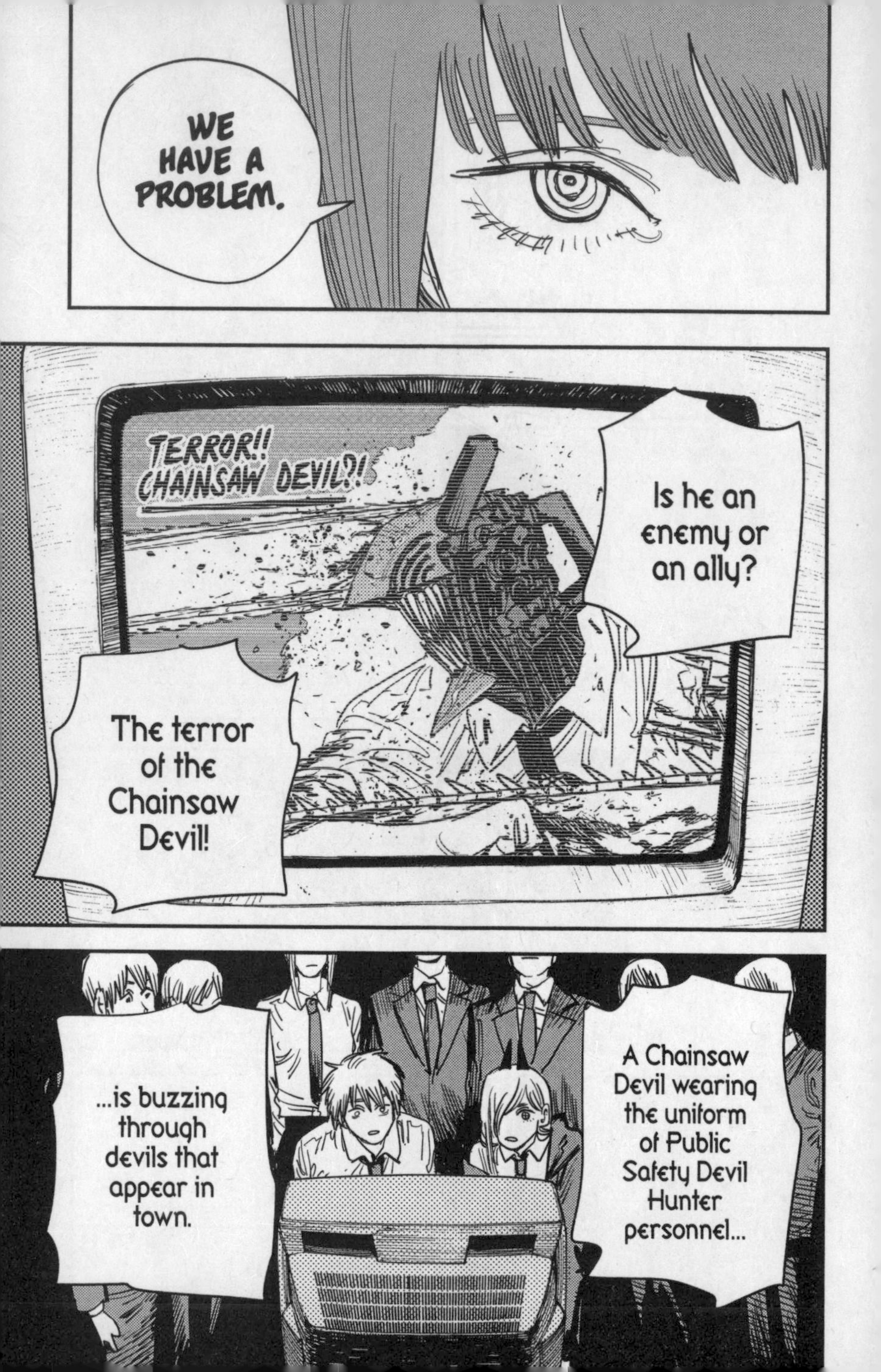
WE HAVE A PROBLEM.
TERROR!! CHAINSAW DEVIL?!
Is he an enemy or an ally?
The terror of the Chainsaw Devil!
A Chainsaw Devil wearing the uniform of Public Safety Devil Hunter personnel...
...is buzzing through devils that appear in town.

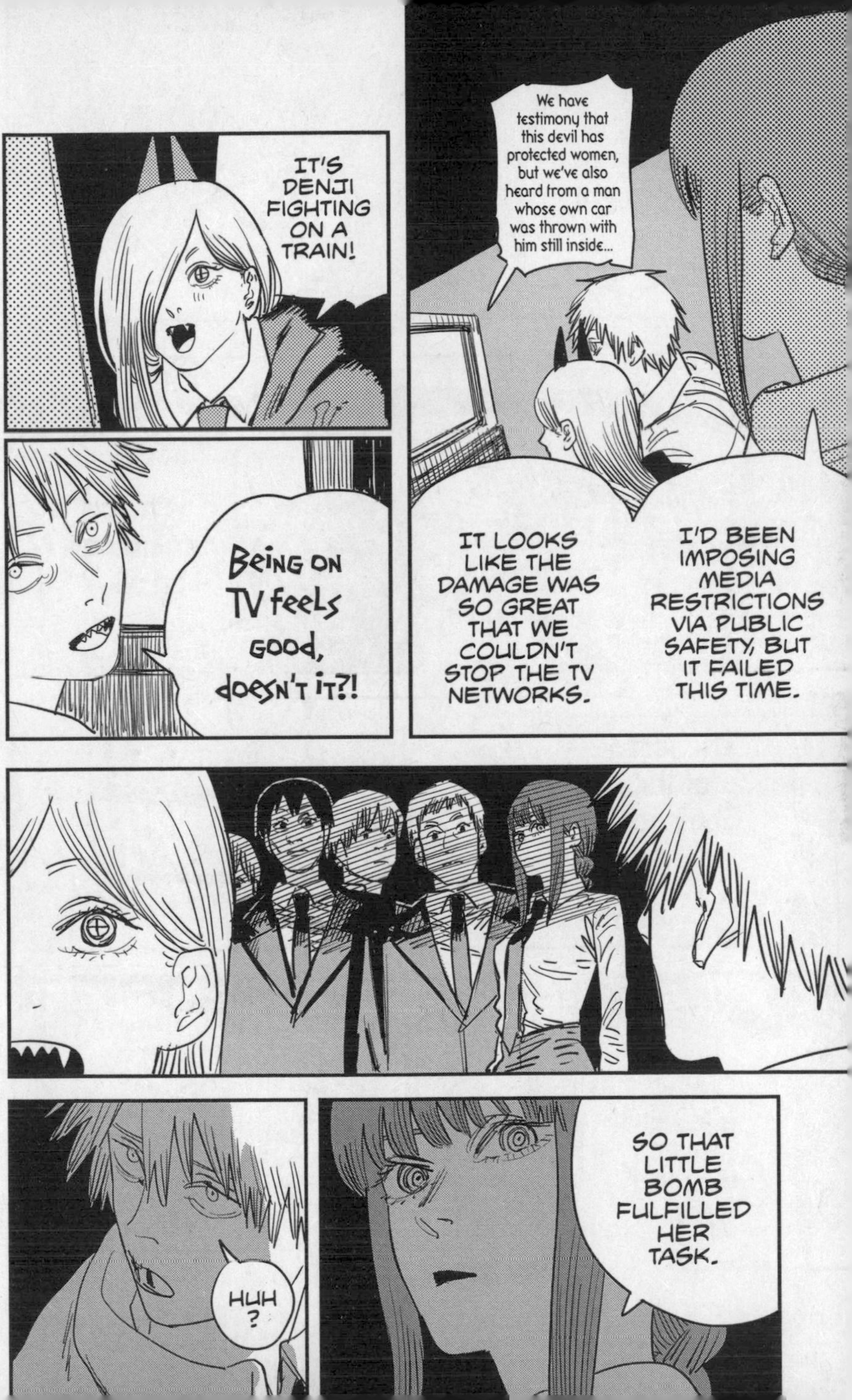

We have testimony that this devil has protected women, but we've also heard from a man whose own car was thrown with him still inside...
I'D BEEN IMPOSING MEDIA RESTRICTIONS VIA PUBLIC SAFETY, BUT IT FAILED THIS TIME.
IT LOOKS LIKE THE DAMAGE WAS SO GREAT THAT WE COULDN'T STOP THE TV NETWORKS.
IT'S DENJI FIGHTING ON A TRAIN!
Being on TV feels good, doesn't it?!
SO THAT LITTLE BOMB FULFILLED HER TASK.
HUH?

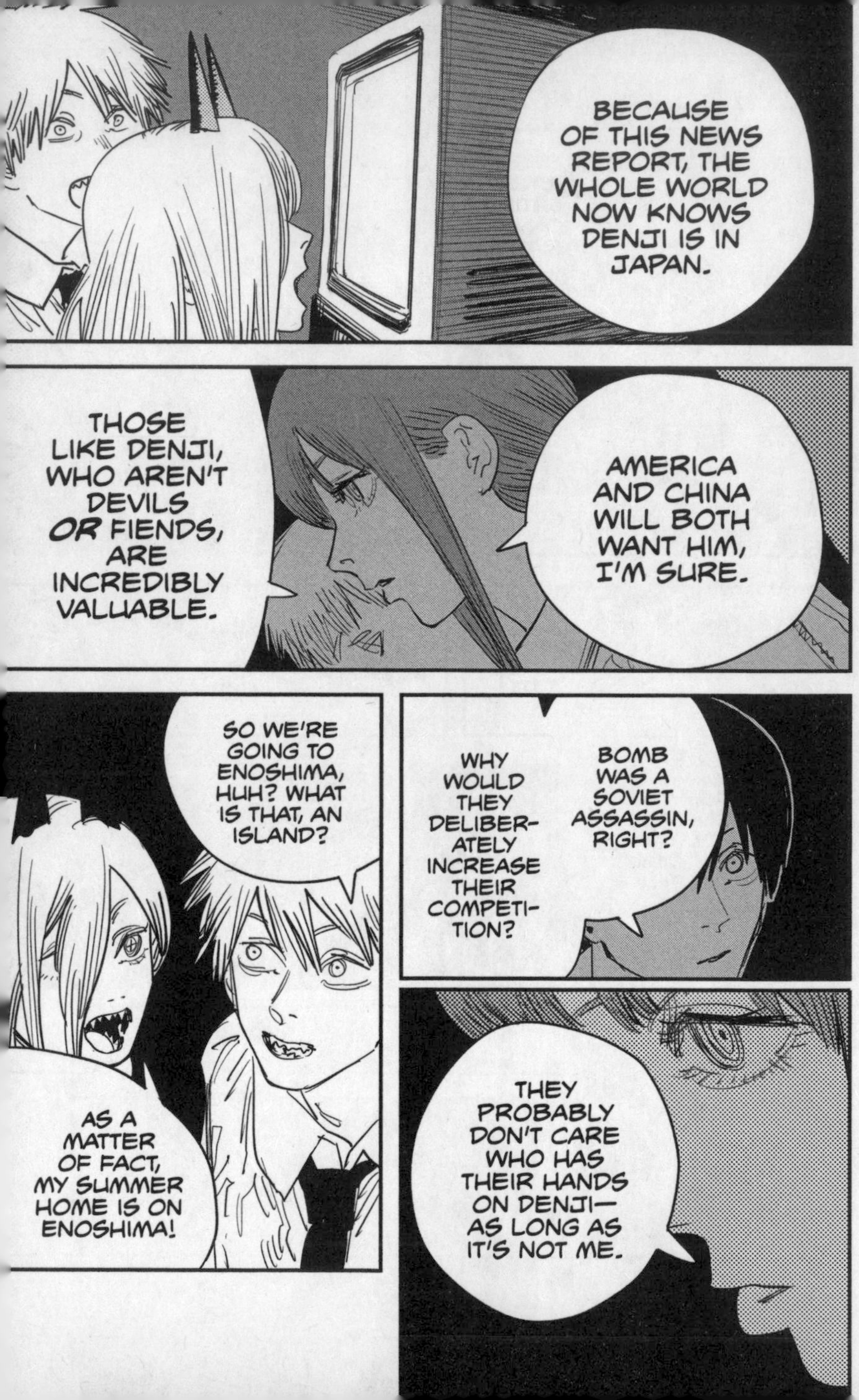
BECAUSE OF THIS NEWS REPORT, THE WHOLE WORLD NOW KNOWS DENJI IS IN JAPAN.
AMERICA AND CHINA WILL BOTH WANT HIM, I'M SURE.
THOSE LIKE DENJI, WHO AREN'T DEVILS *OR* FIENDS, ARE INCREDIBLY VALUABLE.
BOMB WAS A SOVIET ASSASSIN, RIGHT?
WHY WOULD THEY DELIBER-ATELY INCREASE THEIR COMPETI-TION?
THEY PROBABLY DON'T CARE WHO HAS THEIR HANDS ON DENJI— AS LONG AS IT'S NOT ME.
SO WE'RE GOING TO ENOSHIMA, HUH? WHAT IS THAT, AN ISLAND?
AS A MATTER OF FACT, MY SUMMER HOME IS ON ENOSHIMA!

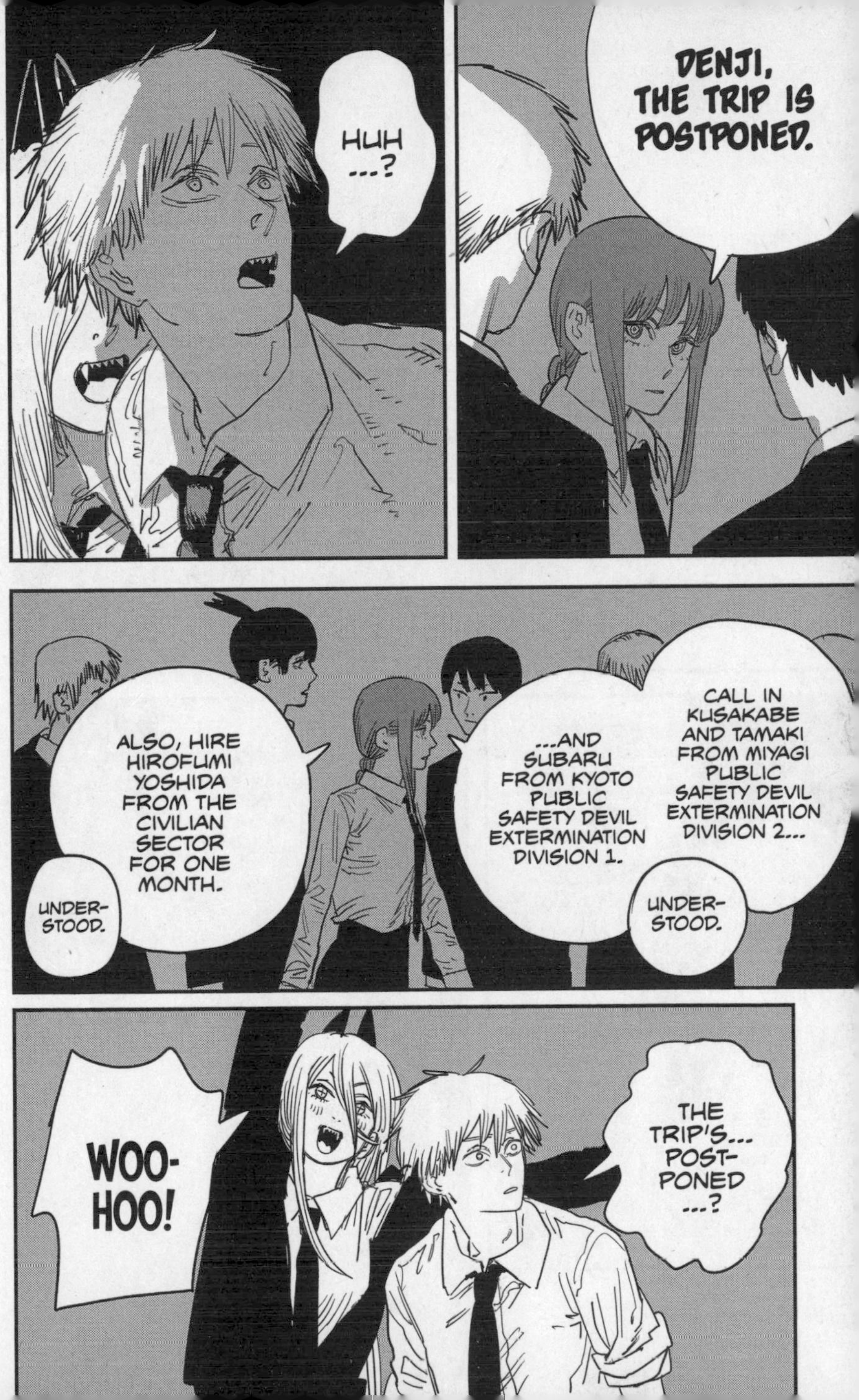
DENJI, THE TRIP IS POSTPONED.
HUH ...?
CALL IN KUSAKABE AND TAMAKI FROM MIYAGI PUBLIC SAFETY DEVIL EXTERMINATION DIVISION 2...
UNDERSTOOD.
...AND SUBARU FROM KYOTO PUBLIC SAFETY DEVIL EXTERMINATION DIVISION 1.
ALSO, HIRE HIROFUMI YOSHIDA FROM THE CIVILIAN SECTOR FOR ONE MONTH.
UNDERSTOOD.
THE TRIP'S... POSTPONED ...?
WOO-HOO!

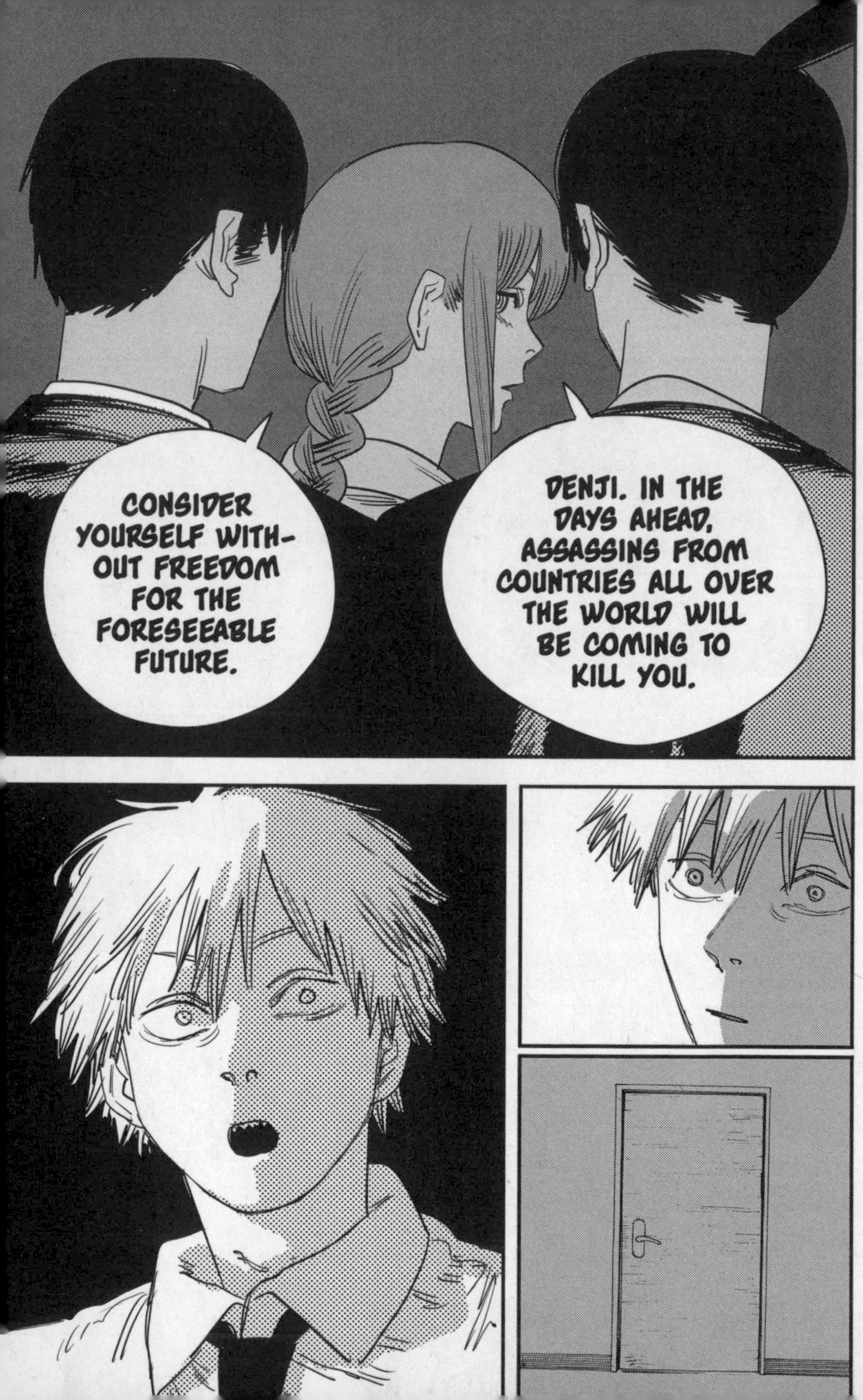
DENJI. IN THE DAYS AHEAD, ASSASSINS FROM COUNTRIES ALL OVER THE WORLD WILL BE COMING TO KILL YOU.
CONSIDER YOURSELF WITH-OUT FREEDOM FOR THE FORESEEABLE FUTURE.

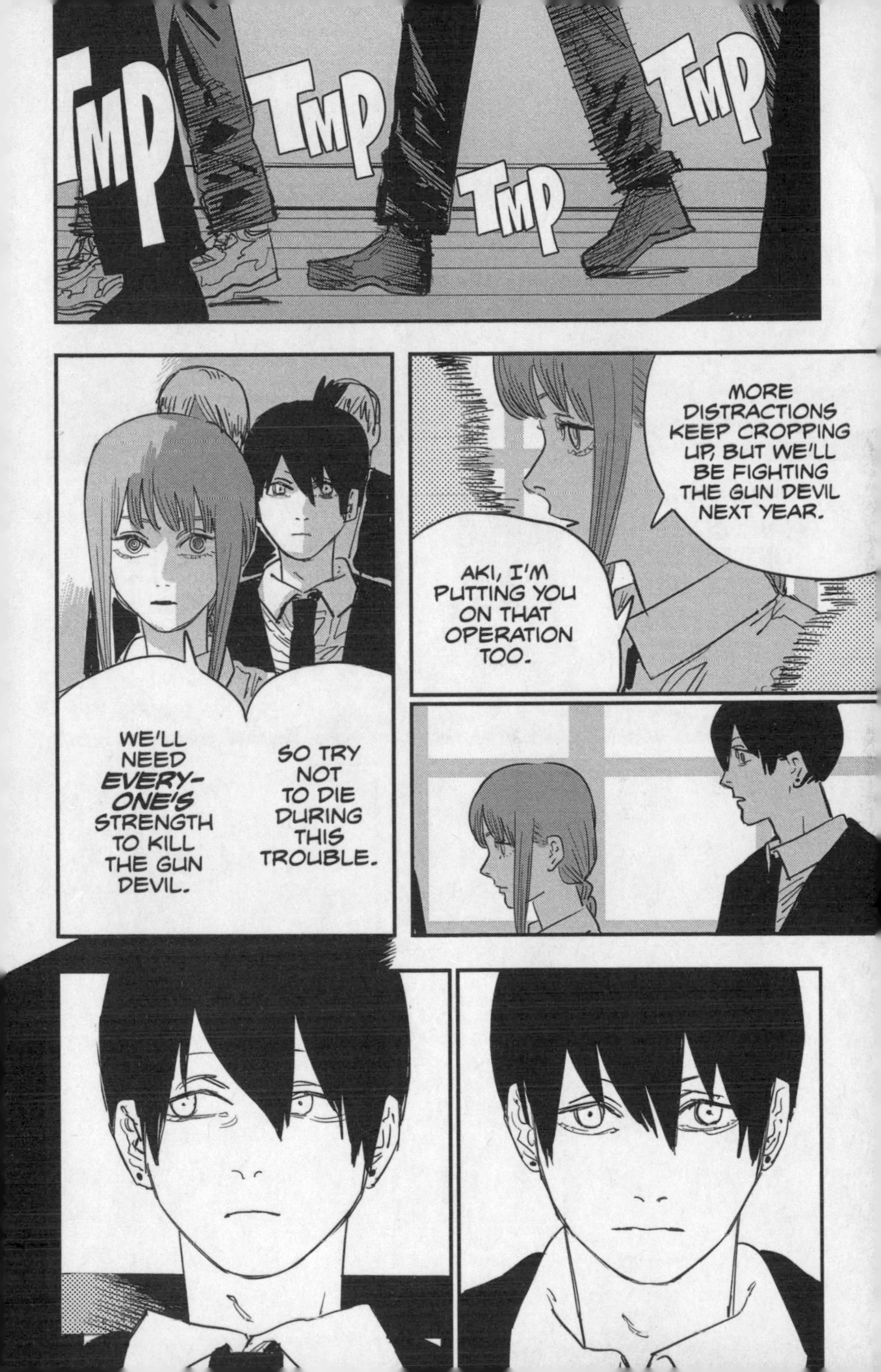
TMP
TMP
TMP
TMP
MORE DISTRACTIONS KEEP CROPPING UP, BUT WE'LL BE FIGHTING THE GUN DEVIL NEXT YEAR.
AKI, I'M PUTTING YOU ON THAT OPERATION TOO.
WE'LL NEED *EVERYONE'S* STRENGTH TO KILL THE GUN DEVIL.
SO TRY NOT TO DIE DURING THIS TROUBLE.

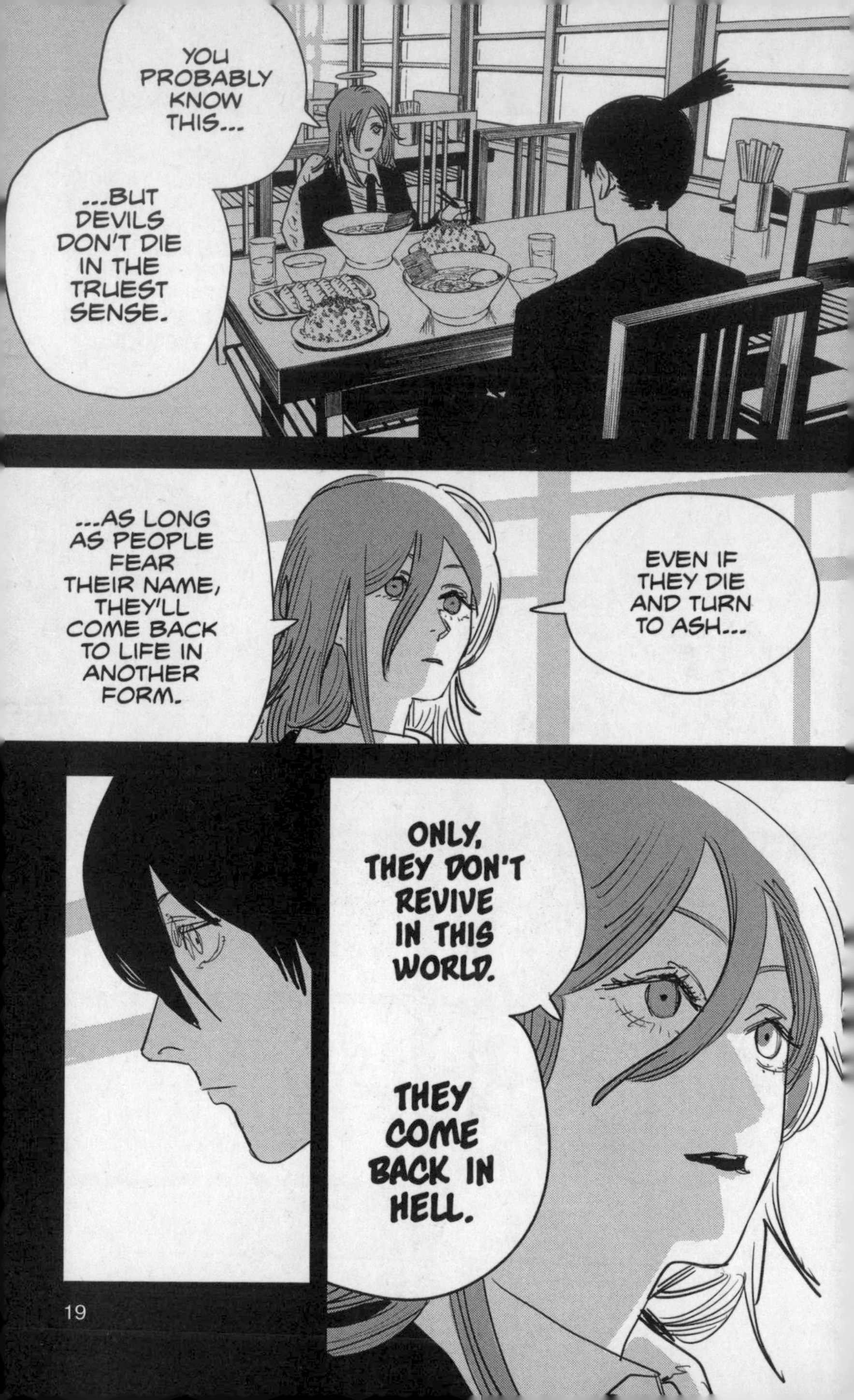
YOU PROBABLY KNOW THIS...
...BUT DEVILS DON'T DIE IN THE TRUEST SENSE.
EVEN IF THEY DIE AND TURN TO ASH...
...AS LONG AS PEOPLE FEAR THEIR NAME, THEY'LL COME BACK TO LIFE IN ANOTHER FORM.
ONLY, THEY DON'T REVIVE IN THIS WORLD.
THEY COME BACK IN HELL.

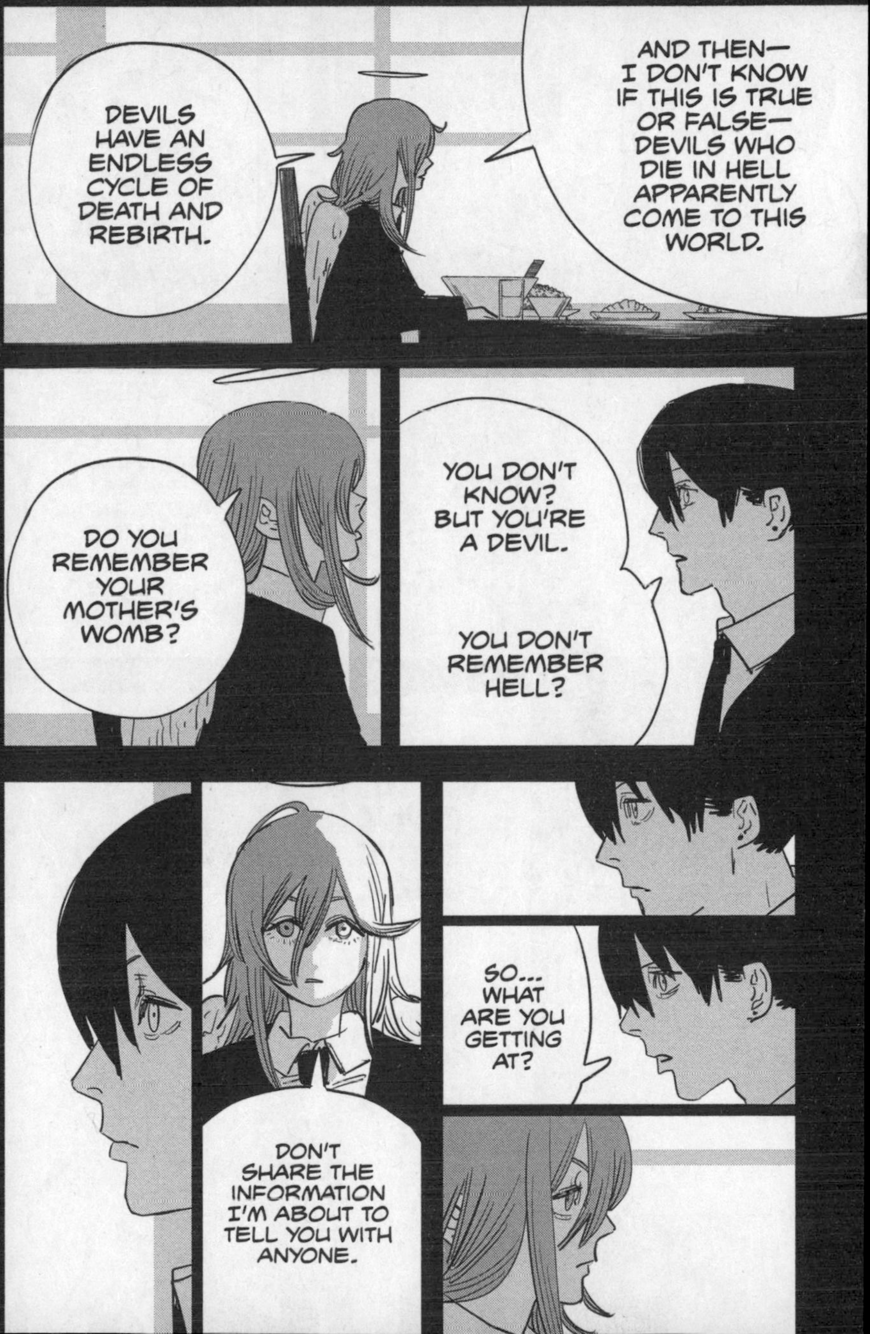
AND THEN— I DON'T KNOW IF THIS IS TRUE OR FALSE— DEVILS WHO DIE IN HELL APPARENTLY COME TO THIS WORLD.
DEVILS HAVE AN ENDLESS CYCLE OF DEATH AND REBIRTH.
YOU DON'T KNOW? BUT YOU'RE A DEVIL.
YOU DON'T REMEMBER HELL?
DO YOU REMEMBER YOUR MOTHER'S WOMB?
SO... WHAT ARE YOU GETTING AT?
DON'T SHARE THE INFORMATION I'M ABOUT TO TELL YOU WITH ANYONE.

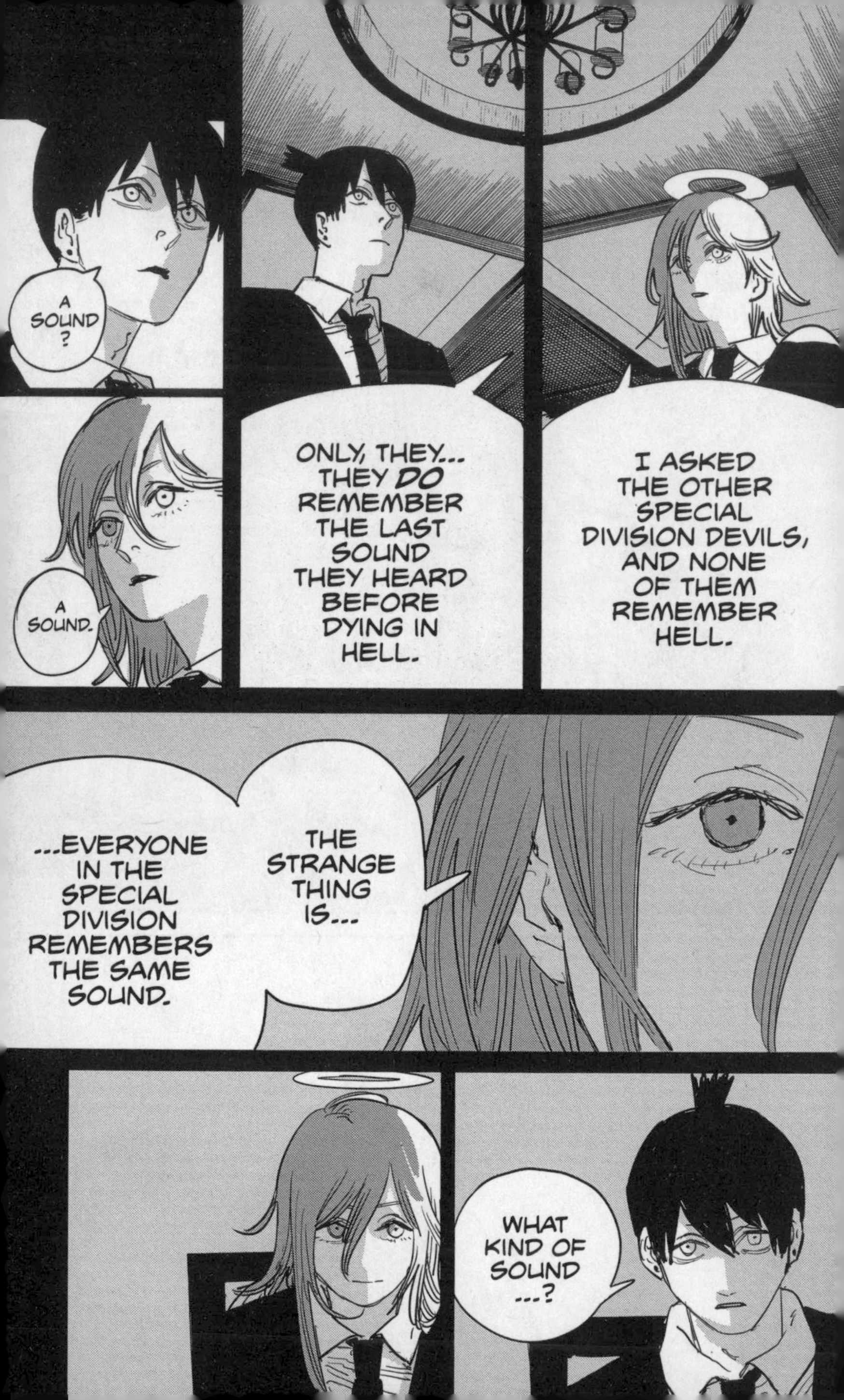

I ASKED THE OTHER SPECIAL DIVISION DEVILS, AND NONE OF THEM REMEMBER HELL.
ONLY, THEY... THEY *DO* REMEMBER THE LAST SOUND THEY HEARD BEFORE DYING IN HELL.
A SOUND?
A SOUND.
THE STRANGE THING IS...
...EVERYONE IN THE SPECIAL DIVISION REMEMBERS THE SAME SOUND.
WHAT KIND OF SOUND...?

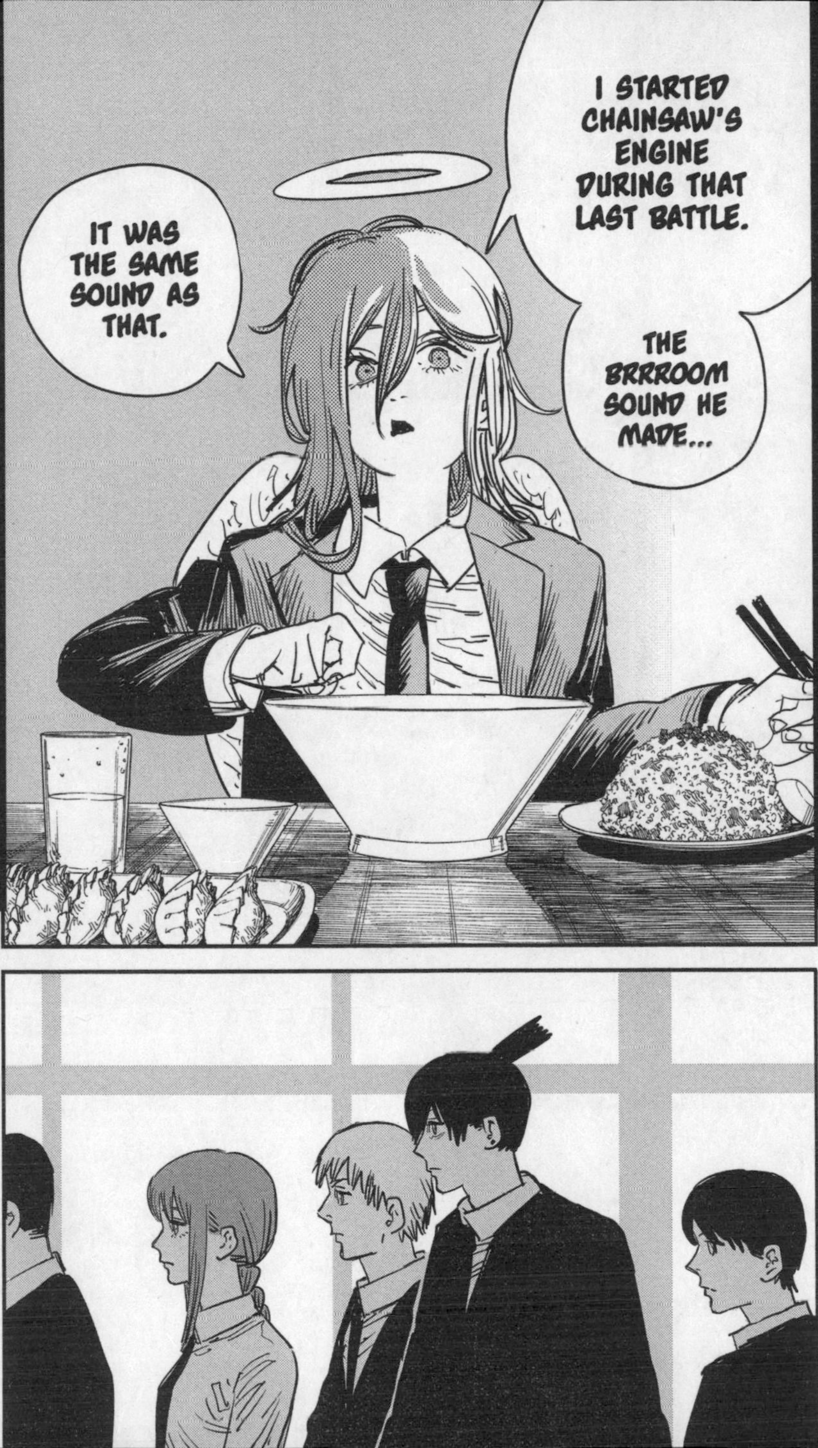
I STARTED CHAINSAW'S ENGINE DURING THAT LAST BATTLE.
THE BRRROOM SOUND HE MADE...
IT WAS THE SAME SOUND AS THAT.

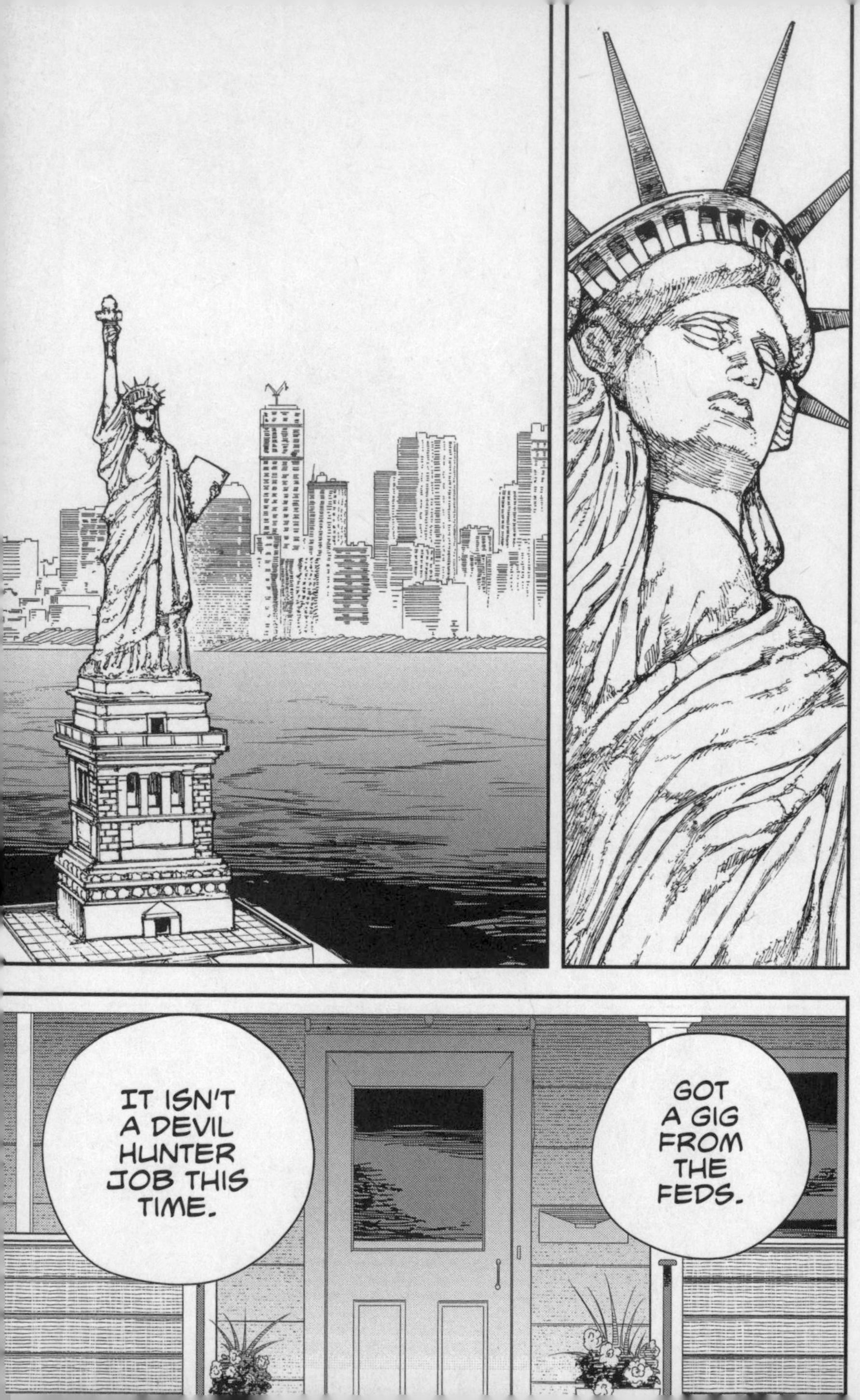
GOT A GIG FROM THE FEDS.
IT ISN'T A DEVIL HUNTER JOB THIS TIME.

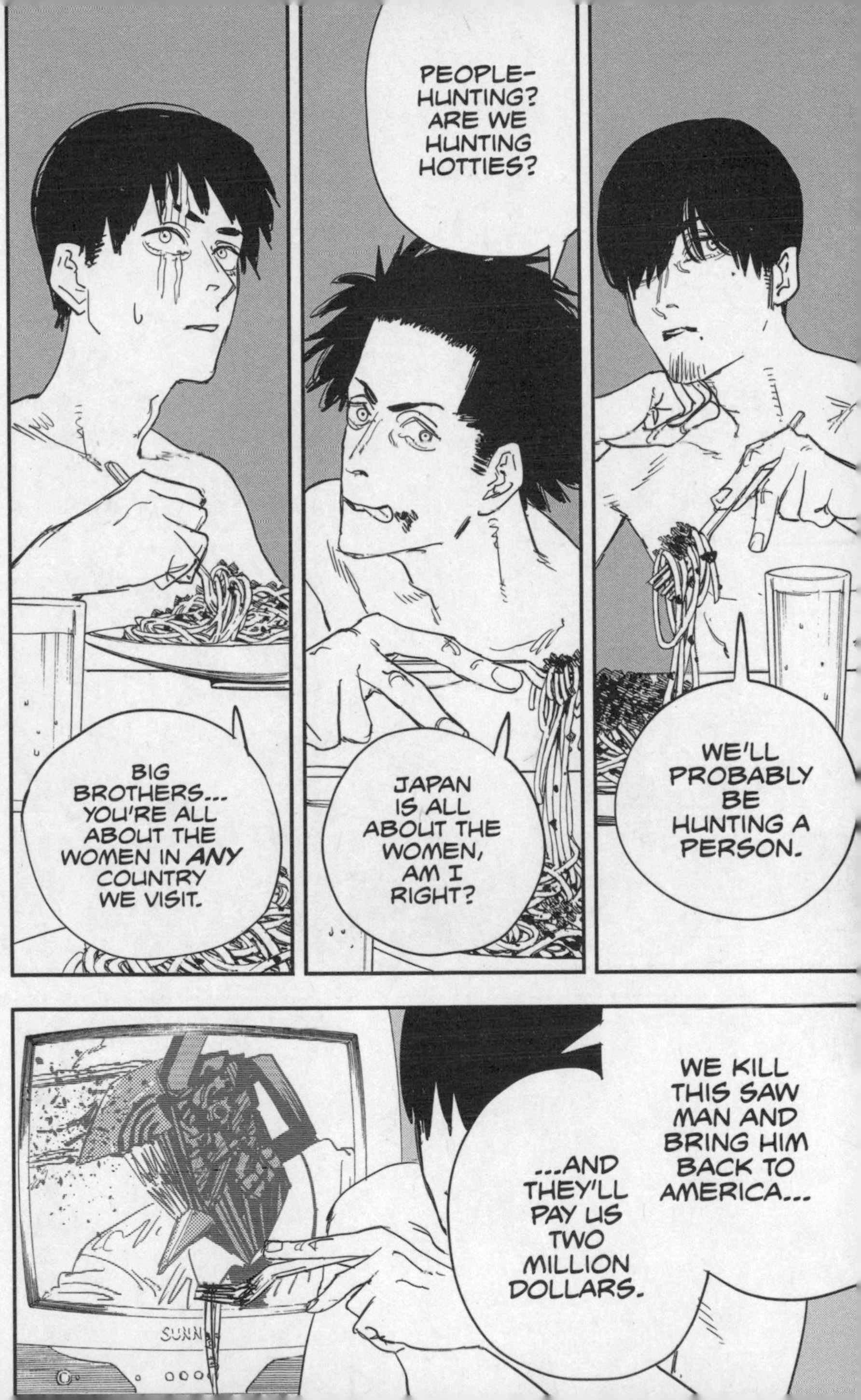
WE'LL PROBABLY BE HUNTING A PERSON.
PEOPLE-HUNTING? ARE WE HUNTING HOTTIES?
JAPAN IS ALL ABOUT THE WOMEN, AM I RIGHT?
BIG BROTHERS... YOU'RE ALL ABOUT THE WOMEN IN *ANY* COUNTRY WE VISIT.
WE KILL THIS SAW MAN AND BRING HIM BACK TO AMERICA...
...AND THEY'LL PAY US TWO MILLION DOLLARS.

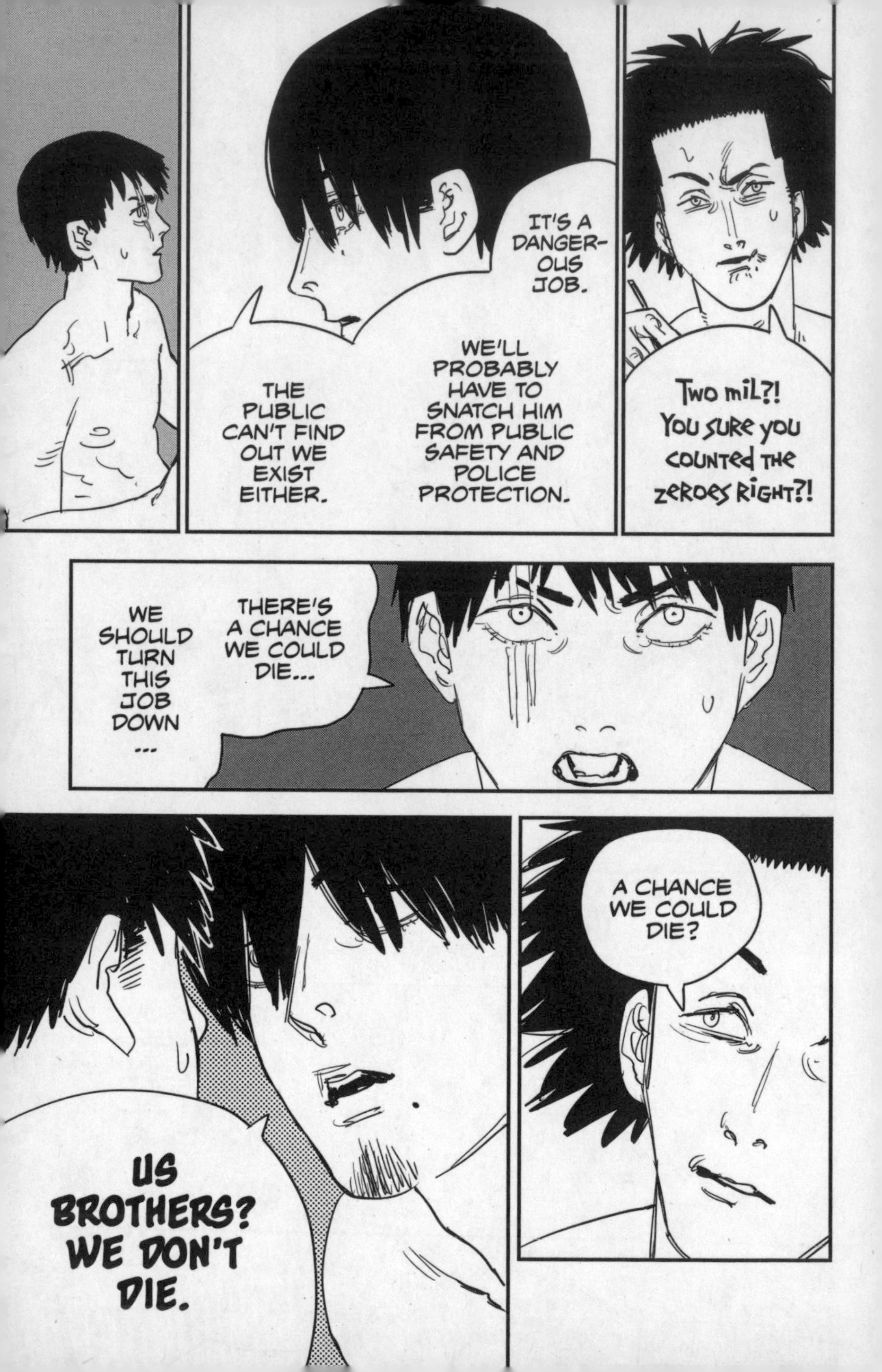
Two mil?! You sure you counted the zeroes right?!
IT'S A DANGER-OUS JOB.
WE'LL PROBABLY HAVE TO SNATCH HIM FROM PUBLIC SAFETY AND POLICE PROTECTION.
THE PUBLIC CAN'T FIND OUT WE EXIST EITHER.
THERE'S A CHANCE WE COULD DIE...
WE SHOULD TURN THIS JOB DOWN ...
A CHANCE WE COULD DIE?
US BROTHERS? WE DON'T DIE.

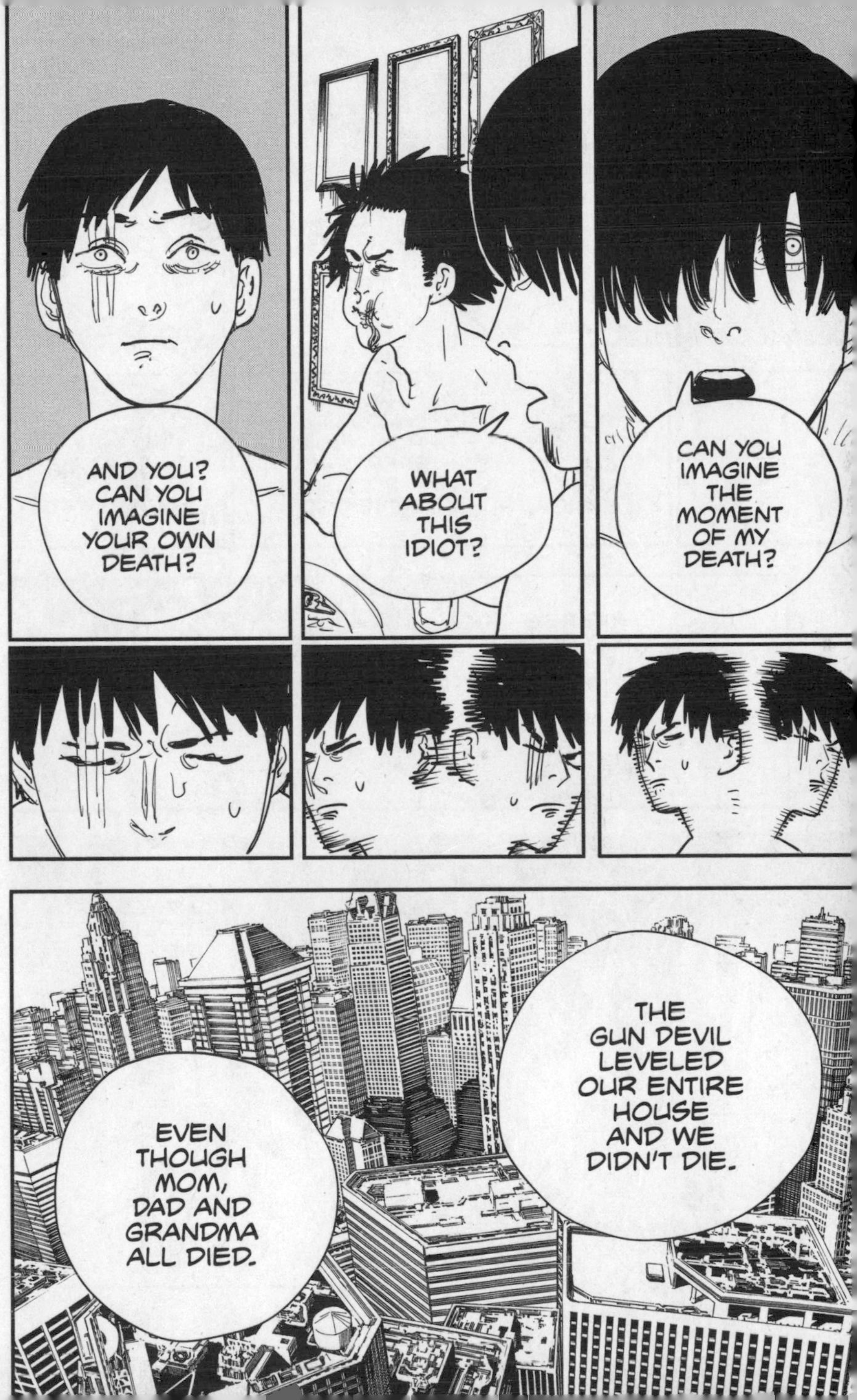
CAN YOU IMAGINE THE MOMENT OF MY DEATH?
WHAT ABOUT THIS IDIOT?
AND YOU? CAN YOU IMAGINE YOUR OWN DEATH?
THE GUN DEVIL LEVELED OUR ENTIRE HOUSE AND WE DIDN'T DIE.
EVEN THOUGH MOM, DAD AND GRANDMA ALL DIED.

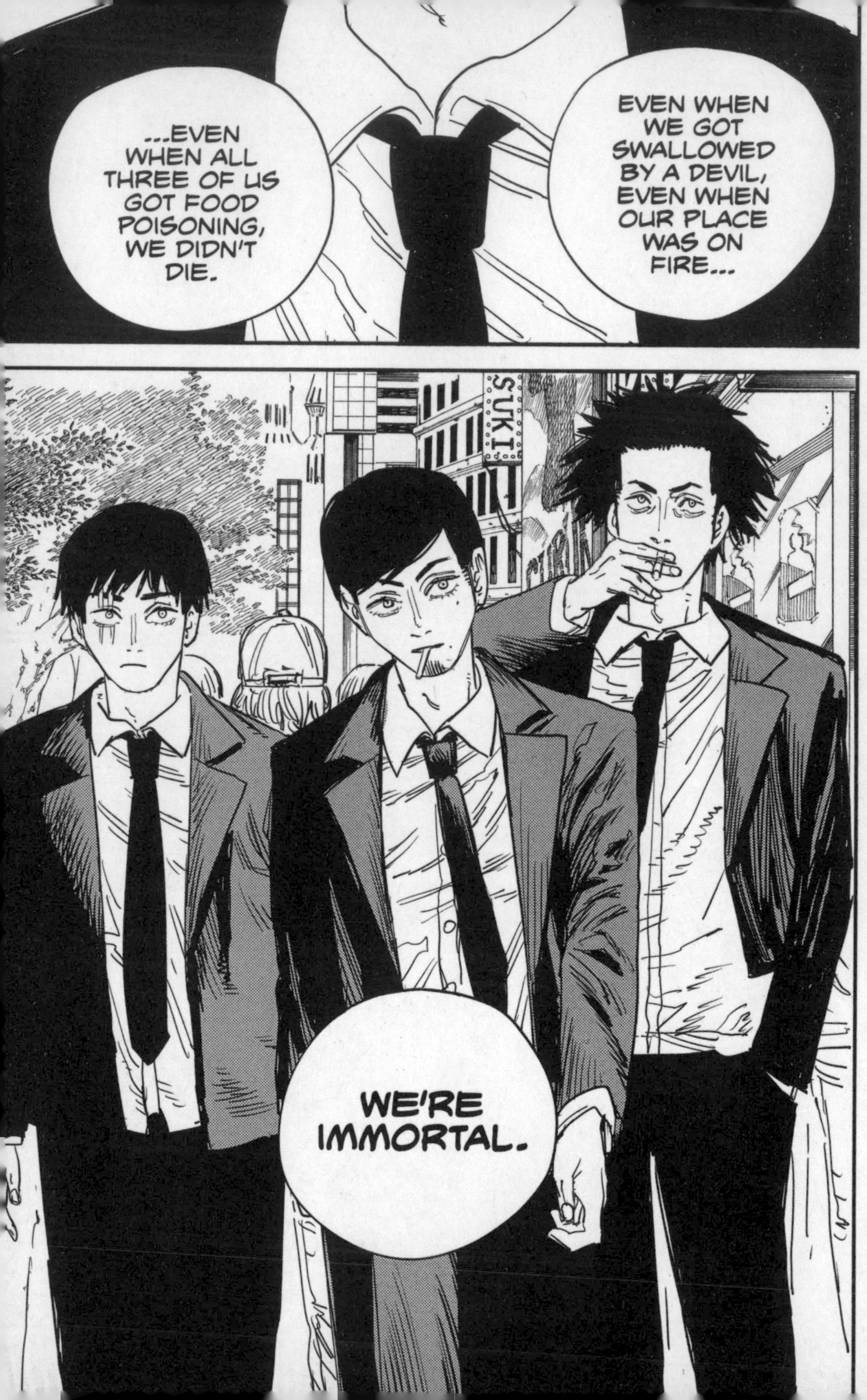
EVEN WHEN WE GOT SWALLOWED BY A DEVIL, EVEN WHEN OUR PLACE WAS ON FIRE...
...EVEN WHEN ALL THREE OF US GOT FOOD POISONING, WE DIDN'T DIE.
SUKI
WE'RE IMMORTAL.

Chain saw man

# Chapter 54: To Go to Enoshima

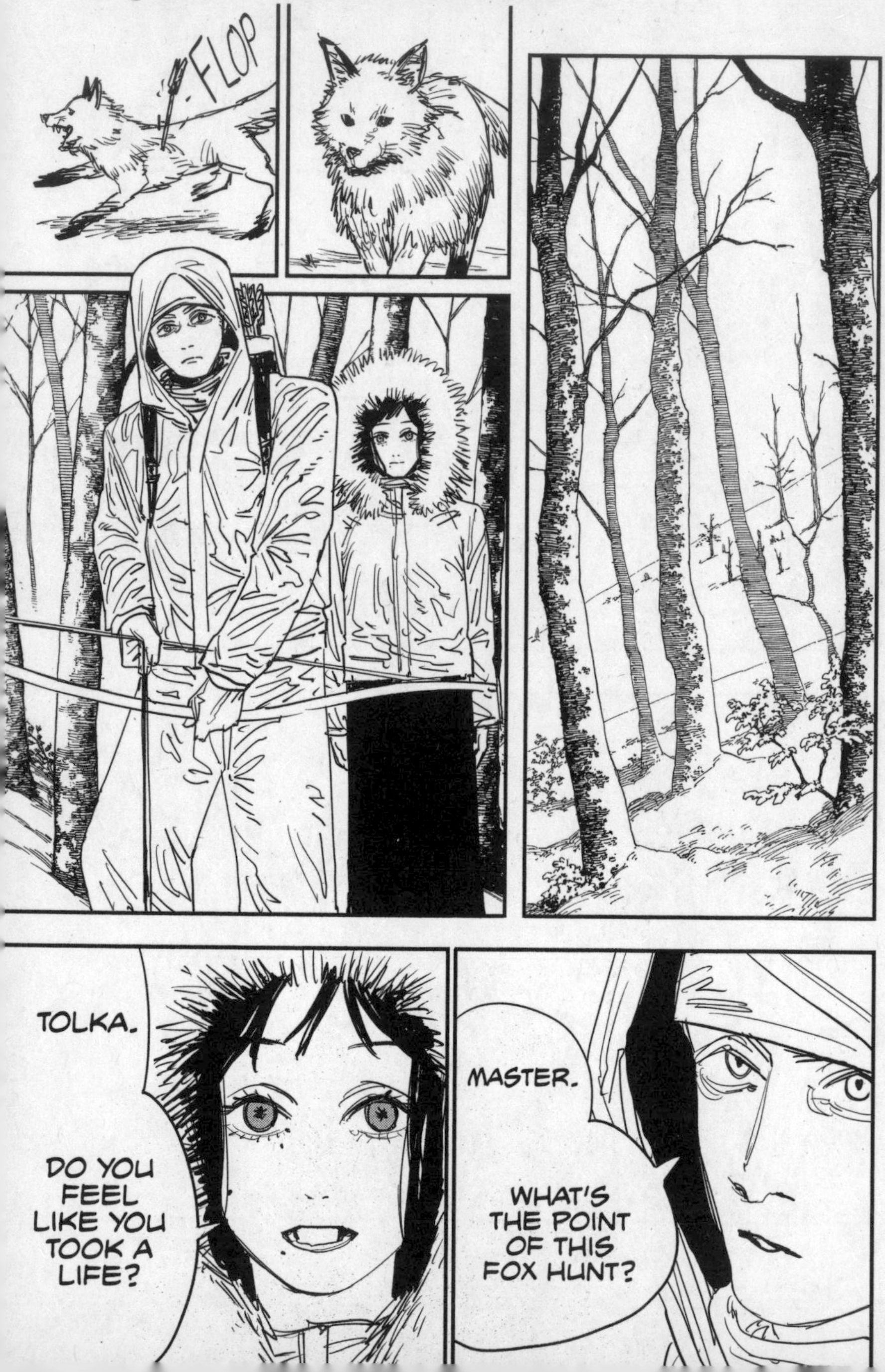
FLOP
MASTER.
WHAT'S THE POINT OF THIS FOX HUNT?
TOLKA.
DO YOU FEEL LIKE YOU TOOK A LIFE?

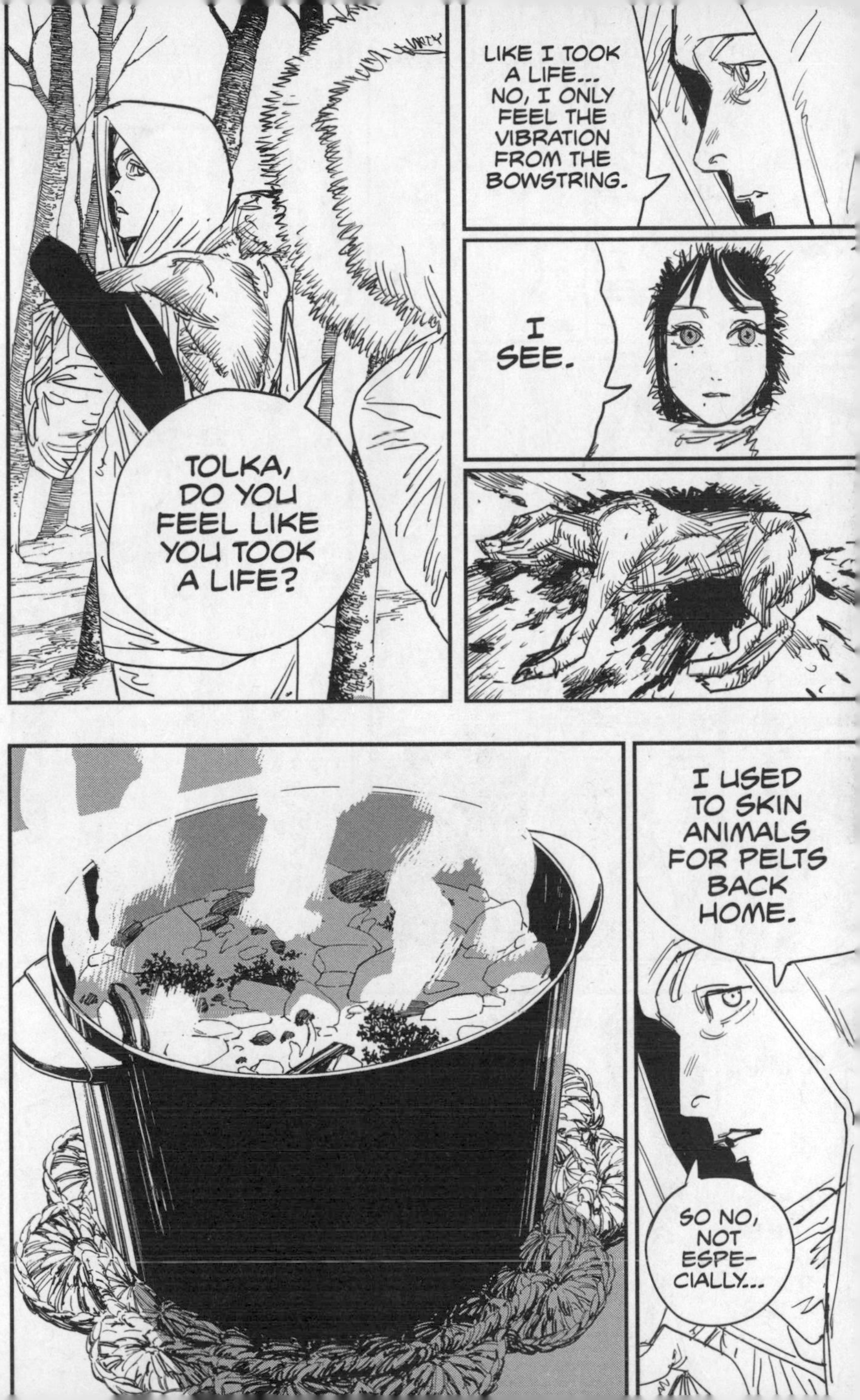
LIKE I TOOK A LIFE... NO, I ONLY FEEL THE VIBRATION FROM THE BOWSTRING.
I SEE.
TOLKA, DO YOU FEEL LIKE YOU TOOK A LIFE?
I USED TO SKIN ANIMALS FOR PELTS BACK HOME.
SO NO, NOT ESPE-CIALLY...

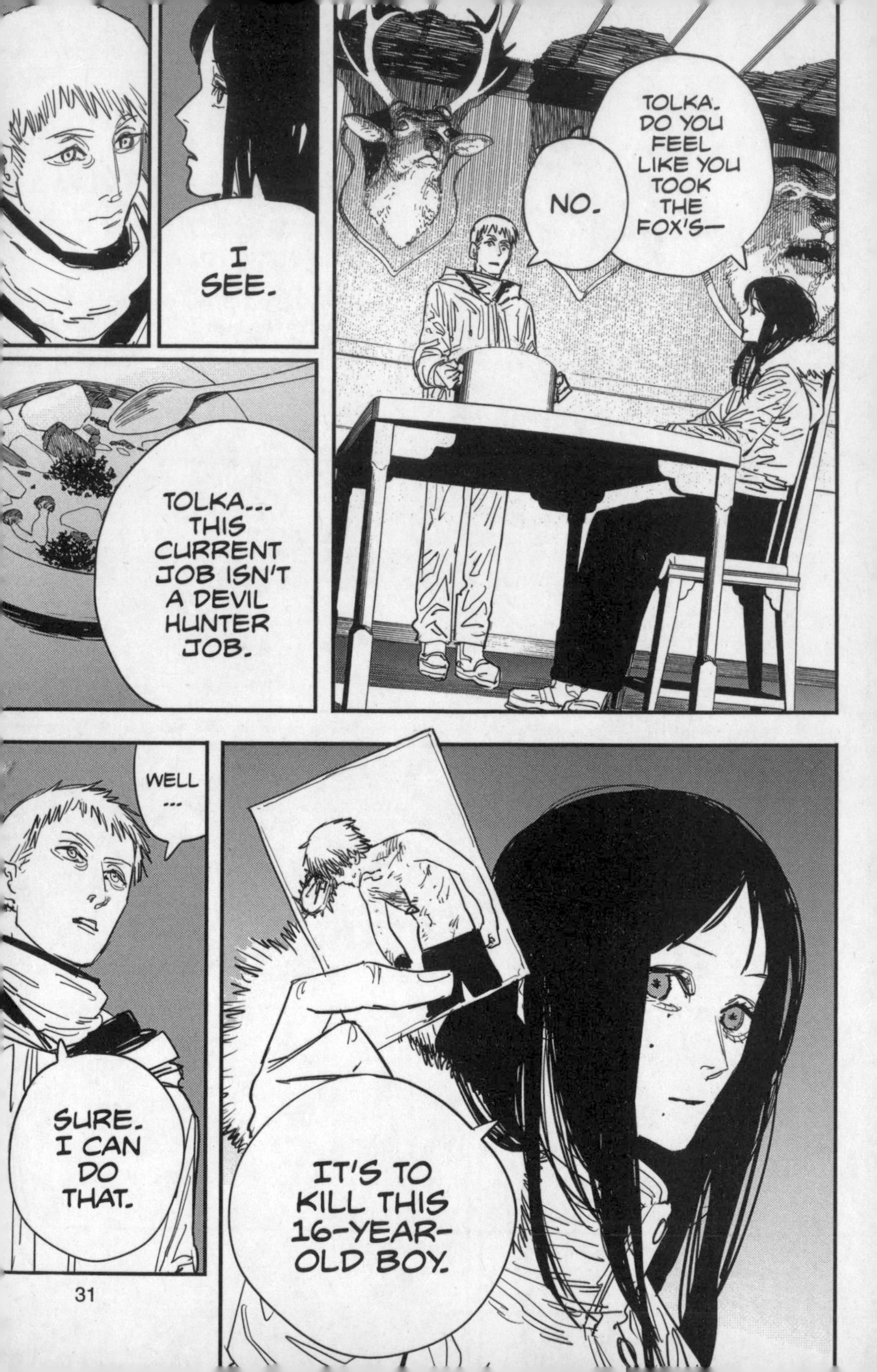
TOLKA. DO YOU FEEL LIKE YOU TOOK THE FOX'S—
NO.
I SEE.
TOLKA... THIS CURRENT JOB ISN'T A DEVIL HUNTER JOB.
IT'S TO KILL THIS 16-YEAR-OLD BOY.
WELL ...
SURE. I CAN DO THAT.

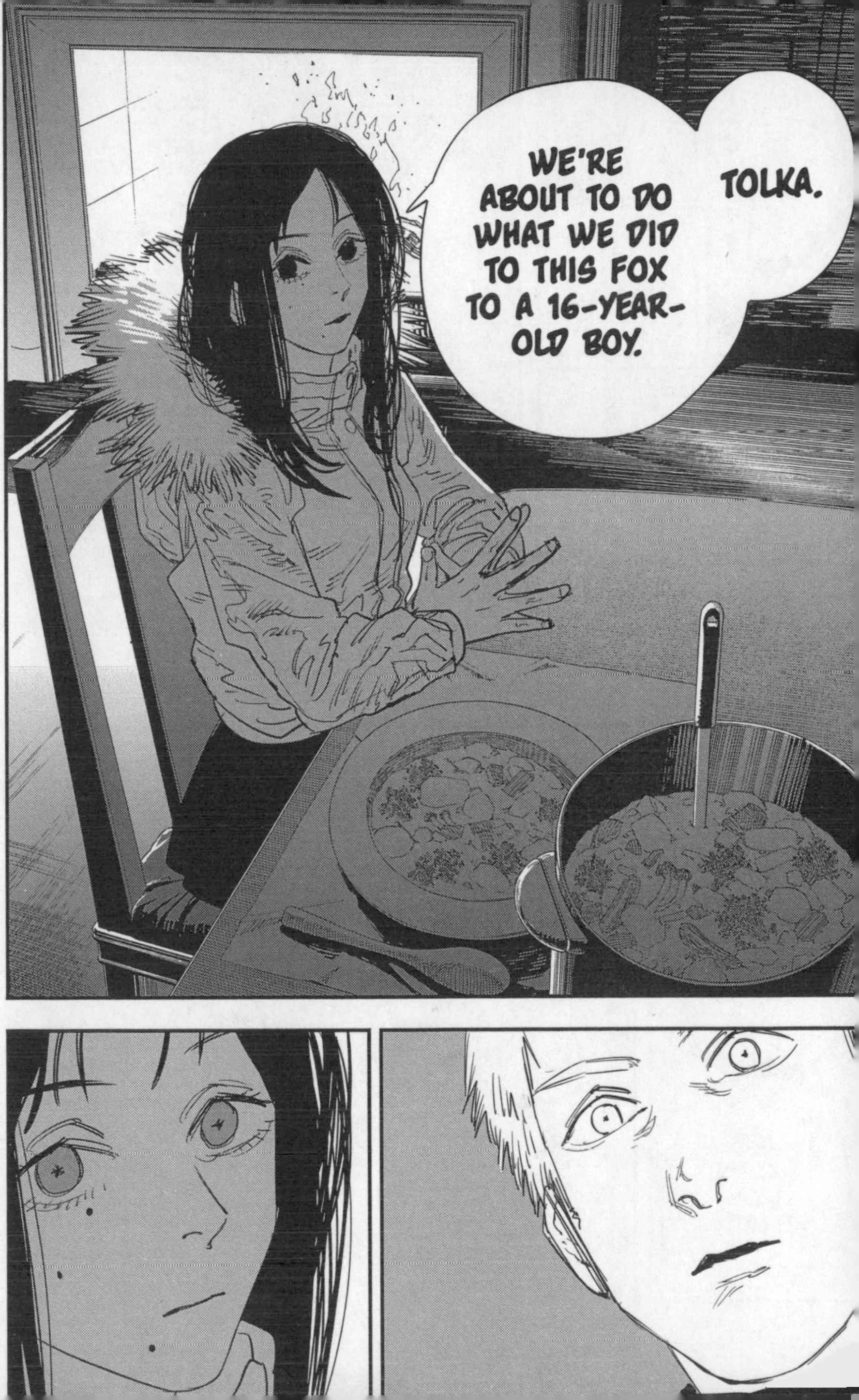
TOLKA.
WE'RE ABOUT TO DO WHAT WE DID TO THIS FOX TO A 16-YEAR-OLD BOY.

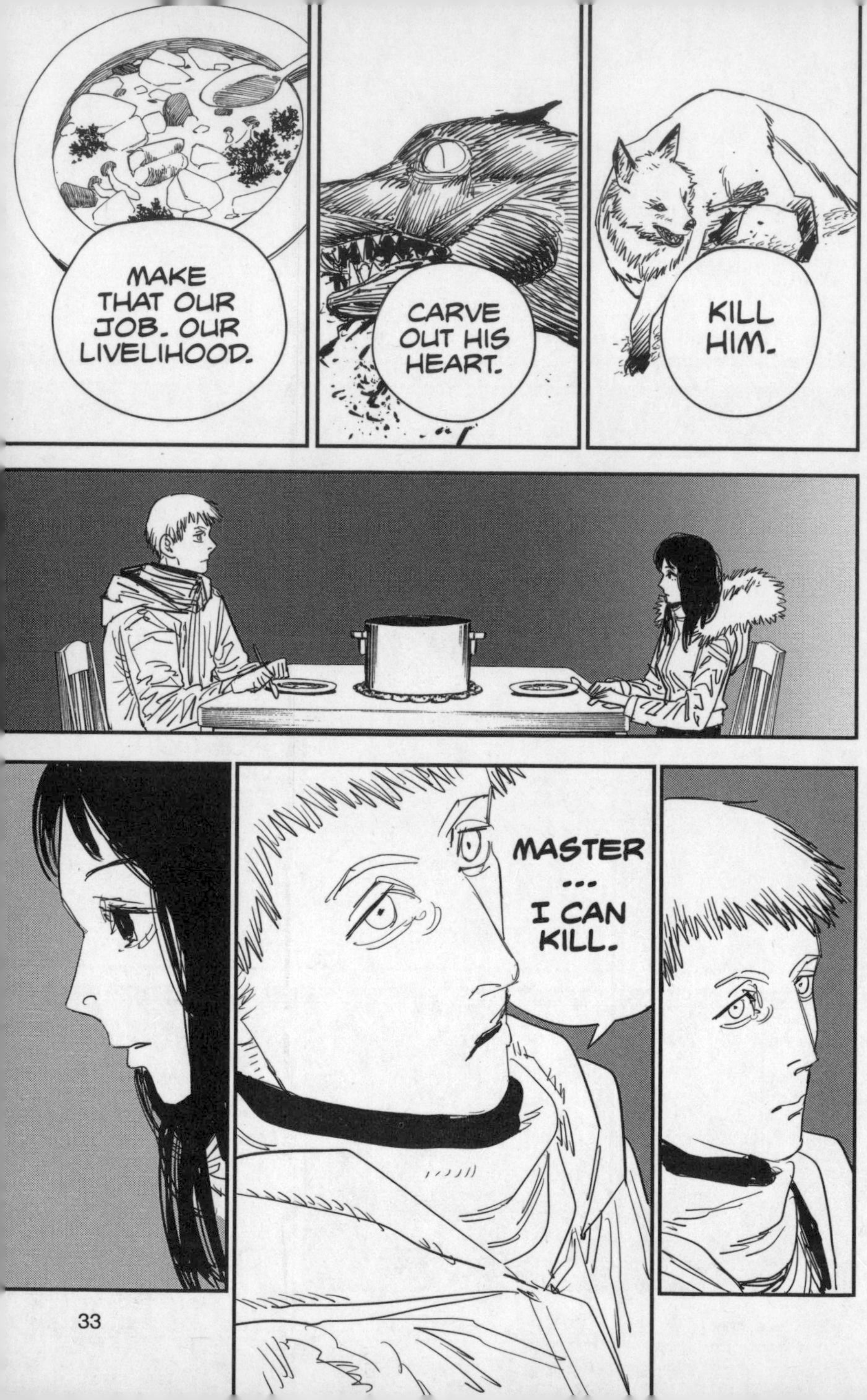
KILL HIM.
CARVE OUT HIS HEART.
MAKE THAT OUR JOB. OUR LIVELIHOOD.
MASTER ... I CAN KILL.

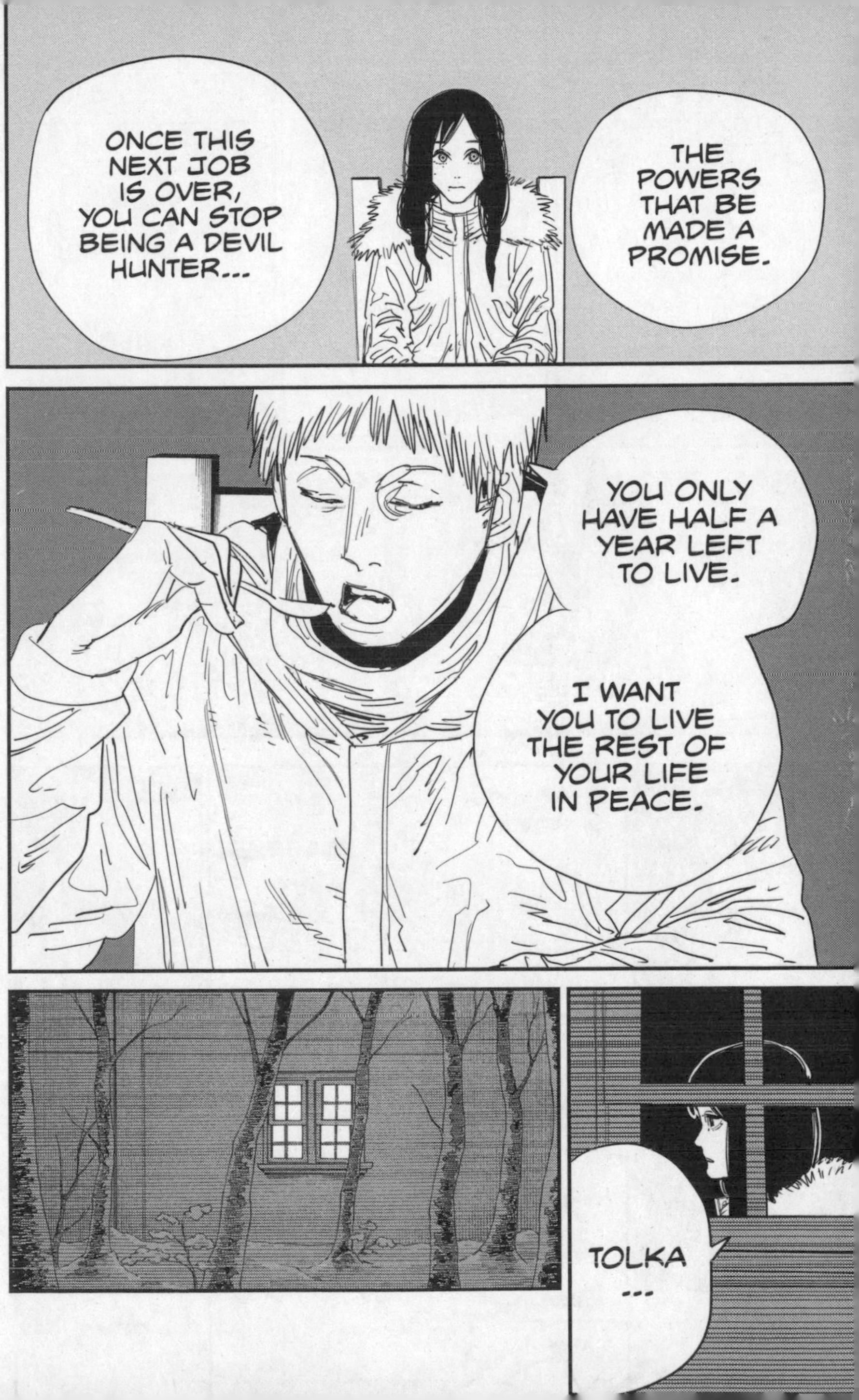
THE POWERS THAT BE MADE A PROMISE.
ONCE THIS NEXT JOB IS OVER, YOU CAN STOP BEING A DEVIL HUNTER...
YOU ONLY HAVE HALF A YEAR LEFT TO LIVE.
I WANT YOU TO LIVE THE REST OF YOUR LIFE IN PEACE.
TOLKA...

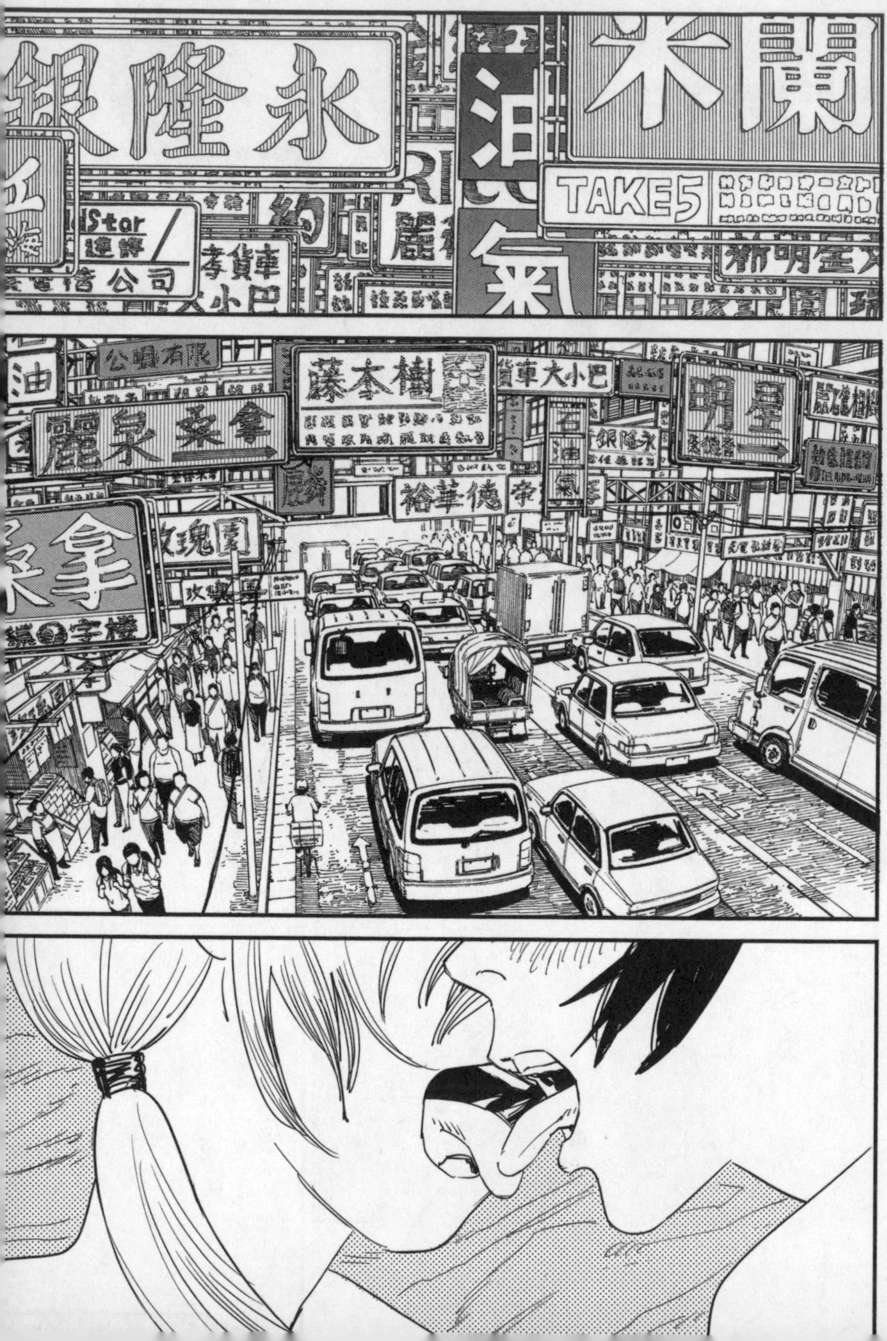
銀隆永
米蘭
油
氣
TAKE5
公司
貨車
小巴
麗泉桑拿
藤本樹
貨車大小巴
明星
裕華德
玫瑰園
桑拿

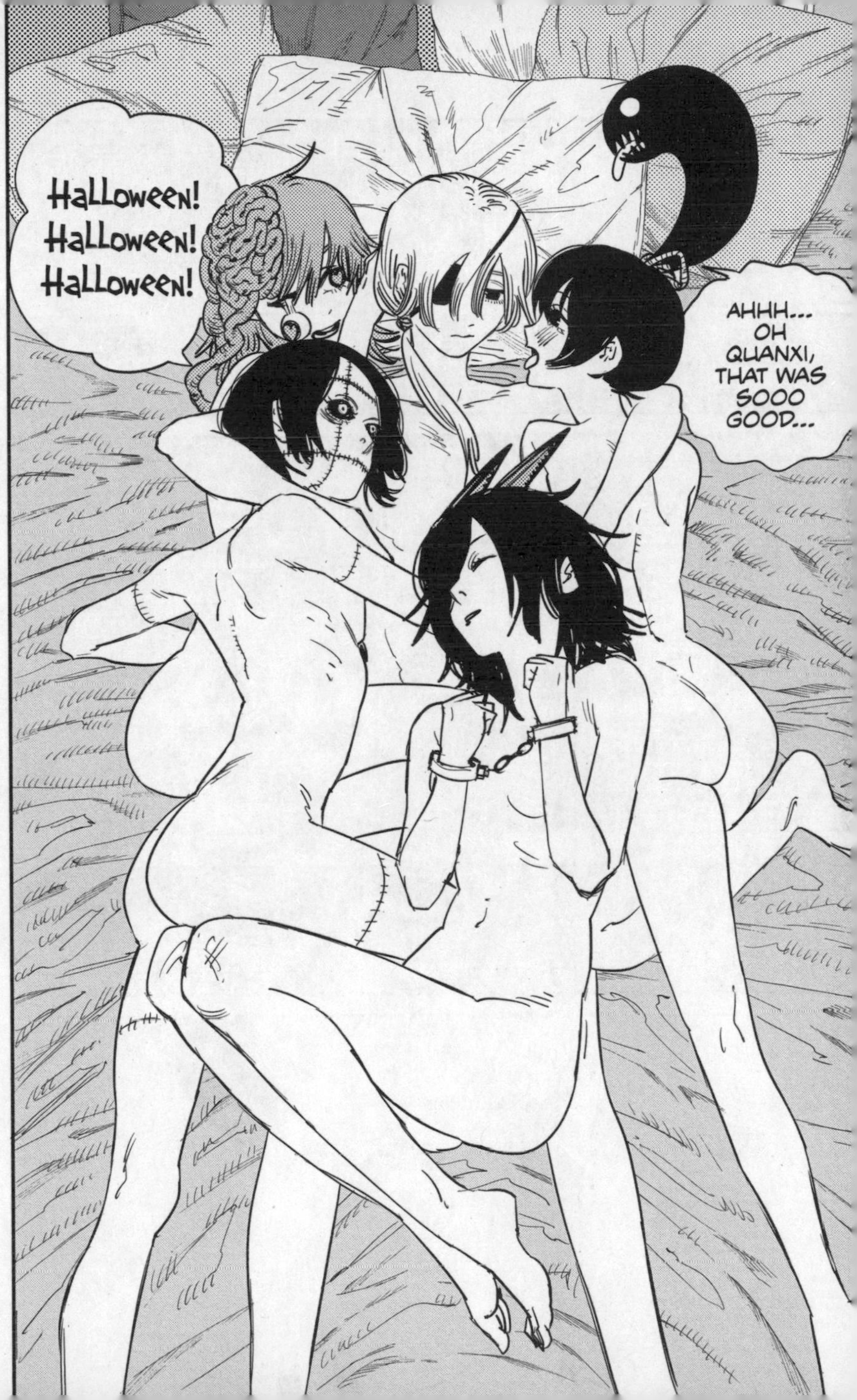
Halloween! Halloween! Halloween!
AHHH... OH QUANXI, THAT WAS SOOO GOOD...

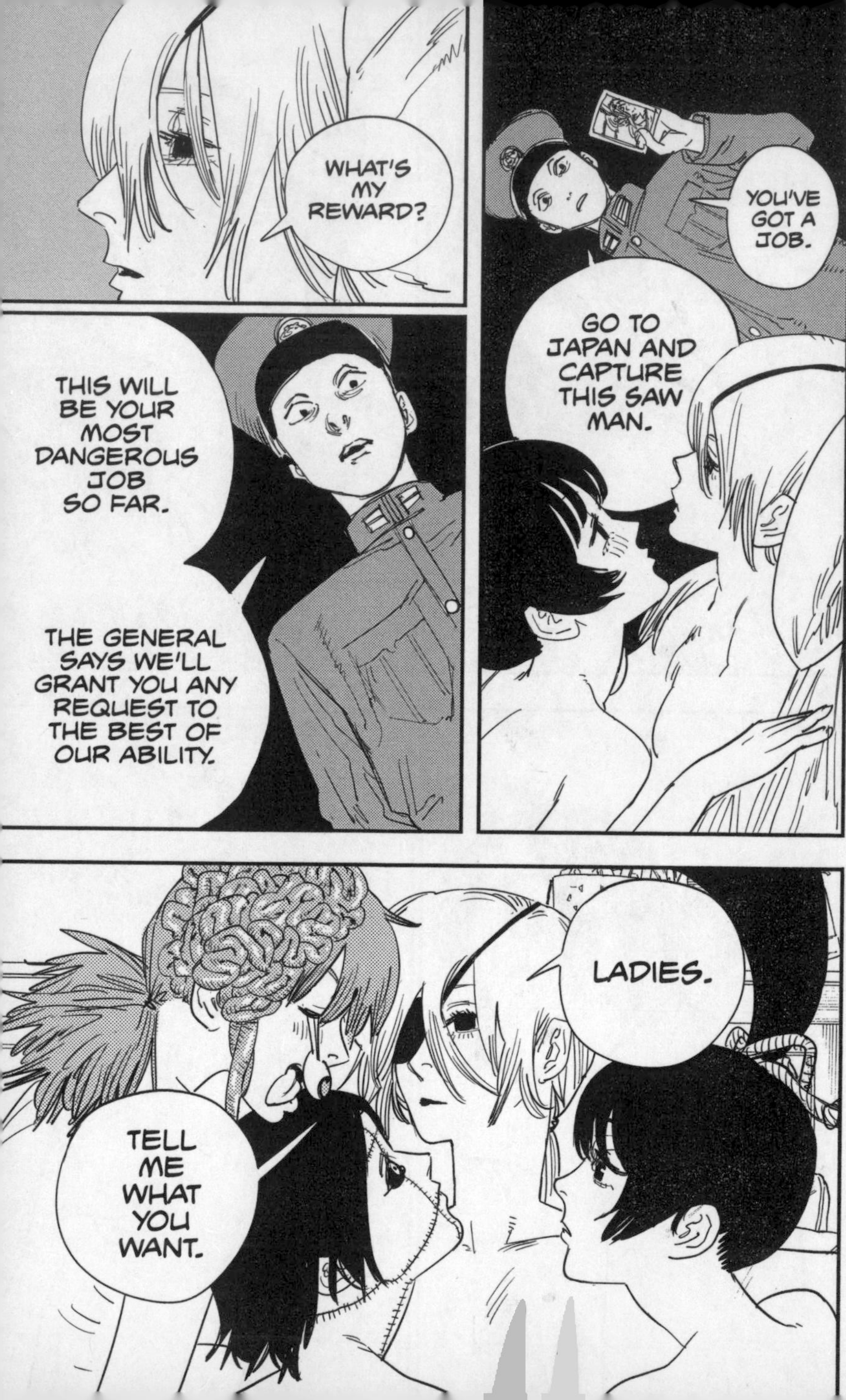
YOU'VE GOT A JOB.
GO TO JAPAN AND CAPTURE THIS SAW MAN.
WHAT'S MY REWARD?
THIS WILL BE YOUR MOST DANGEROUS JOB SO FAR.
THE GENERAL SAYS WE'LL GRANT YOU ANY REQUEST TO THE BEST OF OUR ABILITY.
LADIES.
TELL ME WHAT YOU WANT.

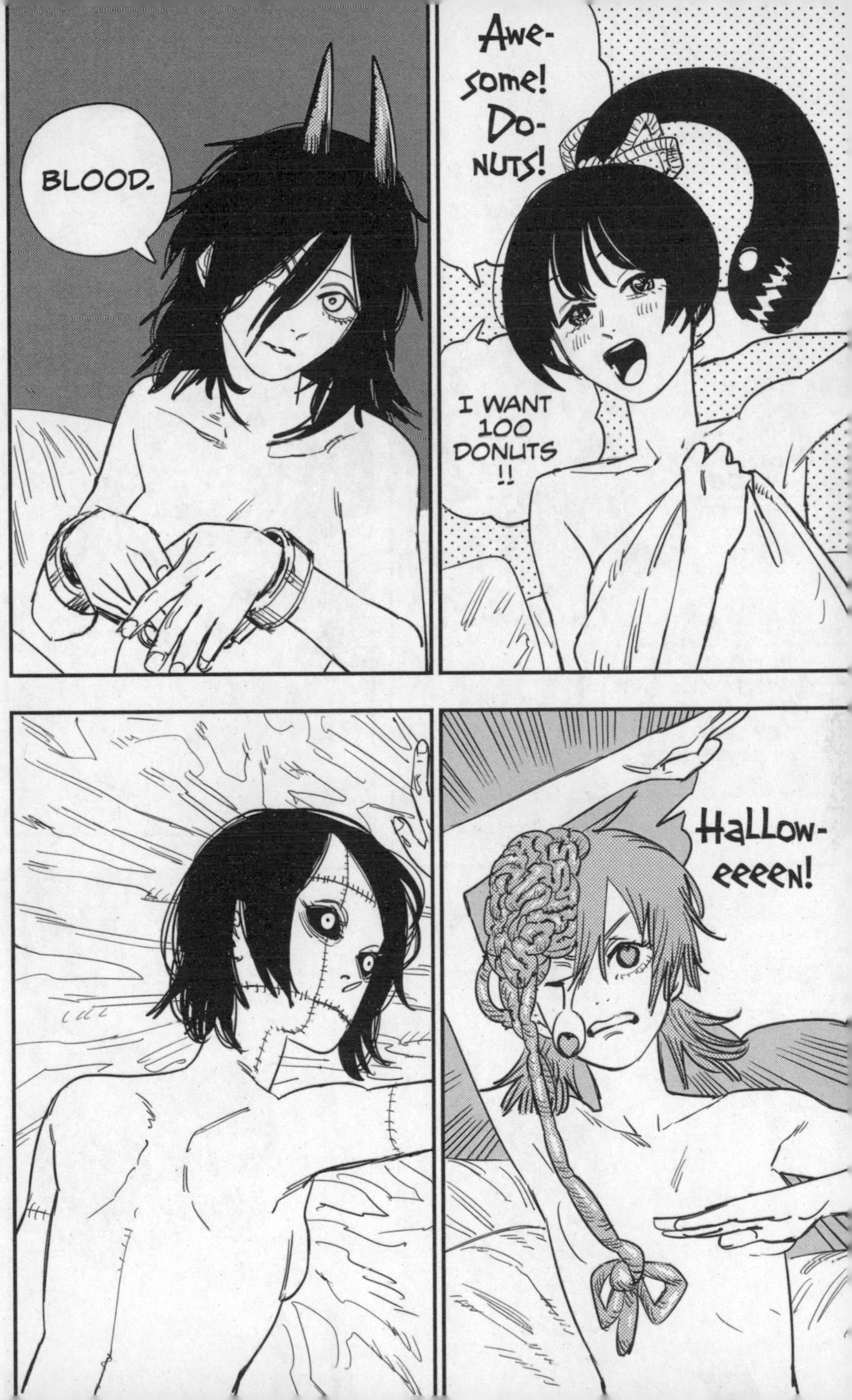
Awe-
some!
Do-
NUTS!
I WANT 100 DONUTS !!
BLOOD.
Hallow-
eeeen!

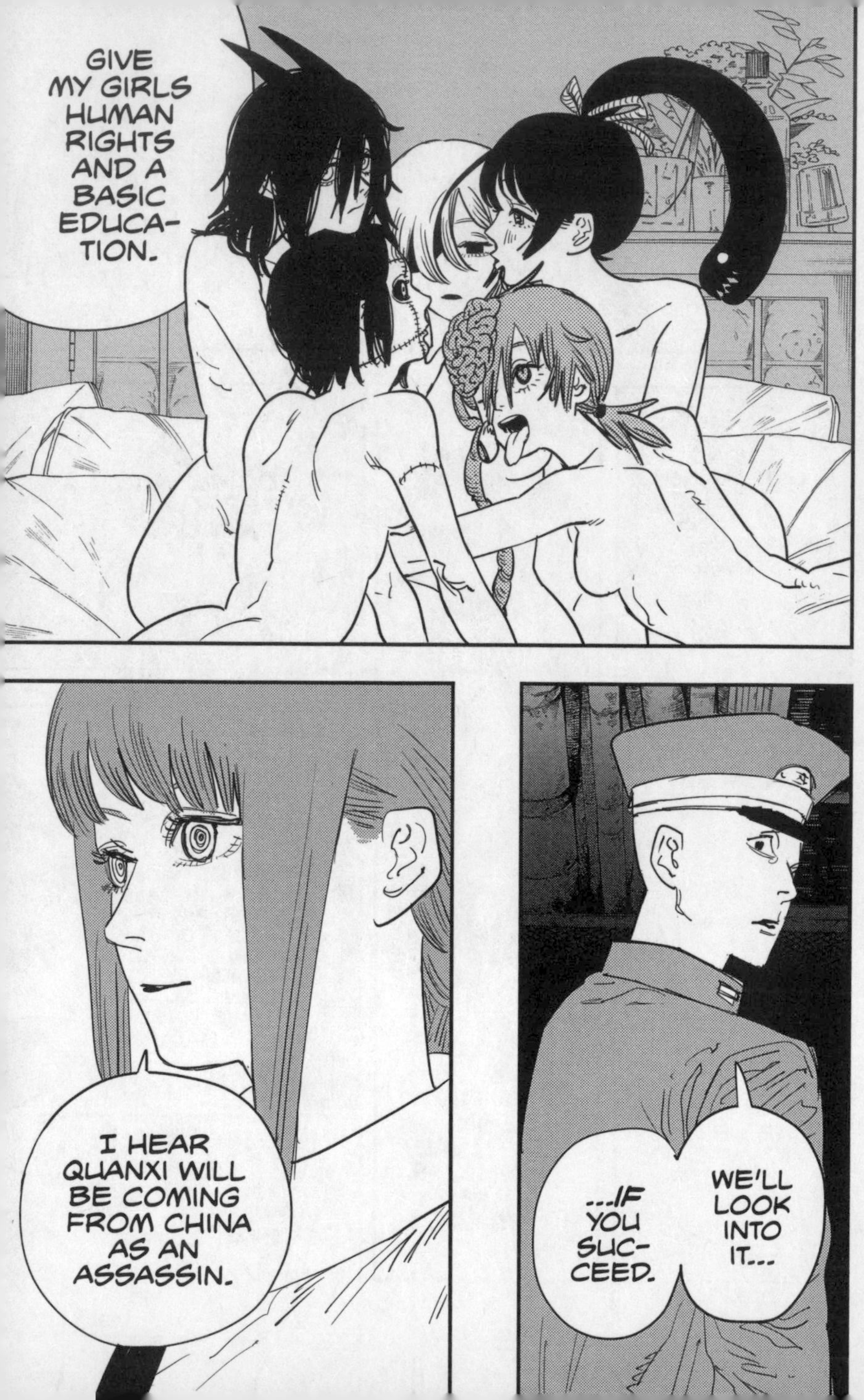
GIVE MY GIRLS HUMAN RIGHTS AND A BASIC EDUCA-TION.
WE'LL LOOK INTO IT...
...IF YOU SUC-CEED.
I HEAR QUANXI WILL BE COMING FROM CHINA AS AN ASSASSIN.

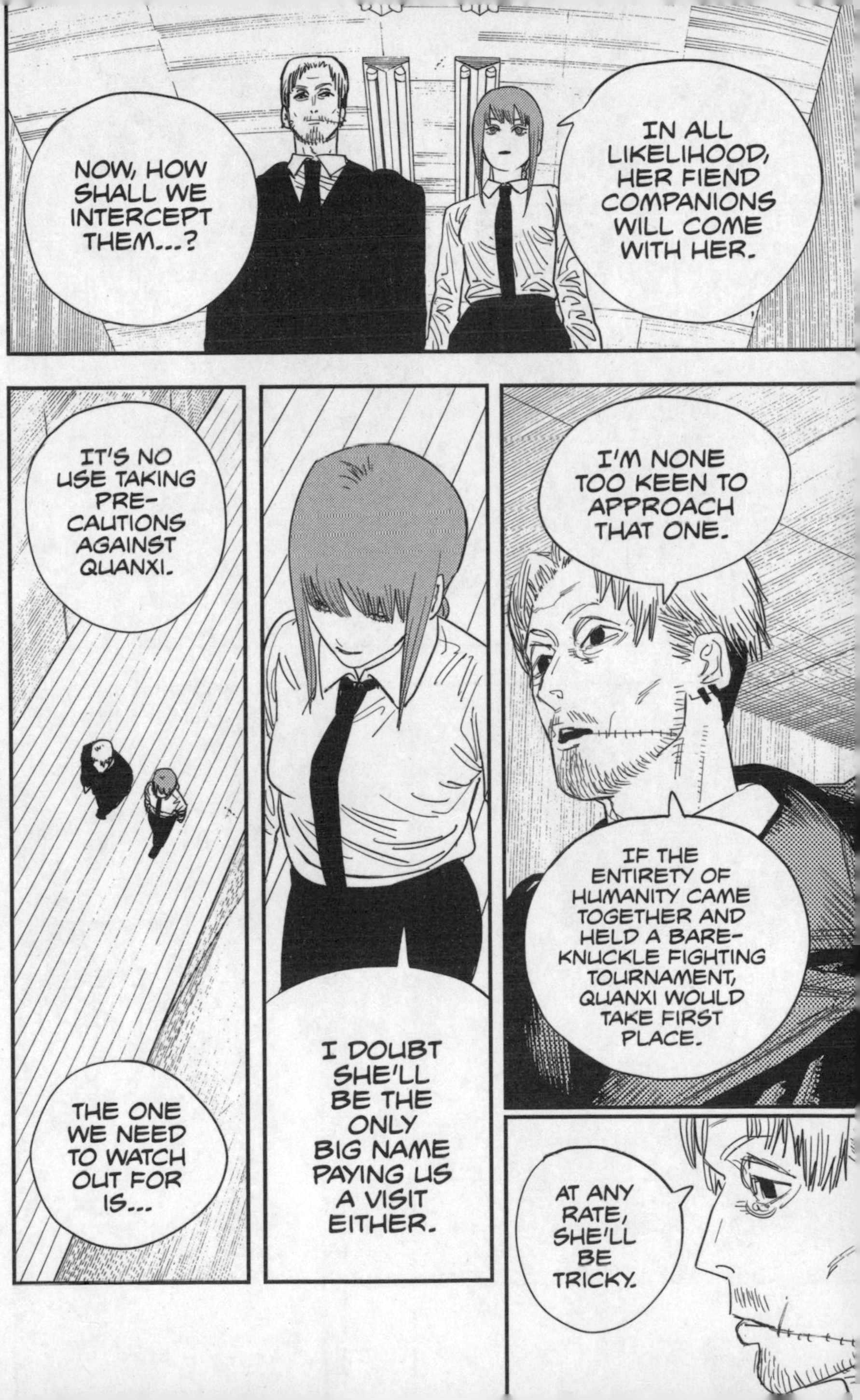
IN ALL LIKELIHOOD, HER FIEND COMPANIONS WILL COME WITH HER.
NOW, HOW SHALL WE INTERCEPT THEM...?
I'M NONE TOO KEEN TO APPROACH THAT ONE.
IF THE ENTIRETY OF HUMANITY CAME TOGETHER AND HELD A BARE-KNUCKLE FIGHTING TOURNAMENT, QUANXI WOULD TAKE FIRST PLACE.
AT ANY RATE, SHE'LL BE TRICKY.
I DOUBT SHE'LL BE THE ONLY BIG NAME PAYING US A VISIT EITHER.
IT'S NO USE TAKING PRE-CAUTIONS AGAINST QUANXI.
THE ONE WE NEED TO WATCH OUT FOR IS...

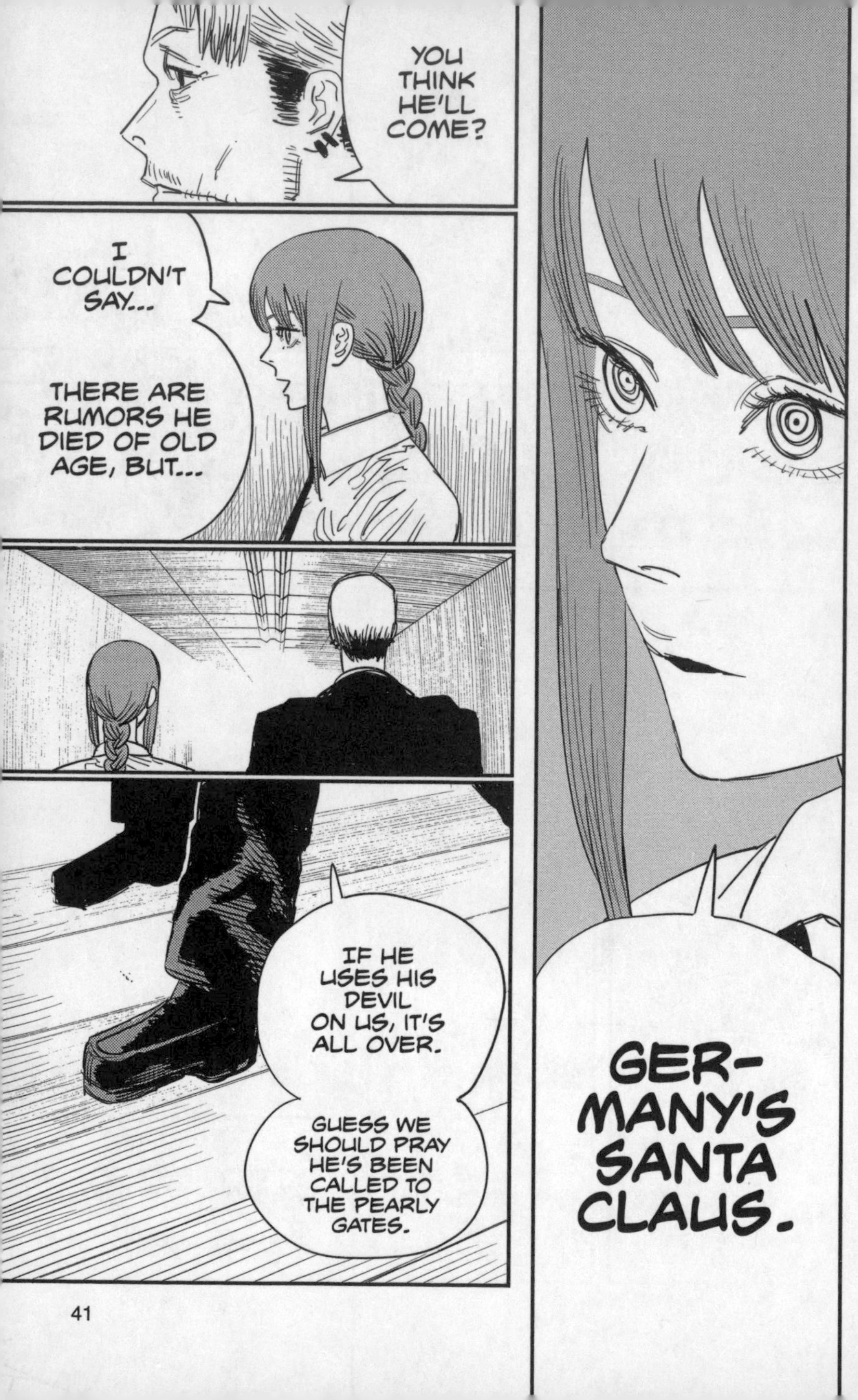
GER-MANY'S SANTA CLAUS.
YOU THINK HE'LL COME?
I COULDN'T SAY...
THERE ARE RUMORS HE DIED OF OLD AGE, BUT...
IF HE USES HIS DEVIL ON US, IT'S ALL OVER.
GUESS WE SHOULD PRAY HE'S BEEN CALLED TO THE PEARLY GATES.

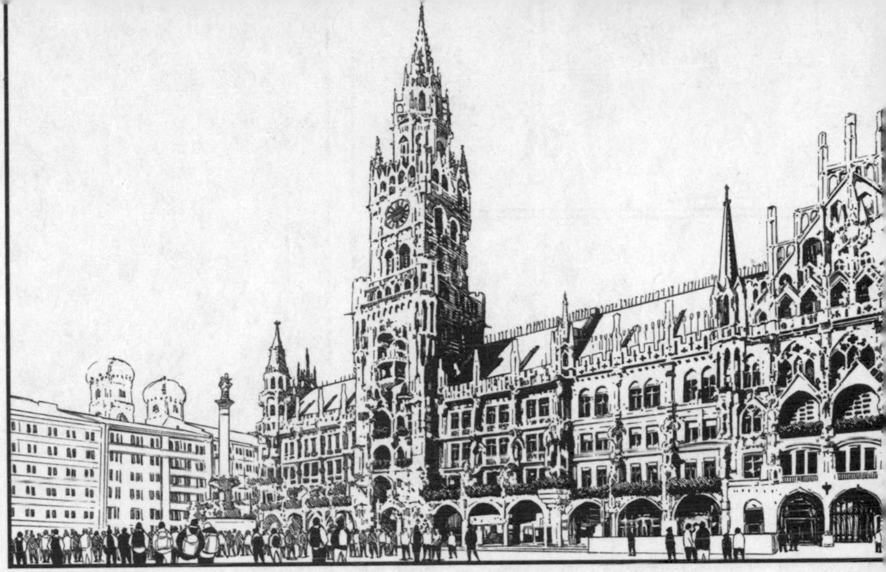
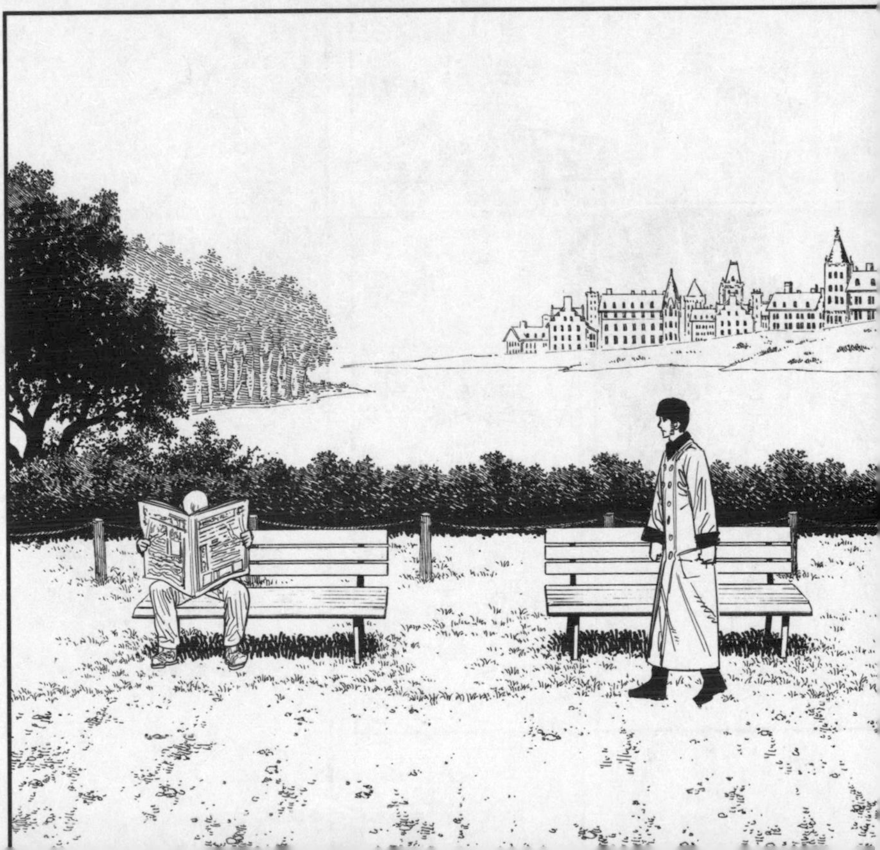

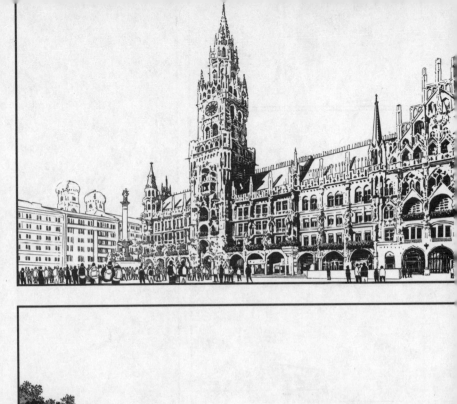

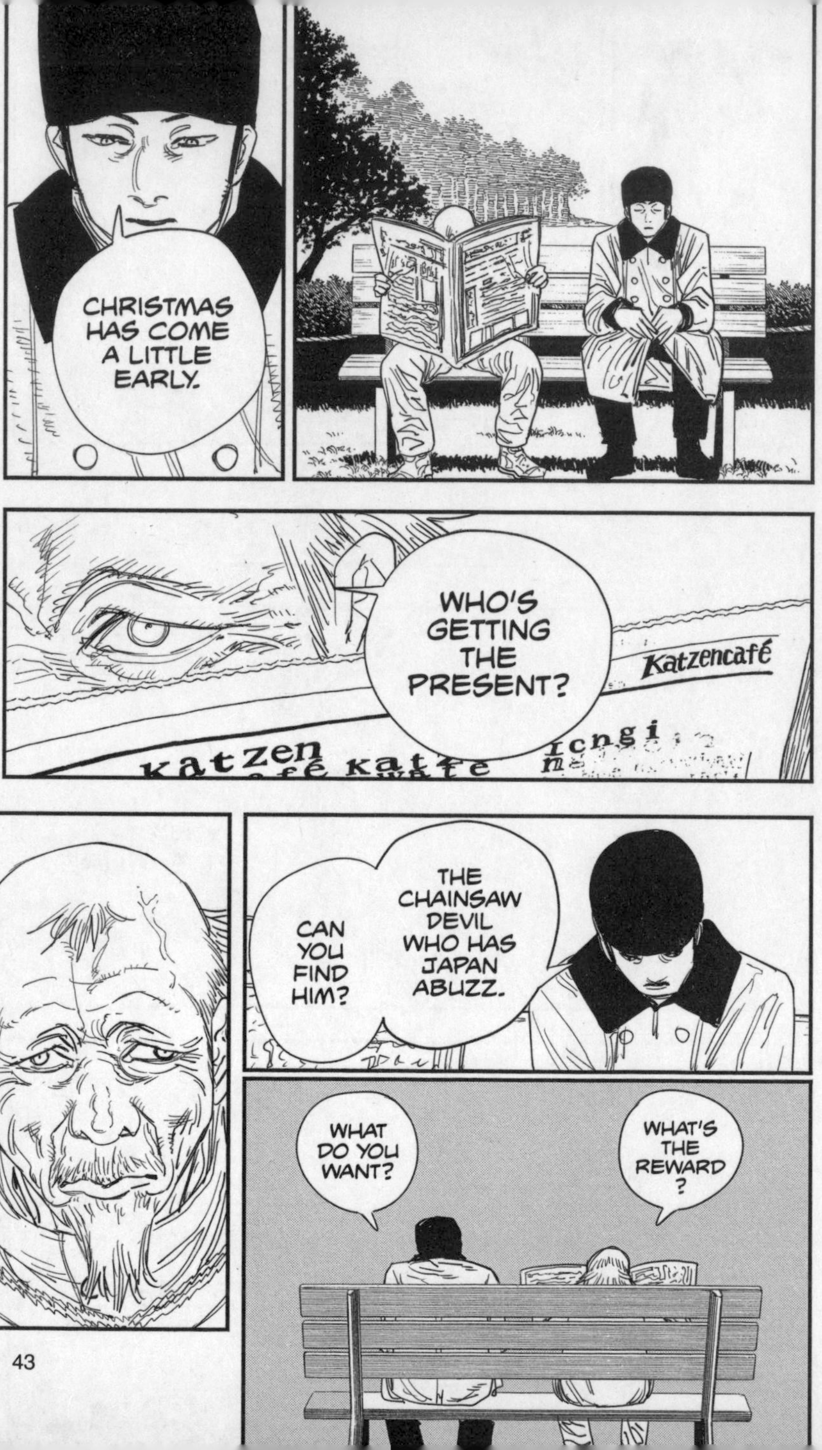
CHRISTMAS HAS COME A LITTLE EARLY.
WHO'S GETTING THE PRESENT?
Katzencafé
THE CHAINSAW DEVIL WHO HAS JAPAN ABUZZ.
CAN YOU FIND HIM?
WHAT'S THE REWARD?
WHAT DO YOU WANT?

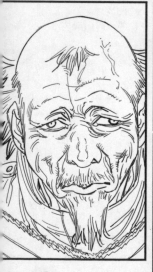

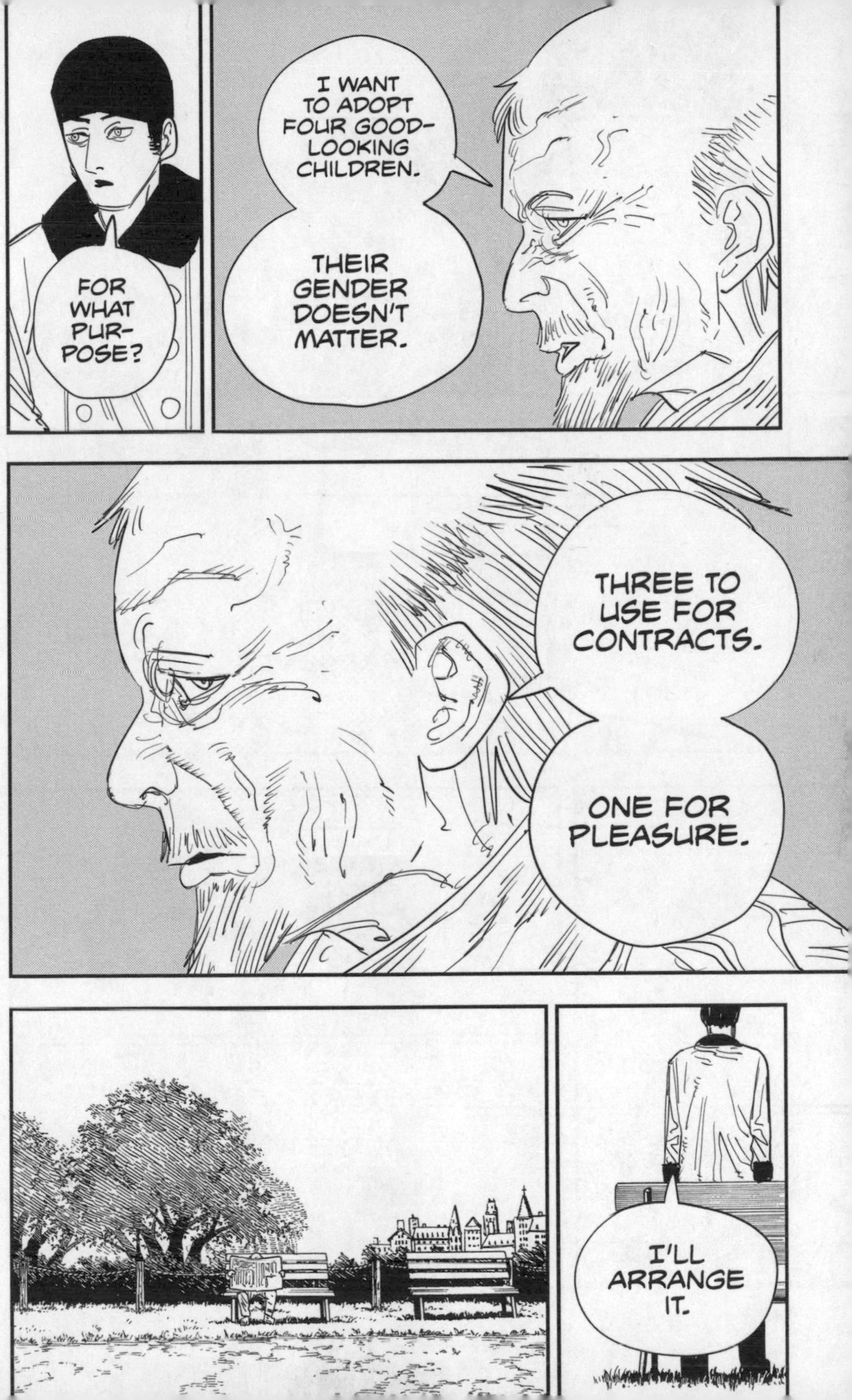
I WANT TO ADOPT FOUR GOOD-LOOKING CHILDREN.
THEIR GENDER DOESN'T MATTER.
FOR WHAT PUR-POSE?
THREE TO USE FOR CONTRACTS.
ONE FOR PLEASURE.
I'LL ARRANGE IT.

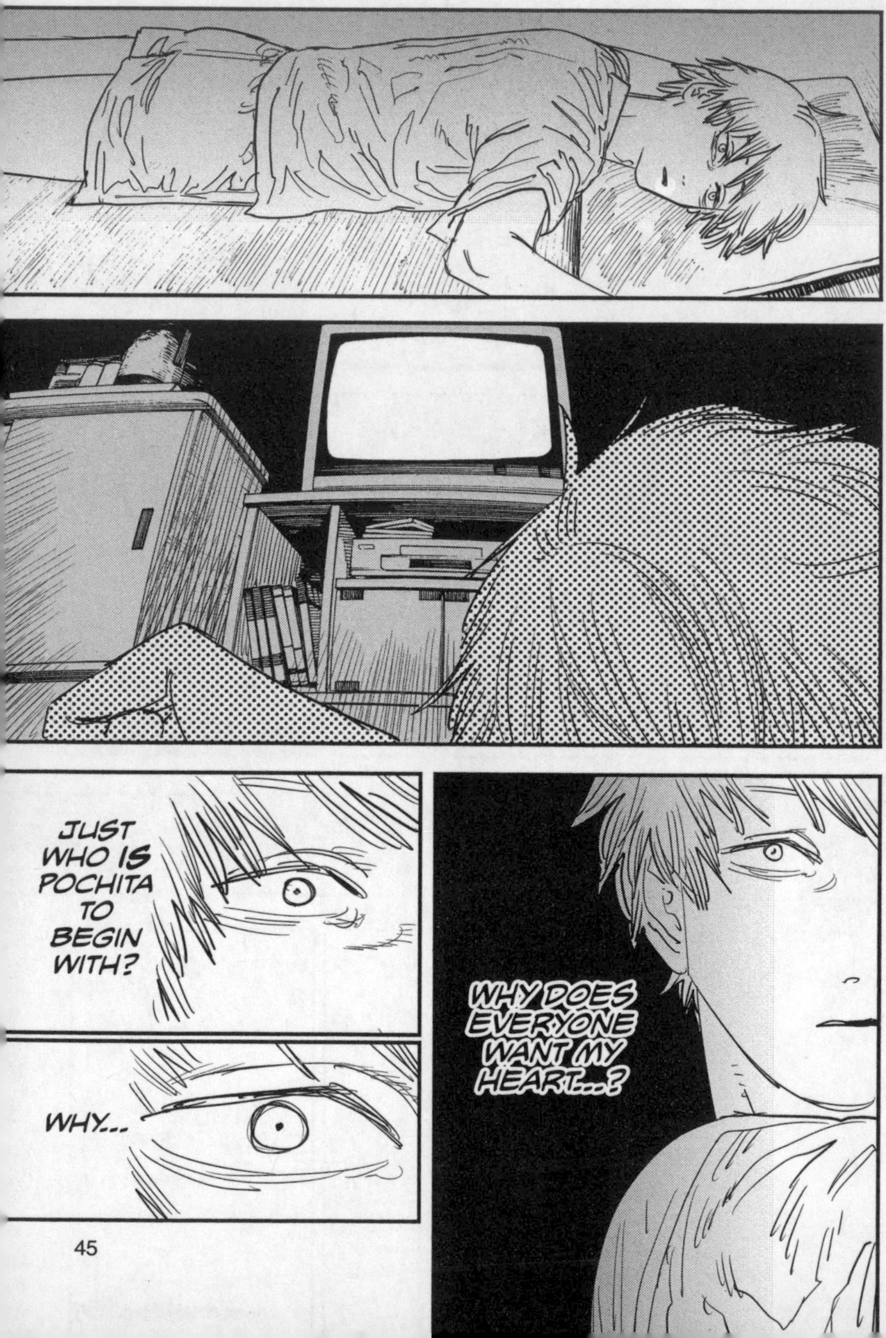
WHY DOES EVERYONE WANT MY HEART...?
JUST WHO IS POCHITA TO BEGIN WITH?
WHY...

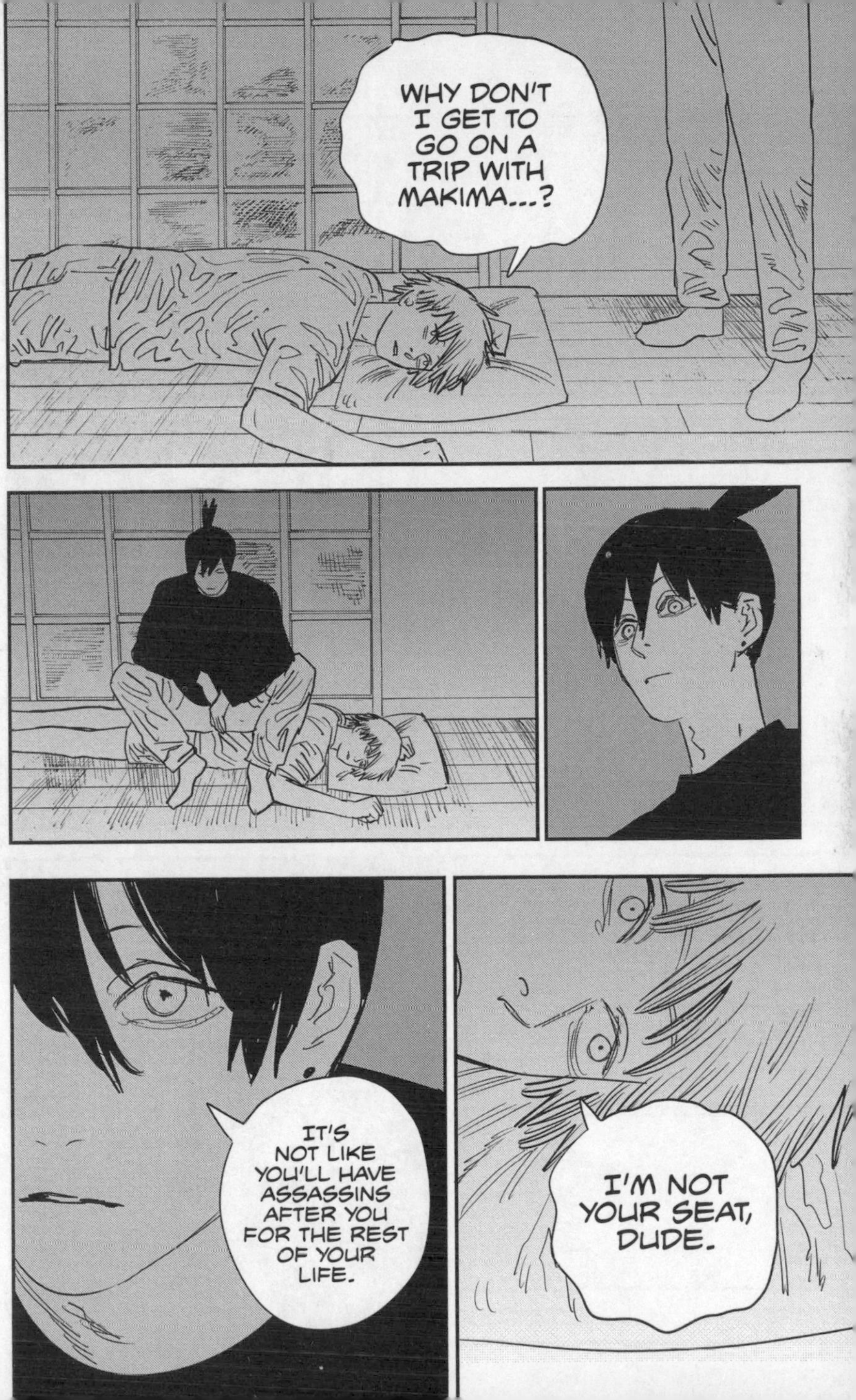
WHY DON'T I GET TO GO ON A TRIP WITH MAKIMA...?
I'M NOT YOUR SEAT, DUDE.
IT'S NOT LIKE YOU'LL HAVE ASSASSINS AFTER YOU FOR THE REST OF YOUR LIFE.

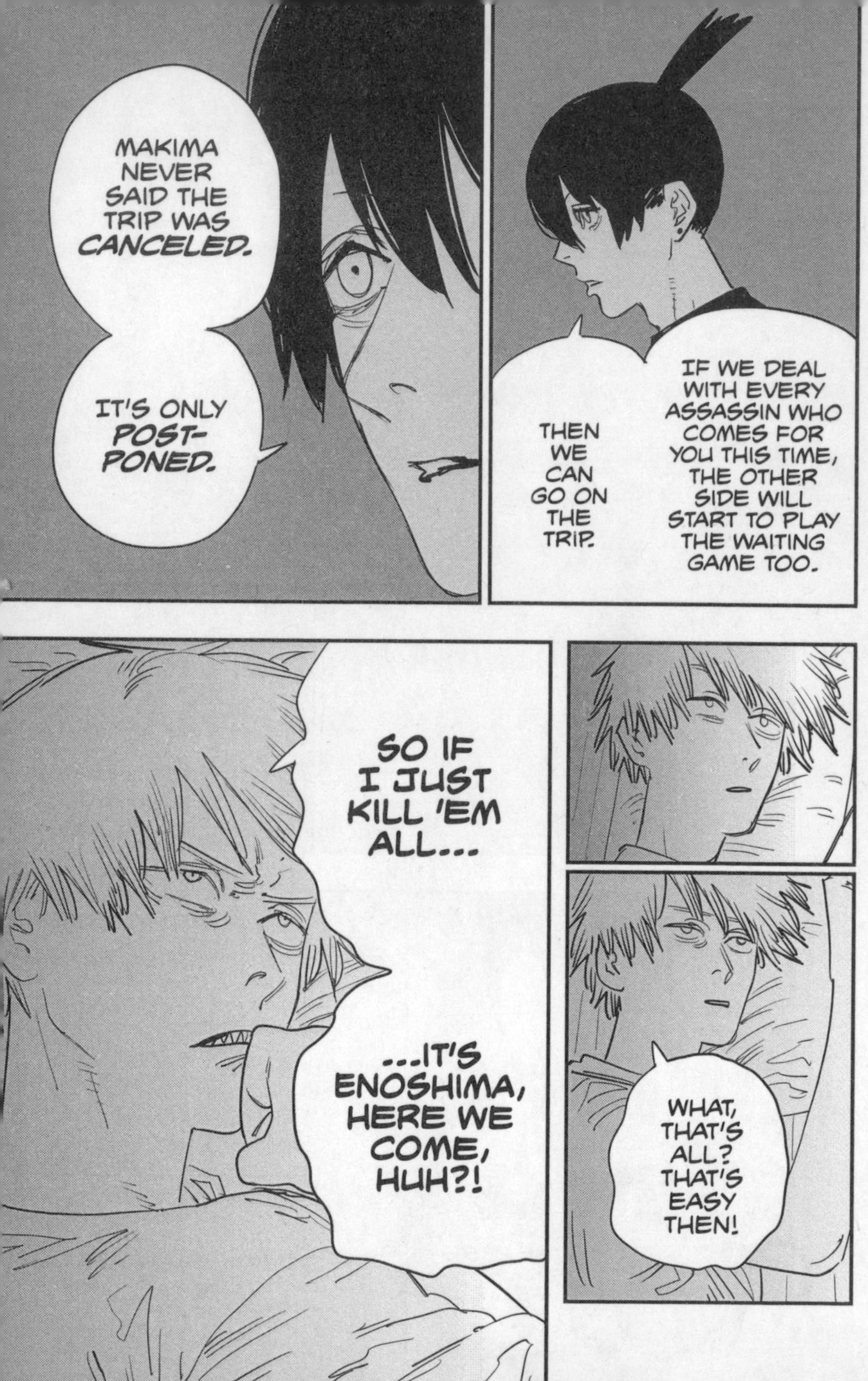
IF WE DEAL WITH EVERY ASSASSIN WHO COMES FOR YOU THIS TIME, THE OTHER SIDE WILL START TO PLAY THE WAITING GAME TOO.
THEN WE CAN GO ON THE TRIP.
MAKIMA NEVER SAID THE TRIP WAS CANCELED.
IT'S ONLY POSTPONED.
WHAT, THAT'S ALL? THAT'S EASY THEN!
SO IF I JUST KILL 'EM ALL...
...IT'S ENOSHIMA, HERE WE COME, HUH?!

*Chain saw man*

# Chapter 55: Let's Go

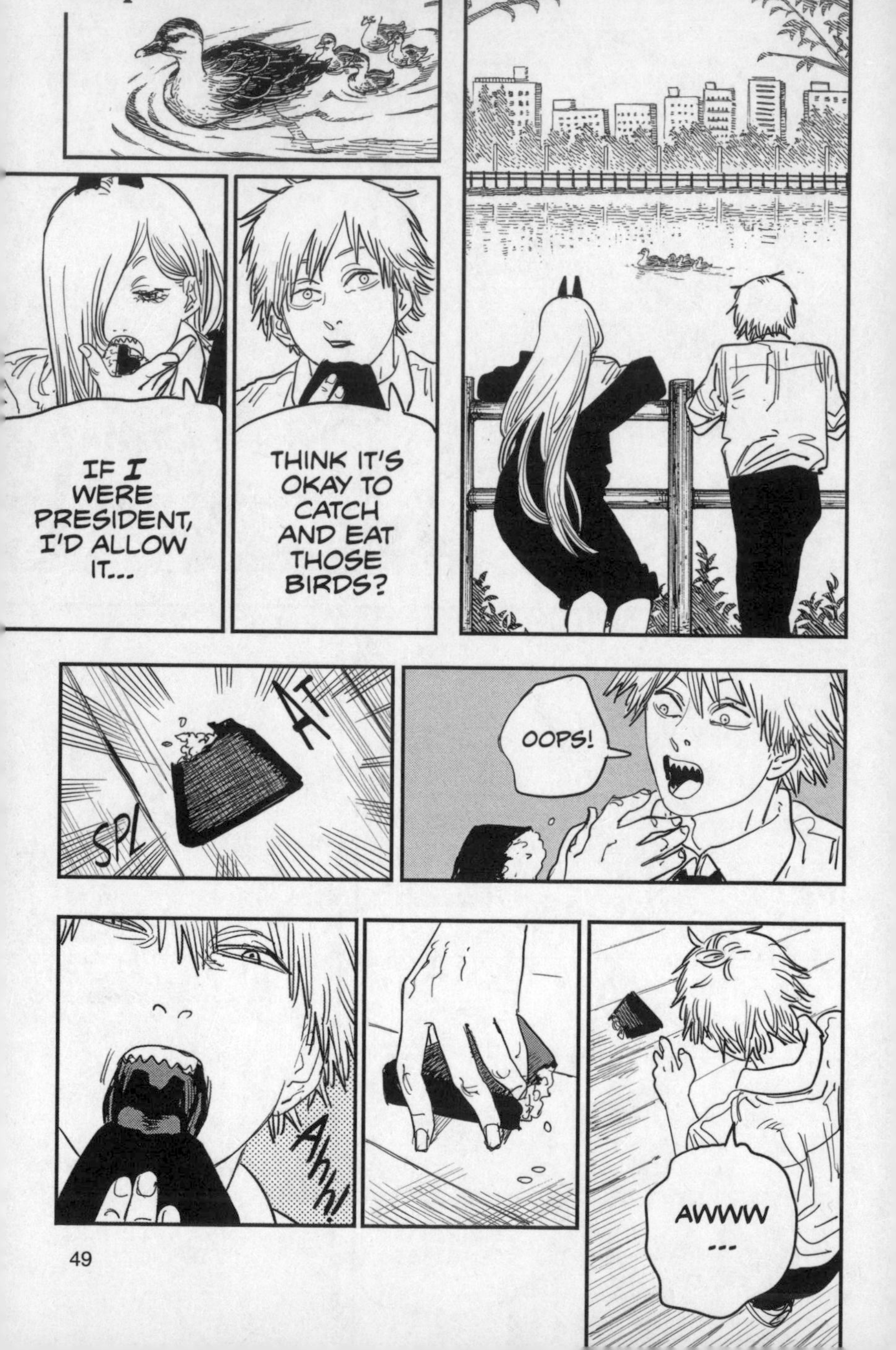

THINK IT'S OKAY TO CATCH AND EAT THOSE BIRDS?
IF I WERE PRESIDENT, I'D ALLOW IT...
OOPS!
SPL
AT
AWWW...
Ahh!

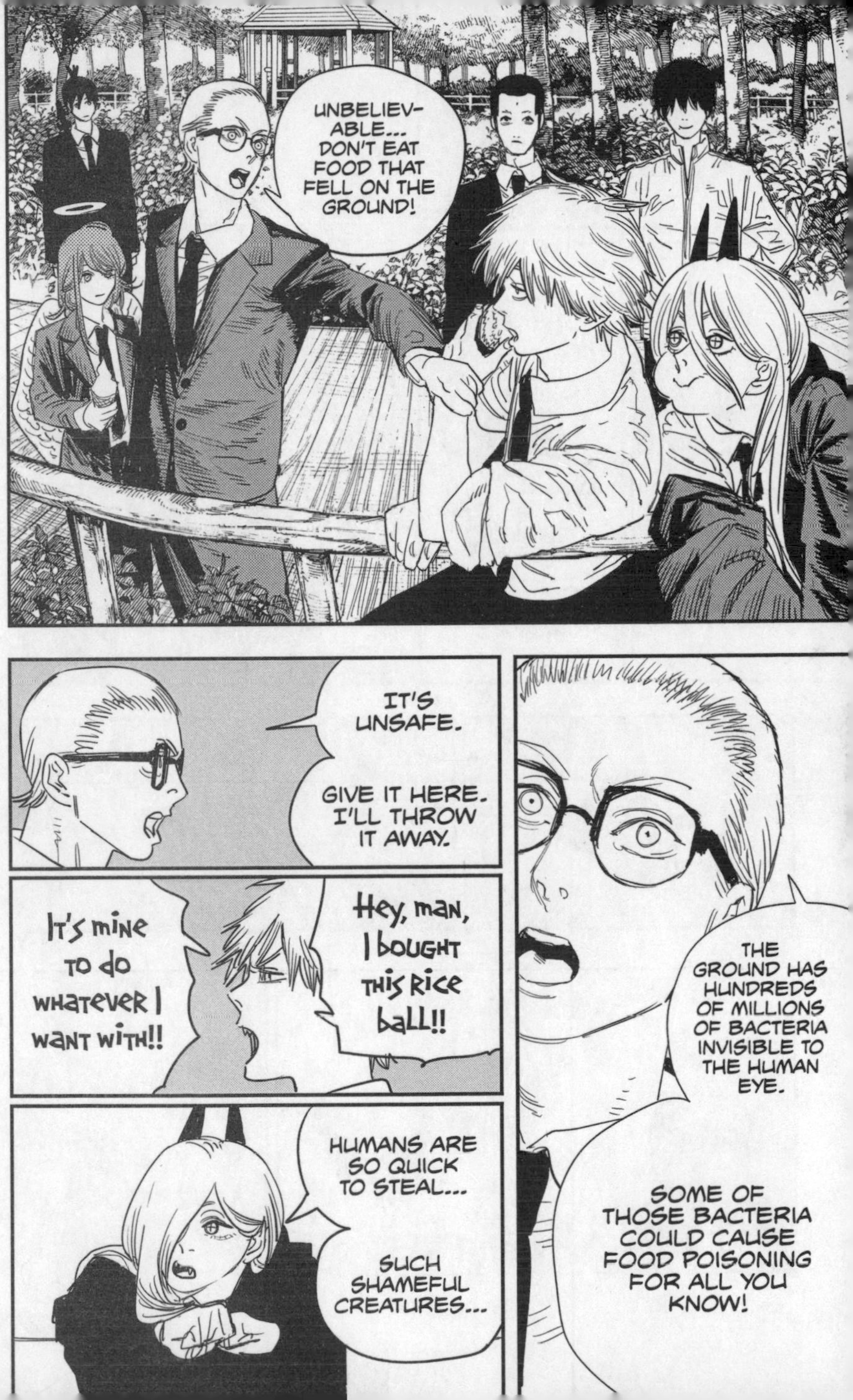
UNBELIEVABLE... DON'T EAT FOOD THAT FELL ON THE GROUND!
THE GROUND HAS HUNDREDS OF MILLIONS OF BACTERIA INVISIBLE TO THE HUMAN EYE.
SOME OF THOSE BACTERIA COULD CAUSE FOOD POISONING FOR ALL YOU KNOW!
IT'S UNSAFE.
GIVE IT HERE. I'LL THROW IT AWAY.
Hey, man, I bought this rice ball!!
It's mine to do whatever I want with!!
HUMANS ARE SO QUICK TO STEAL...
SUCH SHAMEFUL CREATURES...

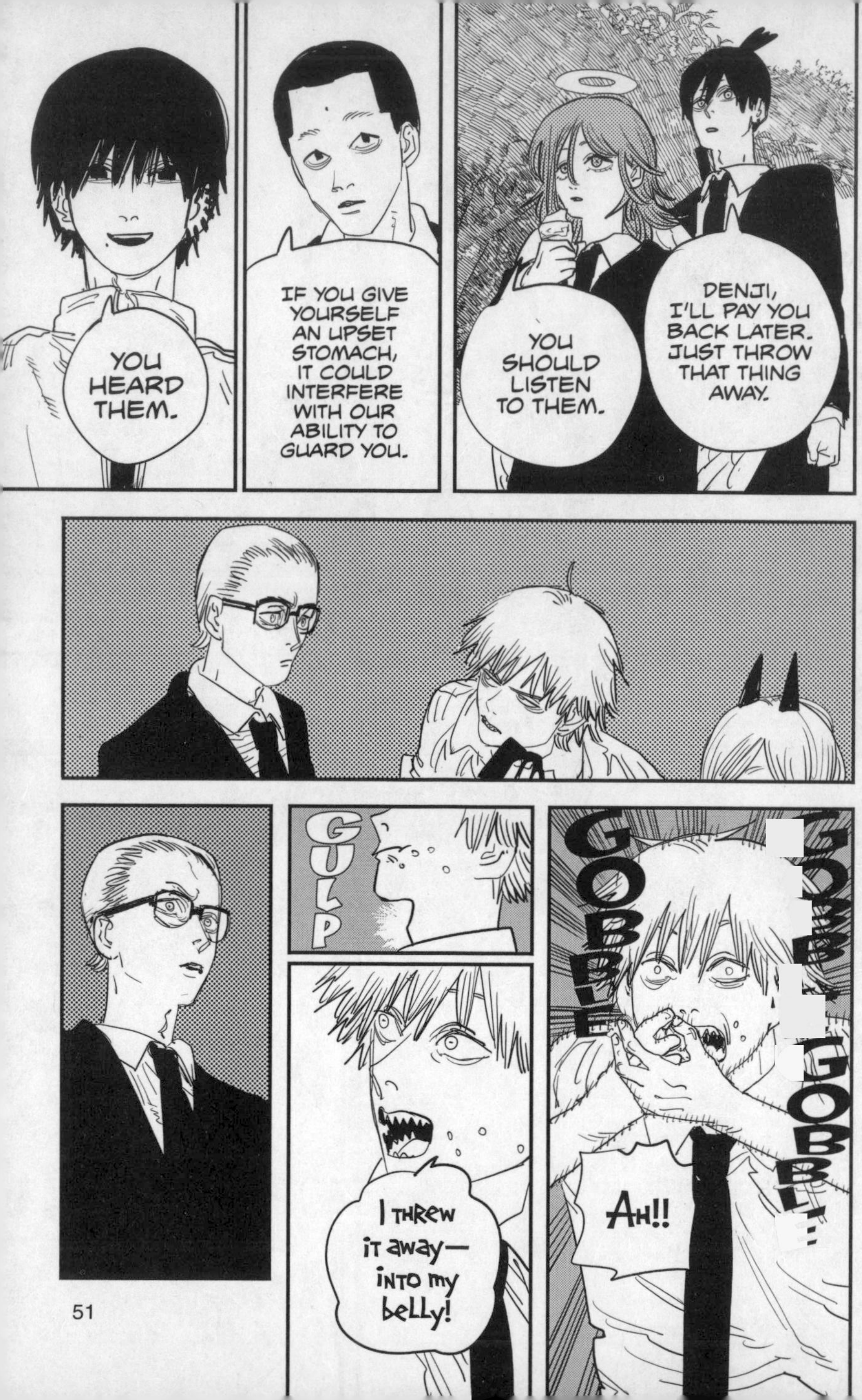
DENJI, I'LL PAY YOU BACK LATER. JUST THROW THAT THING AWAY.
YOU SHOULD LISTEN TO THEM.
IF YOU GIVE YOURSELF AN UPSET STOMACH, IT COULD INTERFERE WITH OUR ABILITY TO GUARD YOU.
YOU HEARD THEM.
GOBBLE
GOBBLE
AH!!
GULP
I THREW IT AWAY— INTO MY BELLY!

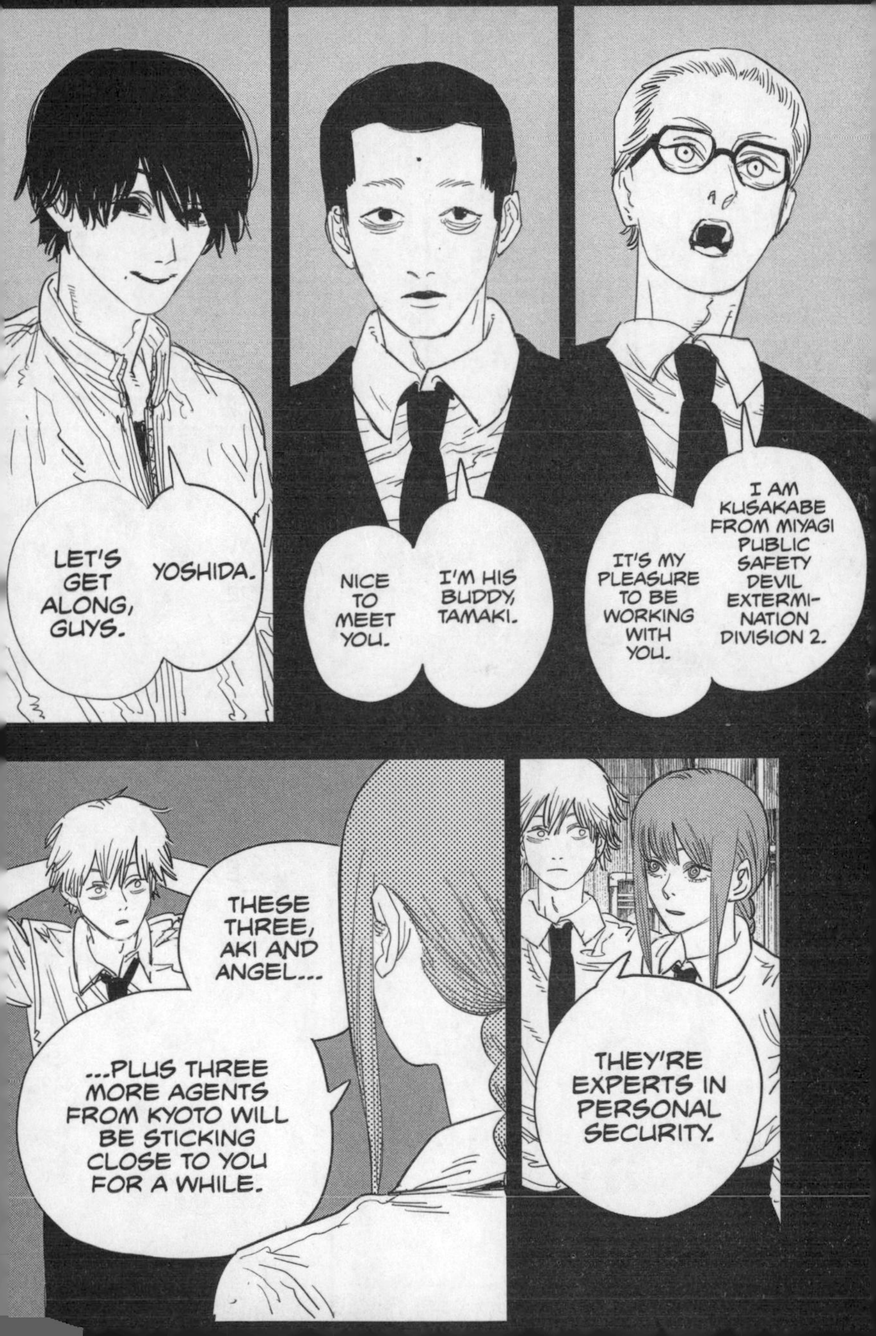
I AM KUSAKABE FROM MIYAGI PUBLIC SAFETY DEVIL EXTERMINATION DIVISION 2.
IT'S MY PLEASURE TO BE WORKING WITH YOU.
I'M HIS BUDDY, TAMAKI.
NICE TO MEET YOU.
YOSHIDA.
LET'S GET ALONG, GUYS.
THEY'RE EXPERTS IN PERSONAL SECURITY.
THESE THREE, AKI AND ANGEL...
...PLUS THREE MORE AGENTS FROM KYOTO WILL BE STICKING CLOSE TO YOU FOR A WHILE.

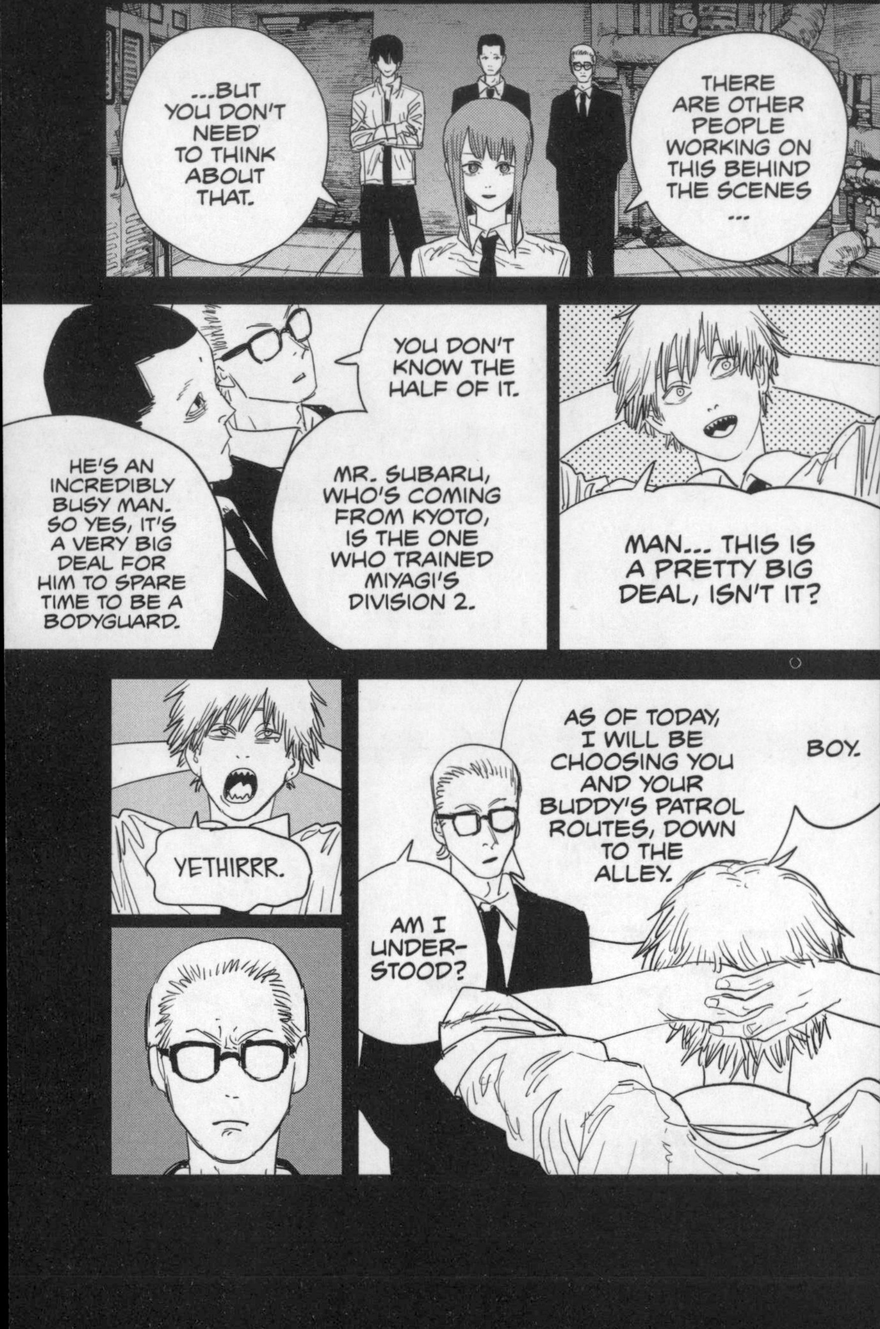
THERE ARE OTHER PEOPLE WORKING ON THIS BEHIND THE SCENES ...
...BUT YOU DON'T NEED TO THINK ABOUT THAT.
MAN... THIS IS A PRETTY BIG DEAL, ISN'T IT?
YOU DON'T KNOW THE HALF OF IT.
MR. SUBARU, WHO'S COMING FROM KYOTO, IS THE ONE WHO TRAINED MIYAGI'S DIVISION 2.
HE'S AN INCREDIBLY BUSY MAN. SO YES, IT'S A VERY BIG DEAL FOR HIM TO SPARE TIME TO BE A BODYGUARD.
BOY.
AS OF TODAY, I WILL BE CHOOSING YOU AND YOUR BUDDY'S PATROL ROUTES, DOWN TO THE ALLEY.
AM I UNDERSTOOD?
YETHIRRR.

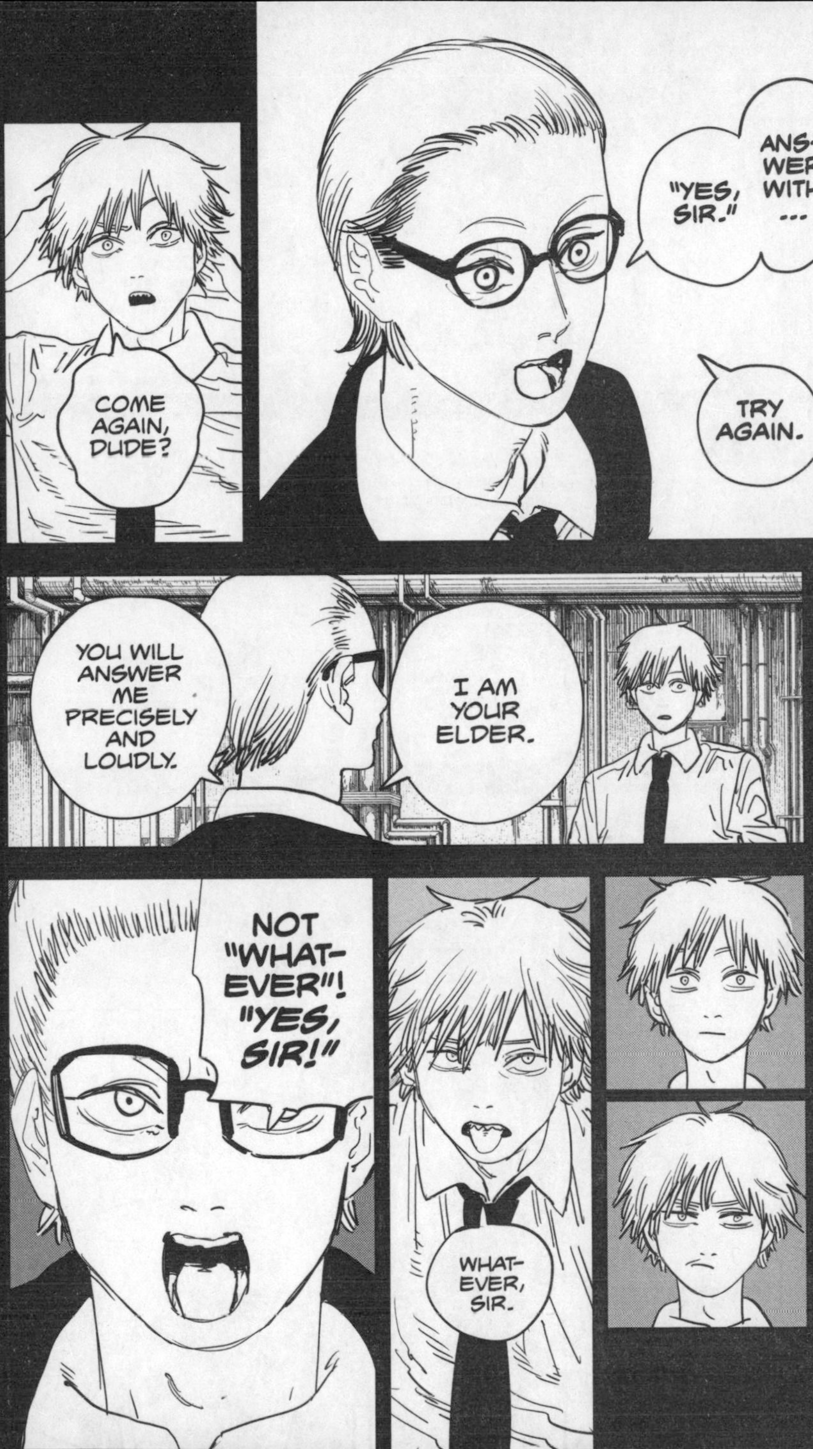
ANSWER WITH... "YES, SIR."
TRY AGAIN.
COME AGAIN, DUDE?
I AM YOUR ELDER.
YOU WILL ANSWER ME PRECISELY AND LOUDLY.
WHATEVER, SIR.
NOT "WHATEVER"! "YES, SIR!"

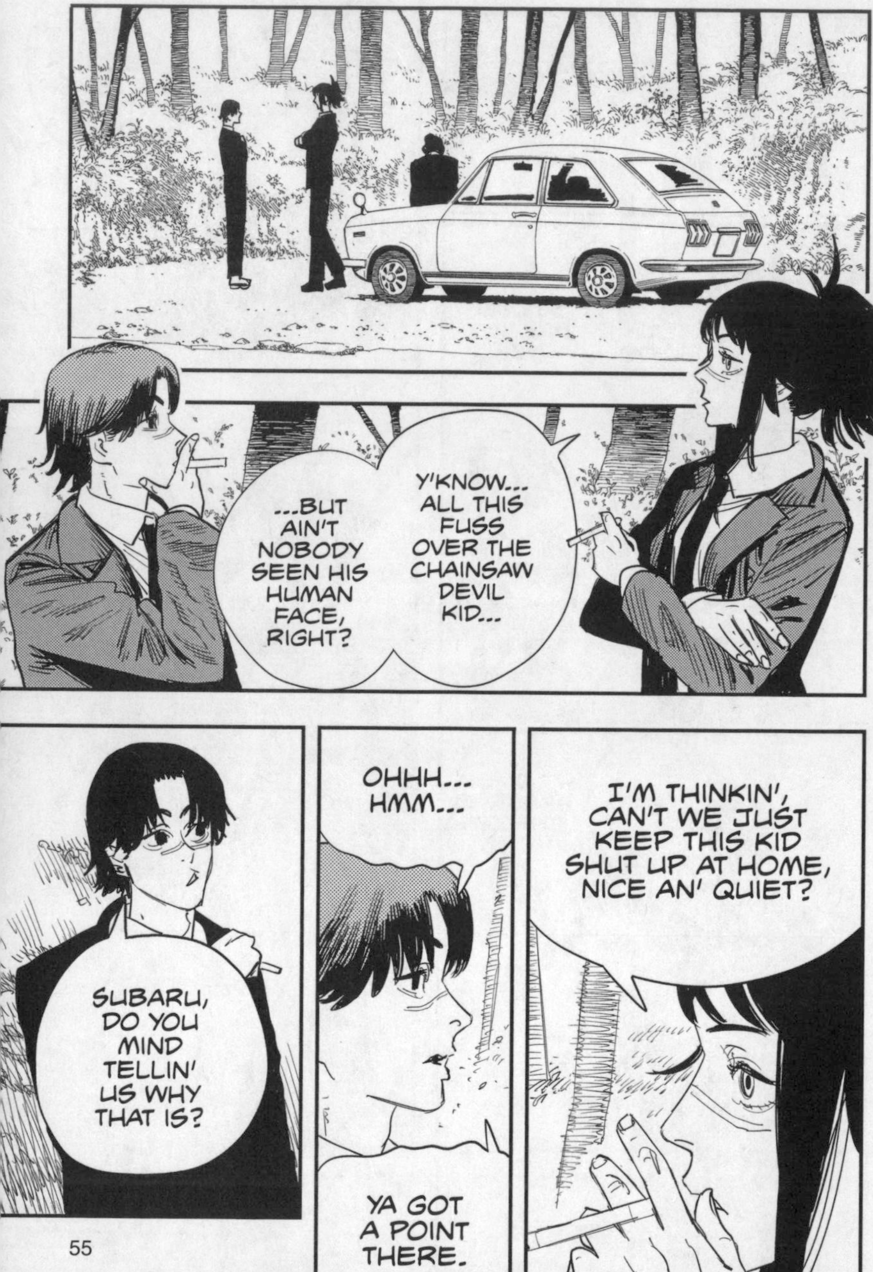
Y'KNOW... ALL THIS FUSS OVER THE CHAINSAW DEVIL KID...
...BUT AIN'T NOBODY SEEN HIS HUMAN FACE, RIGHT?
I'M THINKIN', CAN'T WE JUST KEEP THIS KID SHUT UP AT HOME, NICE AN' QUIET?
OHHH... HMM...
YA GOT A POINT THERE.
SUBARU, DO YOU MIND TELLIN' US WHY THAT IS?

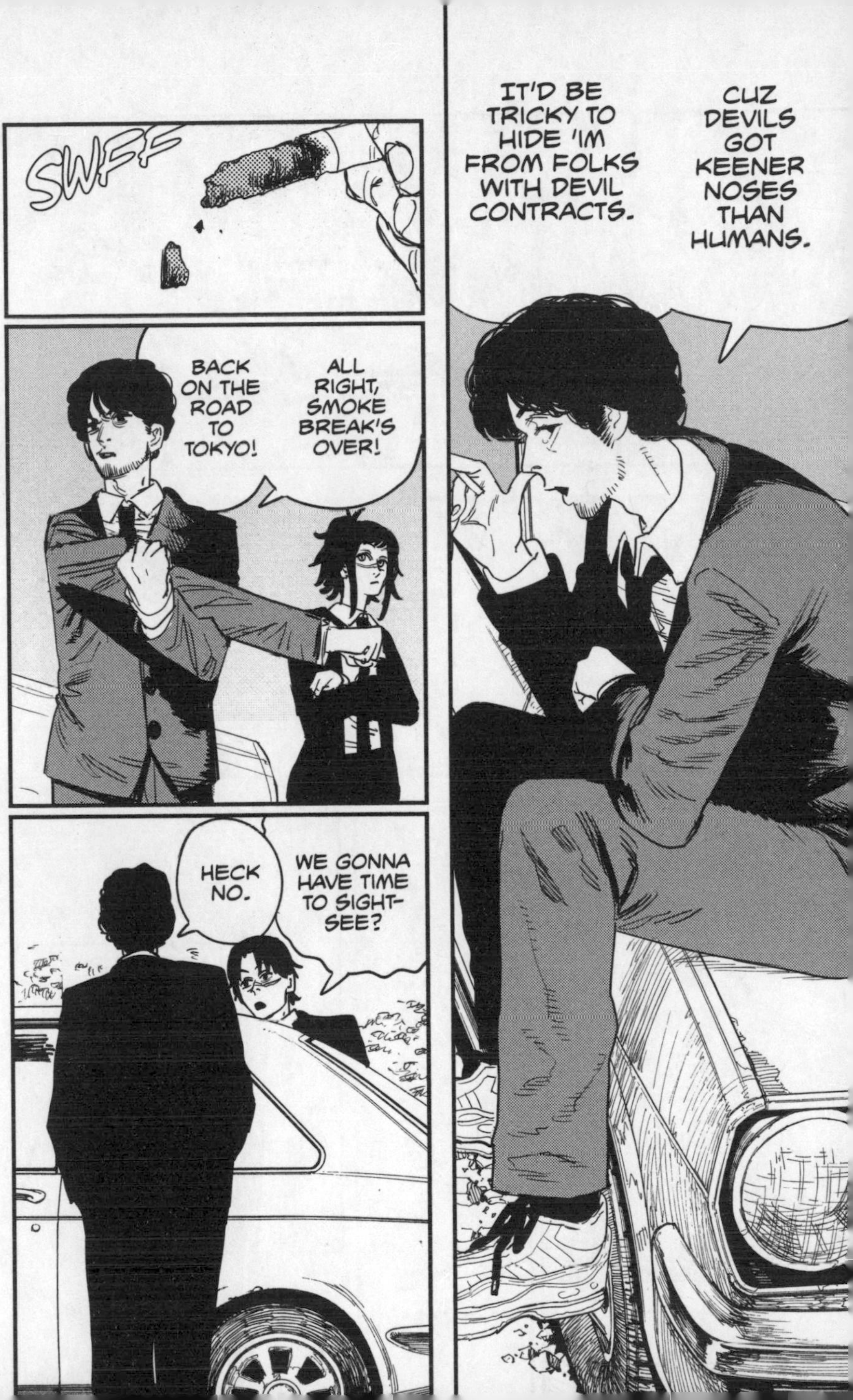
IT'D BE TRICKY TO HIDE 'IM FROM FOLKS WITH DEVIL CONTRACTS.
CUZ DEVILS GOT KEENER NOSES THAN HUMANS.
SWFF
ALL RIGHT, SMOKE BREAK'S OVER!
BACK ON THE ROAD TO TOKYO!
WE GONNA HAVE TIME TO SIGHT-SEE?
HECK NO.

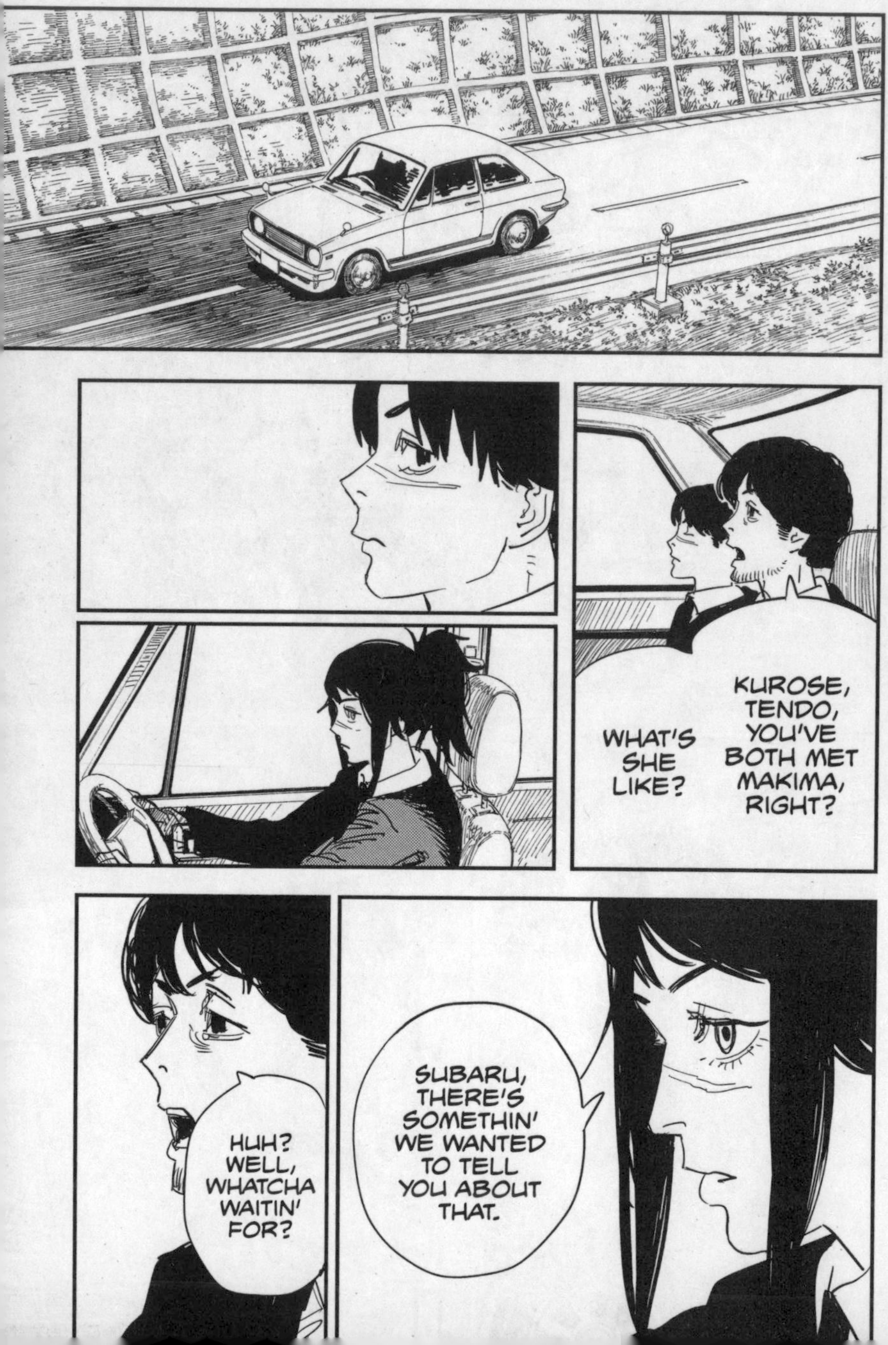
KUROSE, TENDO, YOU'VE BOTH MET MAKIMA, RIGHT?
WHAT'S SHE LIKE?
SUBARU, THERE'S SOMETHIN' WE WANTED TO TELL YOU ABOUT THAT.
HUH? WELL, WHATCHA WAITIN' FOR?

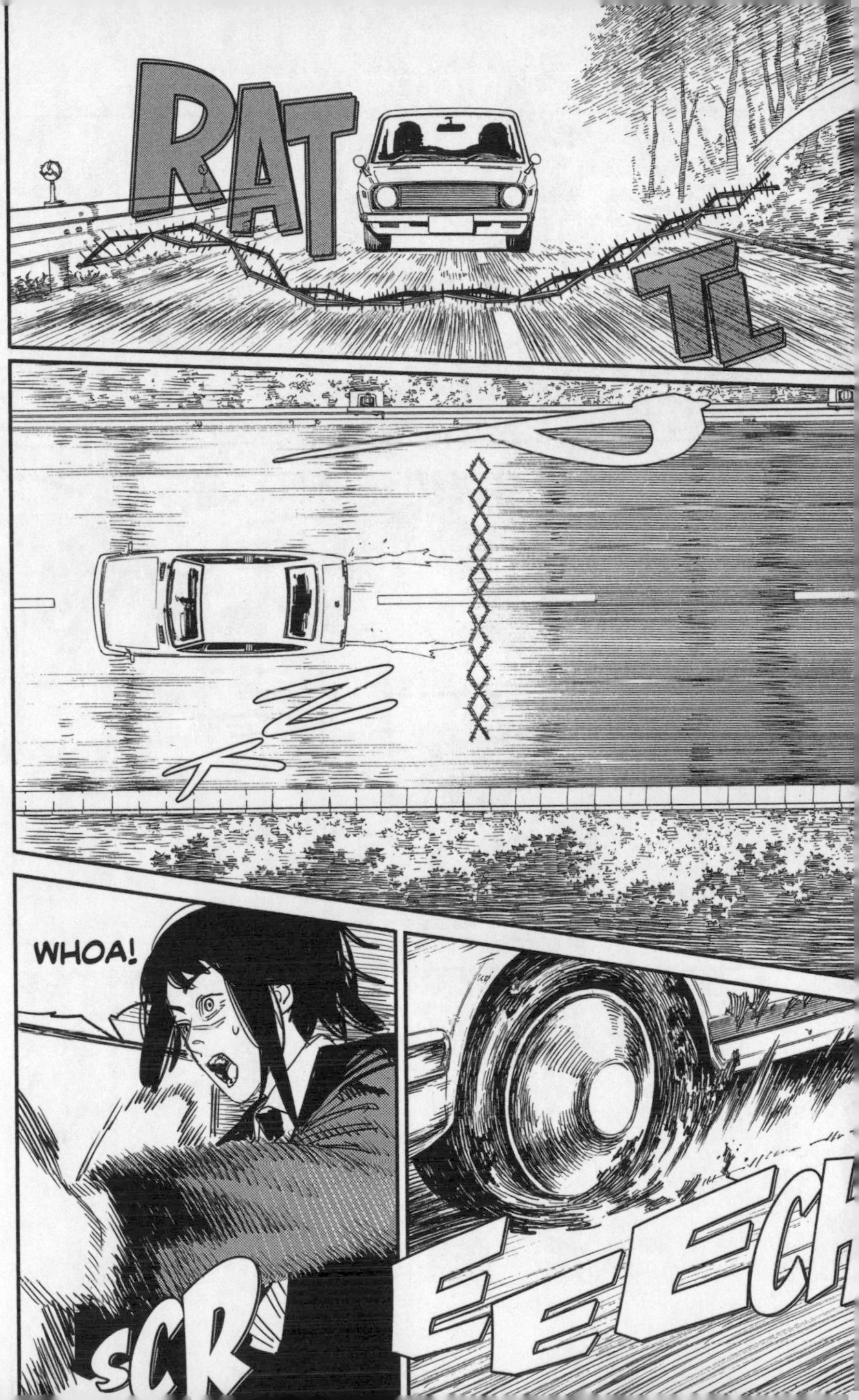
RATTL
WHOA!
SCREEECH

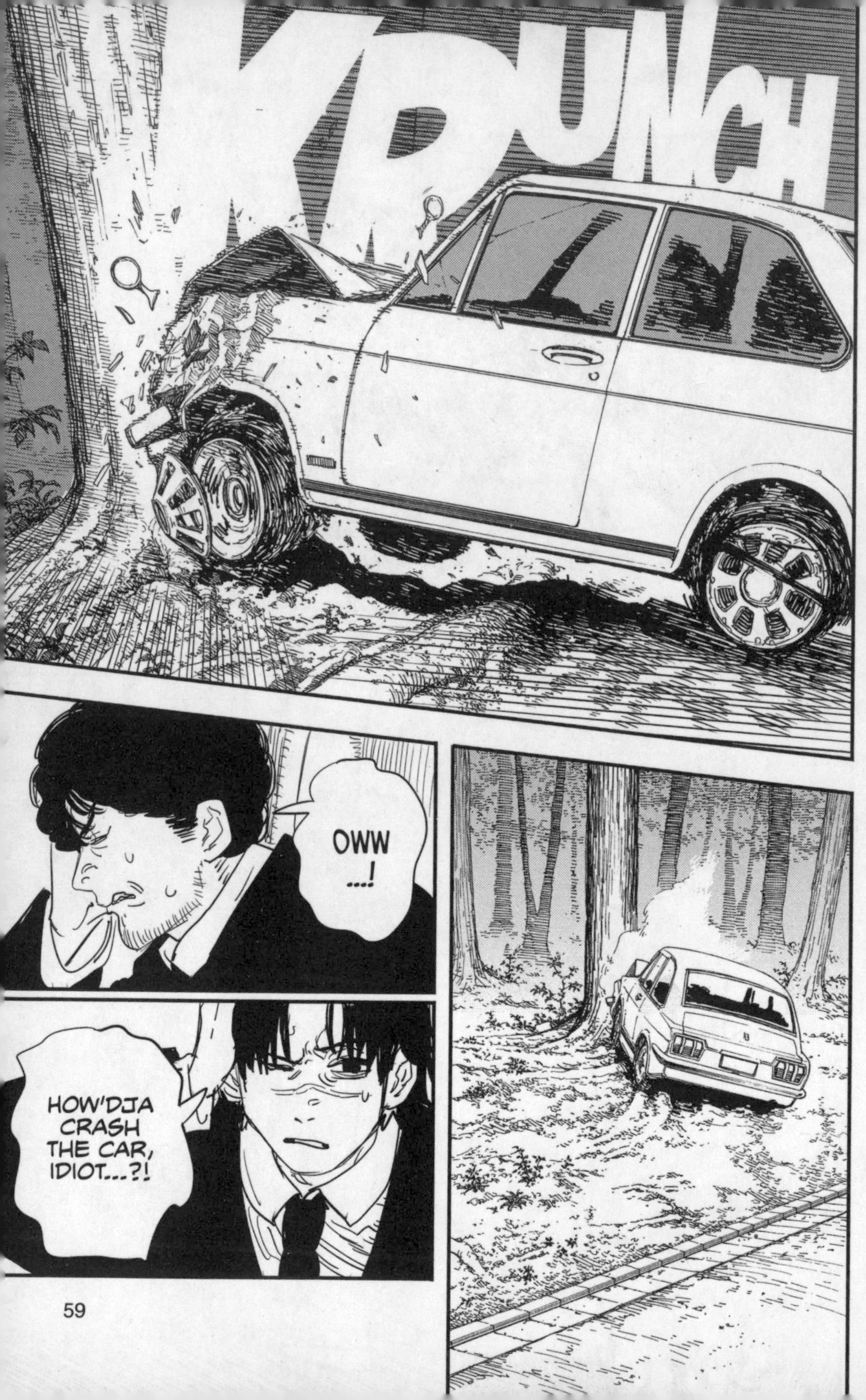
KRUNCH
OWW ...!
HOW'DJA CRASH THE CAR, IDIOT...?!

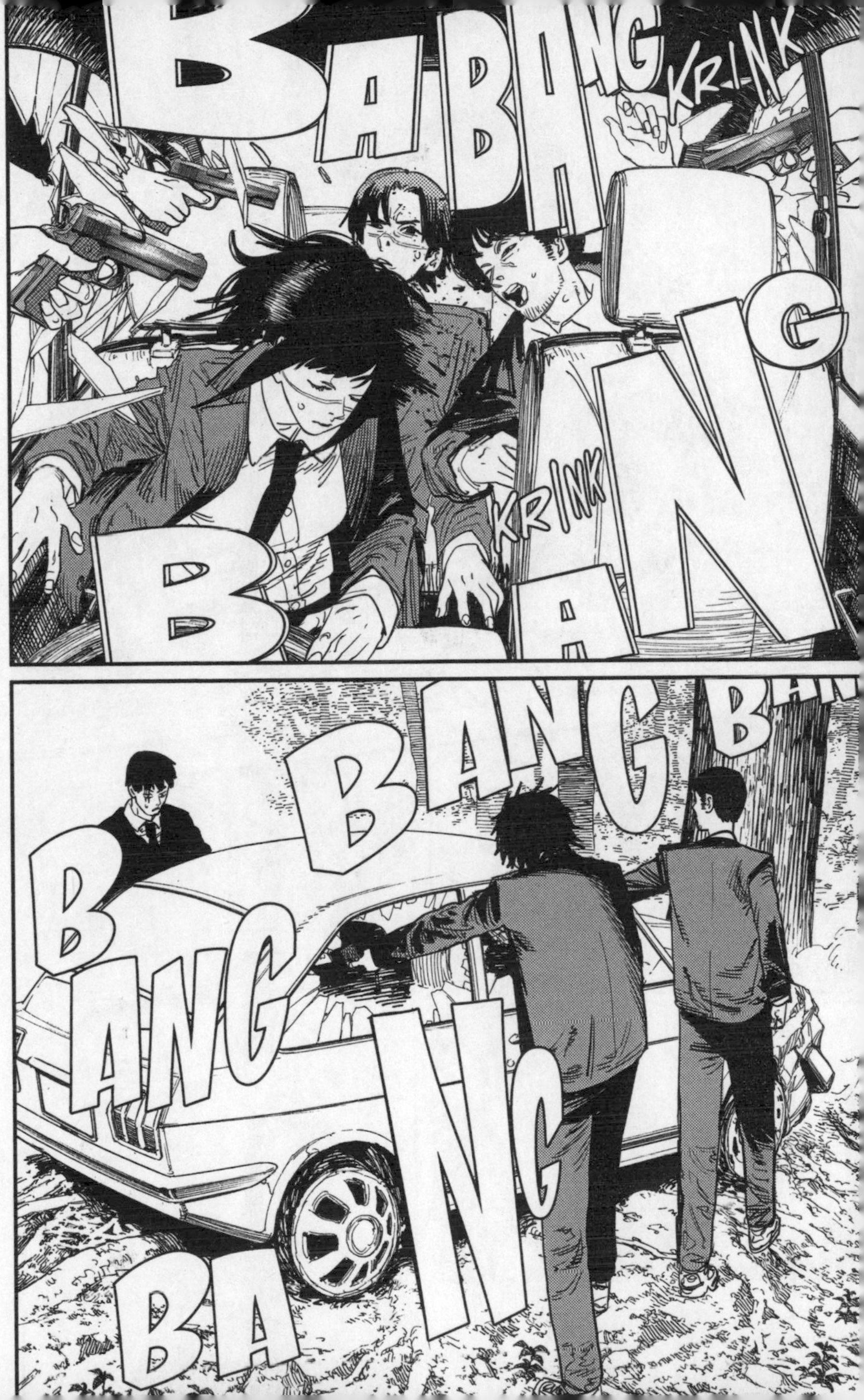

KRINK
BABANG
KRINK
BANG
BAN
BANG
BANG
BANG

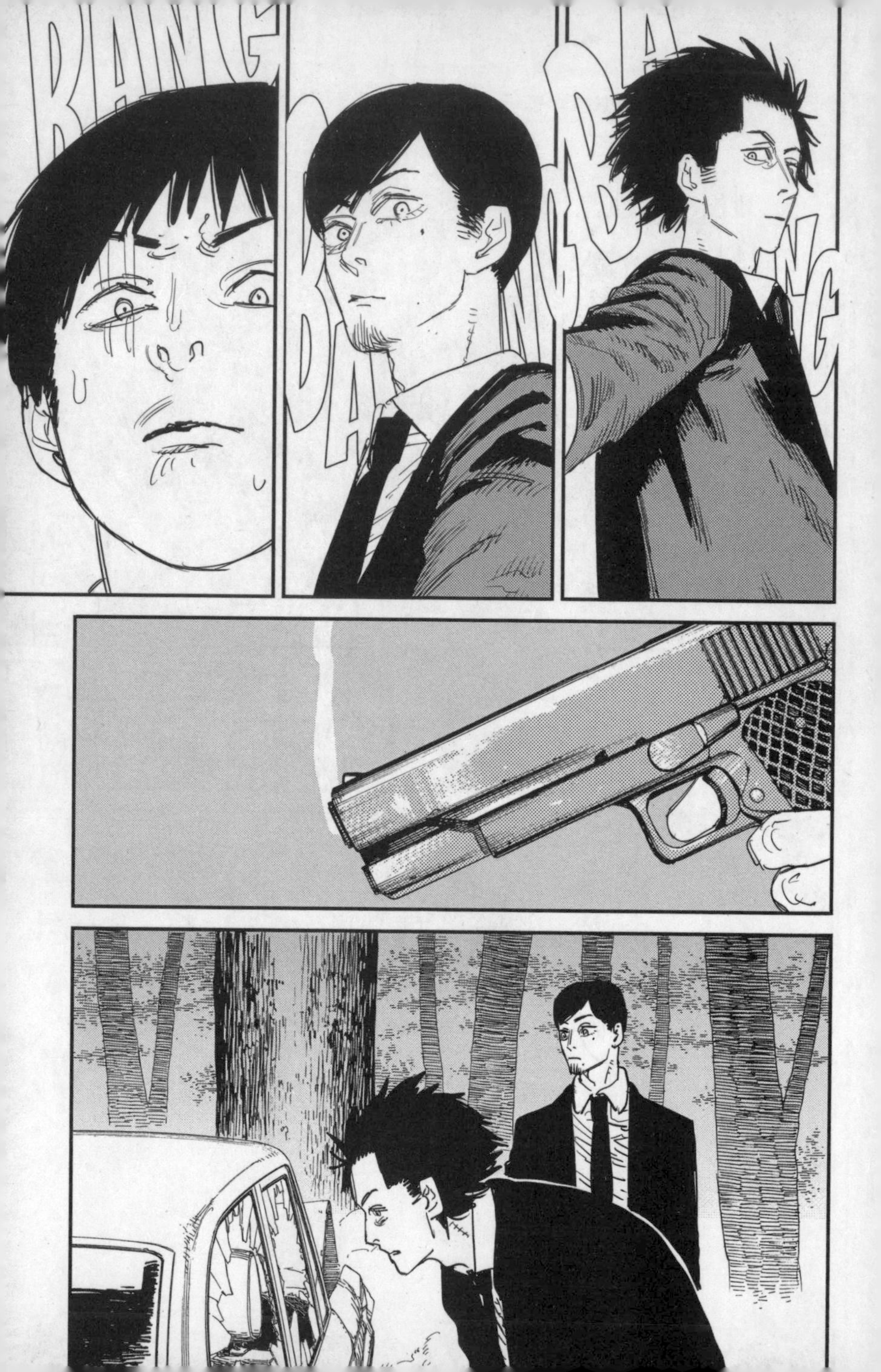
BANG
BANG
BANG

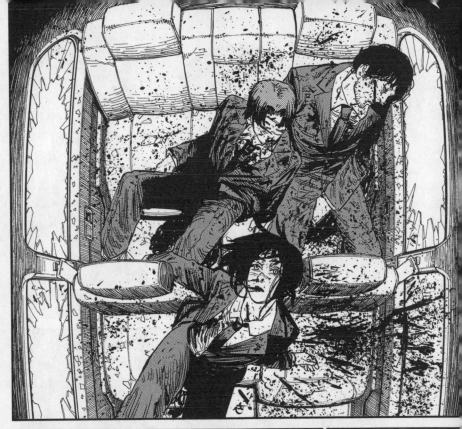

DAMN, THE WOMAN WAS FINE. TOO BAD WE KILLED HER.

LET ME GET A LOOK... OHHH...

NOT MY TYPE. I LIKE MY WOMEN SHORTER THAN ME.

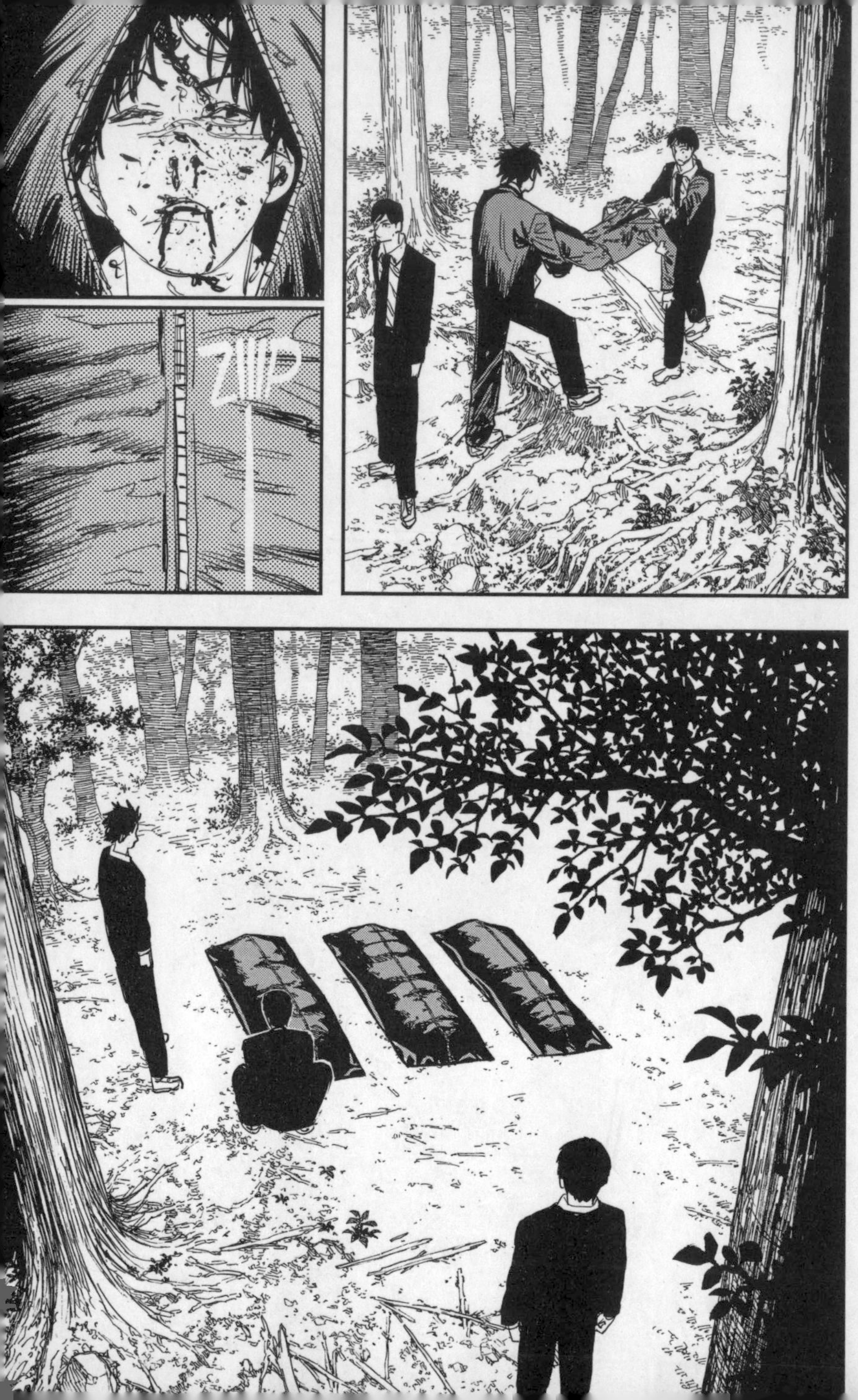
ZIIP

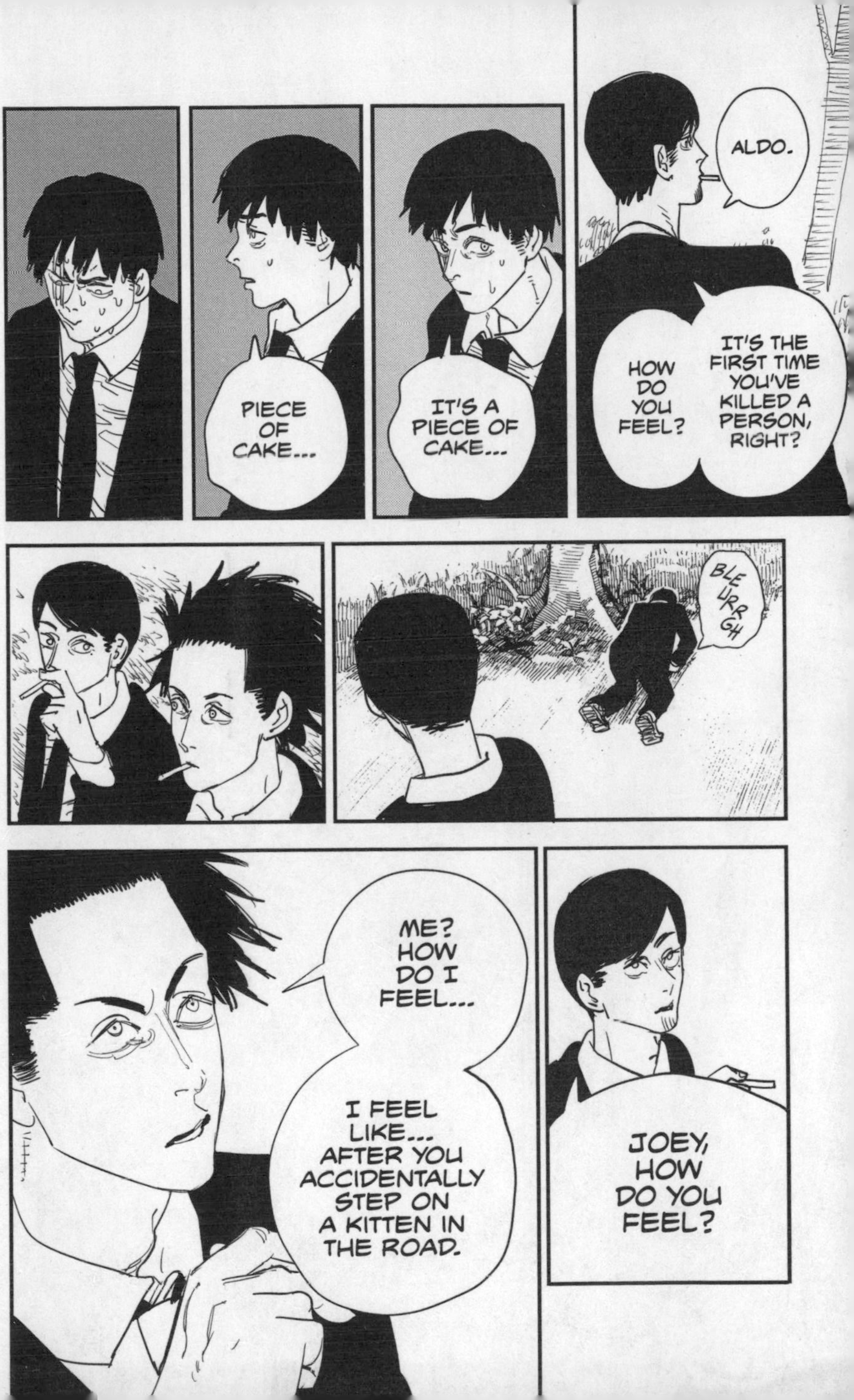

ALDO.
IT'S THE FIRST TIME YOU'VE KILLED A PERSON, RIGHT?
HOW DO YOU FEEL?
IT'S A PIECE OF CAKE...
PIECE OF CAKE...
BLEURRGH
JOEY, HOW DO YOU FEEL?
ME? HOW DO I FEEL...
I FEEL LIKE... AFTER YOU ACCIDENTALLY STEP ON A KITTEN IN THE ROAD.

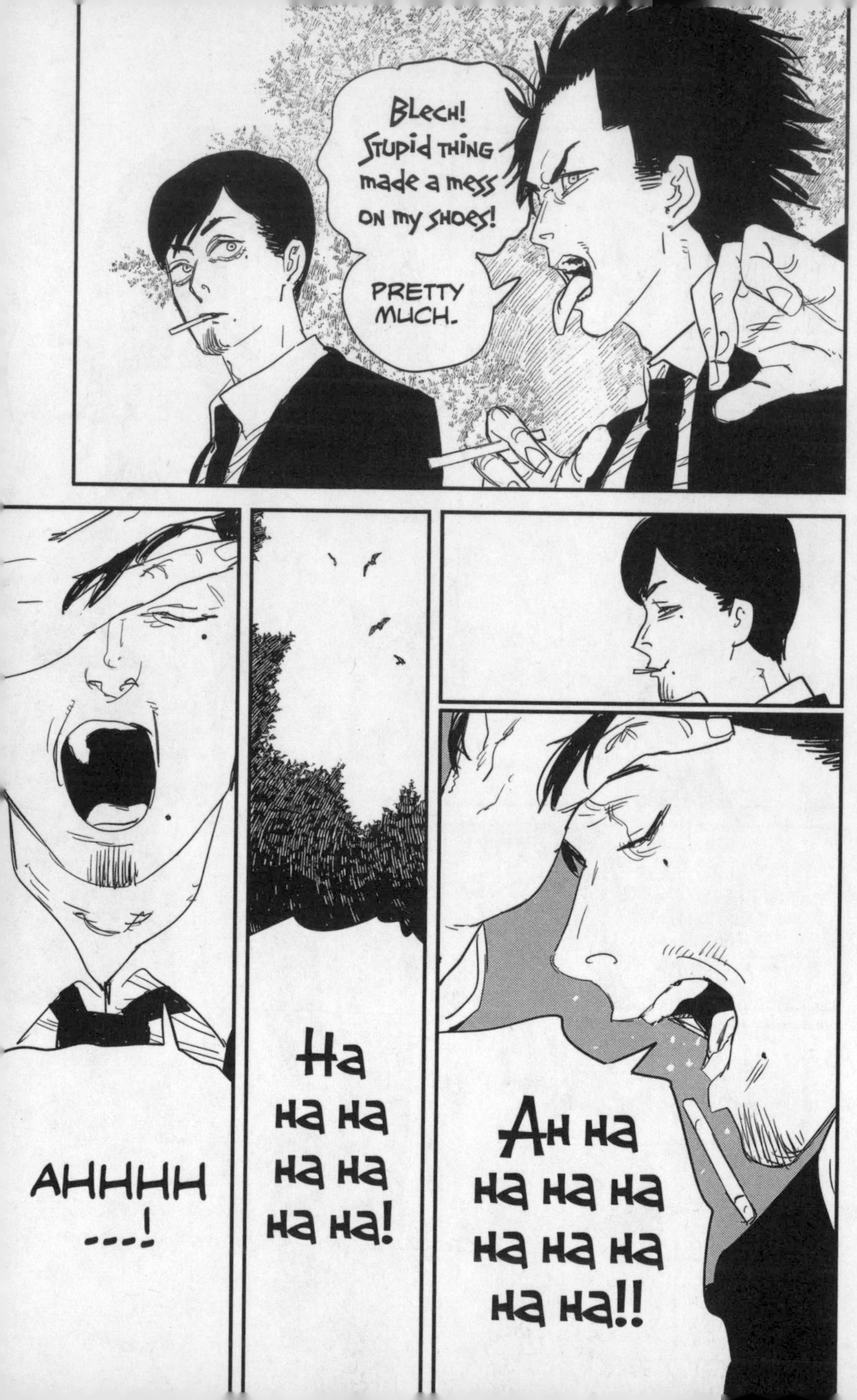
Blech! Stupid thing made a mess on my shoes!
PRETTY MUCH.
Ah ha ha ha ha ha ha ha ha ha!!
Ha ha ha ha ha ha ha!
AHHHH ---!

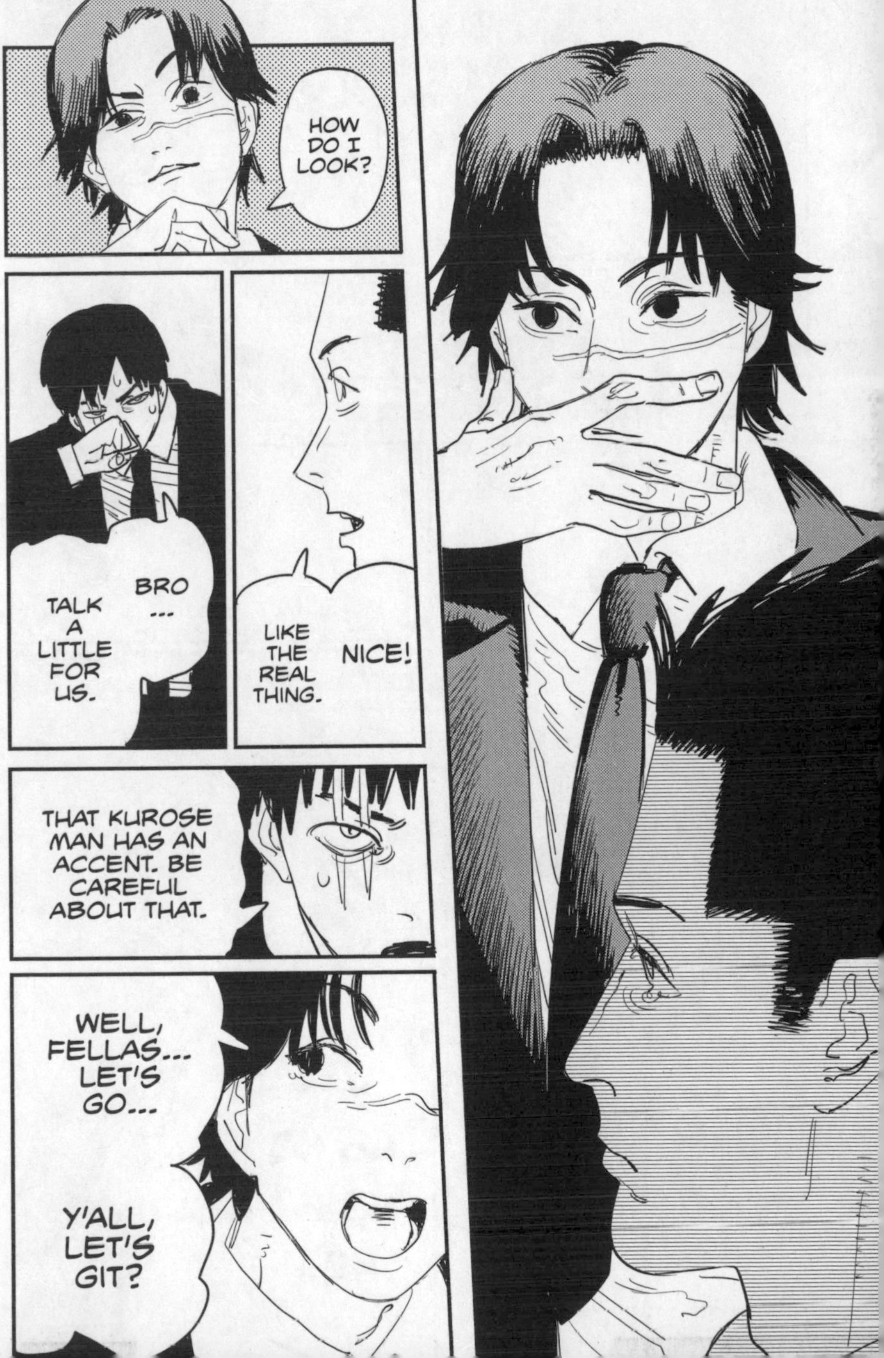
HOW DO I LOOK?
NICE!
LIKE THE REAL THING.
BRO...
TALK A LITTLE FOR US.
THAT KUROSE MAN HAS AN ACCENT. BE CAREFUL ABOUT THAT.
WELL, FELLAS... LET'S GO...
Y'ALL, LET'S GIT?

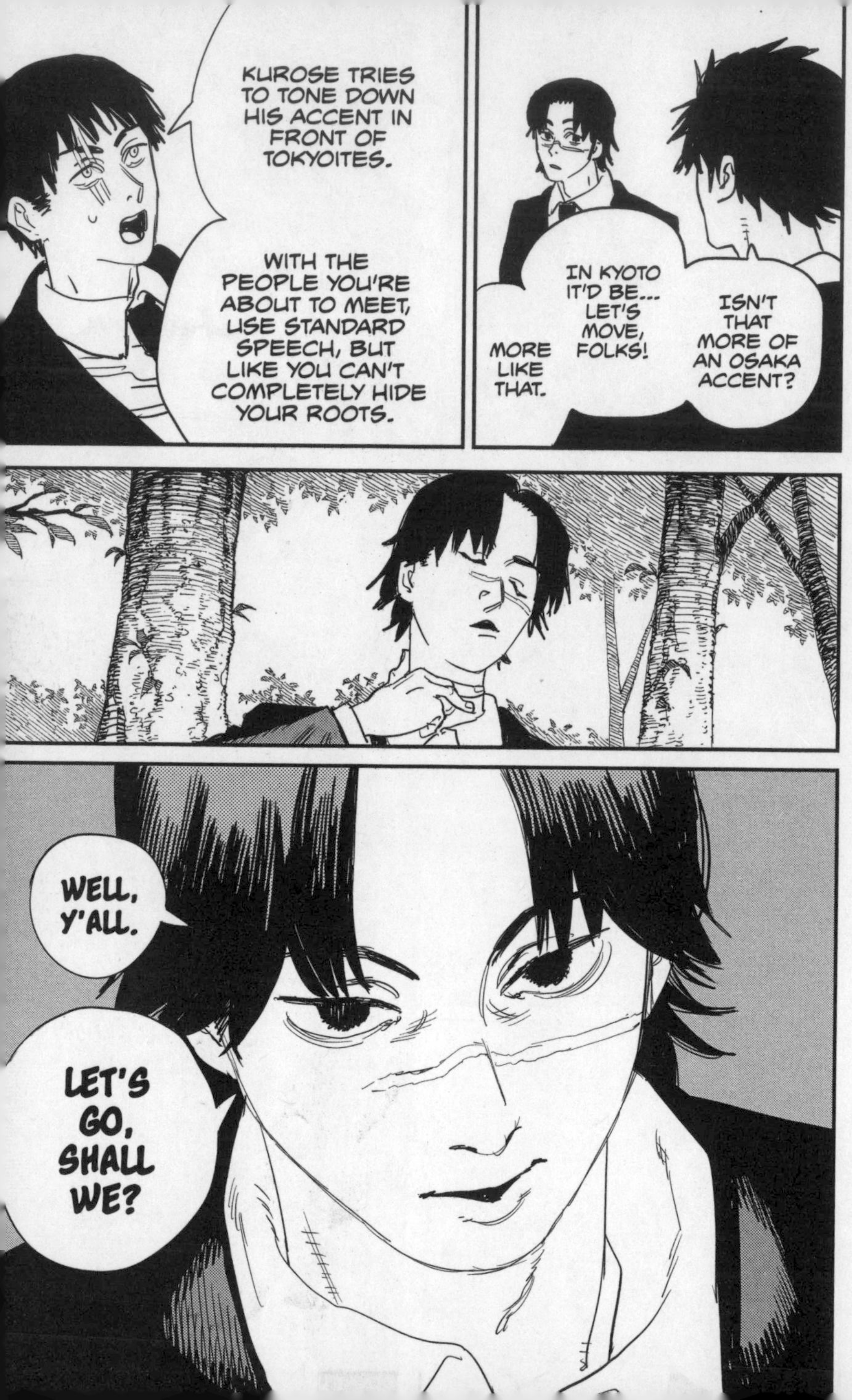
ISN'T THAT MORE OF AN OSAKA ACCENT?
IN KYOTO IT'D BE... LET'S MOVE, FOLKS!
MORE LIKE THAT.
KUROSE TRIES TO TONE DOWN HIS ACCENT IN FRONT OF TOKYOITES.
WITH THE PEOPLE YOU'RE ABOUT TO MEET, USE STANDARD SPEECH, BUT LIKE YOU CAN'T COMPLETELY HIDE YOUR ROOTS.
WELL, Y'ALL.
LET'S GO, SHALL WE?

Chain saw man

# Chapter 56: A Curse and a First

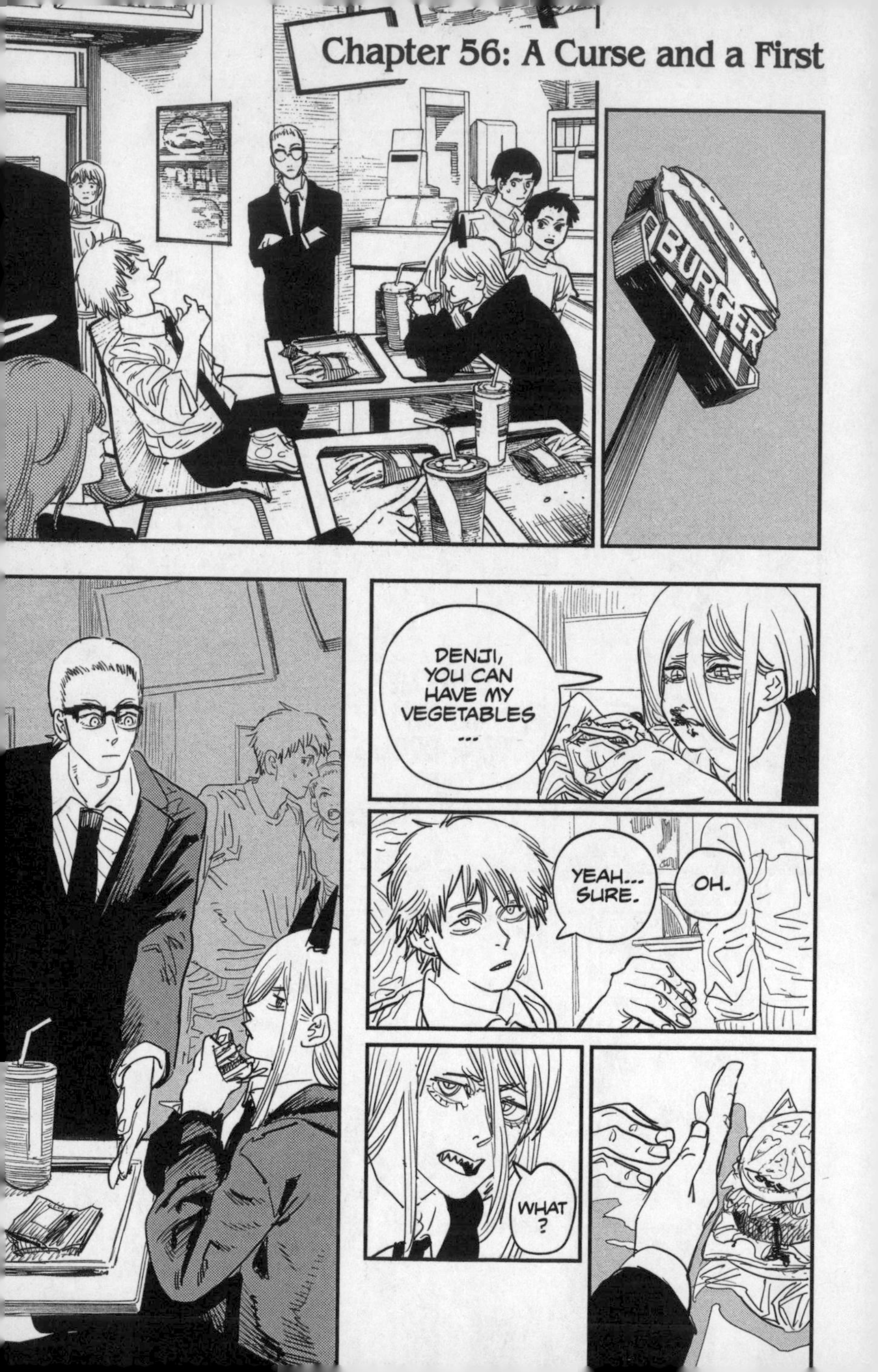
BURGER
DENJI, YOU CAN HAVE MY VEGETABLES...
OH.
YEAH... SURE.
WHAT?

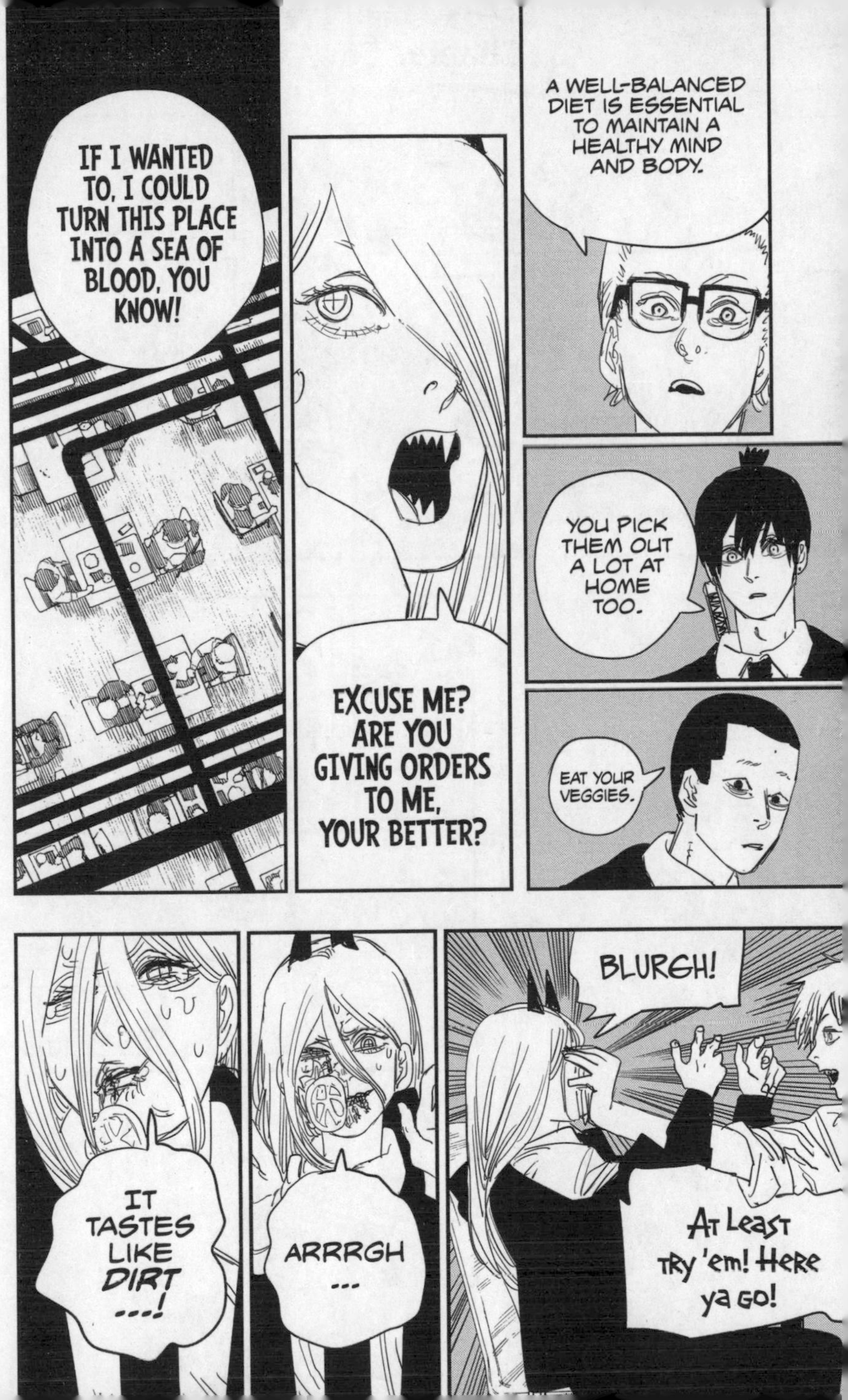
A WELL-BALANCED DIET IS ESSENTIAL TO MAINTAIN A HEALTHY MIND AND BODY.
YOU PICK THEM OUT A LOT AT HOME TOO.
EAT YOUR VEGGIES.
EXCUSE ME? ARE YOU GIVING ORDERS TO ME, YOUR BETTER?
IF I WANTED TO, I COULD TURN THIS PLACE INTO A SEA OF BLOOD, YOU KNOW!
BLURGH!
At Least try 'em! Here ya go!
ARRRGH ...
IT TASTES LIKE *DIRT* ...!

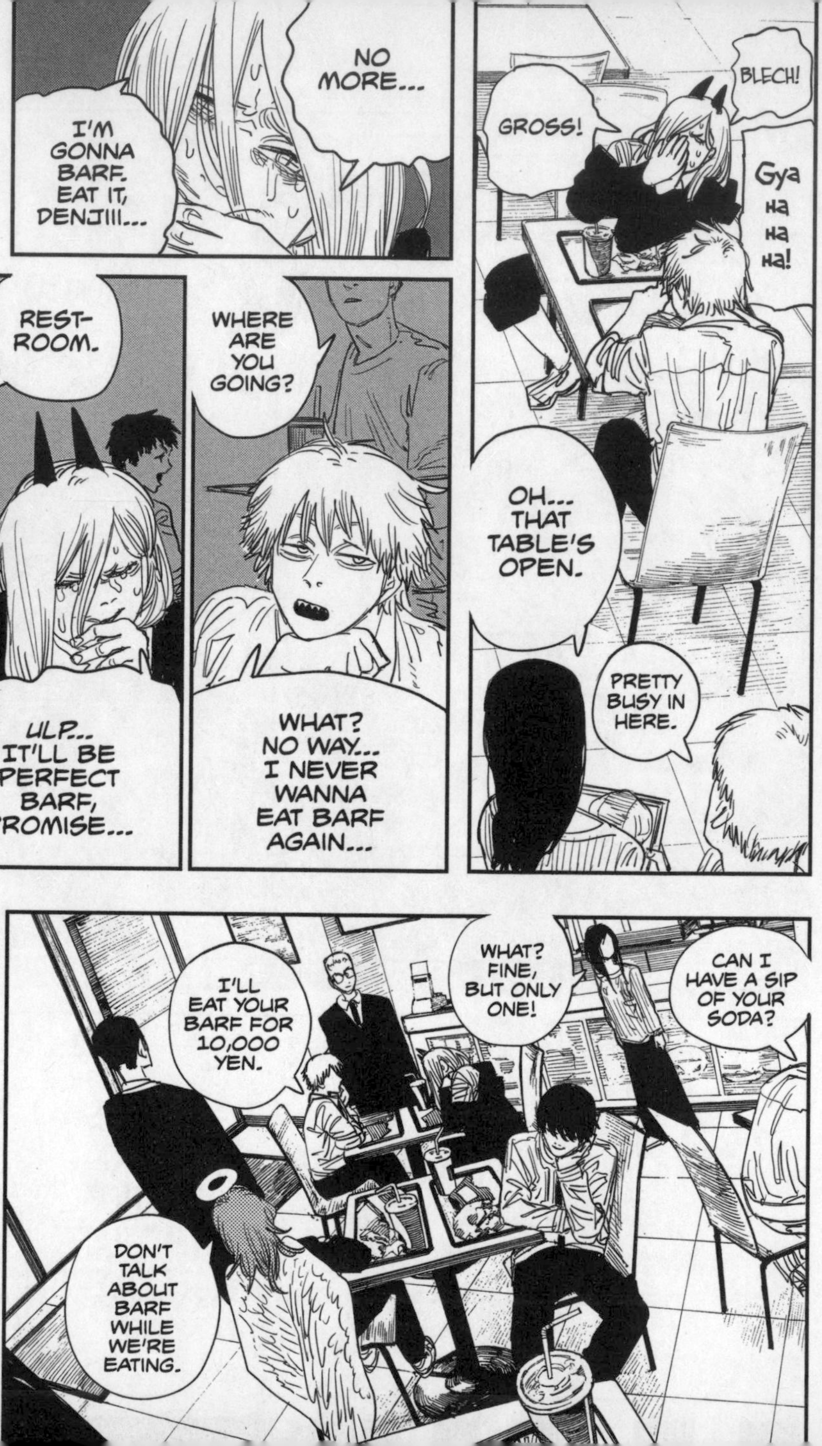
BLECH!
Gya ha ha ha!
GROSS!
OH... THAT TABLE'S OPEN.
PRETTY BUSY IN HERE.
NO MORE...
I'M GONNA BARF. EAT IT, DENJIII...
WHERE ARE YOU GOING?
WHAT? NO WAY... I NEVER WANNA EAT BARF AGAIN...
REST-ROOM.
ULP... IT'LL BE PERFECT BARF, PROMISE...
CAN I HAVE A SIP OF YOUR SODA?
WHAT? FINE, BUT ONLY ONE!
I'LL EAT YOUR BARF FOR 10,000 YEN.
DON'T TALK ABOUT BARF WHILE WE'RE EATING.

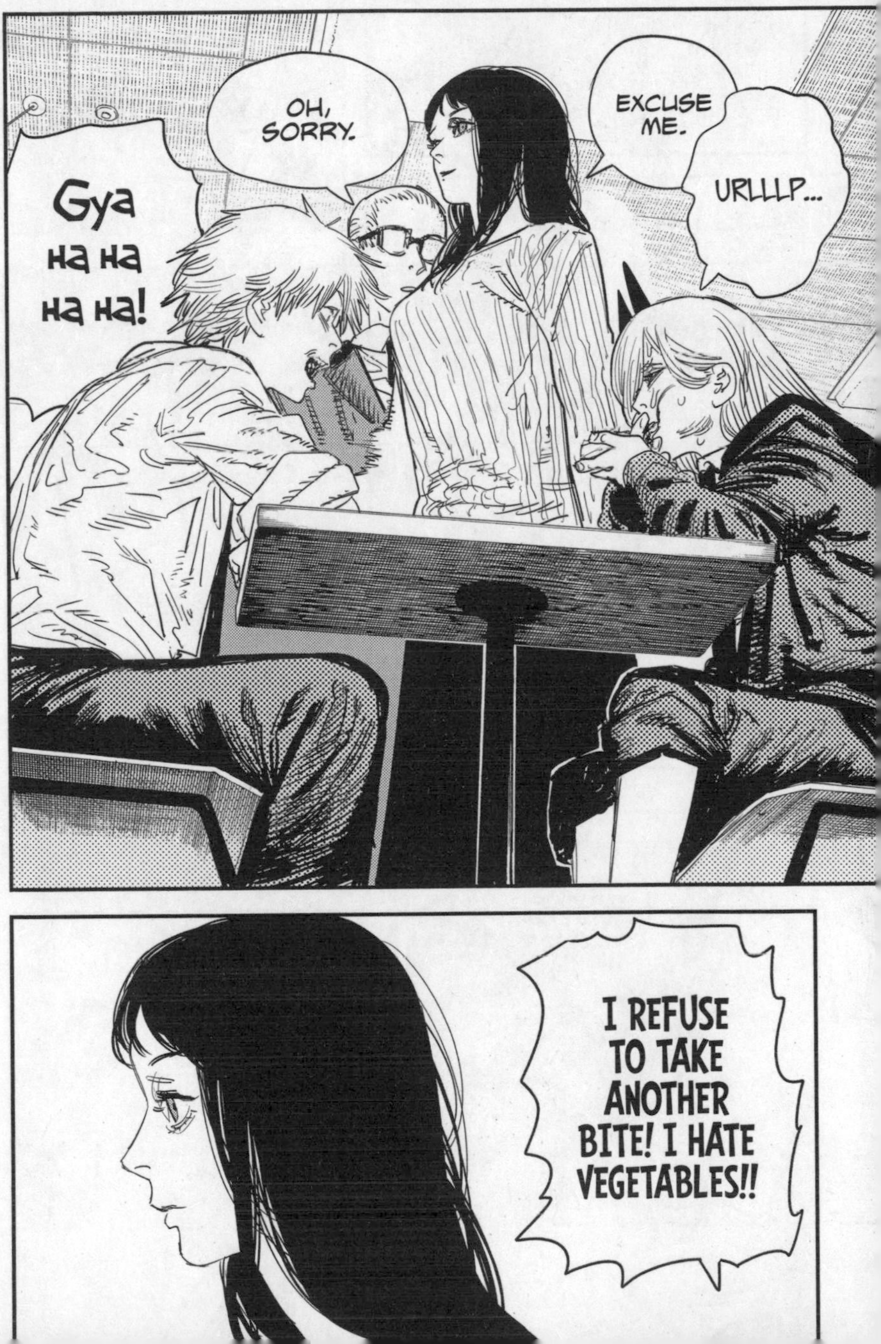
EXCUSE ME.
OH, SORRY.
URLLLP...
Gya ha ha ha ha!
I REFUSE TO TAKE ANOTHER BITE! I HATE VEGETABLES!!

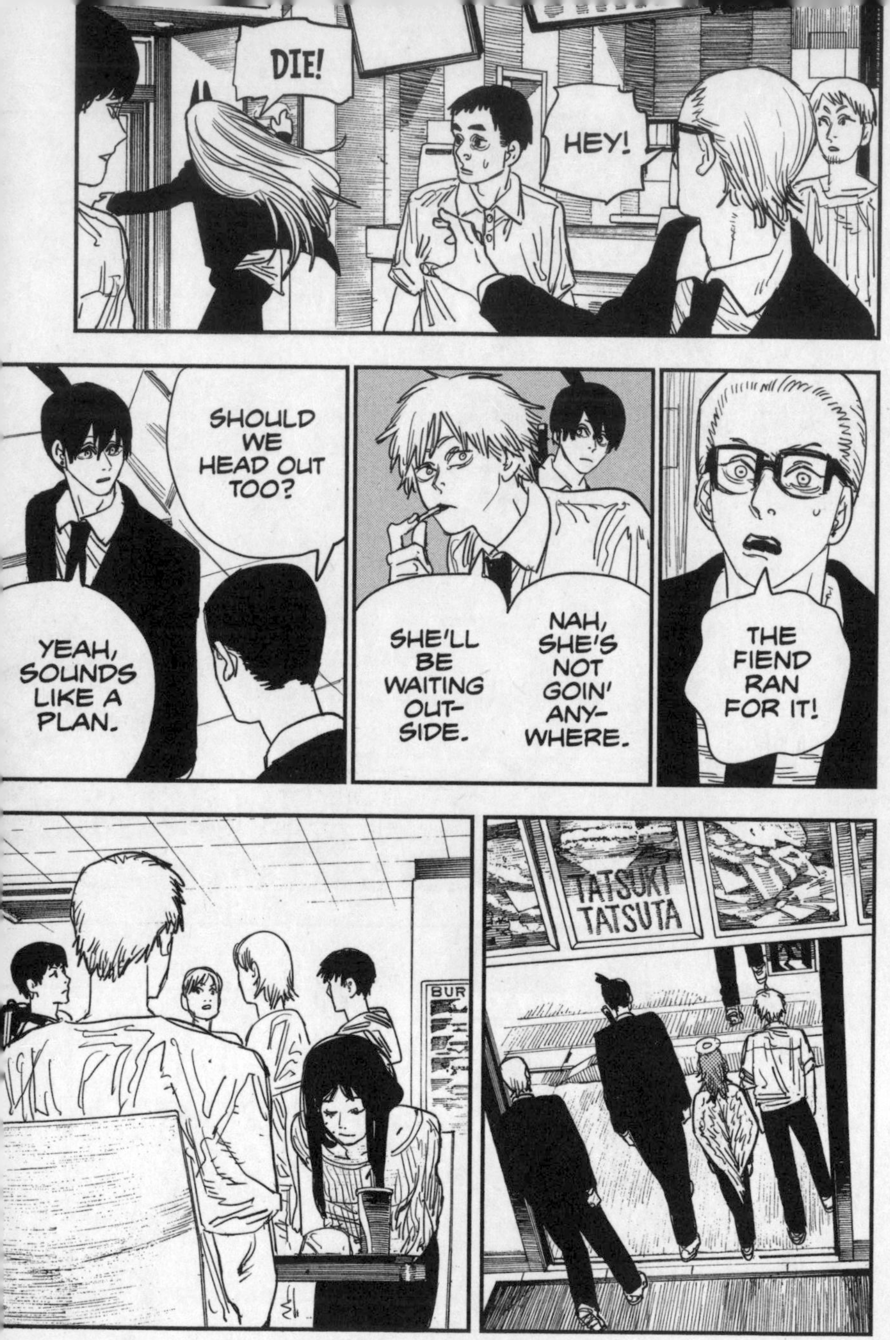
DIE!
HEY!
THE FIEND RAN FOR IT!
NAH, SHE'S NOT GOIN' ANYWHERE.
SHE'LL BE WAITING OUTSIDE.
SHOULD WE HEAD OUT TOO?
YEAH, SOUNDS LIKE A PLAN.
TATSUKI TATSUTA
BUR

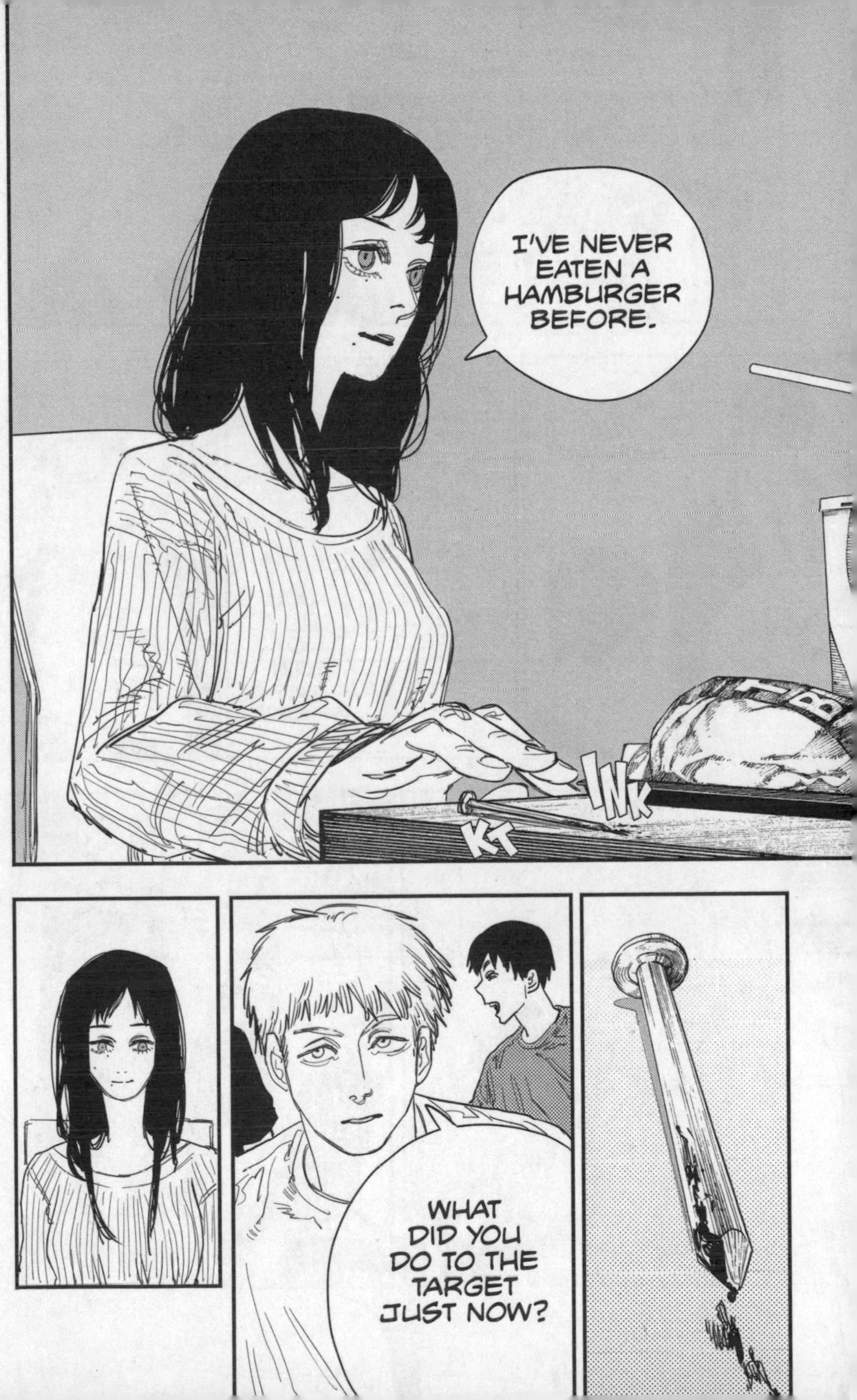
I'VE NEVER EATEN A HAMBURGER BEFORE.
INK
KT
WHAT DID YOU DO TO THE TARGET JUST NOW?

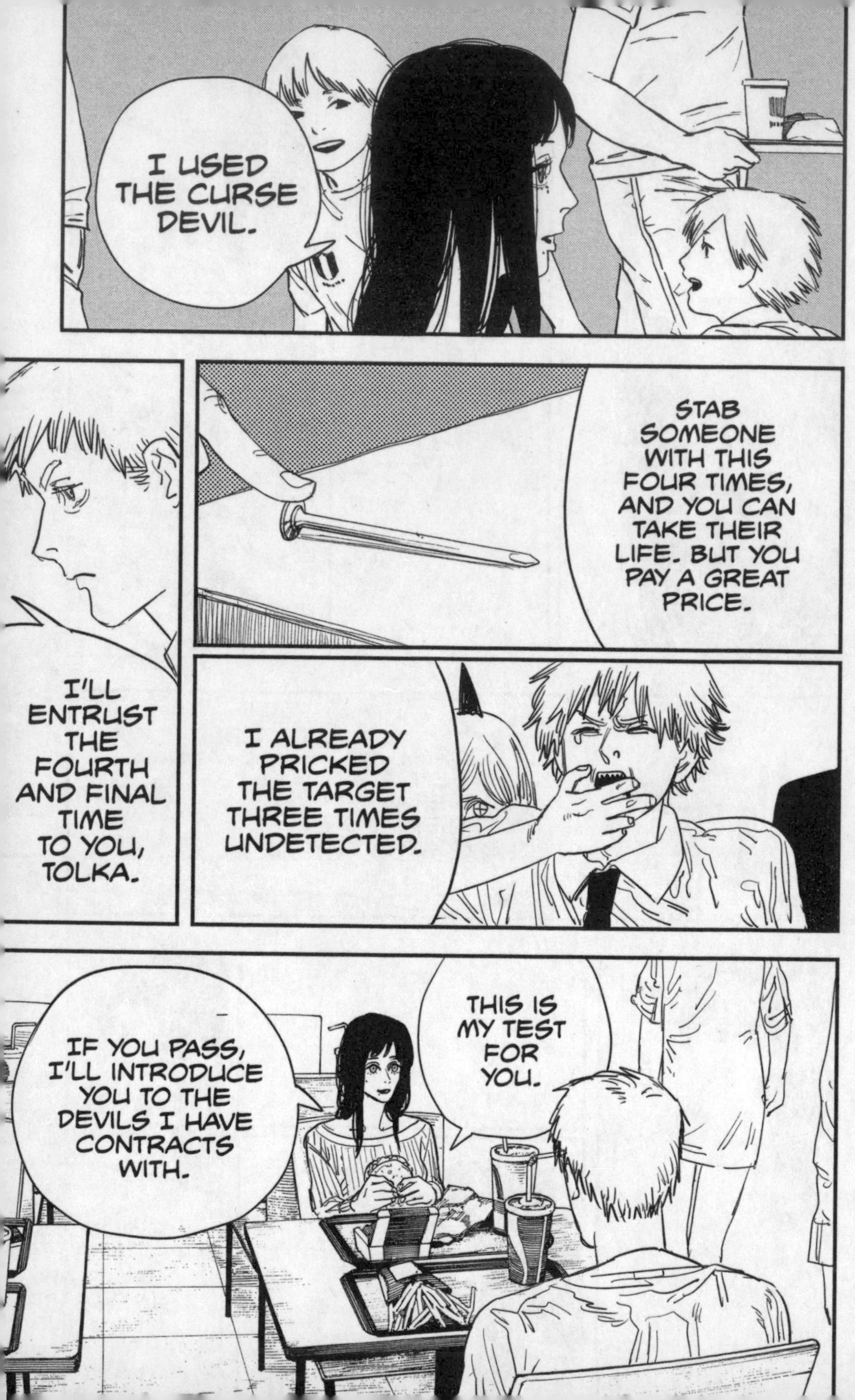
I USED THE CURSE DEVIL.
STAB SOMEONE WITH THIS FOUR TIMES, AND YOU CAN TAKE THEIR LIFE. BUT YOU PAY A GREAT PRICE.
I ALREADY PRICKED THE TARGET THREE TIMES UNDETECTED.
I'LL ENTRUST THE FOURTH AND FINAL TIME TO YOU, TOLKA.
THIS IS MY TEST FOR YOU.
IF YOU PASS, I'LL INTRODUCE YOU TO THE DEVILS I HAVE CONTRACTS WITH.

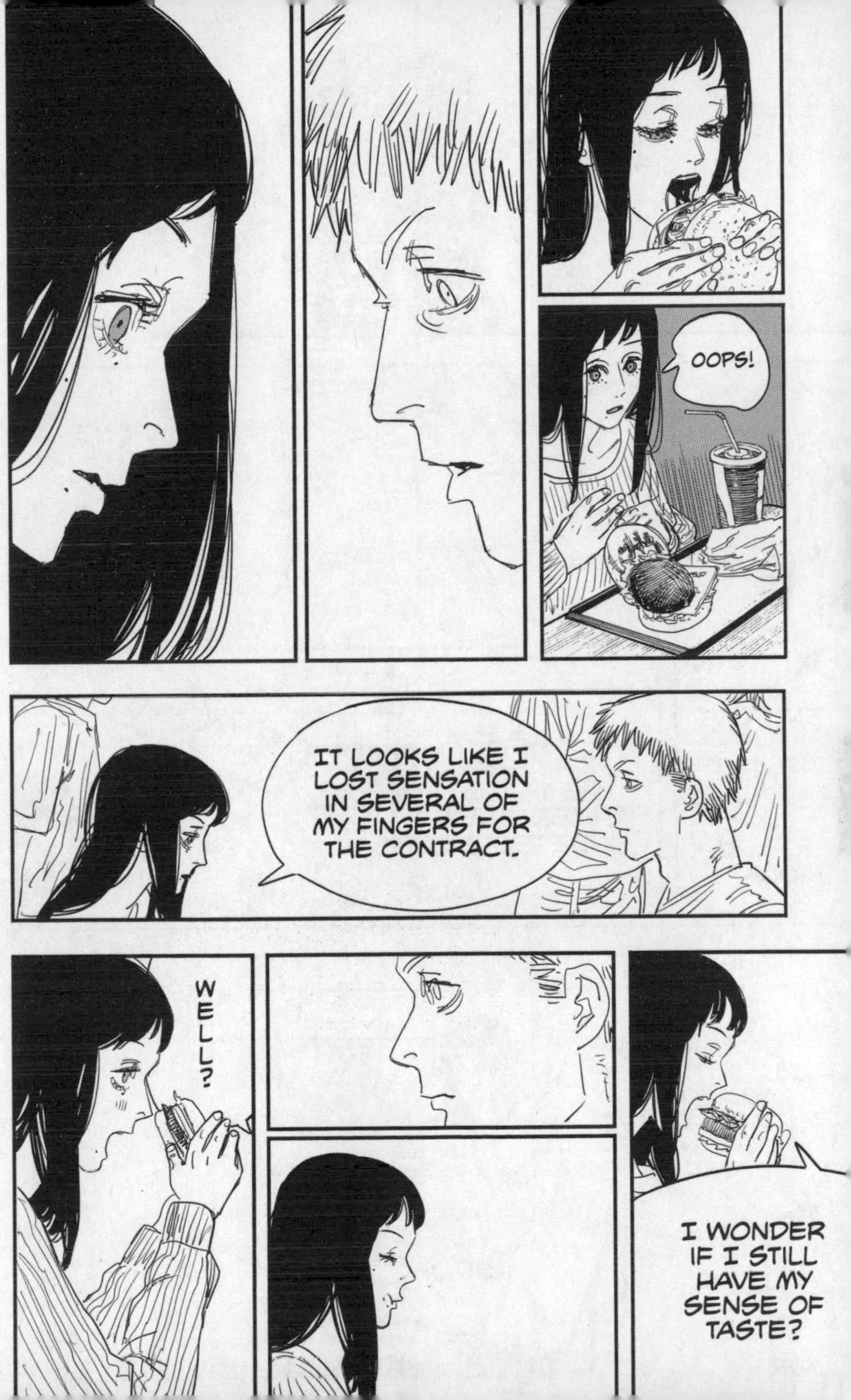
OOPS!
IT LOOKS LIKE I LOST SENSATION IN SEVERAL OF MY FINGERS FOR THE CONTRACT.
I WONDER IF I STILL HAVE MY SENSE OF TASTE?
WELL?

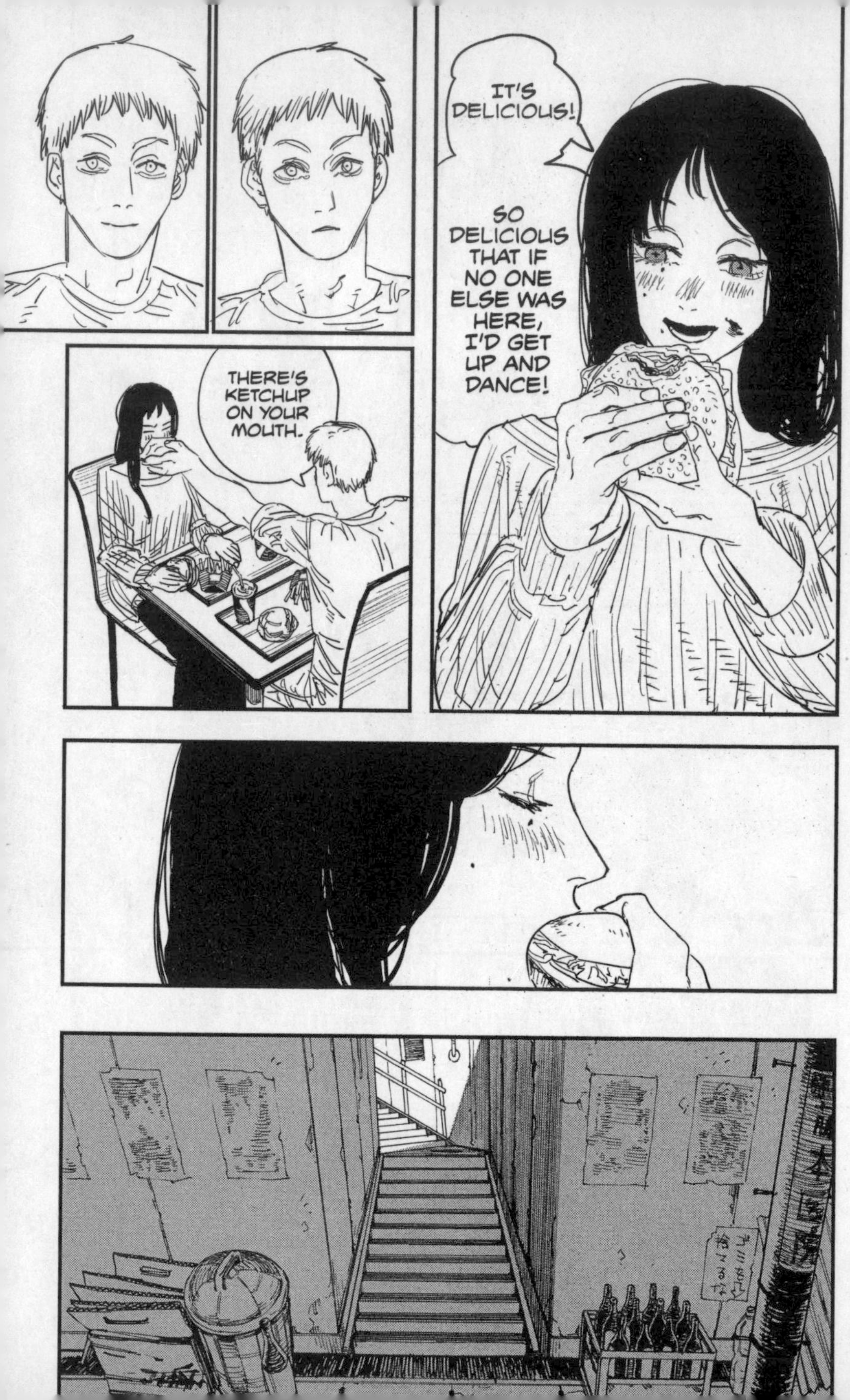
IT'S DELICIOUS!
SO DELICIOUS THAT IF NO ONE ELSE WAS HERE, I'D GET UP AND DANCE!
THERE'S KETCHUP ON YOUR MOUTH.

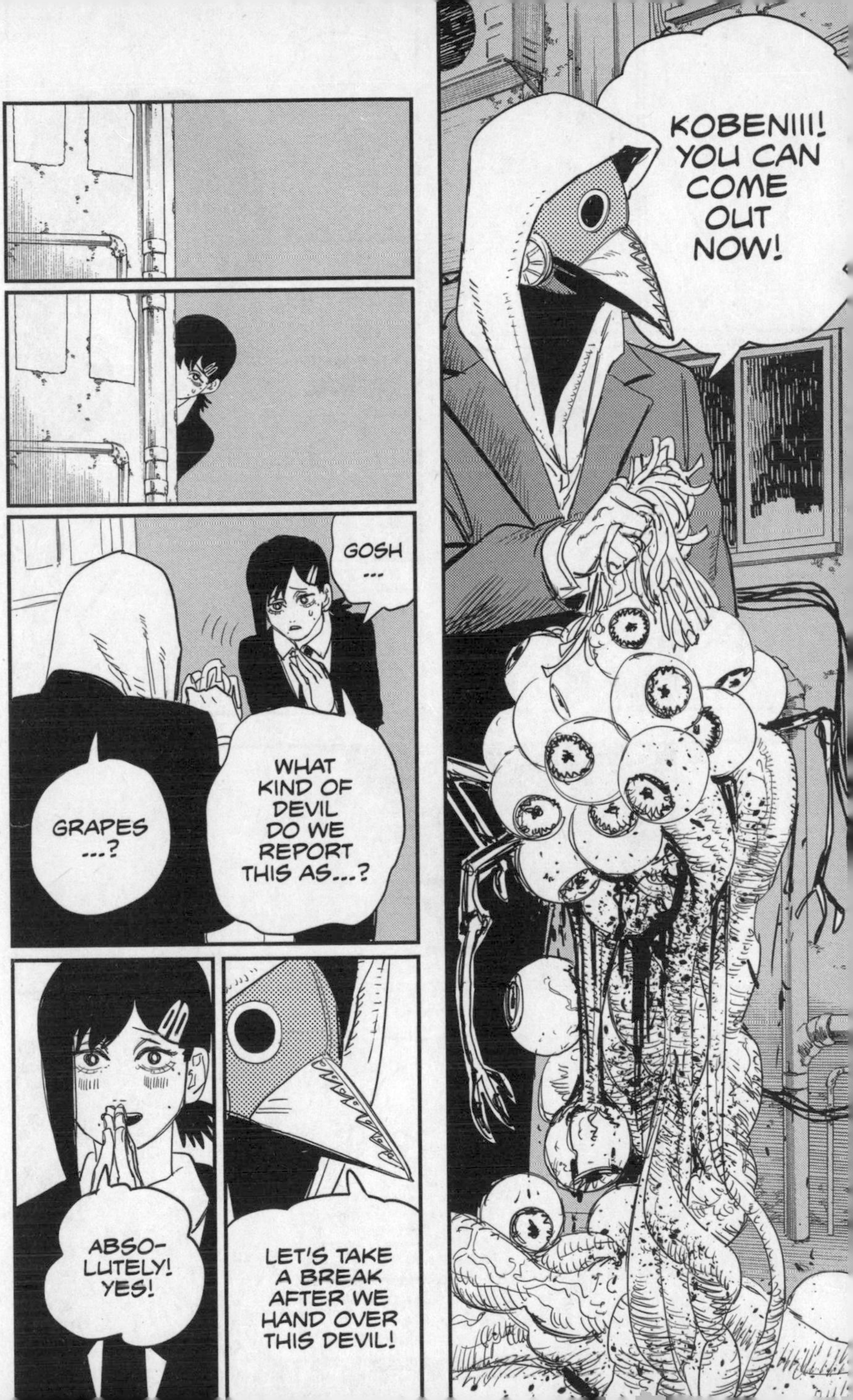
KOBENIIII! YOU CAN COME OUT NOW!
GOSH ...
WHAT KIND OF DEVIL DO WE REPORT THIS AS...?
GRAPES ...?
LET'S TAKE A BREAK AFTER WE HAND OVER THIS DEVIL!
ABSO-LUTELY! YES!

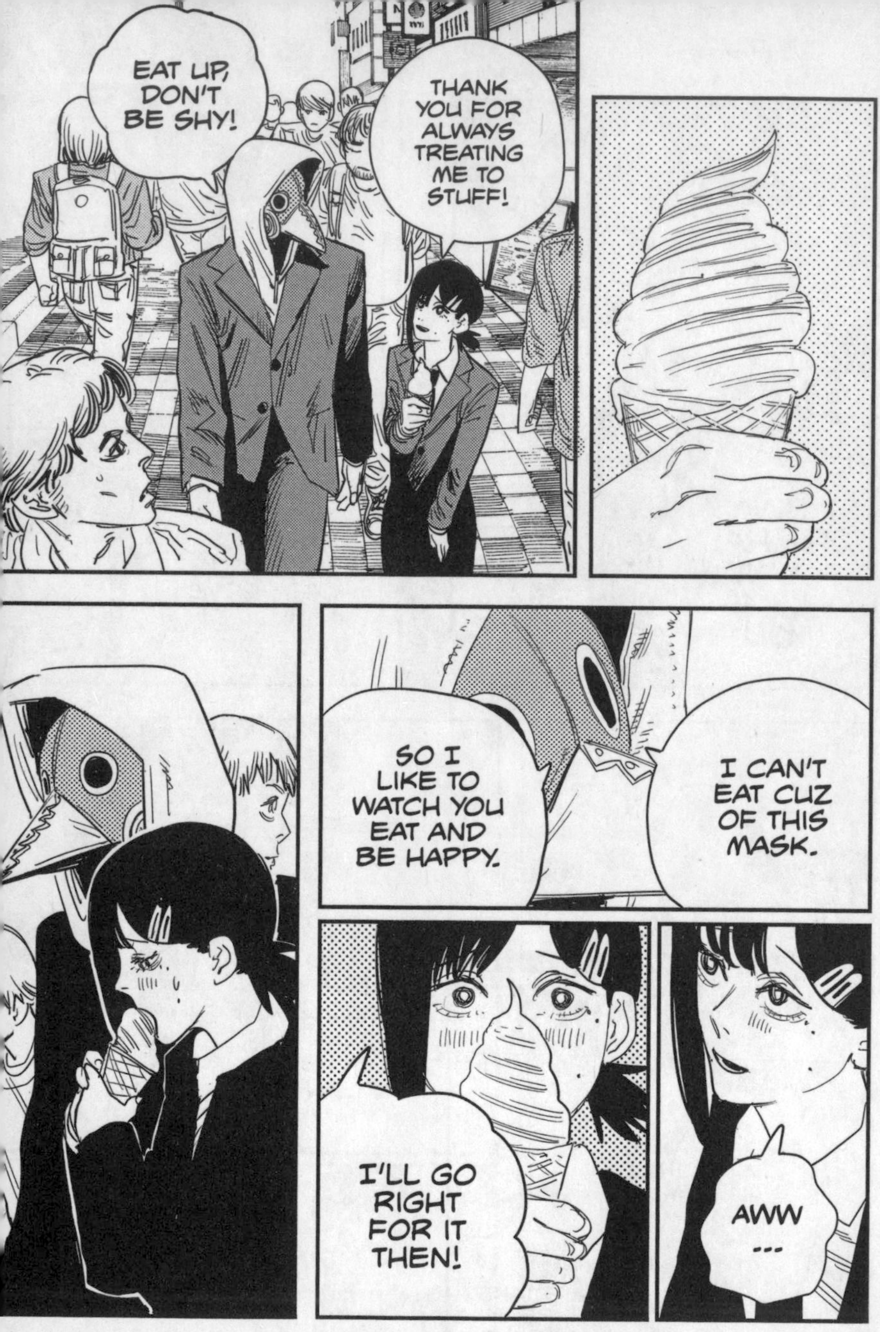
THANK YOU FOR ALWAYS TREATING ME TO STUFF!
EAT UP, DON'T BE SHY!
I CAN'T EAT CUZ OF THIS MASK.
SO I LIKE TO WATCH YOU EAT AND BE HAPPY.
AWW ...
I'LL GO RIGHT FOR IT THEN!

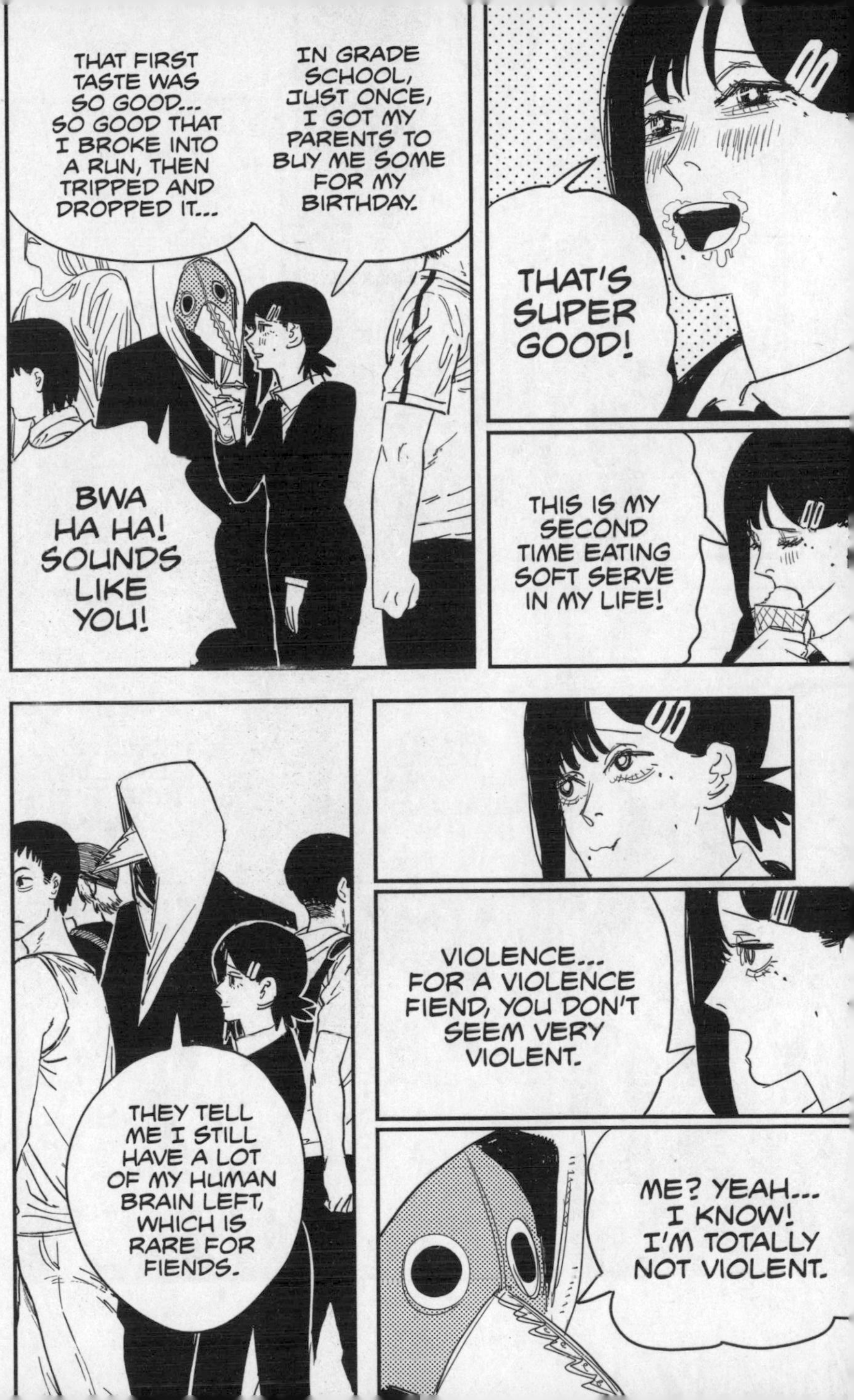
THAT'S SUPER GOOD!
THIS IS MY SECOND TIME EATING SOFT SERVE IN MY LIFE!
IN GRADE SCHOOL, JUST ONCE, I GOT MY PARENTS TO BUY ME SOME FOR MY BIRTHDAY.
THAT FIRST TASTE WAS SO GOOD... SO GOOD THAT I BROKE INTO A RUN, THEN TRIPPED AND DROPPED IT...
BWA HA HA! SOUNDS LIKE YOU!
VIOLENCE... FOR A VIOLENCE FIEND, YOU DON'T SEEM VERY VIOLENT.
ME? YEAH... I KNOW! I'M TOTALLY NOT VIOLENT.
THEY TELL ME I STILL HAVE A LOT OF MY HUMAN BRAIN LEFT, WHICH IS RARE FOR FIENDS.

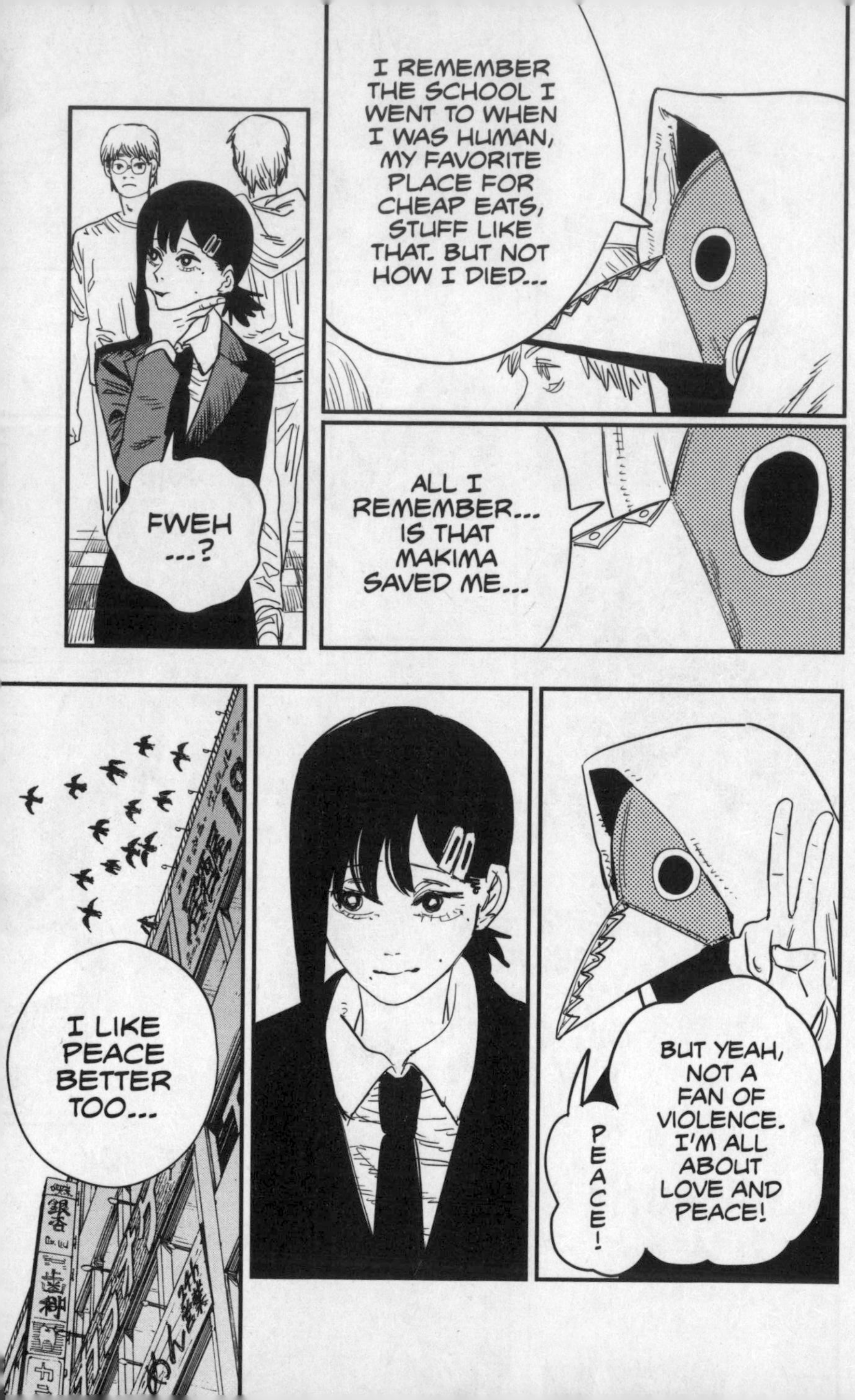
I REMEMBER THE SCHOOL I WENT TO WHEN I WAS HUMAN, MY FAVORITE PLACE FOR CHEAP EATS, STUFF LIKE THAT. BUT NOT HOW I DIED...
ALL I REMEMBER... IS THAT MAKIMA SAVED ME...
FWEH ...?
BUT YEAH, NOT A FAN OF VIOLENCE. I'M ALL ABOUT LOVE AND PEACE!
PEACE!
I LIKE PEACE BETTER TOO...

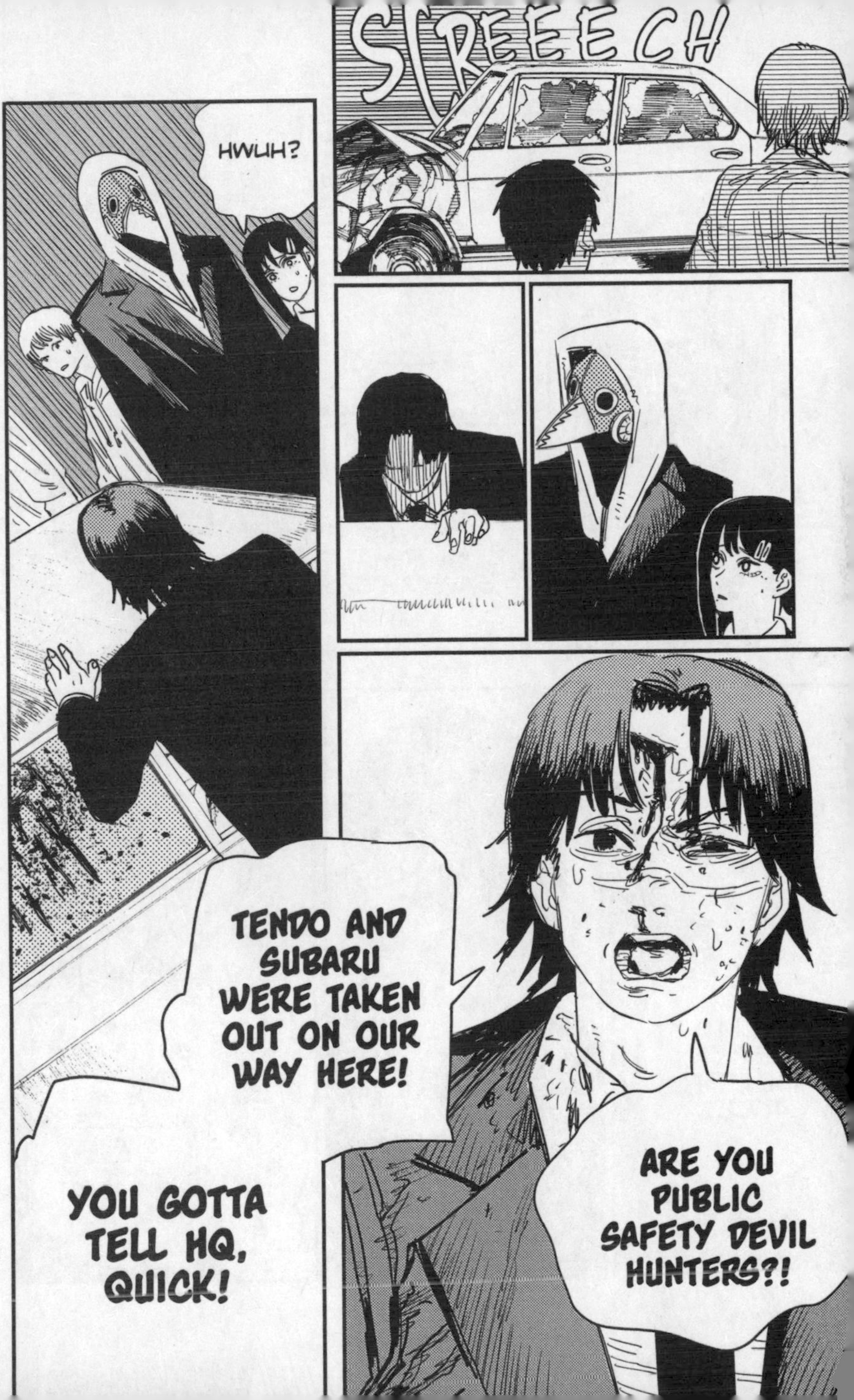
STREEECH
HWUH?
ARE YOU PUBLIC SAFETY DEVIL HUNTERS?!
TENDO AND SUBARU WERE TAKEN OUT ON OUR WAY HERE!
YOU GOTTA TELL HQ, QUICK!

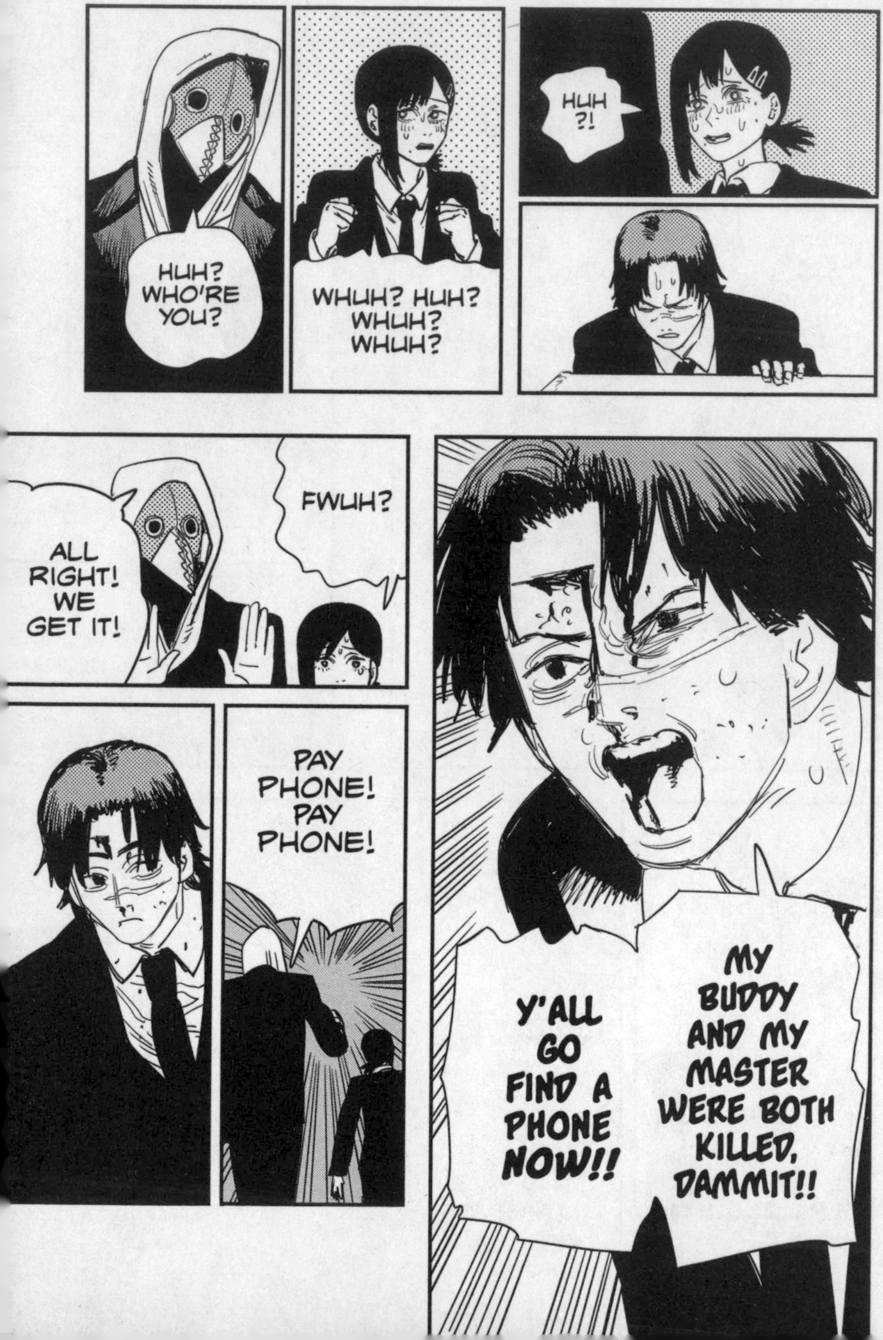
HUH ?!
WHUH? HUH? WHUH? WHUH?
HUH? WHO'RE YOU?
MY BUDDY AND MY MASTER WERE BOTH KILLED, DAMMIT!!
Y'ALL GO FIND A PHONE NOW!!
FWUH?
ALL RIGHT! WE GET IT!
PAY PHONE! PAY PHONE!

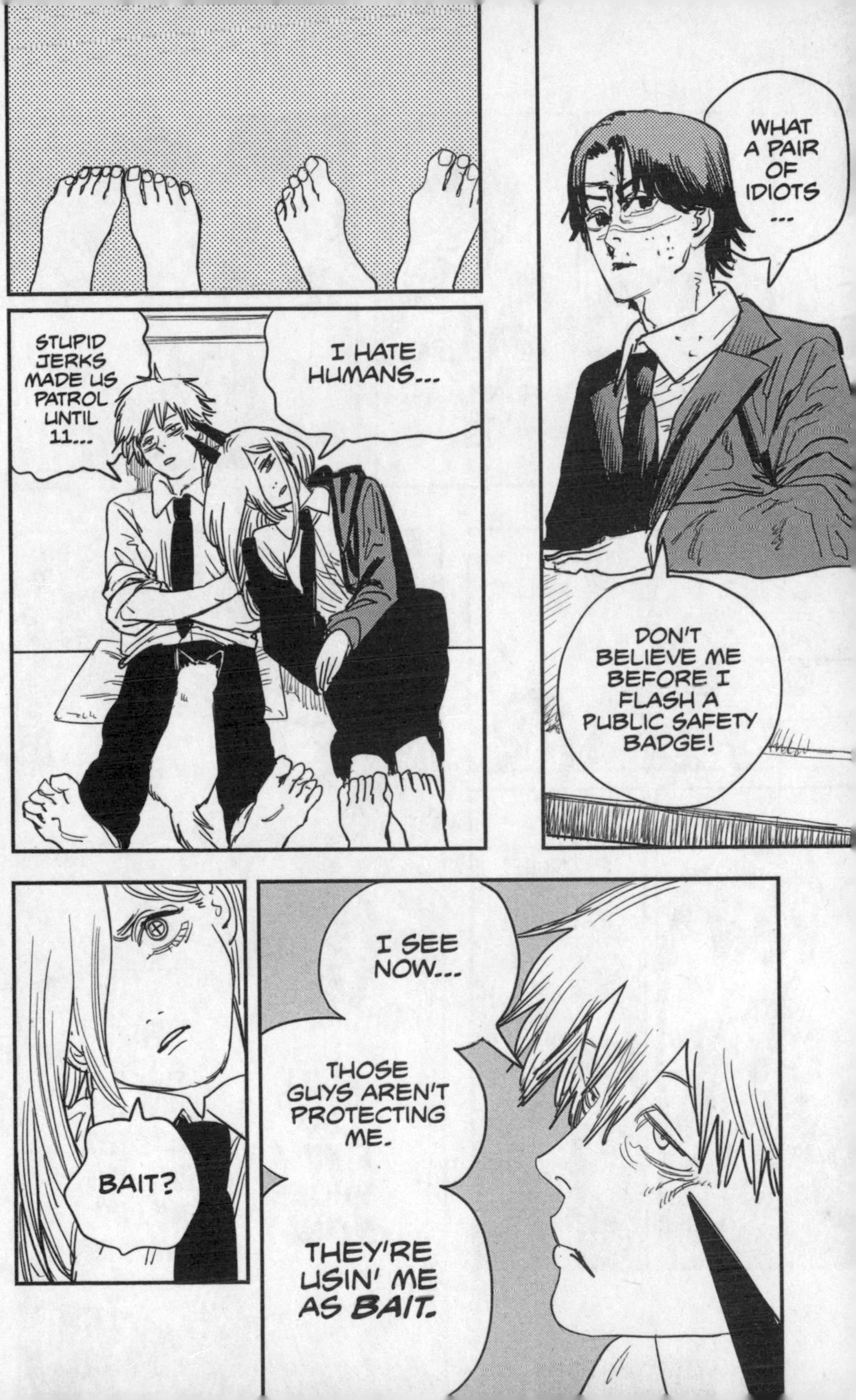
WHAT A PAIR OF IDIOTS ...
DON'T BELIEVE ME BEFORE I FLASH A PUBLIC SAFETY BADGE!
I HATE HUMANS...
STUPID JERKS MADE US PATROL UNTIL 11...
I SEE NOW...
THOSE GUYS AREN'T PROTECTING ME.
THEY'RE USIN' ME AS BAIT.
BAIT?

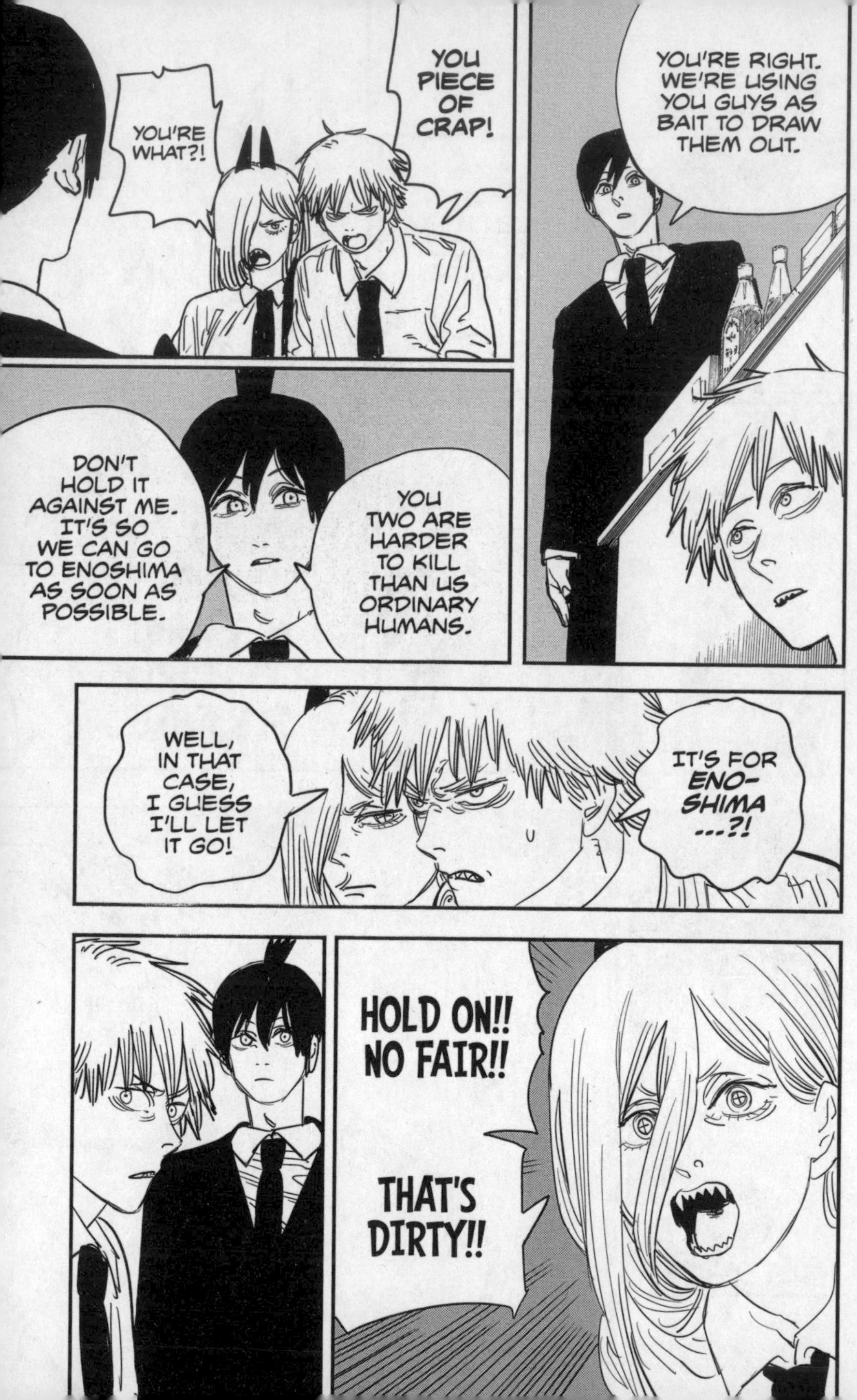
YOU'RE RIGHT. WE'RE USING YOU GUYS AS BAIT TO DRAW THEM OUT.
YOU PIECE OF CRAP!
YOU'RE WHAT?!
YOU TWO ARE HARDER TO KILL THAN US ORDINARY HUMANS.
DON'T HOLD IT AGAINST ME. IT'S SO WE CAN GO TO ENOSHIMA AS SOON AS POSSIBLE.
IT'S FOR ENO-SHIMA...?!
WELL, IN THAT CASE, I GUESS I'LL LET IT GO!
HOLD ON!! NO FAIR!!
THAT'S DIRTY!!

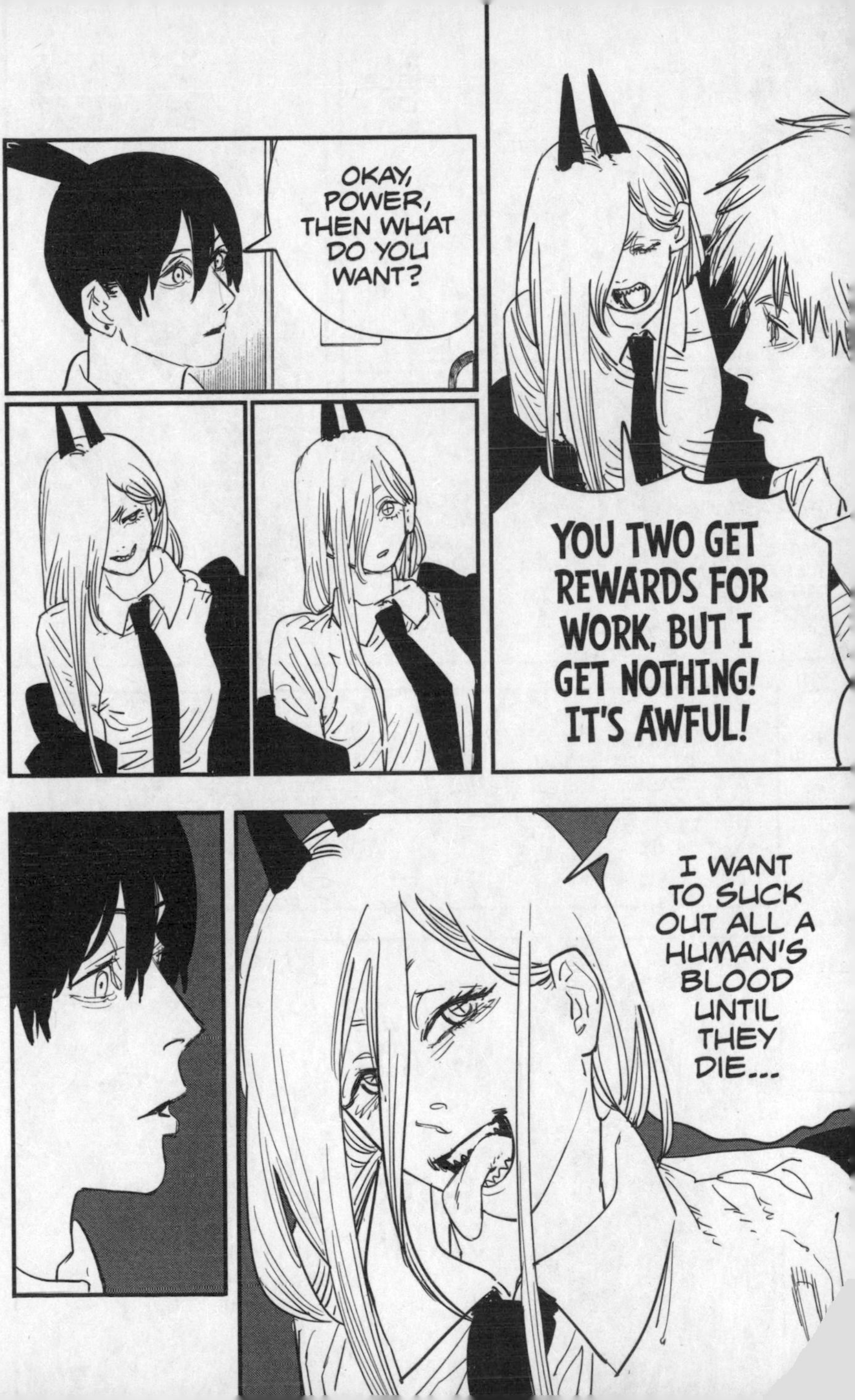
YOU TWO GET REWARDS FOR WORK, BUT I GET NOTHING! IT'S AWFUL!
OKAY, POWER, THEN WHAT DO YOU WANT?
I WANT TO SUCK OUT ALL A HUMAN'S BLOOD UNTIL THEY DIE...

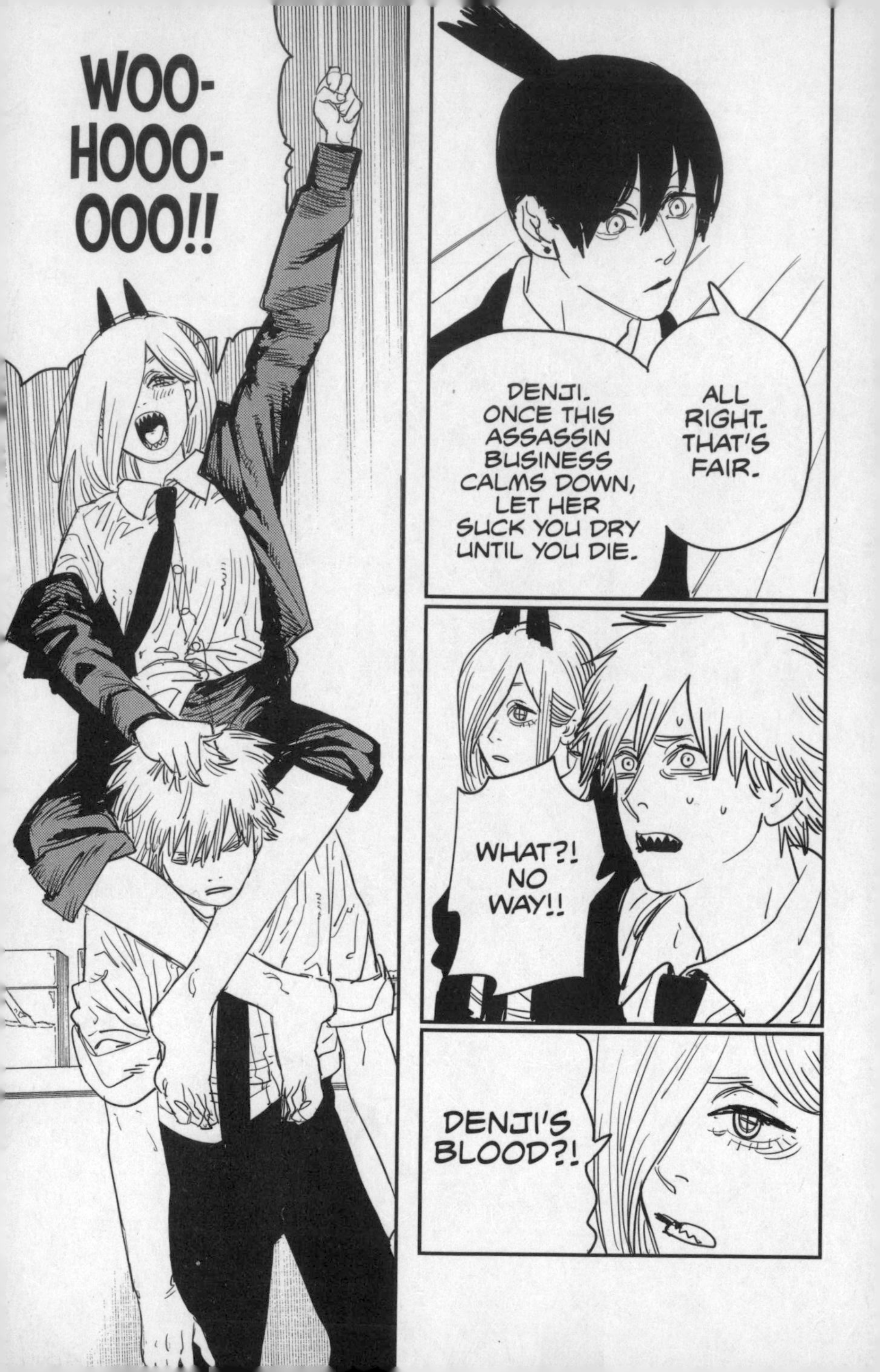
ALL RIGHT. THAT'S FAIR.
DENJI. ONCE THIS ASSASSIN BUSINESS CALMS DOWN, LET HER SUCK YOU DRY UNTIL YOU DIE.
WHAT?! NO WAY!!
DENJI'S BLOOD?!
WOO-HOOOO-OOO!!

Chain saw man

# Chapter 57: Suddenly

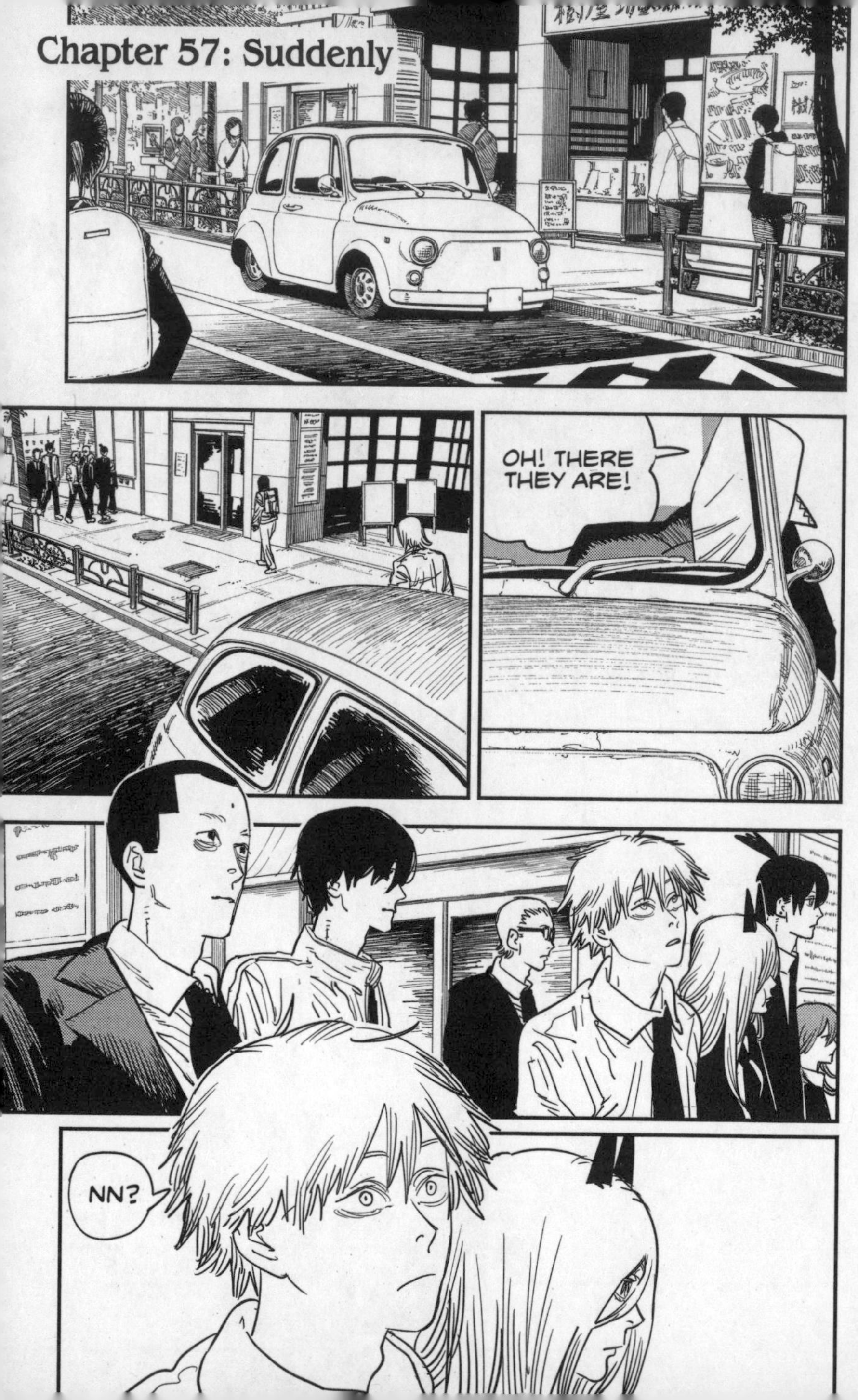
OH! THERE THEY ARE!
NN?

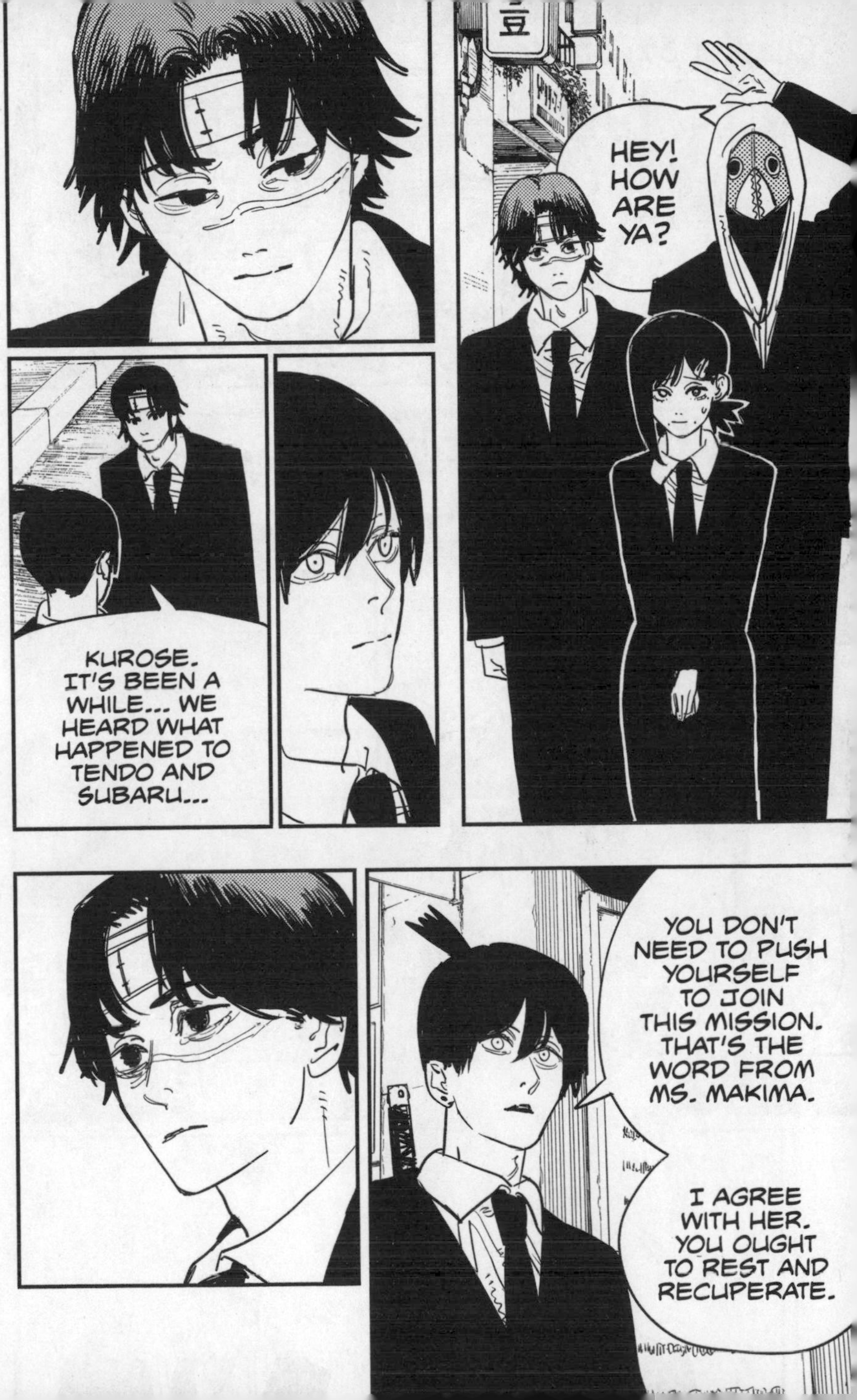

HEY! HOW ARE YA?
KUROSE. IT'S BEEN A WHILE... WE HEARD WHAT HAPPENED TO TENDO AND SUBARU...
YOU DON'T NEED TO PUSH YOURSELF TO JOIN THIS MISSION. THAT'S THE WORD FROM MS. MAKIMA.
I AGREE WITH HER. YOU OUGHT TO REST AND RECUPERATE.

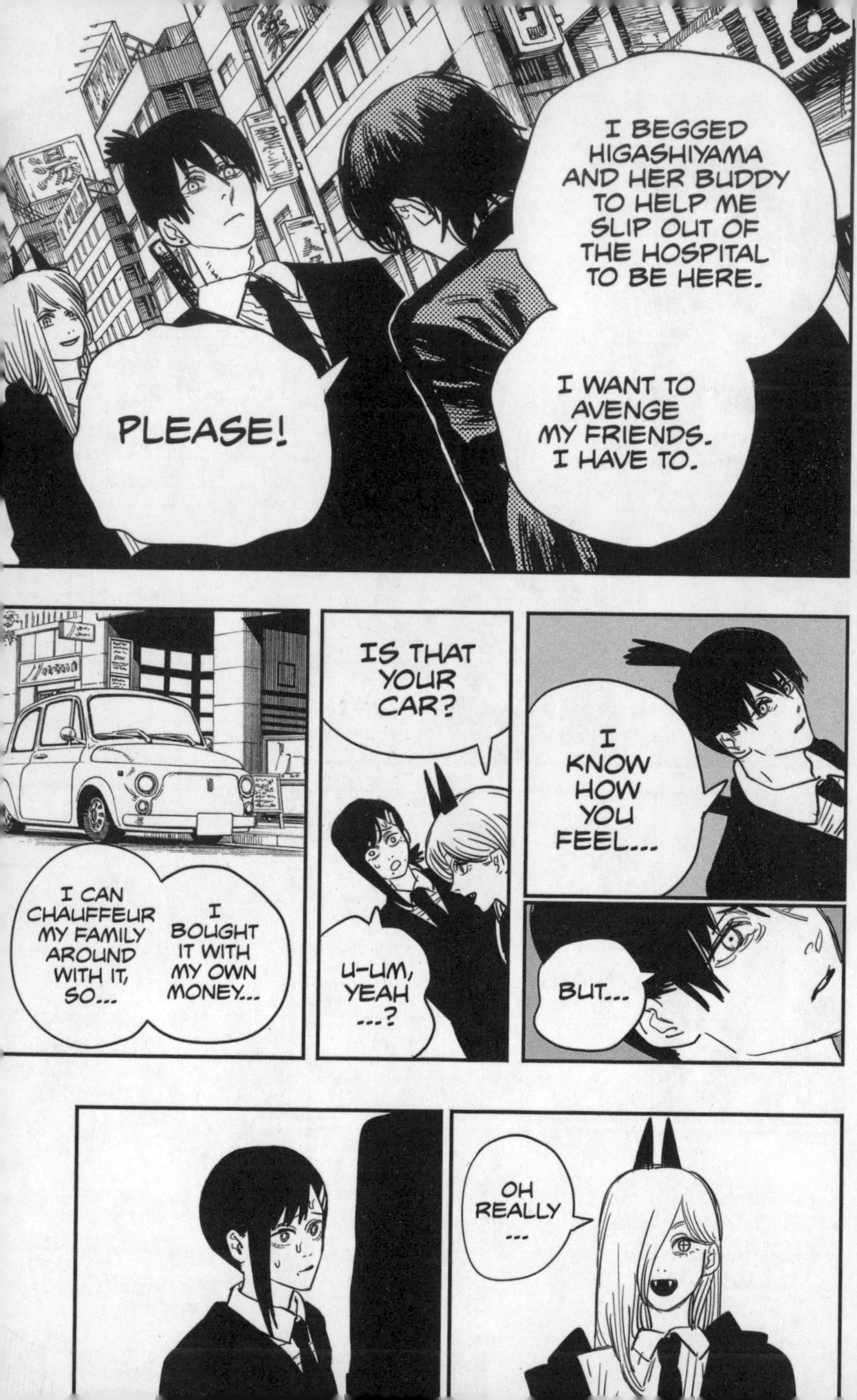
I BEGGED HIGASHIYAMA AND HER BUDDY TO HELP ME SLIP OUT OF THE HOSPITAL TO BE HERE.
I WANT TO AVENGE MY FRIENDS. I HAVE TO.
PLEASE!
I KNOW HOW YOU FEEL...
BUT...
IS THAT YOUR CAR?
U-UM, YEAH ...?
I BOUGHT IT WITH MY OWN MONEY...
I CAN CHAUFFEUR MY FAMILY AROUND WITH IT, SO...
OH REALLY ...

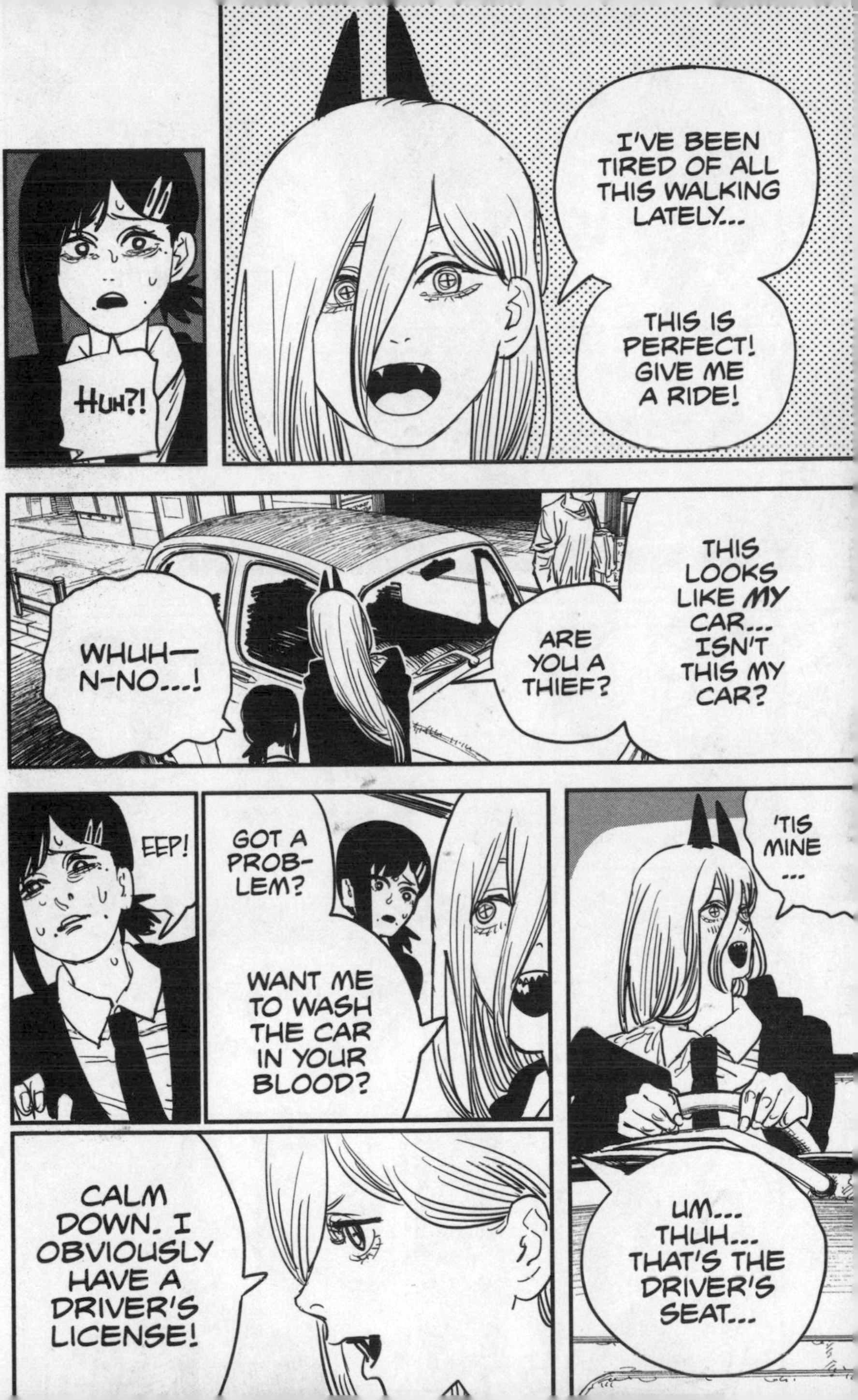
I'VE BEEN TIRED OF ALL THIS WALKING LATELY...
THIS IS PERFECT! GIVE ME A RIDE!
HUH?!
THIS LOOKS LIKE *MY* CAR... ISN'T THIS MY CAR?
ARE YOU A THIEF?
WHUH— N-NO...!
'TIS MINE...
UM... THUH... THAT'S THE DRIVER'S SEAT...
GOT A PROB-LEM?
WANT ME TO WASH THE CAR IN YOUR BLOOD?
EEP!
CALM DOWN. I OBVIOUSLY HAVE A DRIVER'S LICENSE!

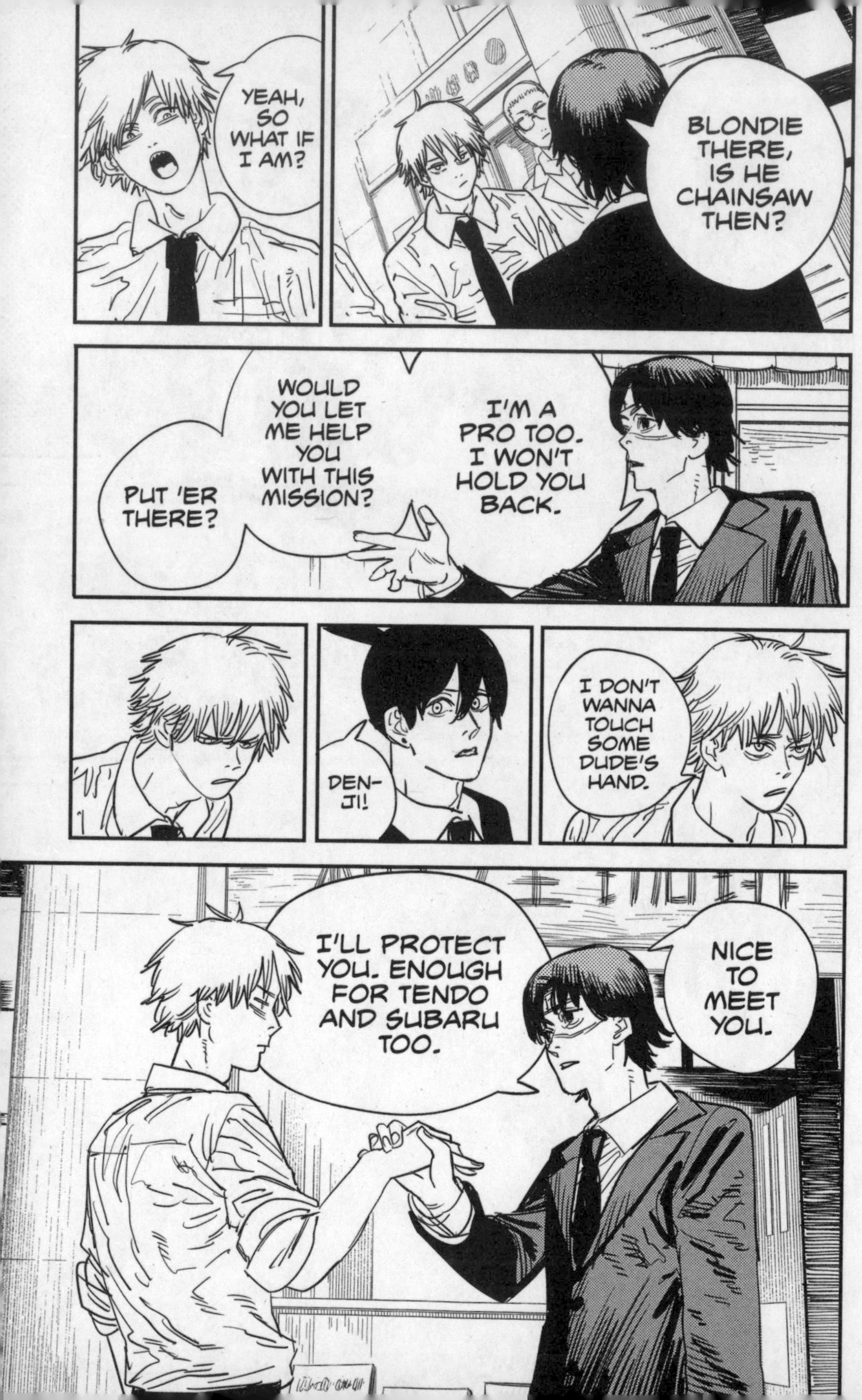
BLONDIE THERE, IS HE CHAINSAW THEN?
YEAH, SO WHAT IF I AM?
I'M A PRO TOO. I WON'T HOLD YOU BACK.
WOULD YOU LET ME HELP YOU WITH THIS MISSION?
PUT 'ER THERE?
I DON'T WANNA TOUCH SOME DUDE'S HAND.
DEN-JI!
NICE TO MEET YOU.
I'LL PROTECT YOU. ENOUGH FOR TENDO AND SUBARU TOO.

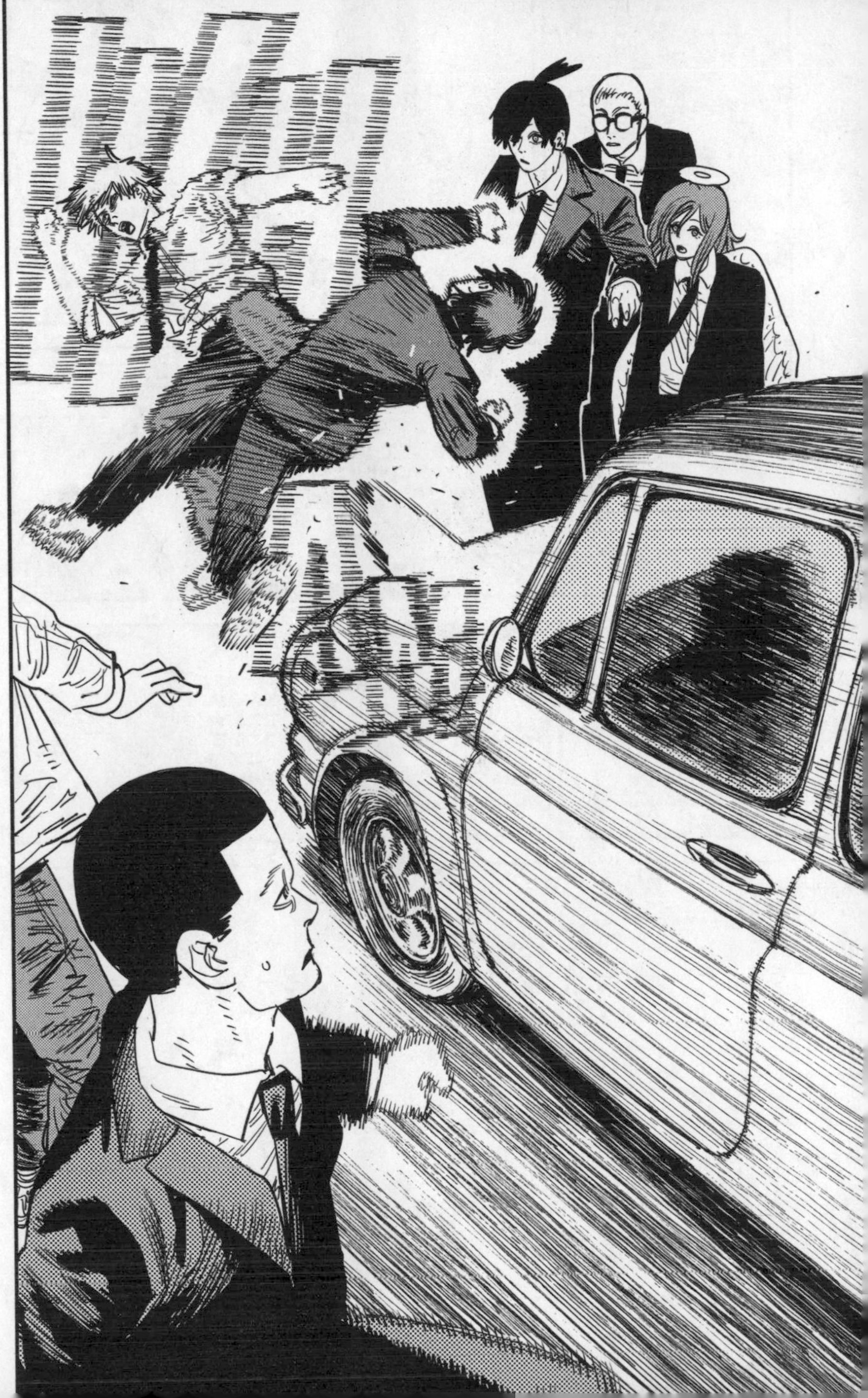

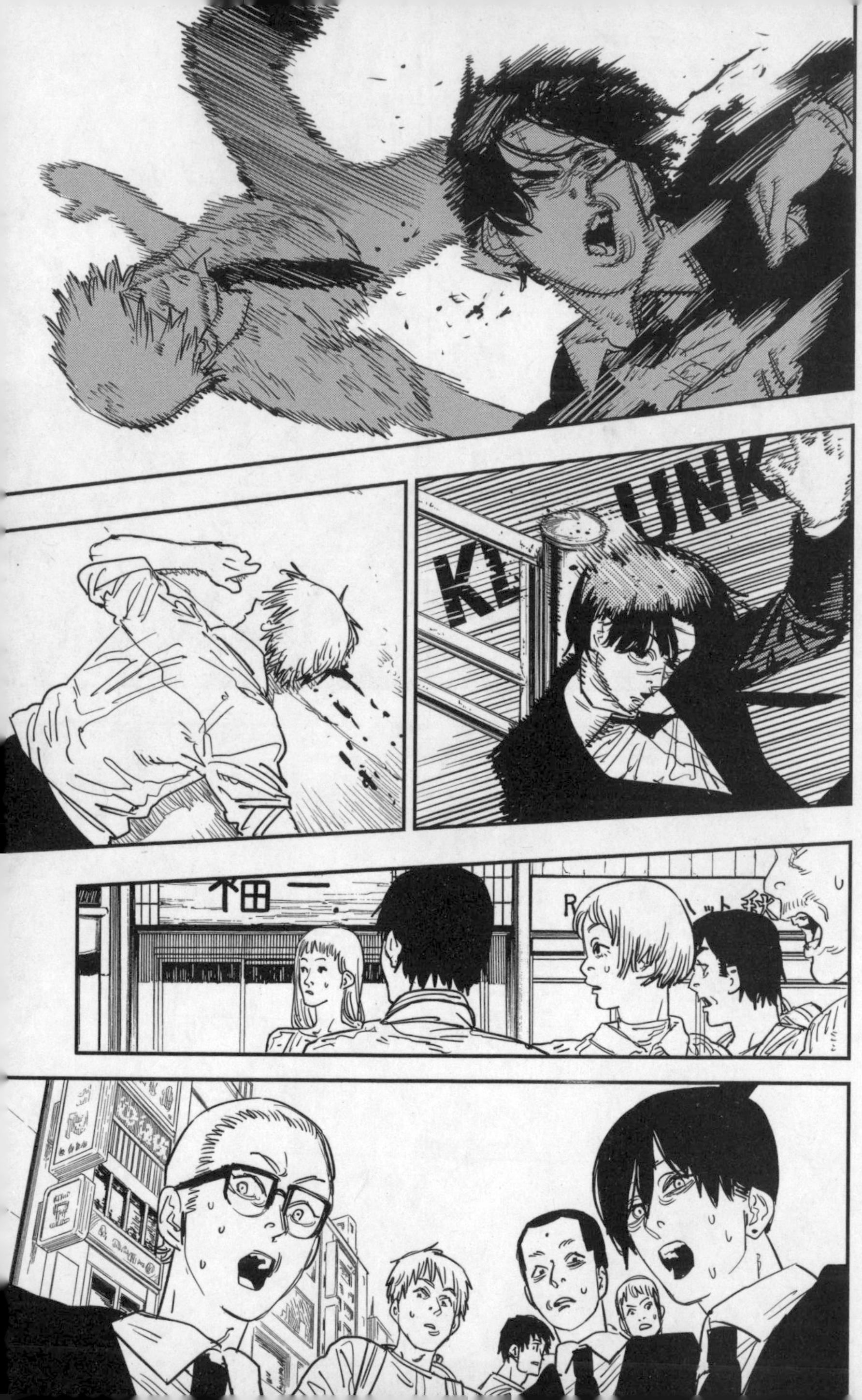
KLUNK

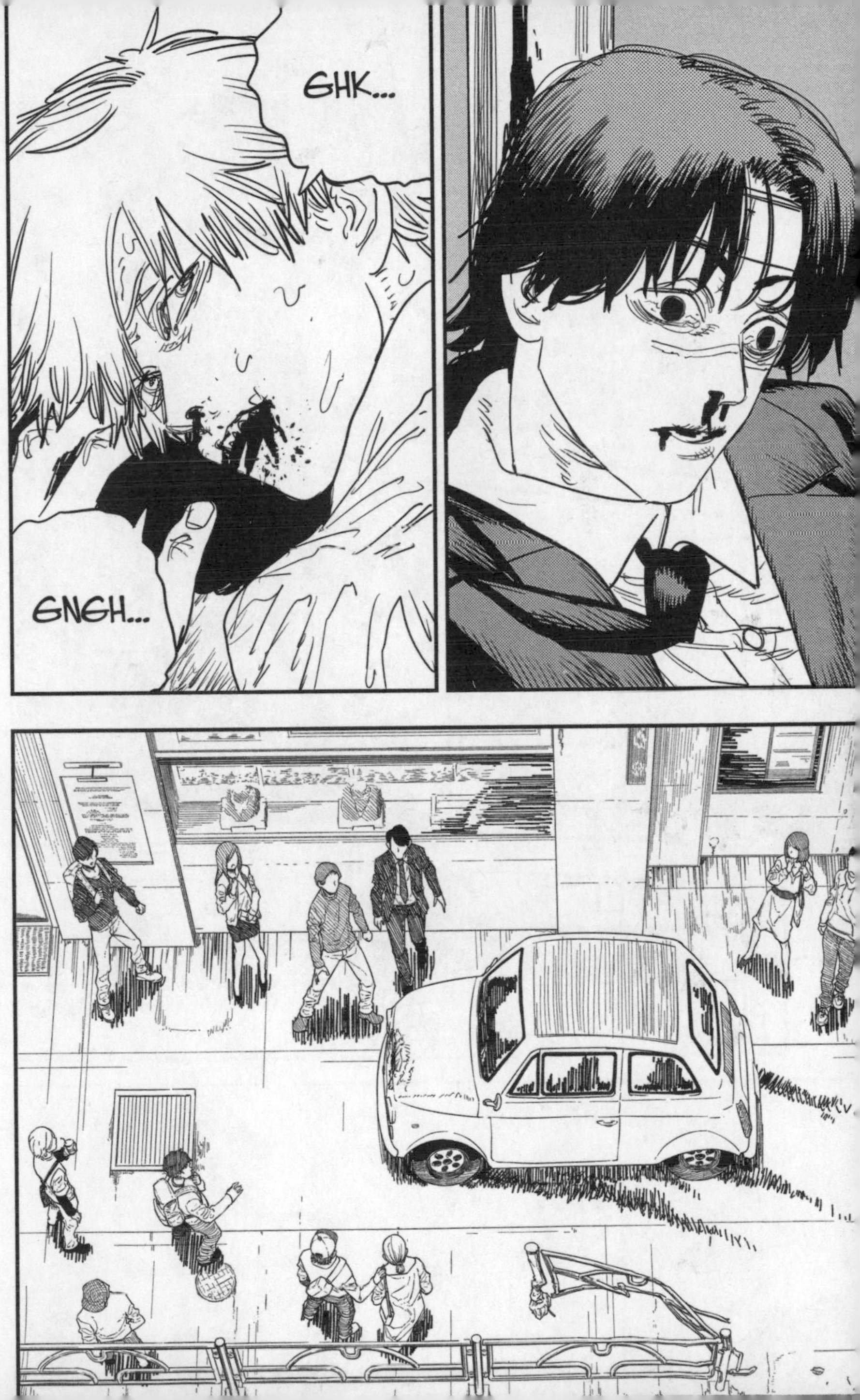
GHK...
GNGH...

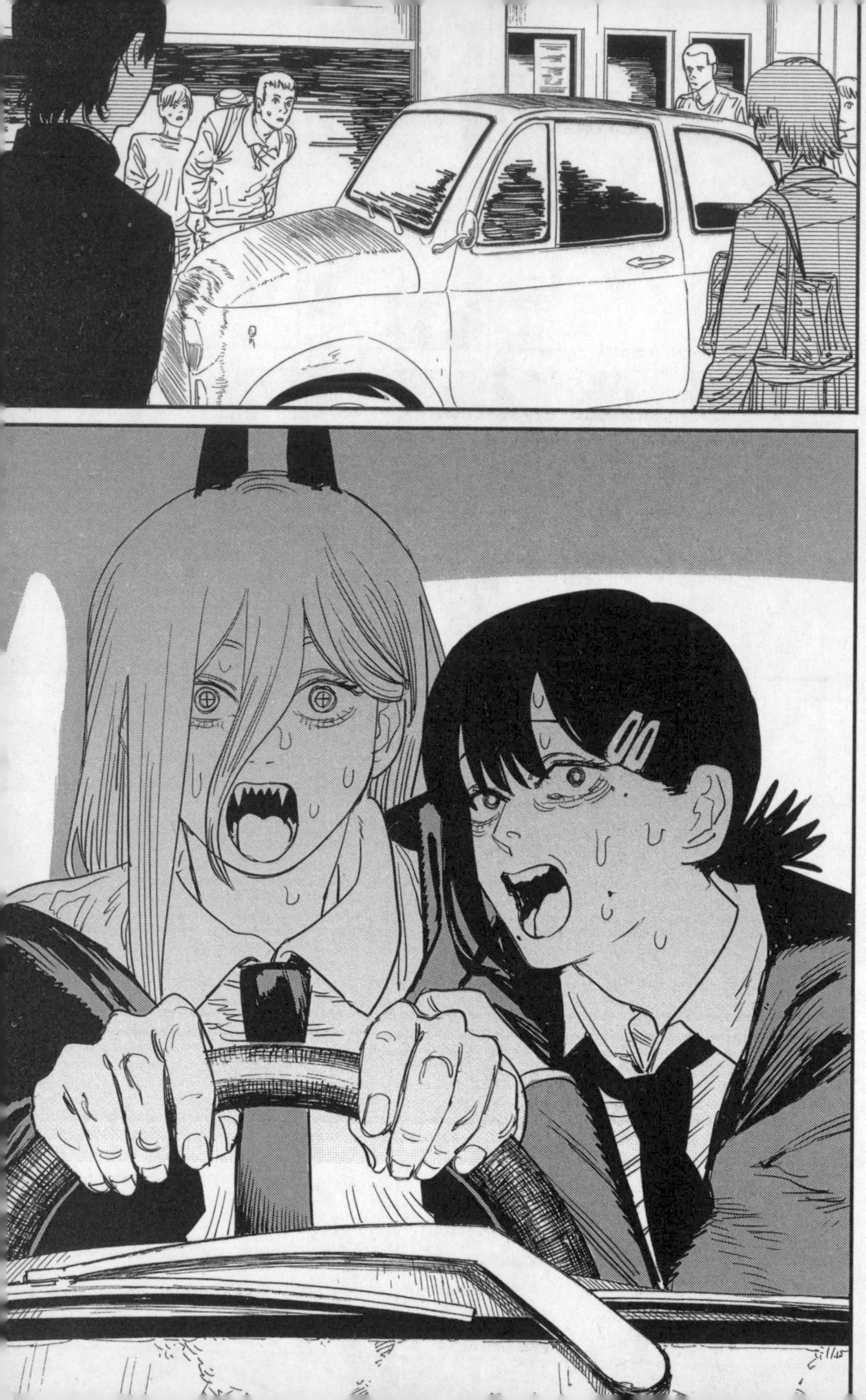

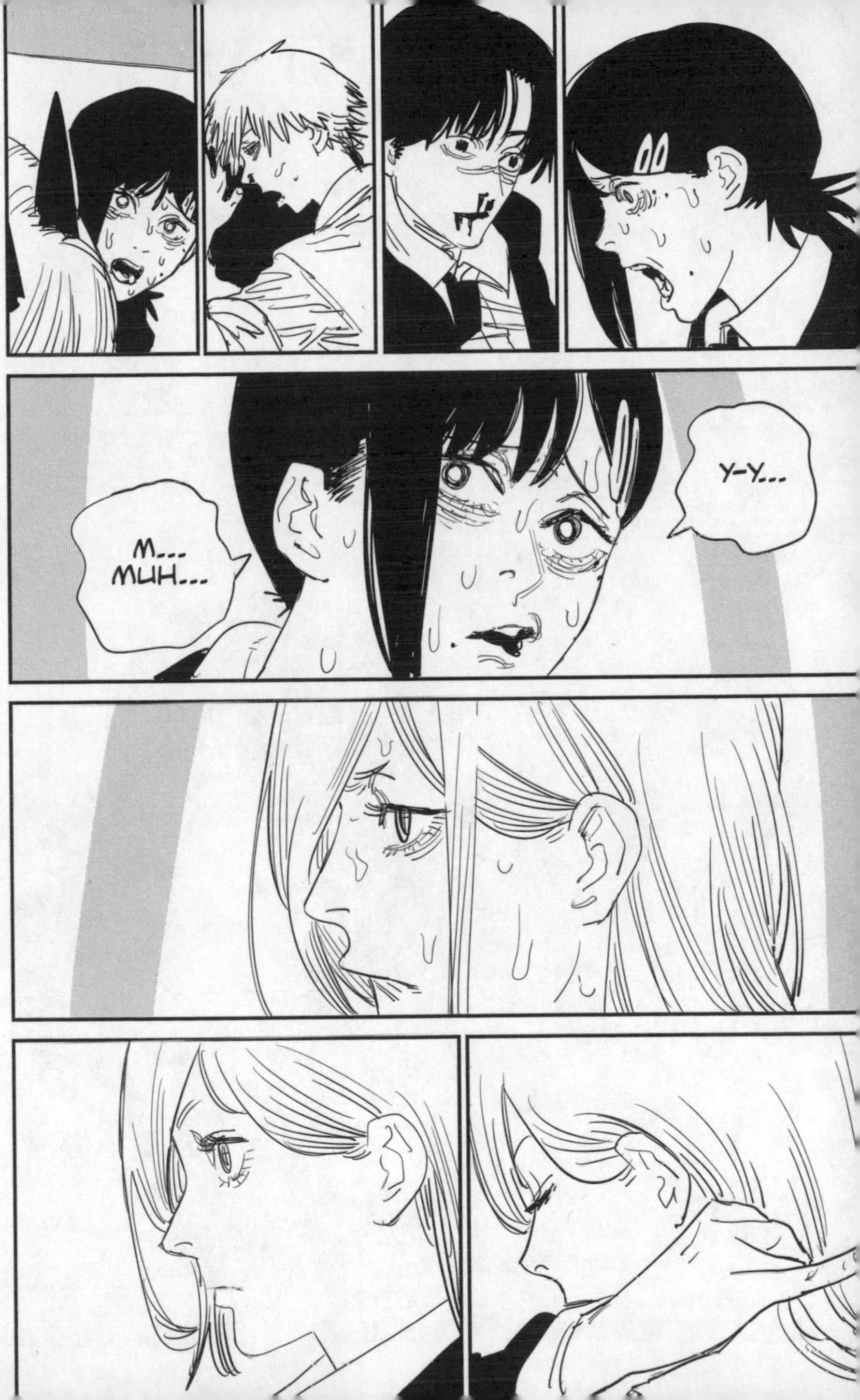
Y-Y...
M... MUH...

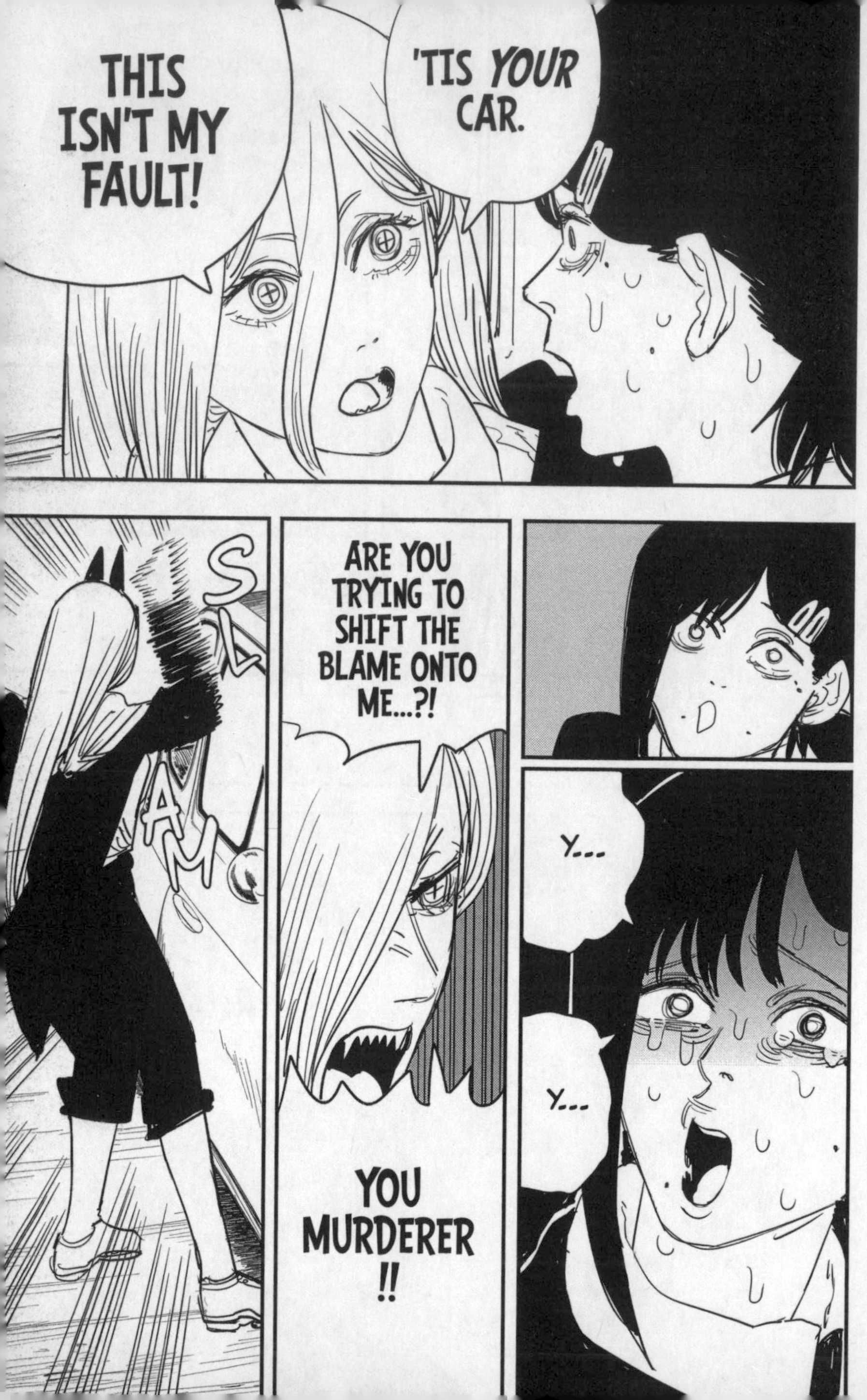
'TIS *YOUR* CAR.
THIS ISN'T MY FAULT!
Y...
Y...
ARE YOU TRYING TO SHIFT THE BLAME ONTO ME...?!
YOU MURDERER!!
SLAM

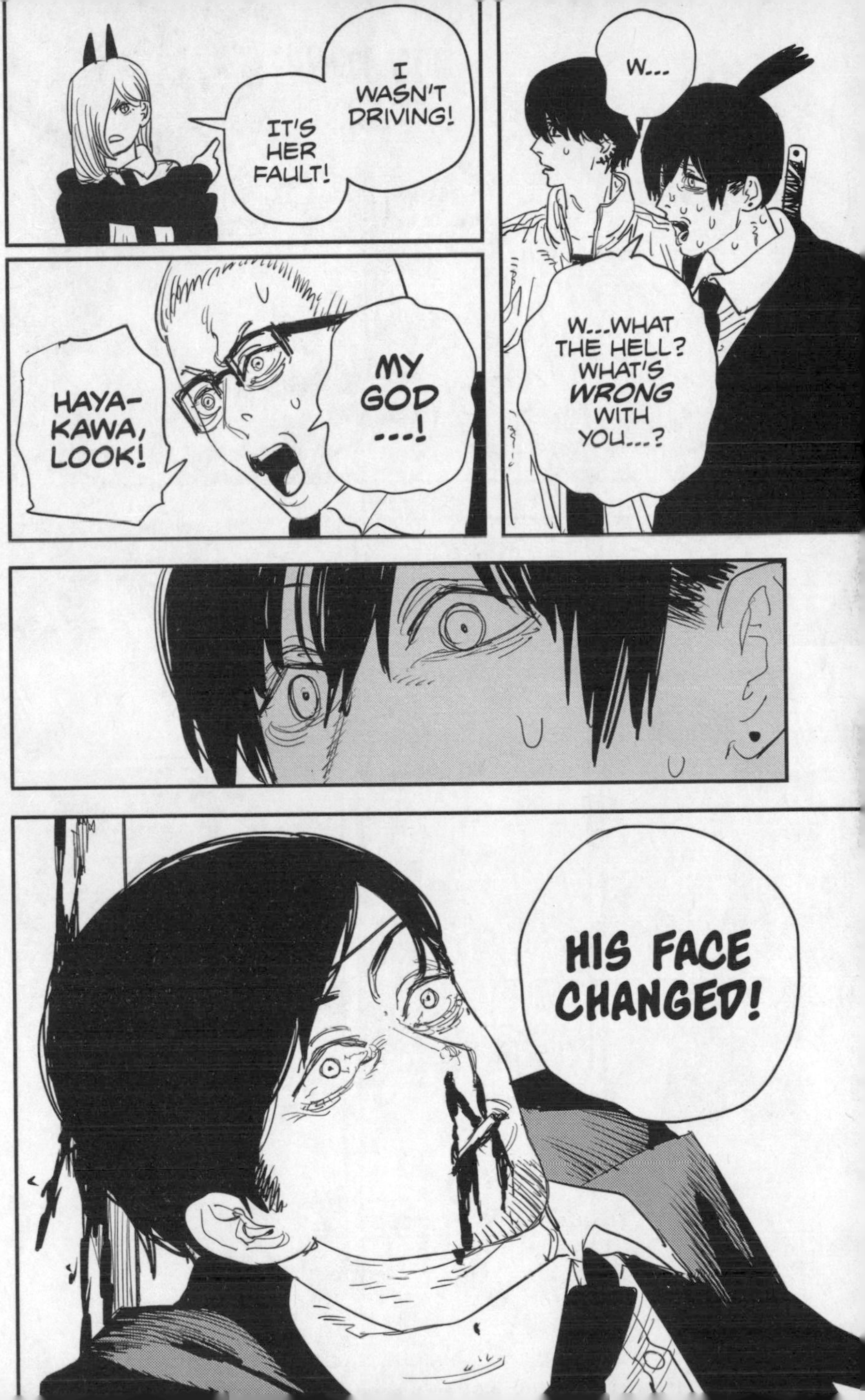
W...
I WASN'T DRIVING!
IT'S HER FAULT!
W...WHAT THE HELL? WHAT'S *WRONG* WITH YOU...?
MY GOD ...!
HAYA-KAWA, LOOK!
HIS FACE CHANGED!

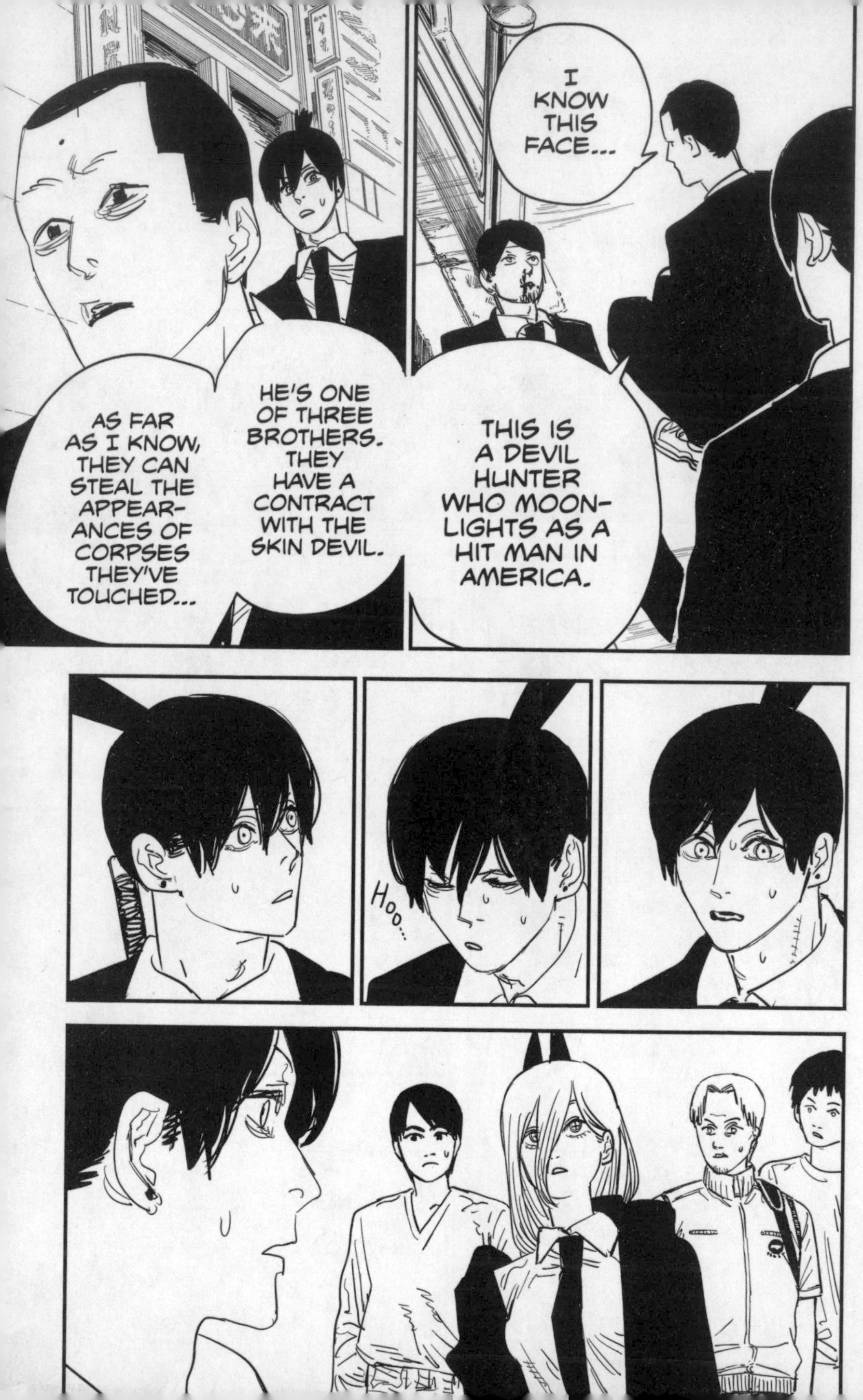
I KNOW THIS FACE...
THIS IS A DEVIL HUNTER WHO MOON-LIGHTS AS A HIT MAN IN AMERICA.
HE'S ONE OF THREE BROTHERS. THEY HAVE A CONTRACT WITH THE SKIN DEVIL.
AS FAR AS I KNOW, THEY CAN STEAL THE APPEAR-ANCES OF CORPSES THEY'VE TOUCHED...
HOO...

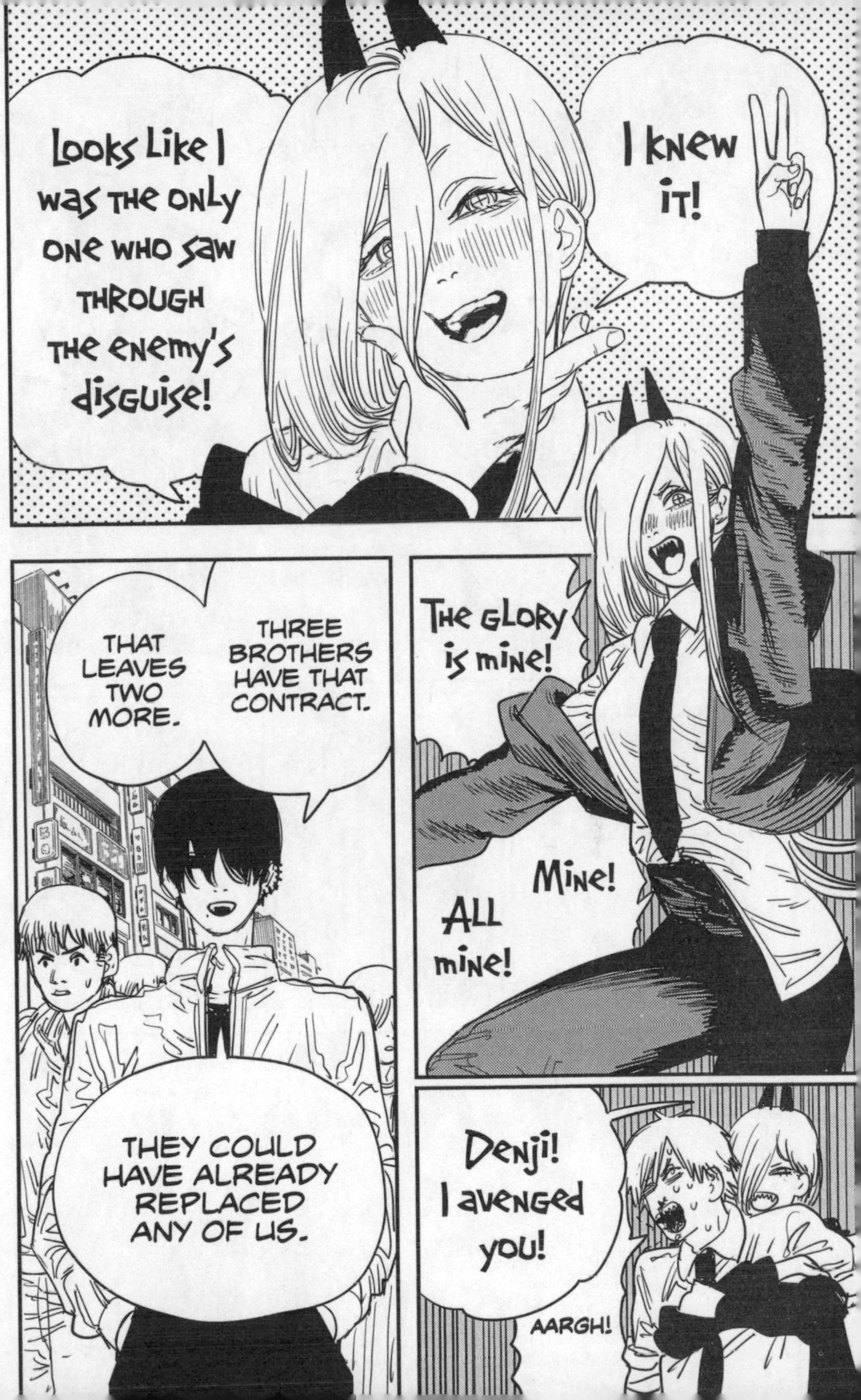
I knew it!
Looks like I was the only one who saw through the enemy's disguise!
The glory is mine!
Mine!
All mine!
Denji! I avenged you!
AARGH!
Three brothers have that contract.
That leaves two more.
They could have already replaced any of us.

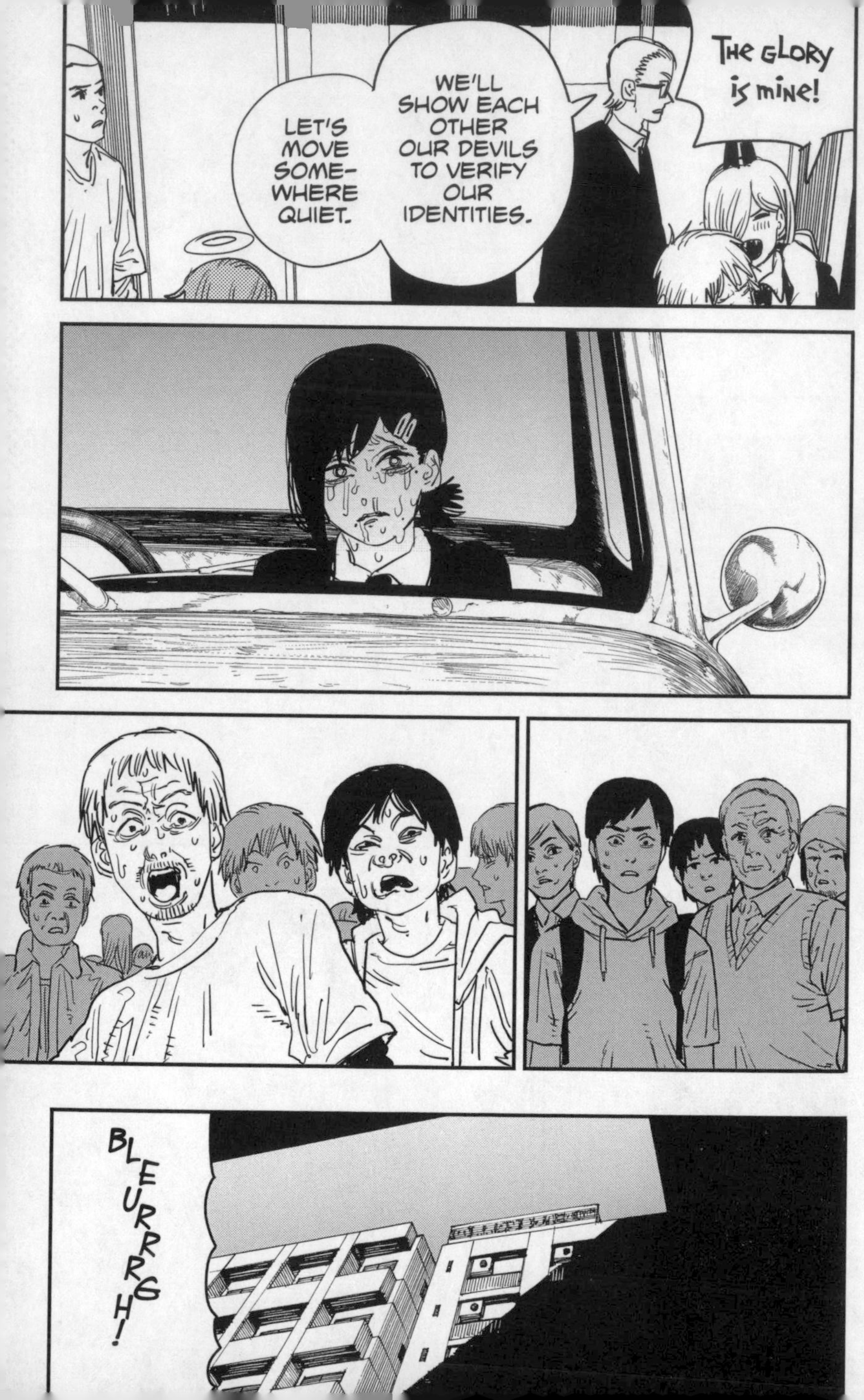
The glory is mine!
WE'LL SHOW EACH OTHER OUR DEVILS TO VERIFY OUR IDENTITIES.
LET'S MOVE SOME-WHERE QUIET.
BLEURRRGH!

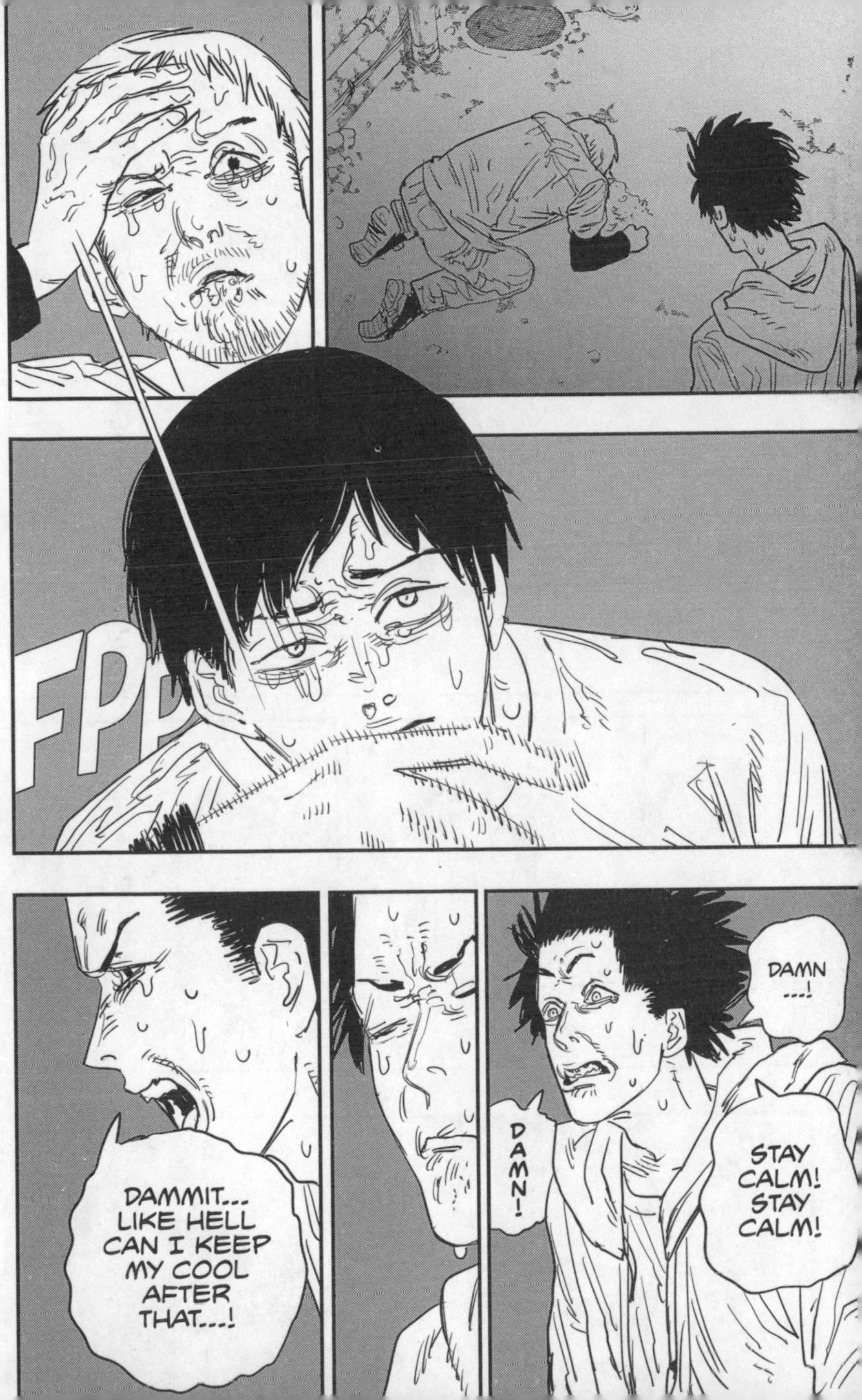
FPP
DAMN...!
STAY CALM! STAY CALM!
DAMN!
DAMMIT... LIKE HELL CAN I KEEP MY COOL AFTER THAT...!

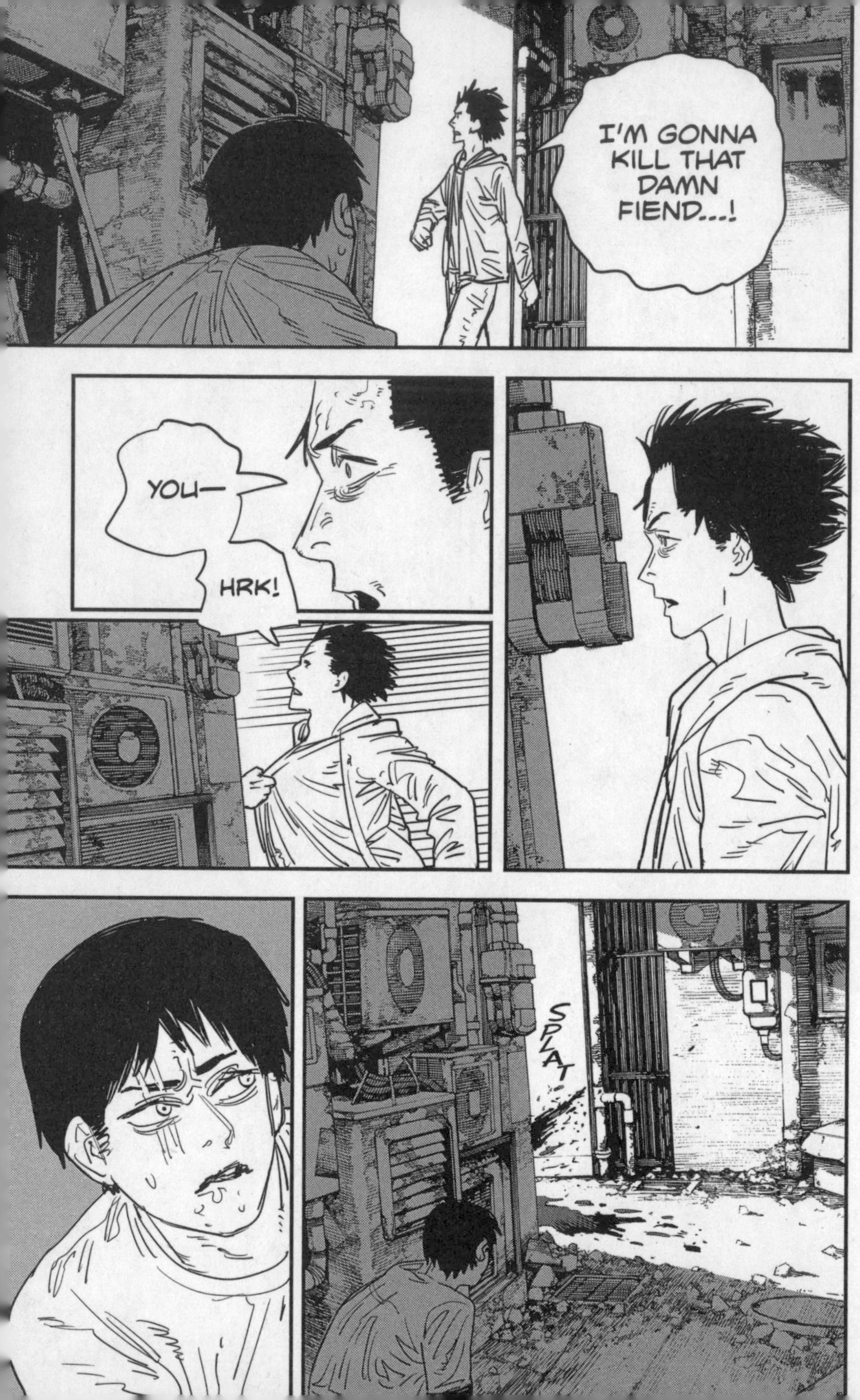
I'M GONNA KILL THAT DAMN FIEND...!
YOU—
HRK!
SPLAT

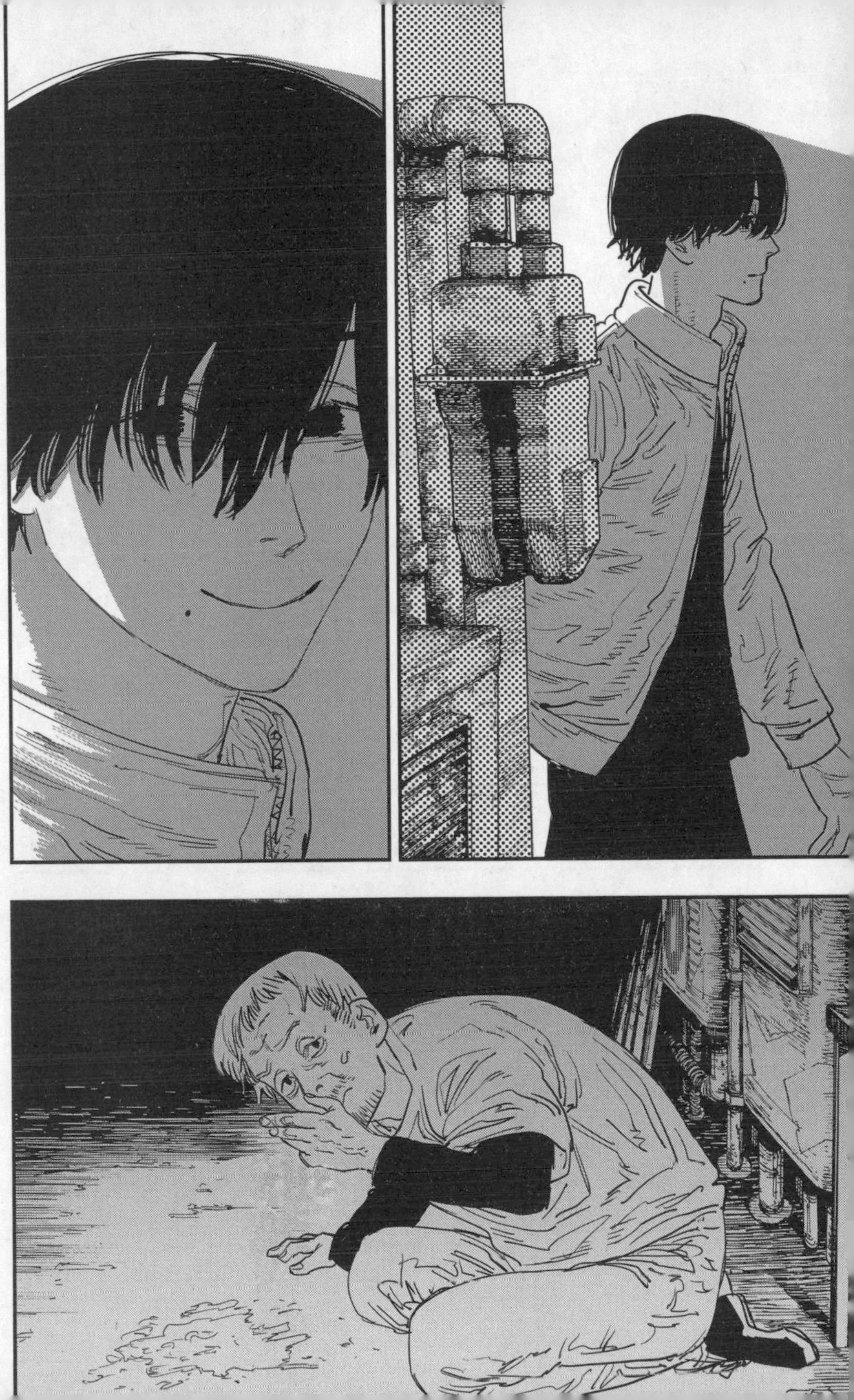

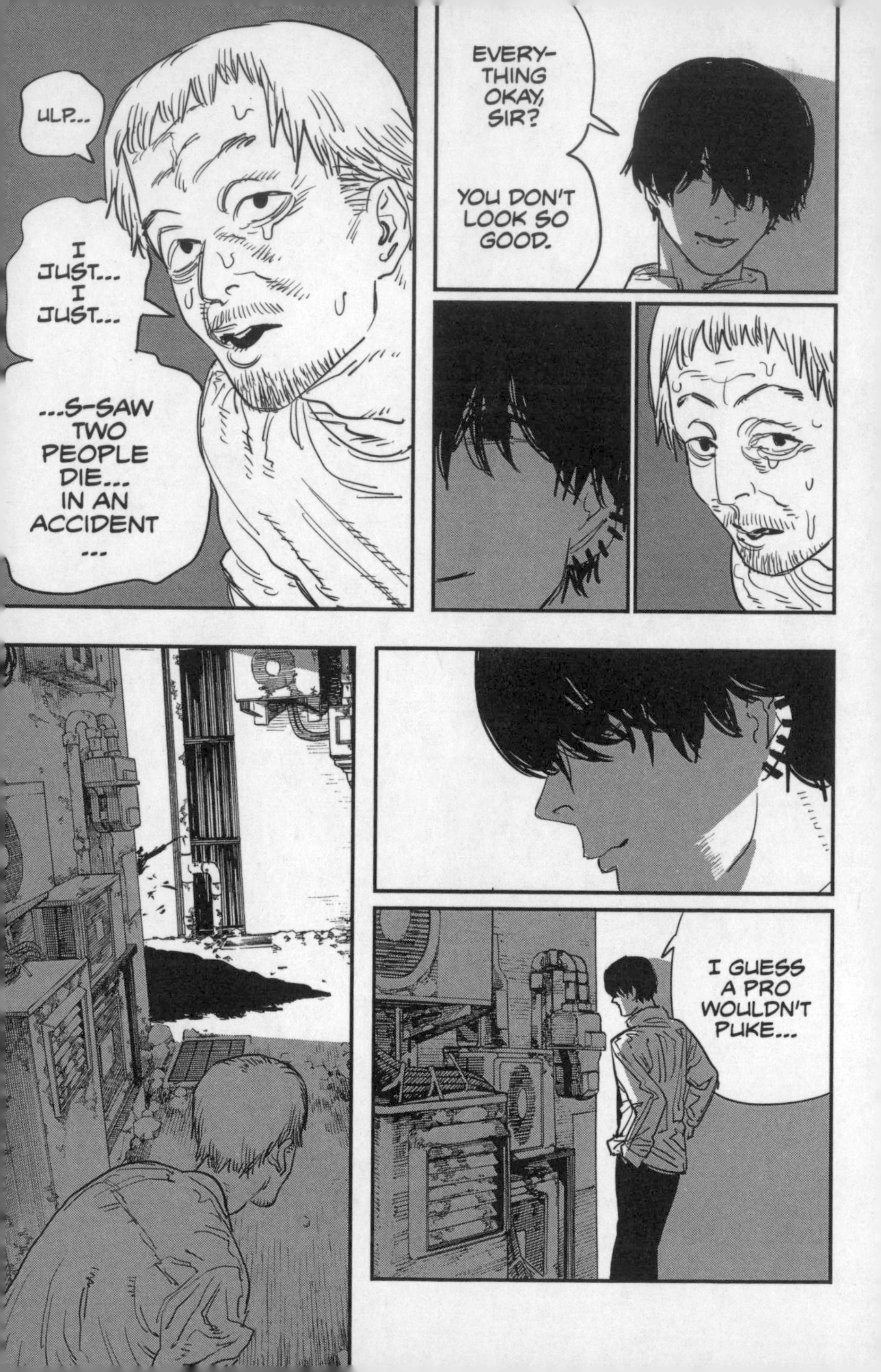
EVERY-THING OKAY, SIR?
YOU DON'T LOOK SO GOOD.
ULP...
I JUST... I JUST...
...S-SAW TWO PEOPLE DIE... IN AN ACCIDENT...
I GUESS A PRO WOULDN'T PUKE...

Chain
s aw  m an

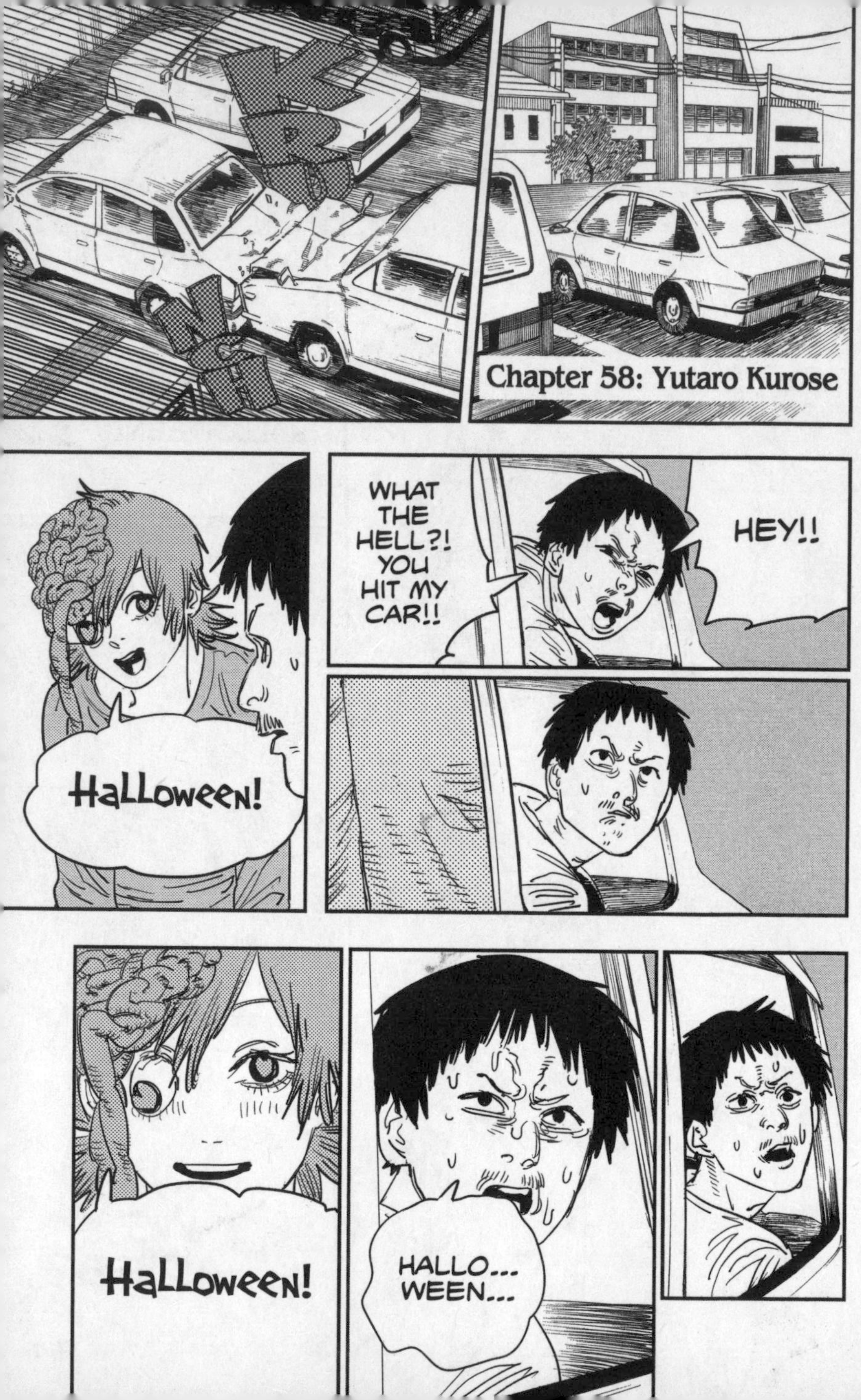
Chapter 58: Yutaro Kurose
HEY!!
WHAT THE HELL?! YOU HIT MY CAR!!
Halloween!
HALLO... WEEN...
Halloween!

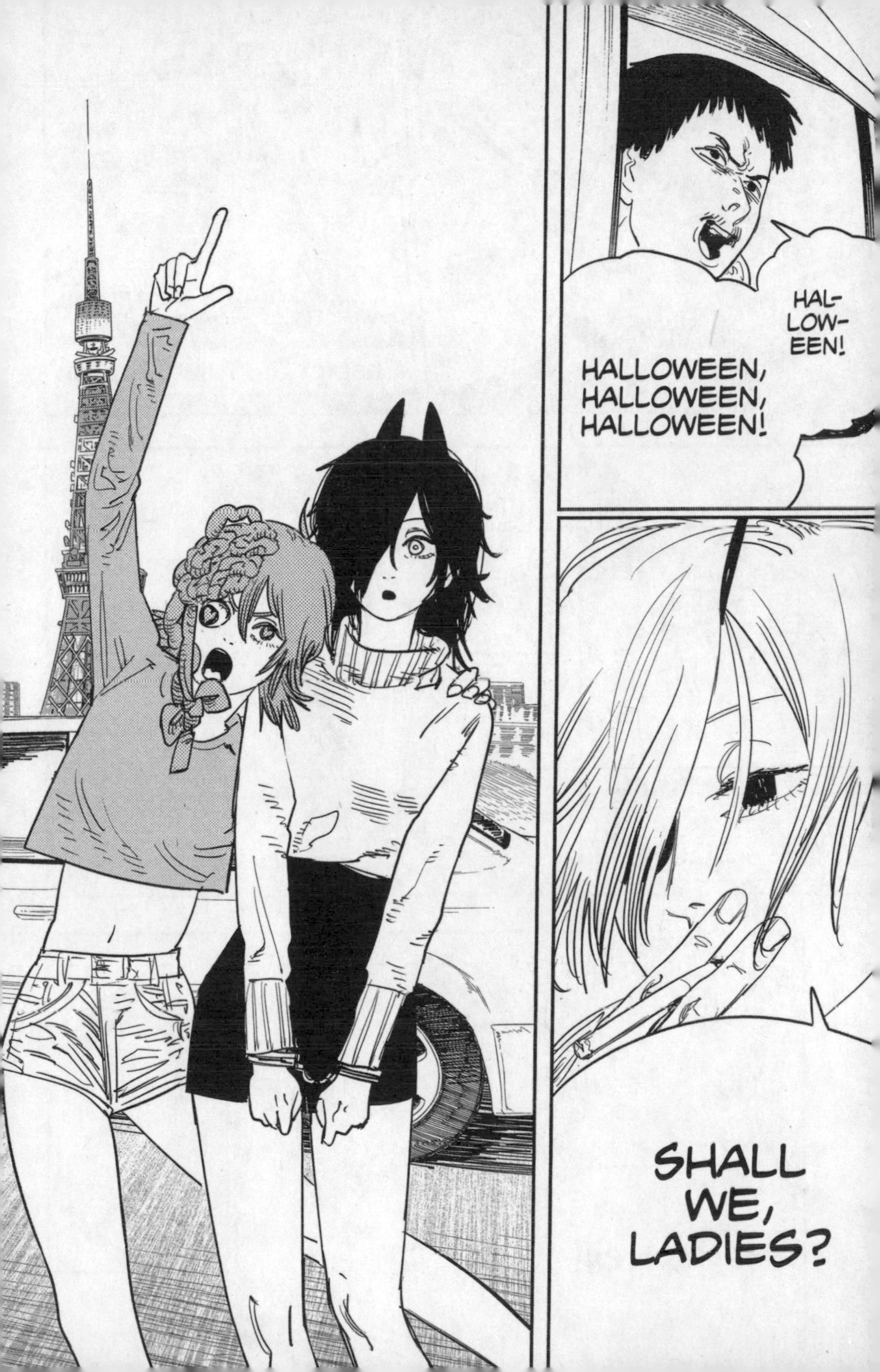
HAL-LOW-EEN!
HALLOWEEN, HALLOWEEN, HALLOWEEN!
SHALL WE, LADIES?

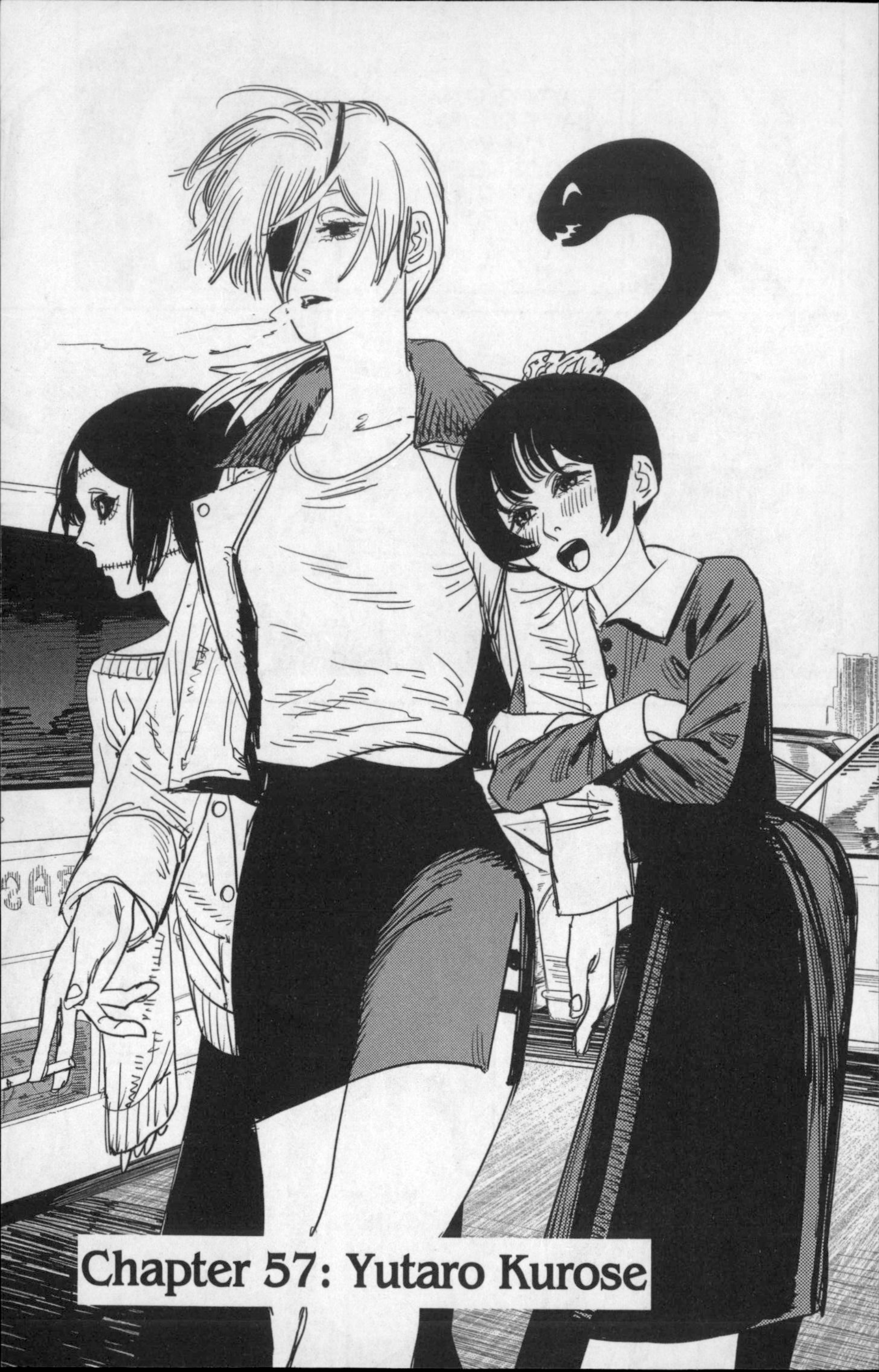

# Chapter 57: Yutaro Kurose

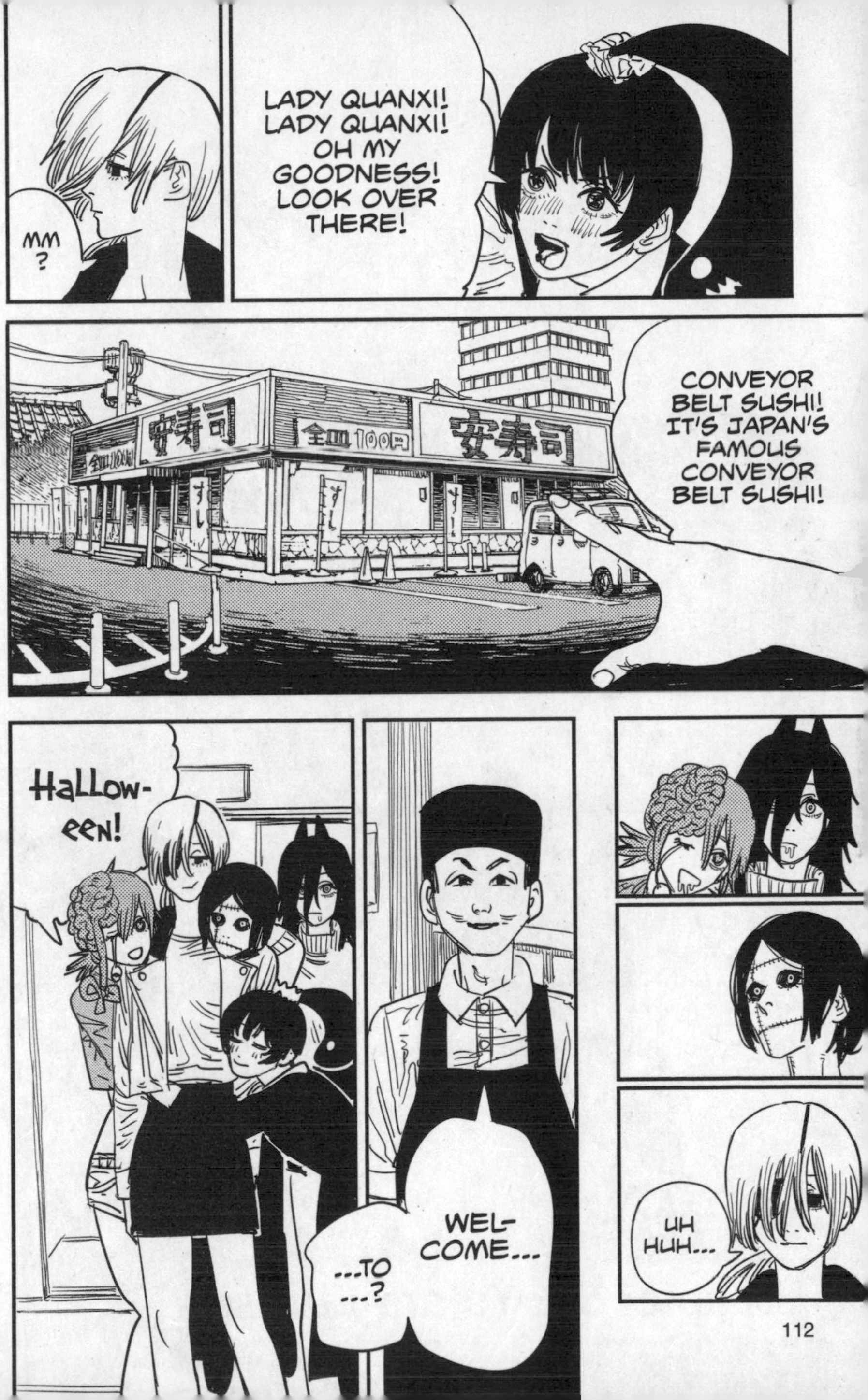
LADY QUANXI! LADY QUANXI! OH MY GOODNESS! LOOK OVER THERE!
MM ?
安寿司
全皿100円
すし
CONVEYOR BELT SUSHI! IT'S JAPAN'S FAMOUS CONVEYOR BELT SUSHI!
UH HUH...
WEL-COME...
...TO ...?
Hallow-een!

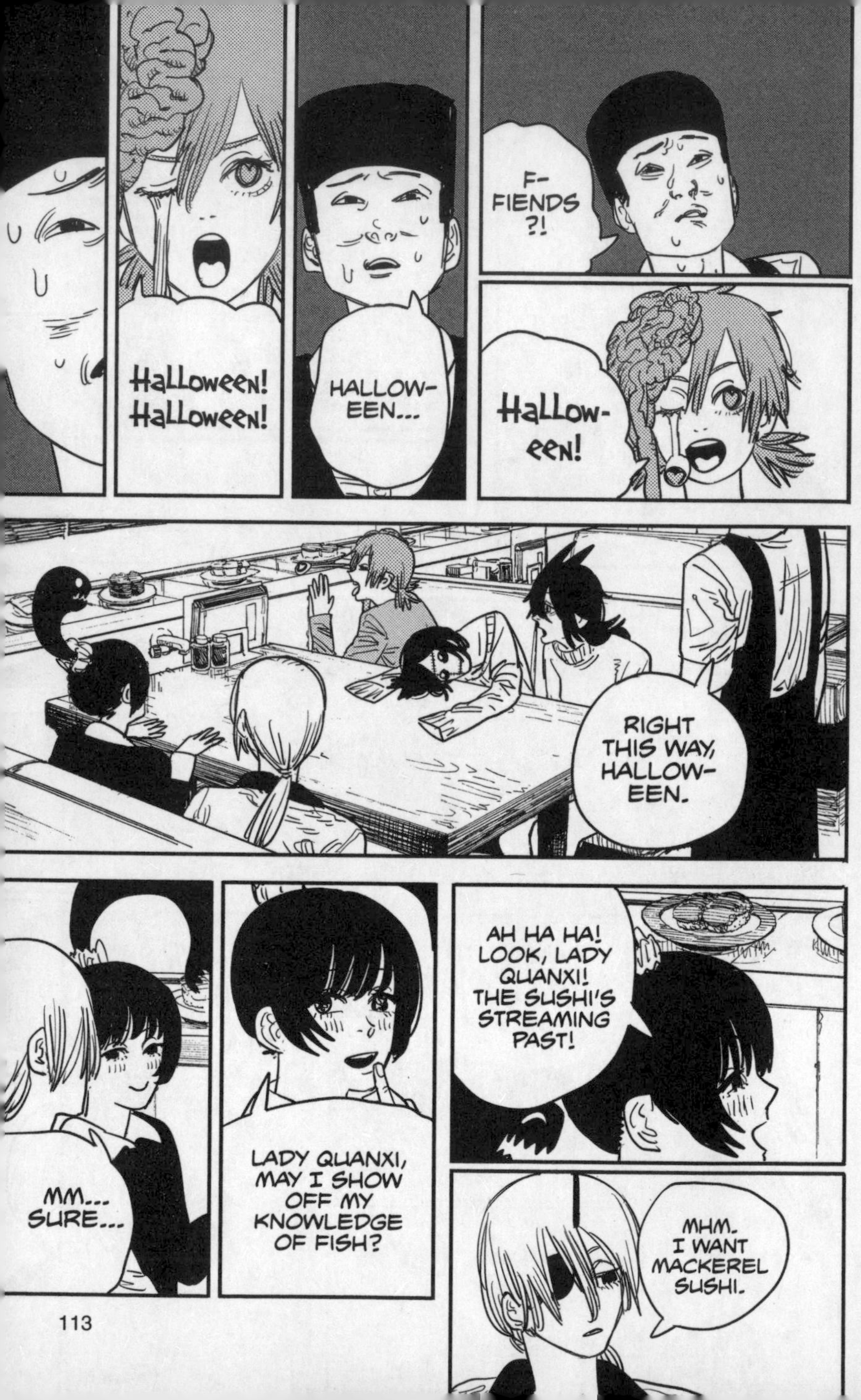
F-FIENDS?!
Hallow-een!
HALLOW-EEN...
Halloween! Halloween!
RIGHT THIS WAY, HALLOW-EEN.
AH HA HA! LOOK, LADY QUANXI! THE SUSHI'S STREAMING PAST!
MHM. I WANT MACKEREL SUSHI.
LADY QUANXI, MAY I SHOW OFF MY KNOWLEDGE OF FISH?
MM... SURE...

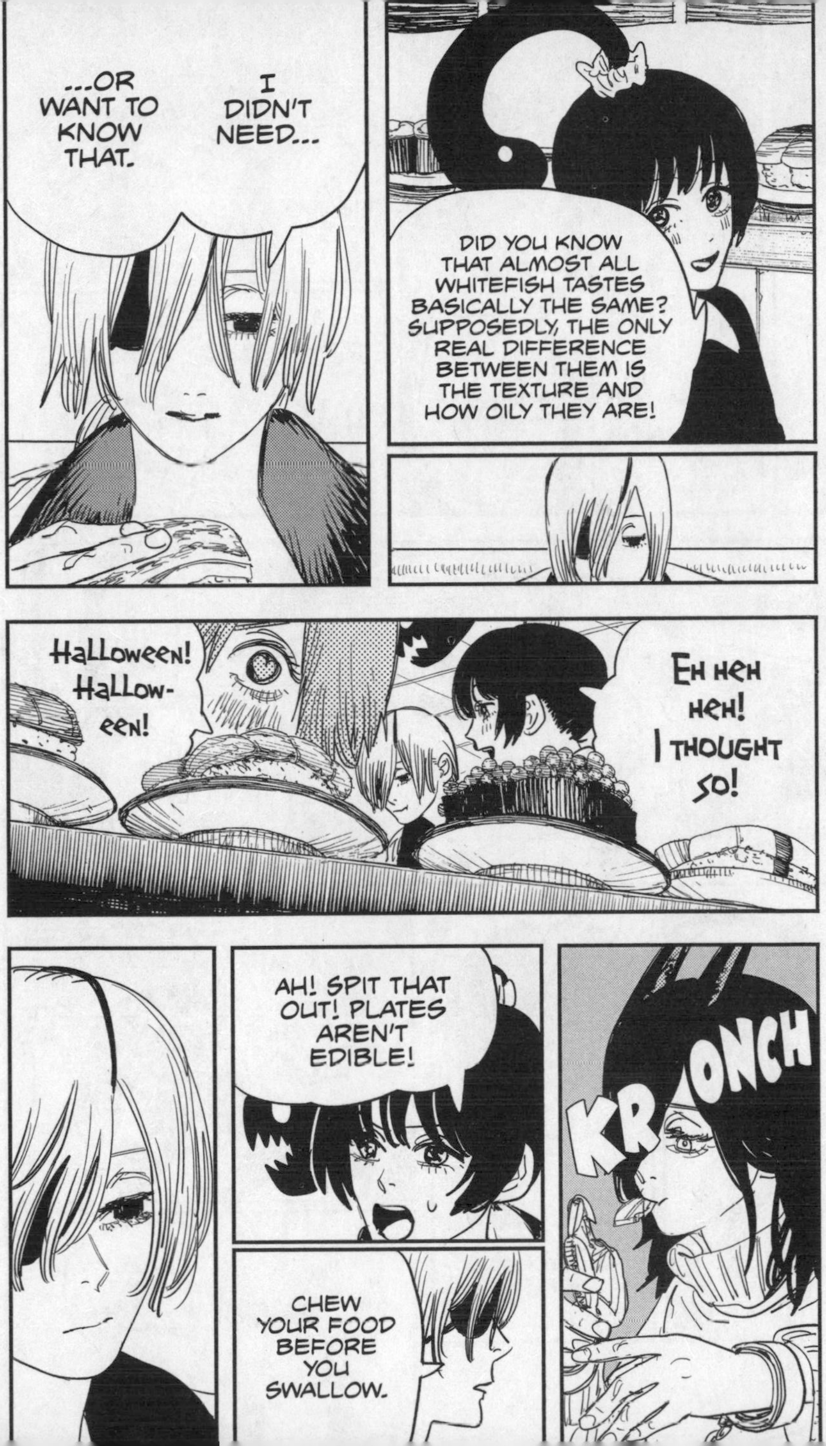
DID YOU KNOW THAT ALMOST ALL WHITEFISH TASTES BASICALLY THE SAME? SUPPOSEDLY, THE ONLY REAL DIFFERENCE BETWEEN THEM IS THE TEXTURE AND HOW OILY THEY ARE!
I DIDN'T NEED...
...OR WANT TO KNOW THAT.
EH HEH HEH! I THOUGHT SO!
Halloween! Hallow-een!
KRONCH
AH! SPIT THAT OUT! PLATES AREN'T EDIBLE!
CHEW YOUR FOOD BEFORE YOU SWALLOW.

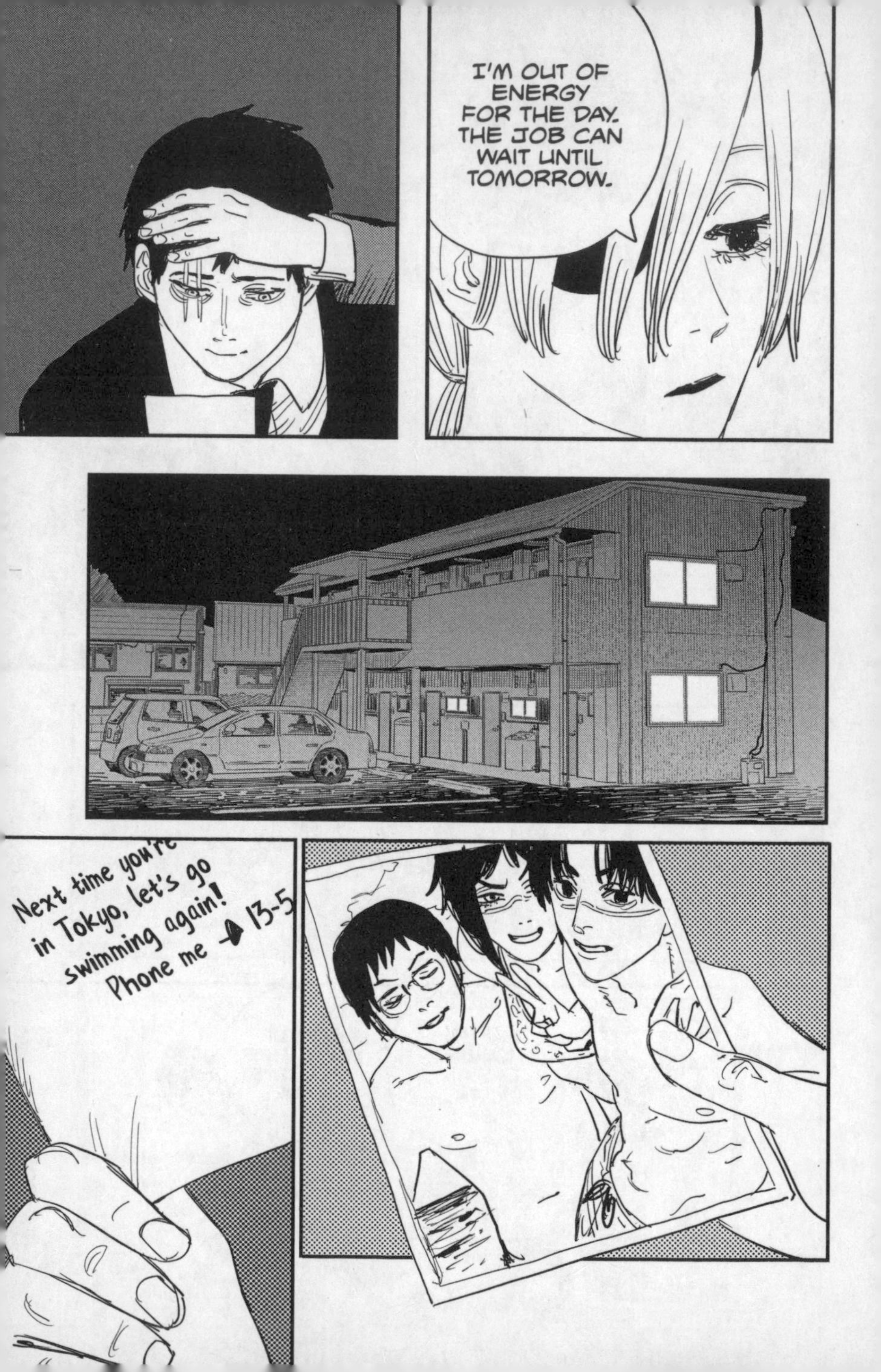
I'M OUT OF ENERGY FOR THE DAY. THE JOB CAN WAIT UNTIL TOMORROW.
Next time you're in Tokyo, let's go swimming again! Phone me → 13-5

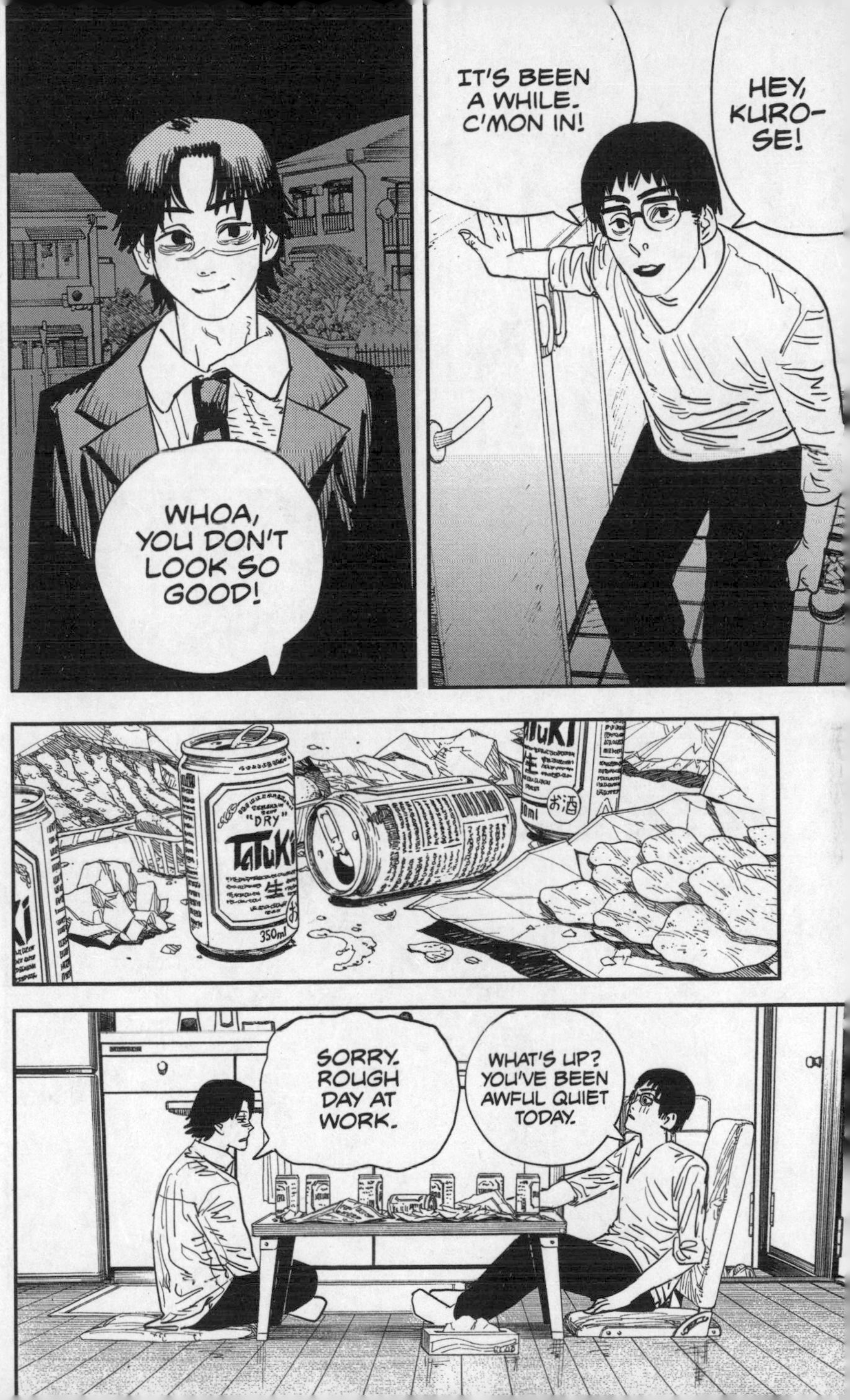
HEY, KURO-SE!
IT'S BEEN A WHILE. C'MON IN!
WHOA, YOU DON'T LOOK SO GOOD!
"DRY"
TaTuKi
生
350ml
お酒
WHAT'S UP? YOU'VE BEEN AWFUL QUIET TODAY.
SORRY. ROUGH DAY AT WORK.

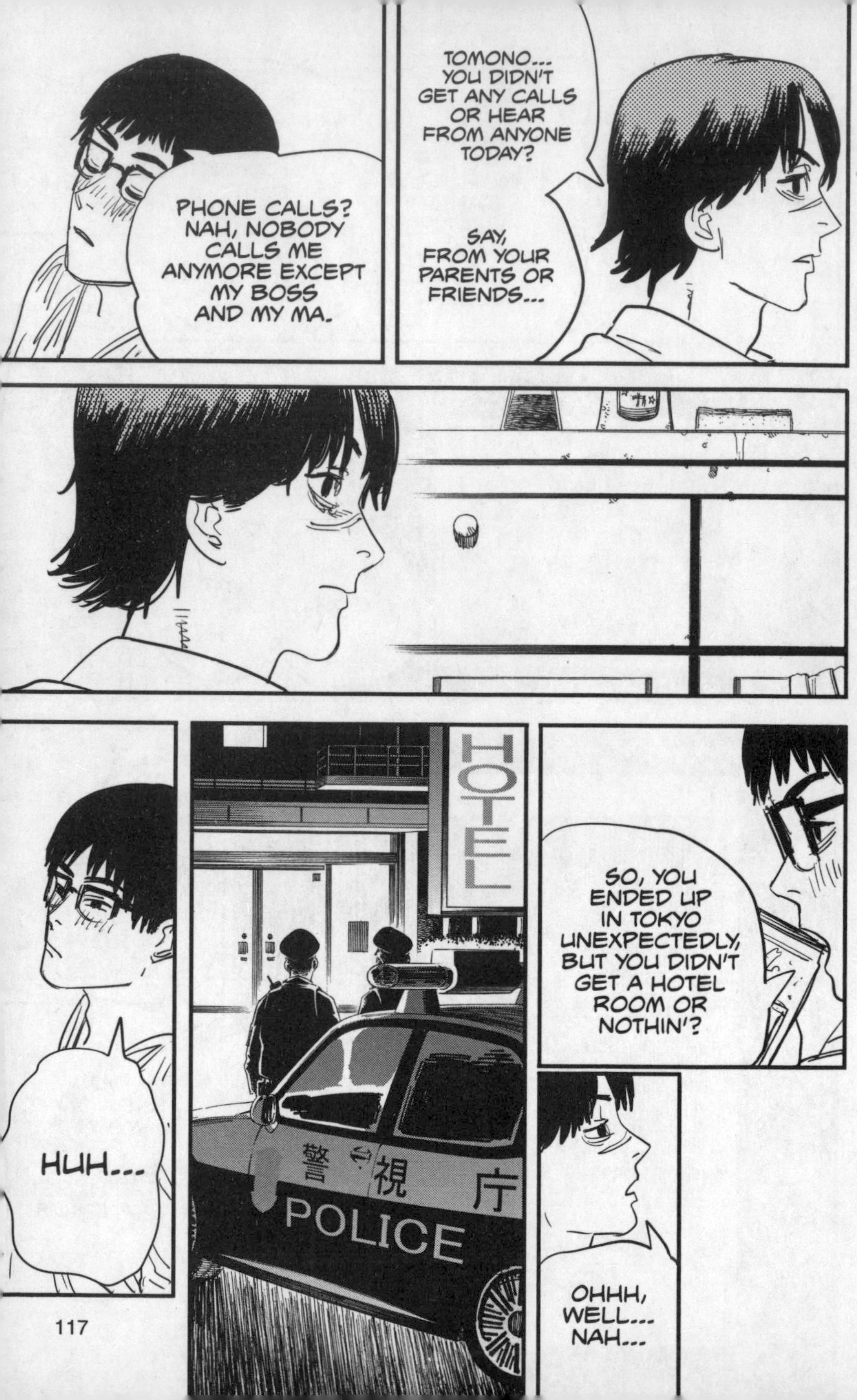
TOMONO... YOU DIDN'T GET ANY CALLS OR HEAR FROM ANYONE TODAY?
SAY, FROM YOUR PARENTS OR FRIENDS...
PHONE CALLS? NAH, NOBODY CALLS ME ANYMORE EXCEPT MY BOSS AND MY MA.
SO, YOU ENDED UP IN TOKYO UNEXPECTEDLY, BUT YOU DIDN'T GET A HOTEL ROOM OR NOTHIN'?
OHHH, WELL... NAH...
HOTEL
警視庁
POLICE
HUH...

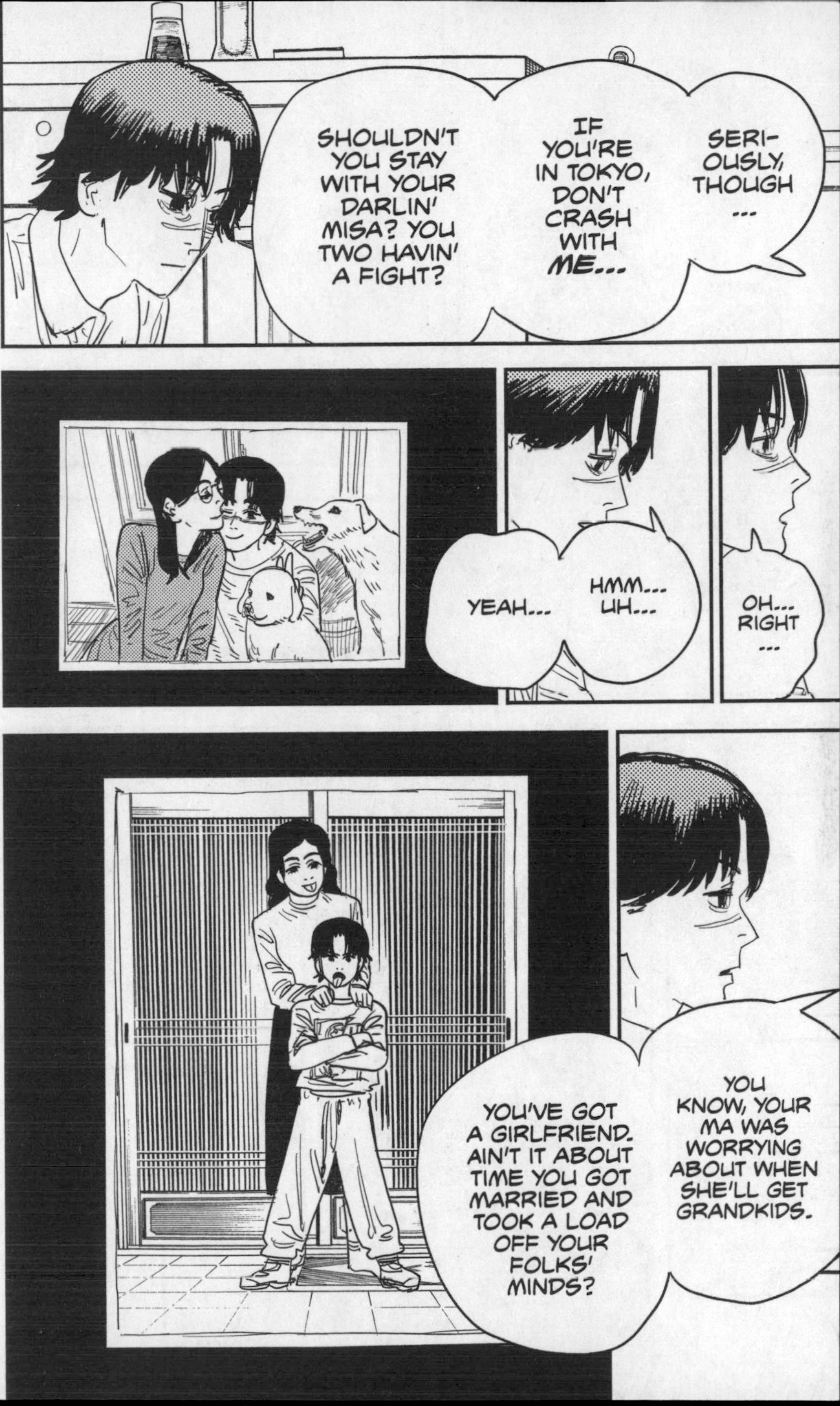
SERIOUSLY, THOUGH...
IF YOU'RE IN TOKYO, DON'T CRASH WITH ME...
SHOULDN'T YOU STAY WITH YOUR DARLIN' MISA? YOU TWO HAVIN' A FIGHT?
OH... RIGHT...
HMM... UH...
YEAH...
YOU KNOW, YOUR MA WAS WORRYING ABOUT WHEN SHE'LL GET GRANDKIDS.
YOU'VE GOT A GIRLFRIEND. AIN'T IT ABOUT TIME YOU GOT MARRIED AND TOOK A LOAD OFF YOUR FOLKS' MINDS?

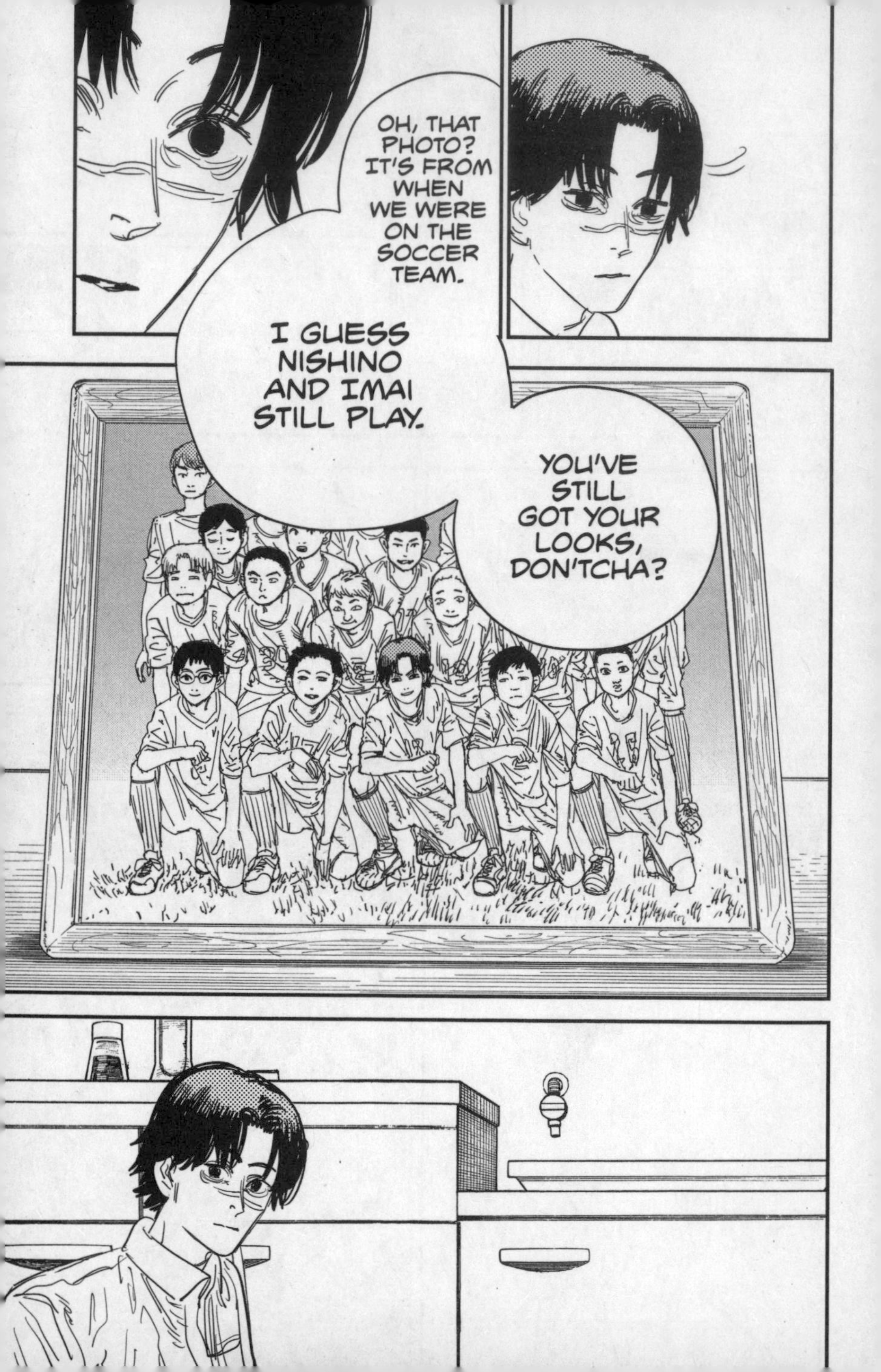
OH, THAT PHOTO? IT'S FROM WHEN WE WERE ON THE SOCCER TEAM.
I GUESS NISHINO AND IMAI STILL PLAY.
YOU'VE STILL GOT YOUR LOOKS, DON'TCHA?

UH, NOTHING...

WHAT?

SORRY ...

I'M SORRY...

I'M SO....

NGH... AH...

AAAAH...! WHAT...
GOD...
WHAT THE HELL...AM I DOING...?!
WHY ARE YOU CRYING?! YOU'RE TOO DRUNK!!

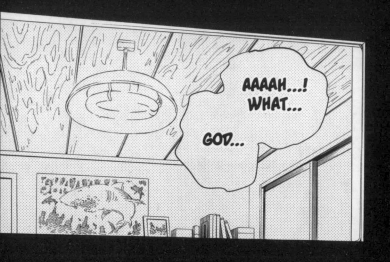

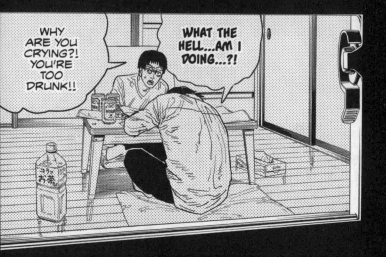

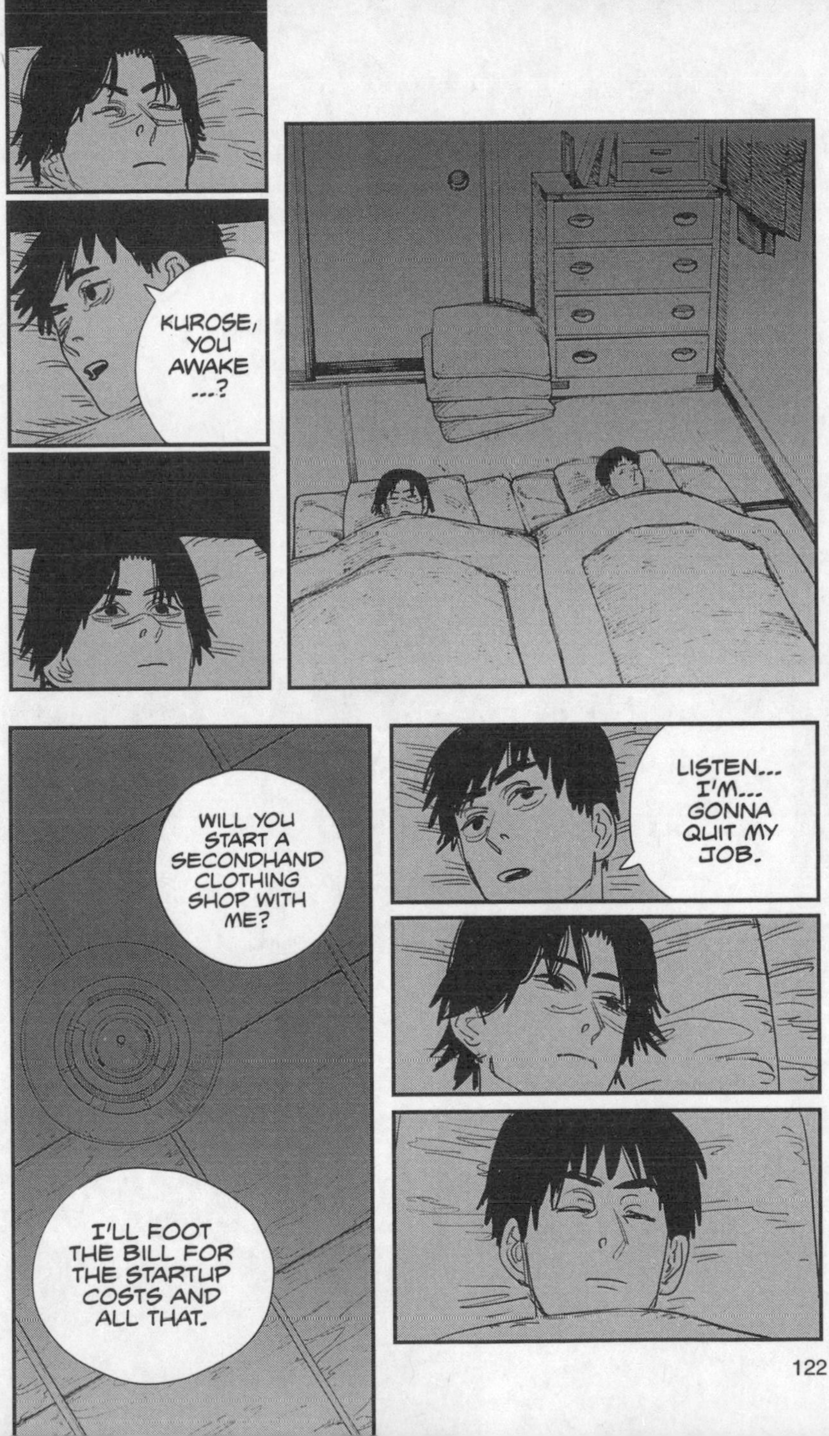
KUROSE, YOU AWAKE ...?
LISTEN... I'M... GONNA QUIT MY JOB.
WILL YOU START A SECONDHAND CLOTHING SHOP WITH ME?
I'LL FOOT THE BILL FOR THE STARTUP COSTS AND ALL THAT.

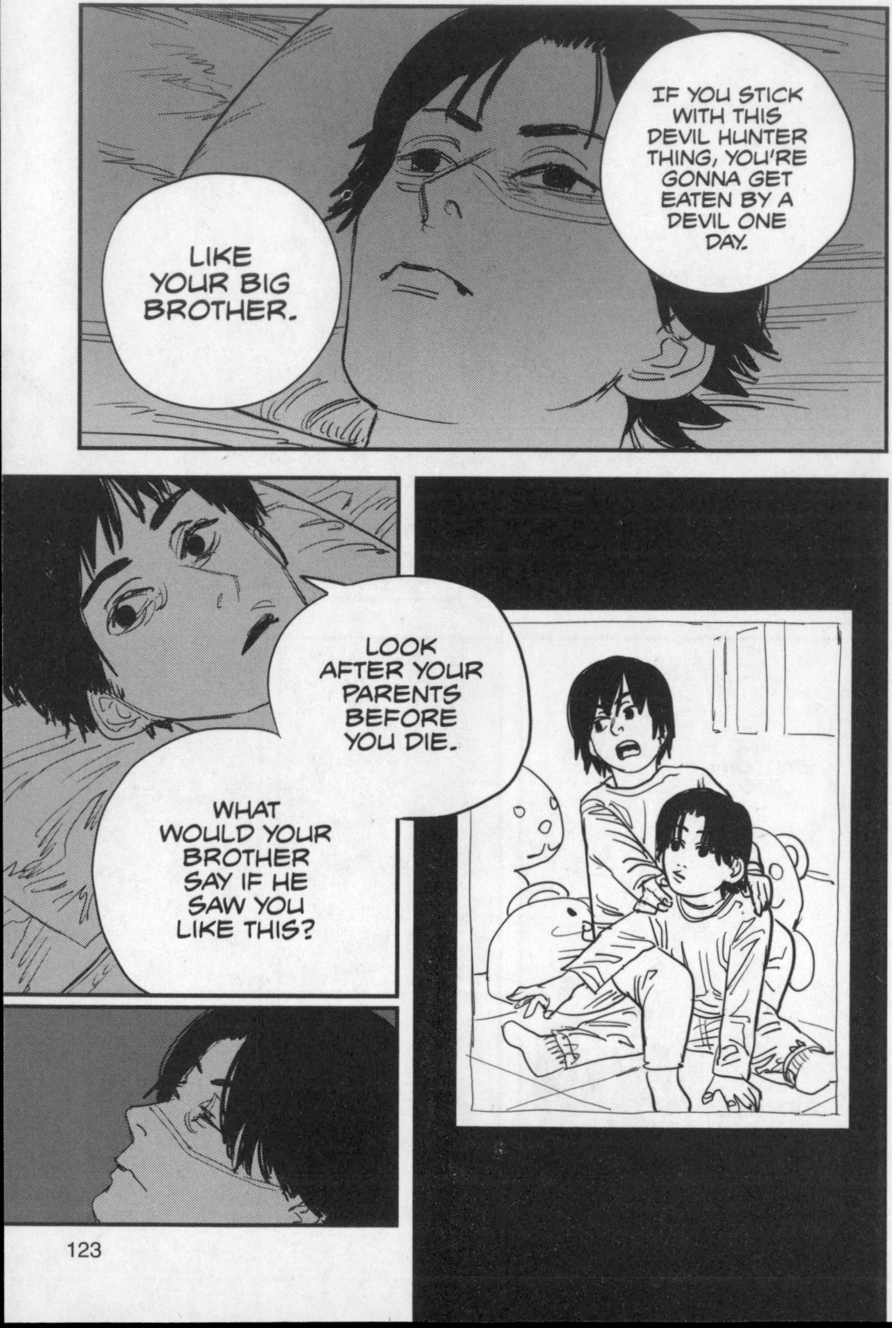
IF YOU STICK WITH THIS DEVIL HUNTER THING, YOU'RE GONNA GET EATEN BY A DEVIL ONE DAY.
LIKE YOUR BIG BROTHER.
LOOK AFTER YOUR PARENTS BEFORE YOU DIE.
WHAT WOULD YOUR BROTHER SAY IF HE SAW YOU LIKE THIS?

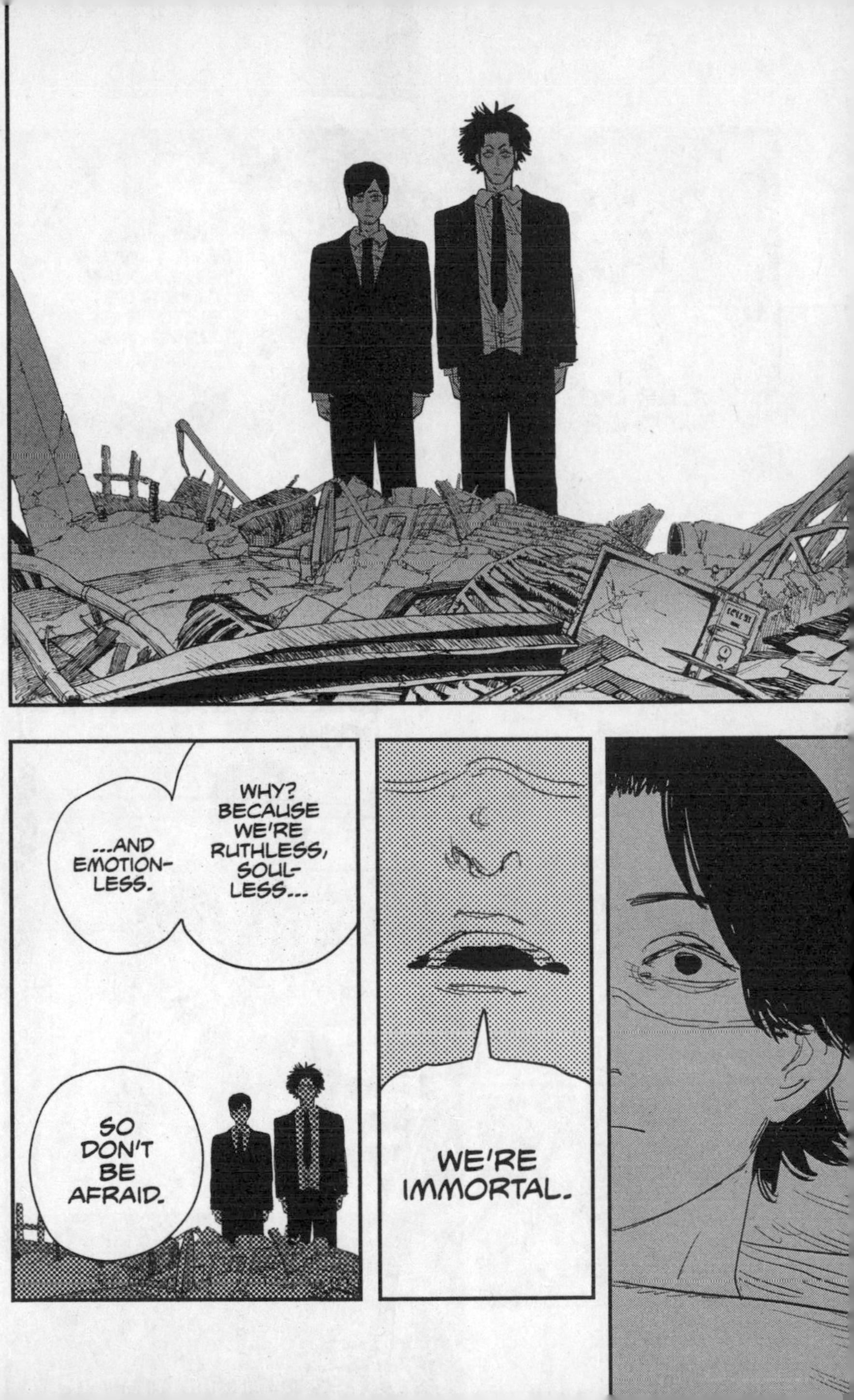
WE'RE IMMORTAL.
WHY? BECAUSE WE'RE RUTHLESS, SOUL-LESS...
...AND EMOTION-LESS.
SO DON'T BE AFRAID.

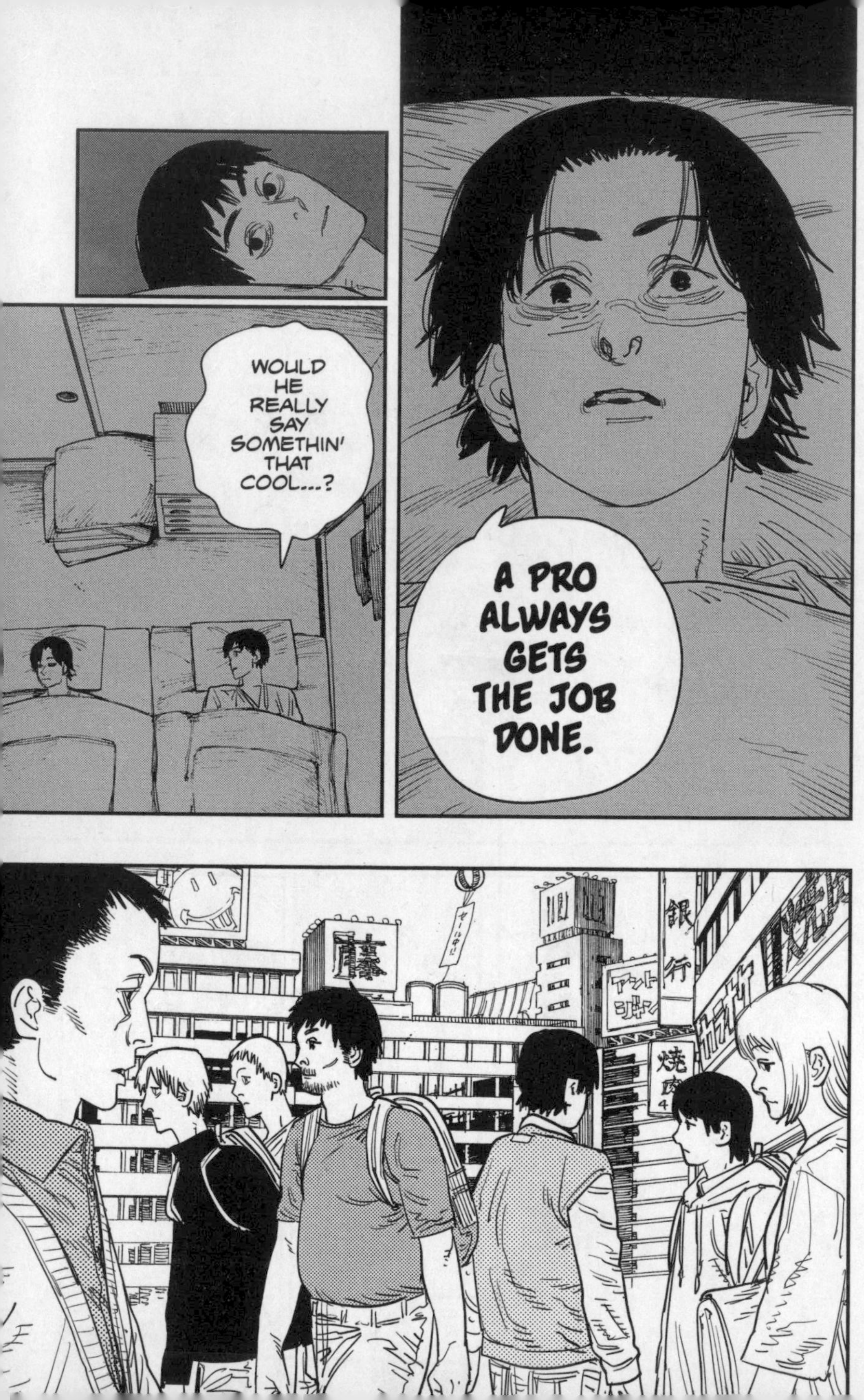
A PRO ALWAYS GETS THE JOB DONE.
WOULD HE REALLY SAY SOMETHIN' THAT COOL...?
銀行

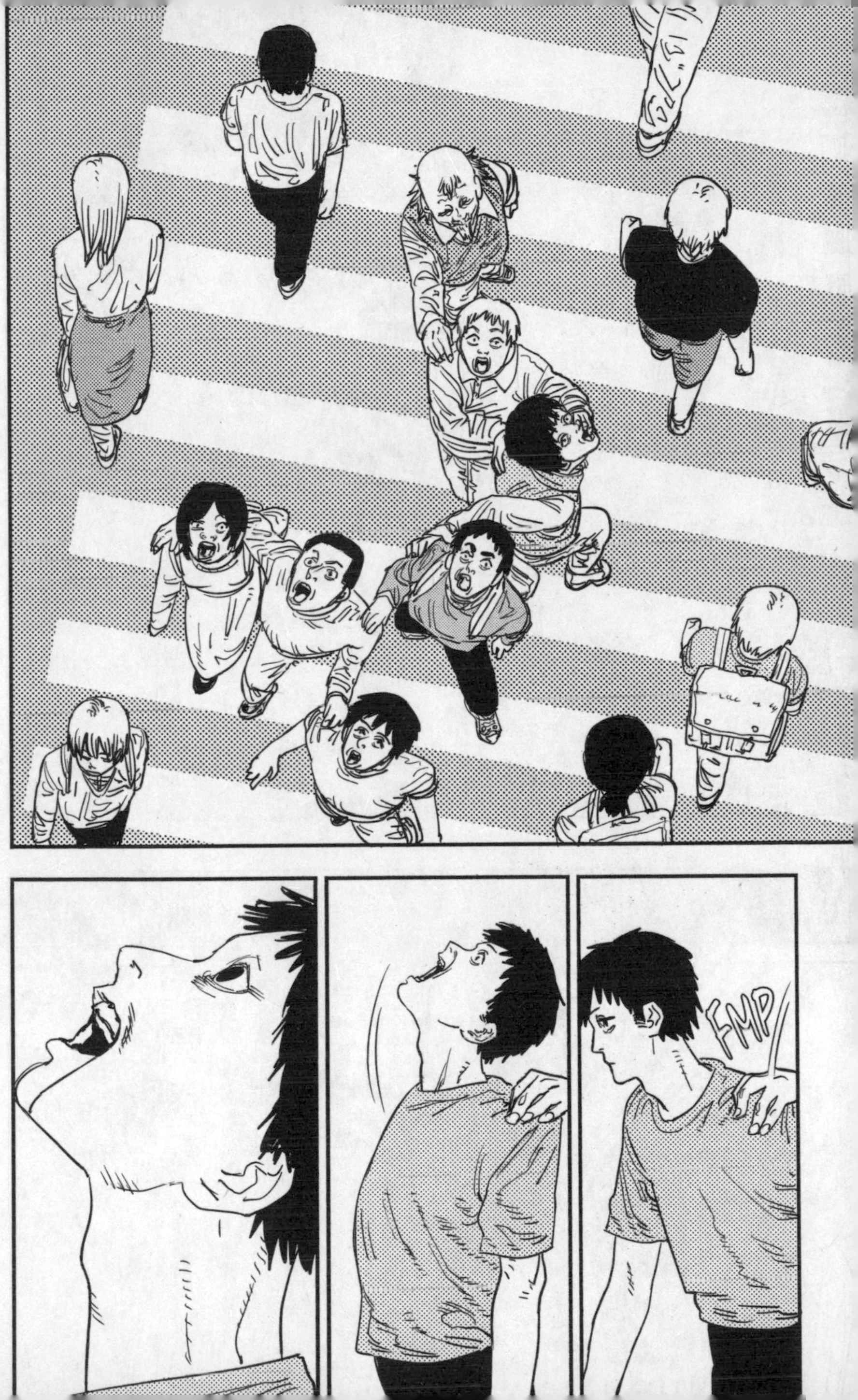
FMP

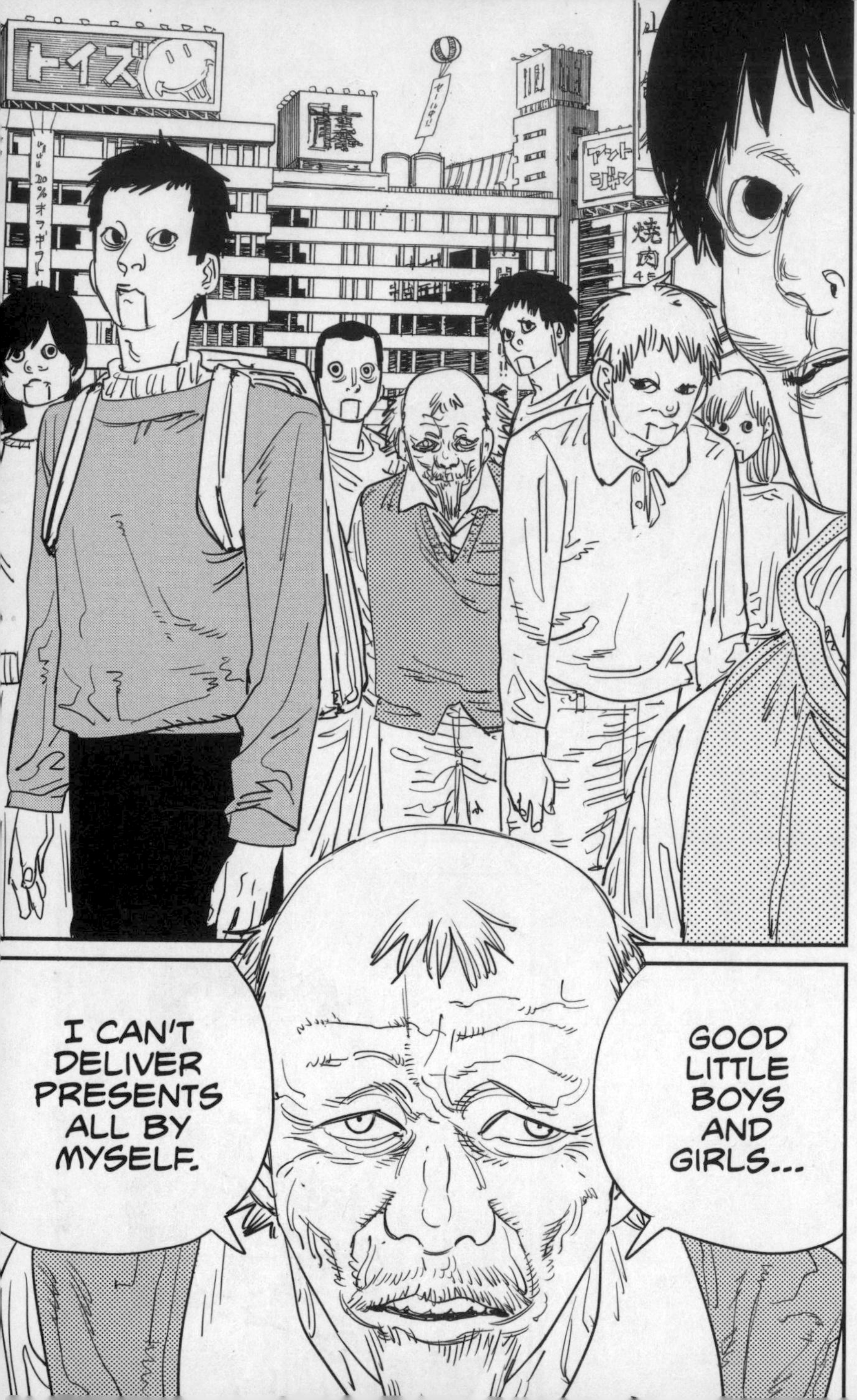
トイズ
焼肉
GOOD LITTLE BOYS AND GIRLS...
I CAN'T DELIVER PRESENTS ALL BY MYSELF.

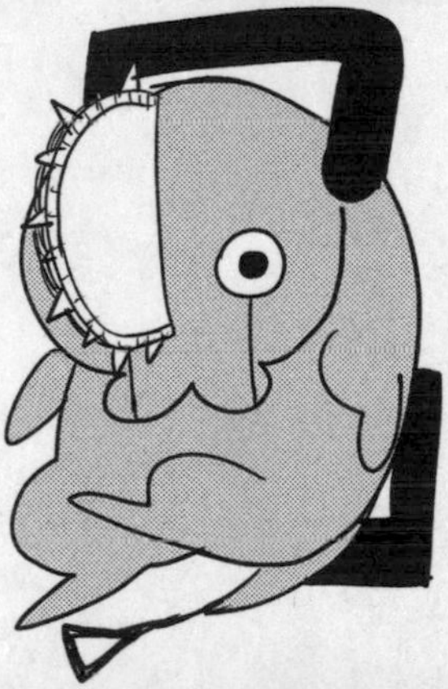

Chain saw man

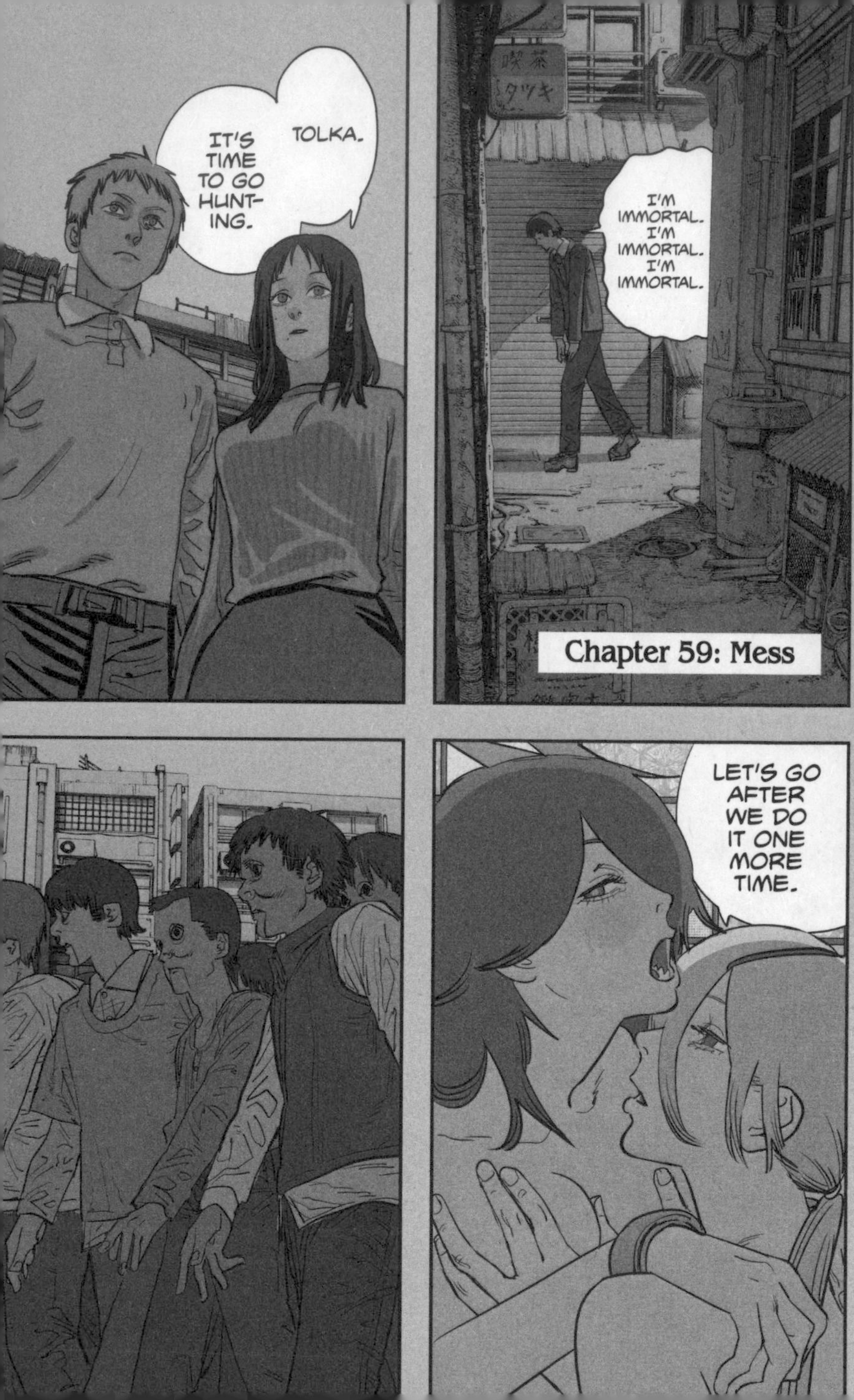
喫茶
タツキ
I'M IMMORTAL. I'M IMMORTAL. I'M IMMORTAL.
Chapter 59: Mess
TOLKA.
IT'S TIME TO GO HUNTING.
LET'S GO AFTER WE DO IT ONE MORE TIME.

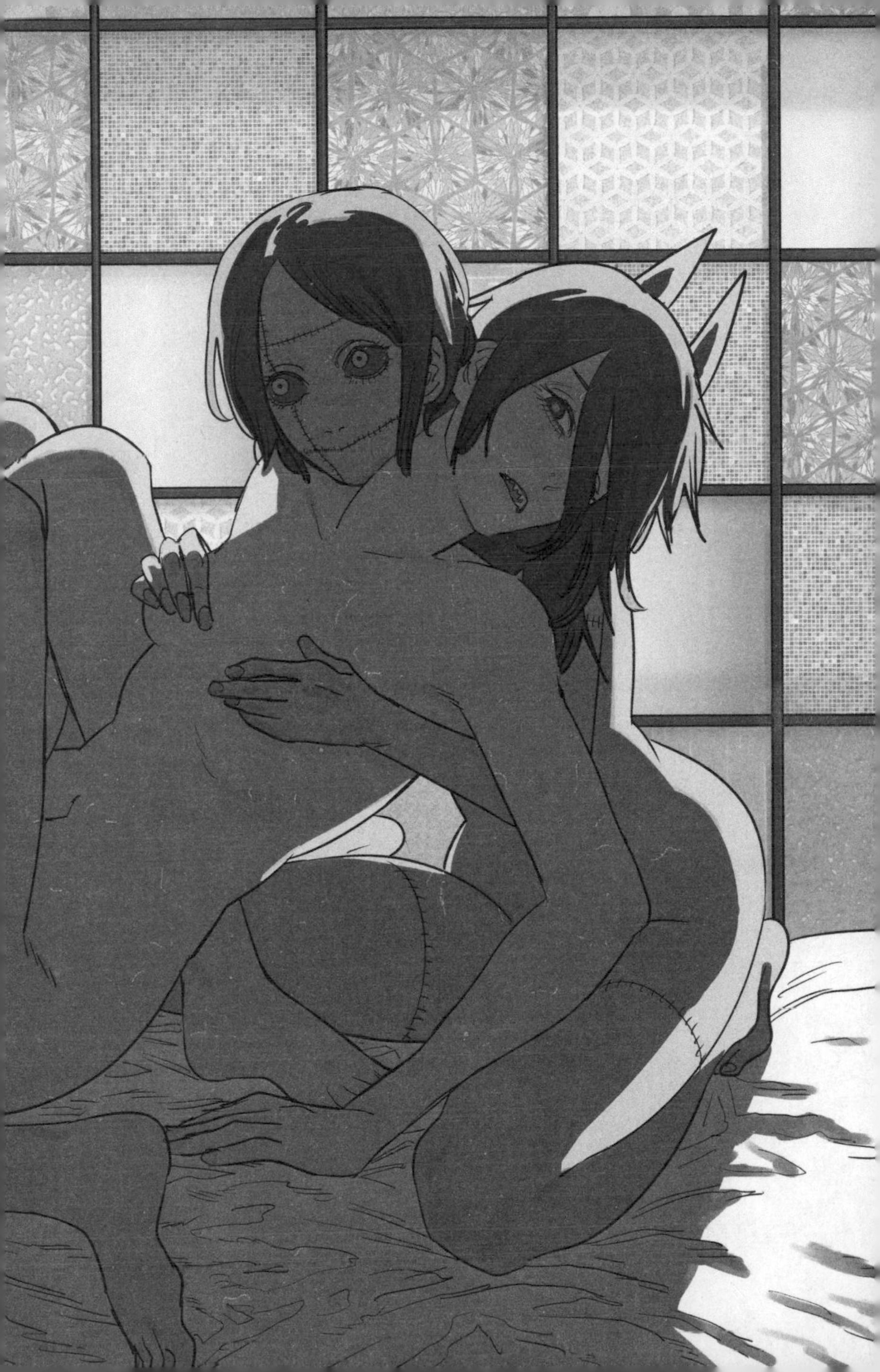

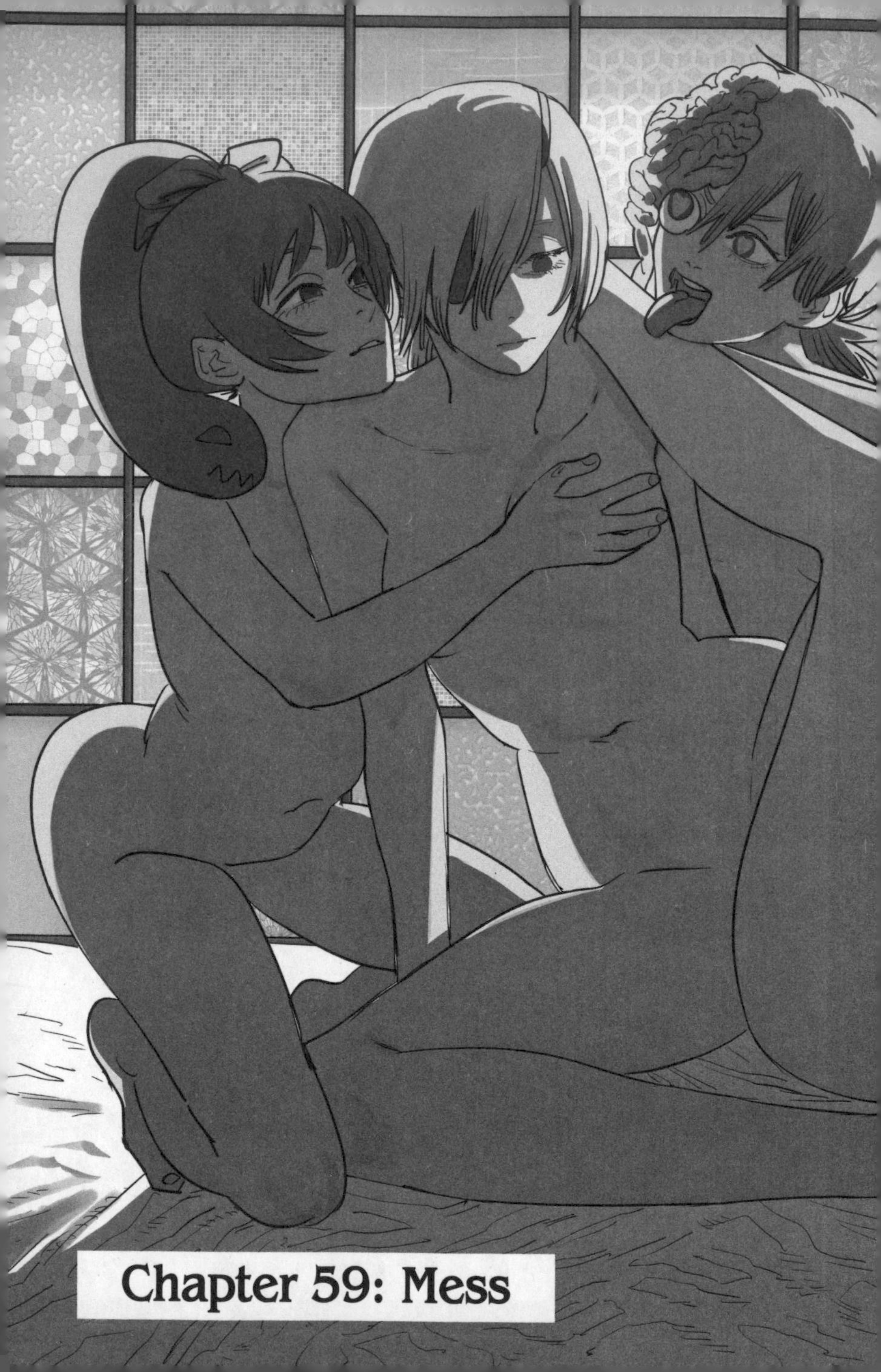

# Chapter 59: Mess

CHAINSAW MAN

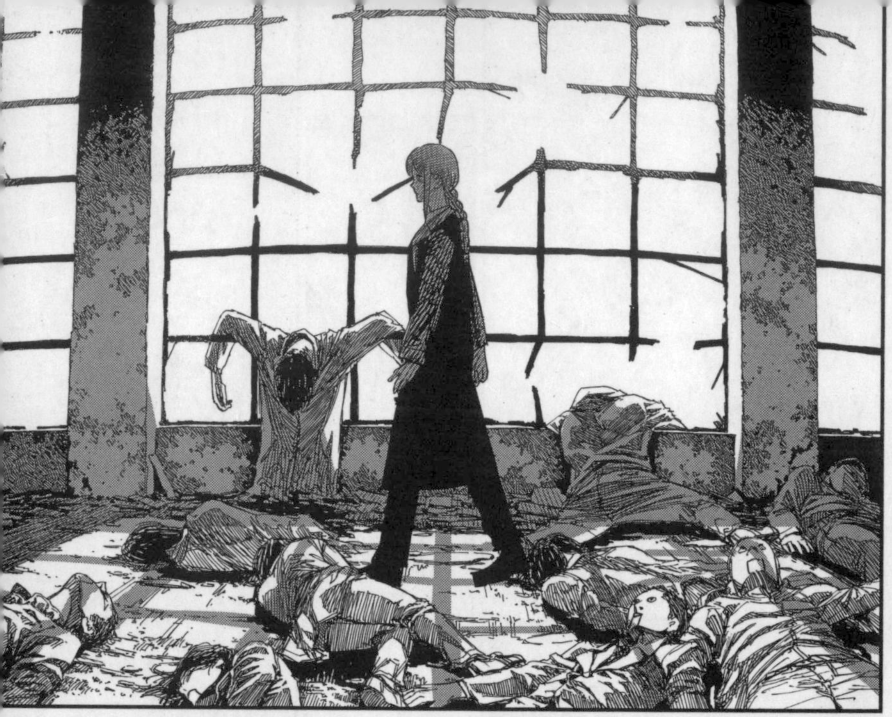

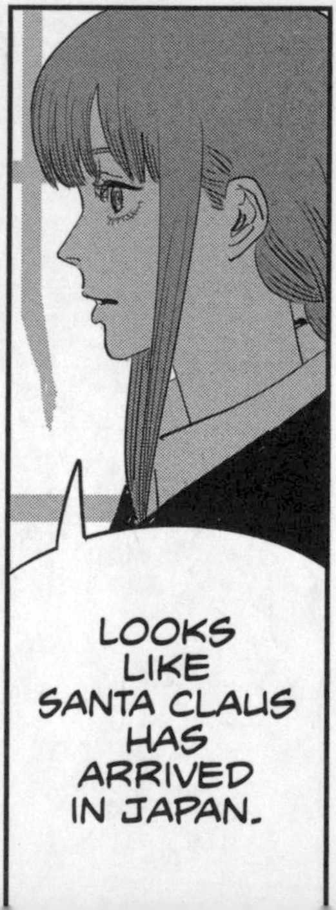
LOOKS LIKE SANTA CLAUS HAS ARRIVED IN JAPAN.

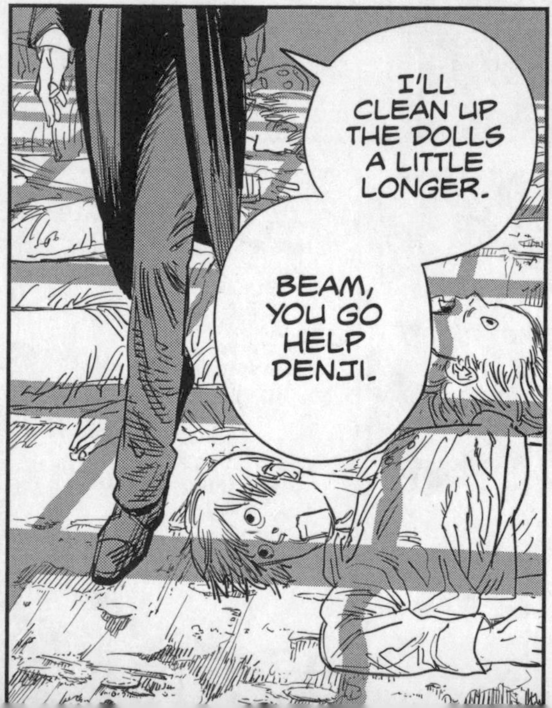
I'LL CLEAN UP THE DOLLS A LITTLE LONGER.
BEAM, YOU GO HELP DENJI.

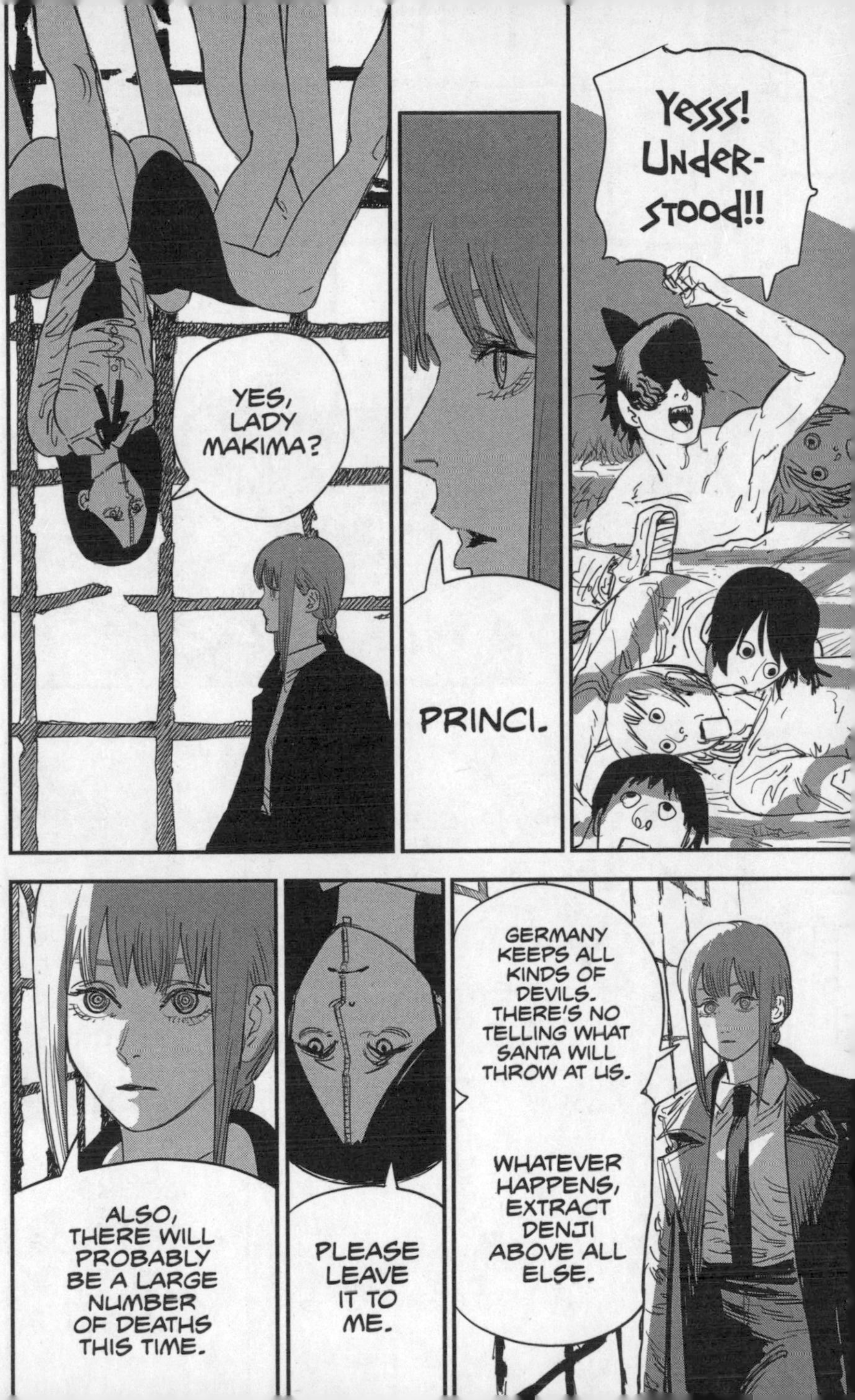
Yessss! Under-stood!!
PRINCI.
YES, LADY MAKIMA?
GERMANY KEEPS ALL KINDS OF DEVILS. THERE'S NO TELLING WHAT SANTA WILL THROW AT US.
WHATEVER HAPPENS, EXTRACT DENJI ABOVE ALL ELSE.
PLEASE LEAVE IT TO ME.
ALSO, THERE WILL PROBABLY BE A LARGE NUMBER OF DEATHS THIS TIME.

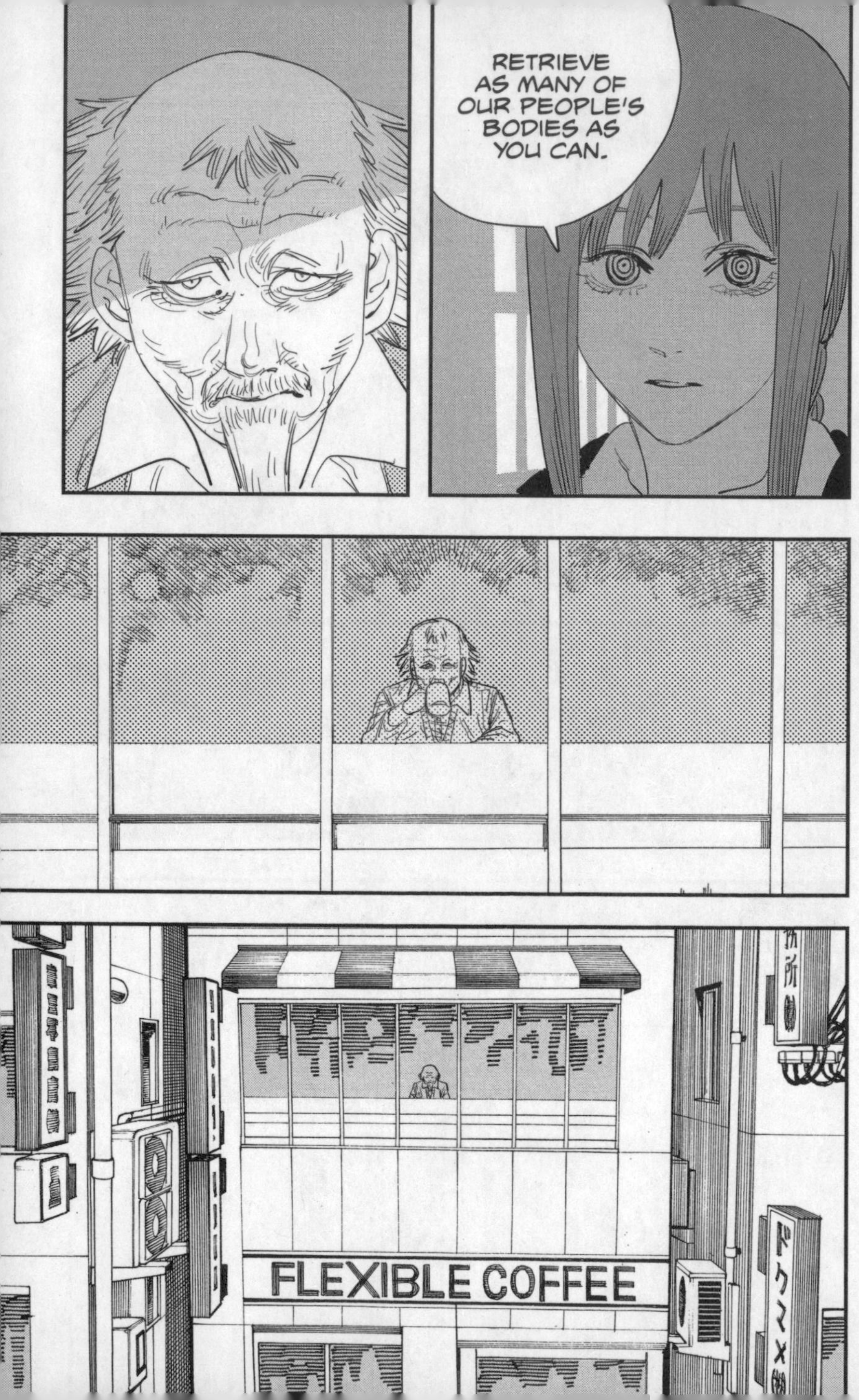
RETRIEVE AS MANY OF OUR PEOPLE'S BODIES AS YOU CAN.
FLEXIBLE COFFEE

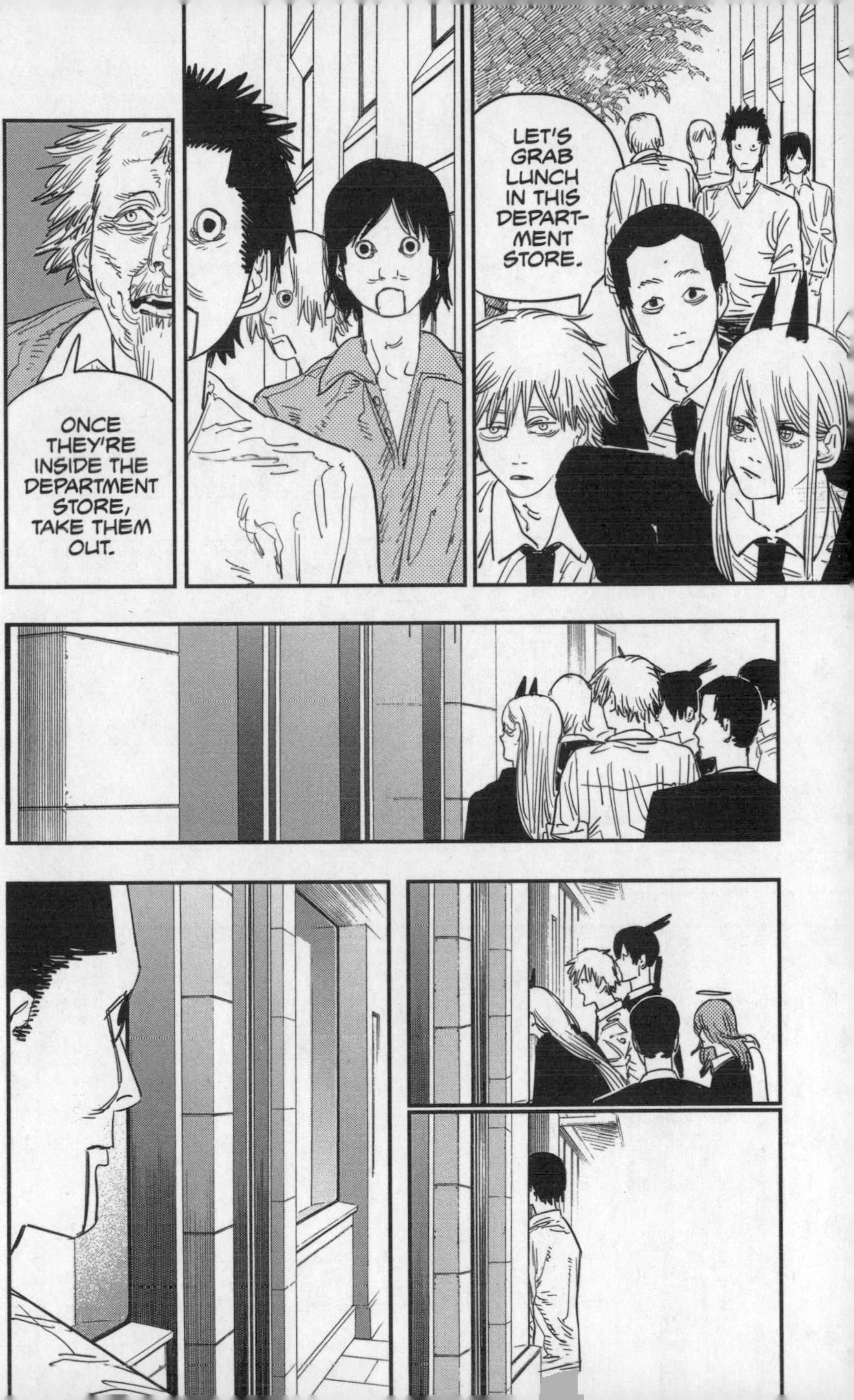
LET'S GRAB LUNCH IN THIS DEPART- MENT STORE.
ONCE THEY'RE INSIDE THE DEPARTMENT STORE, TAKE THEM OUT.

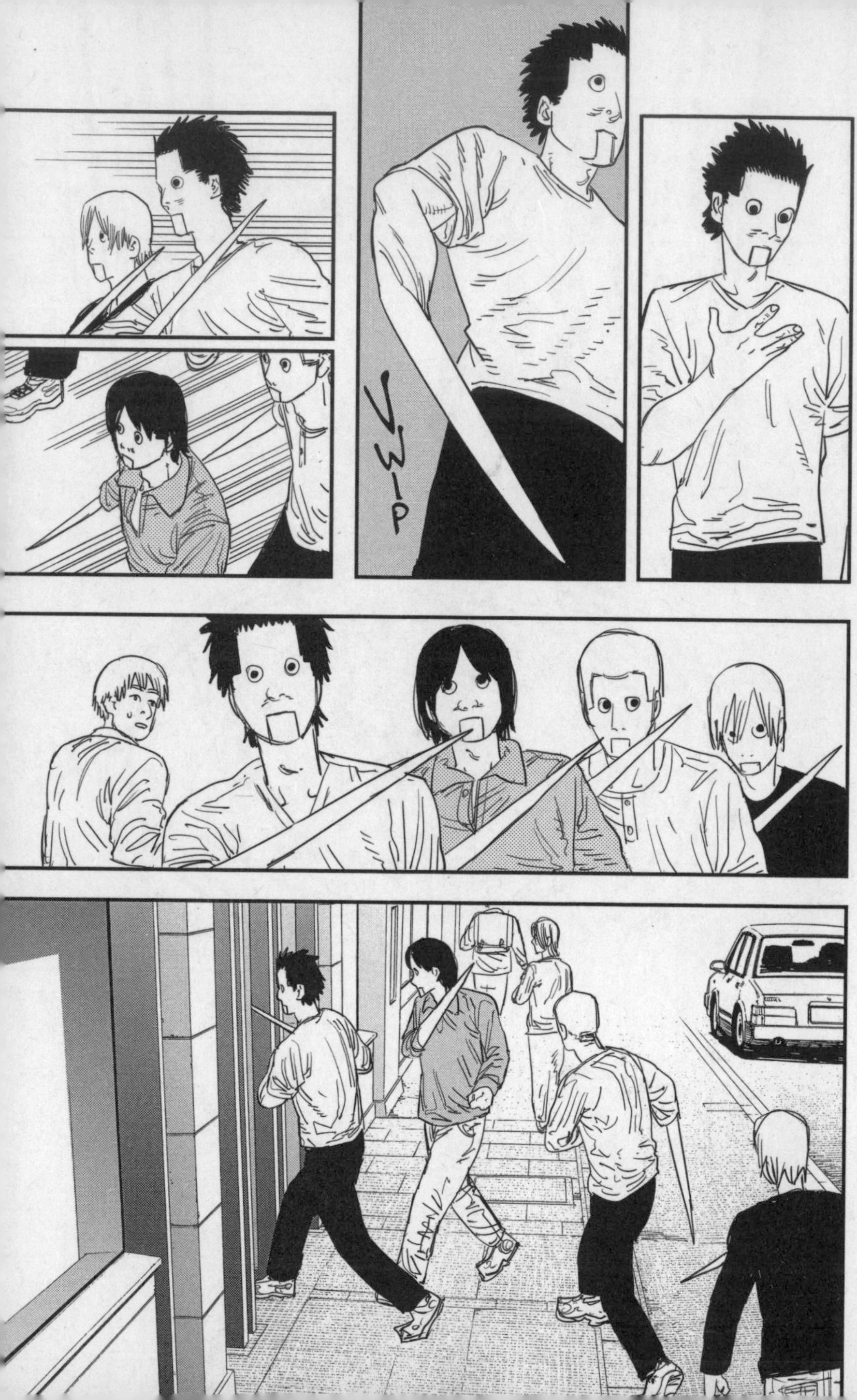
VWIP

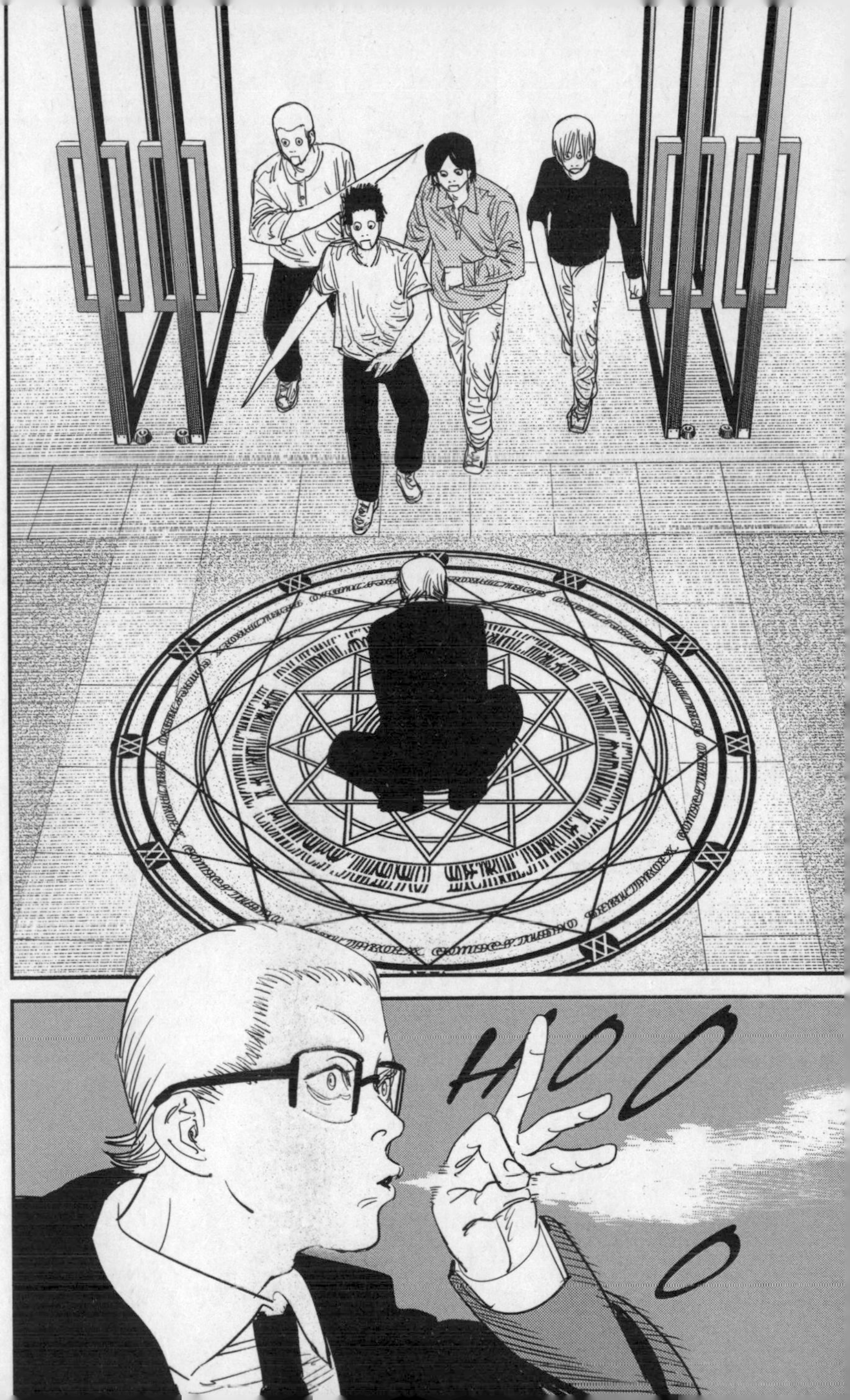
HOOO

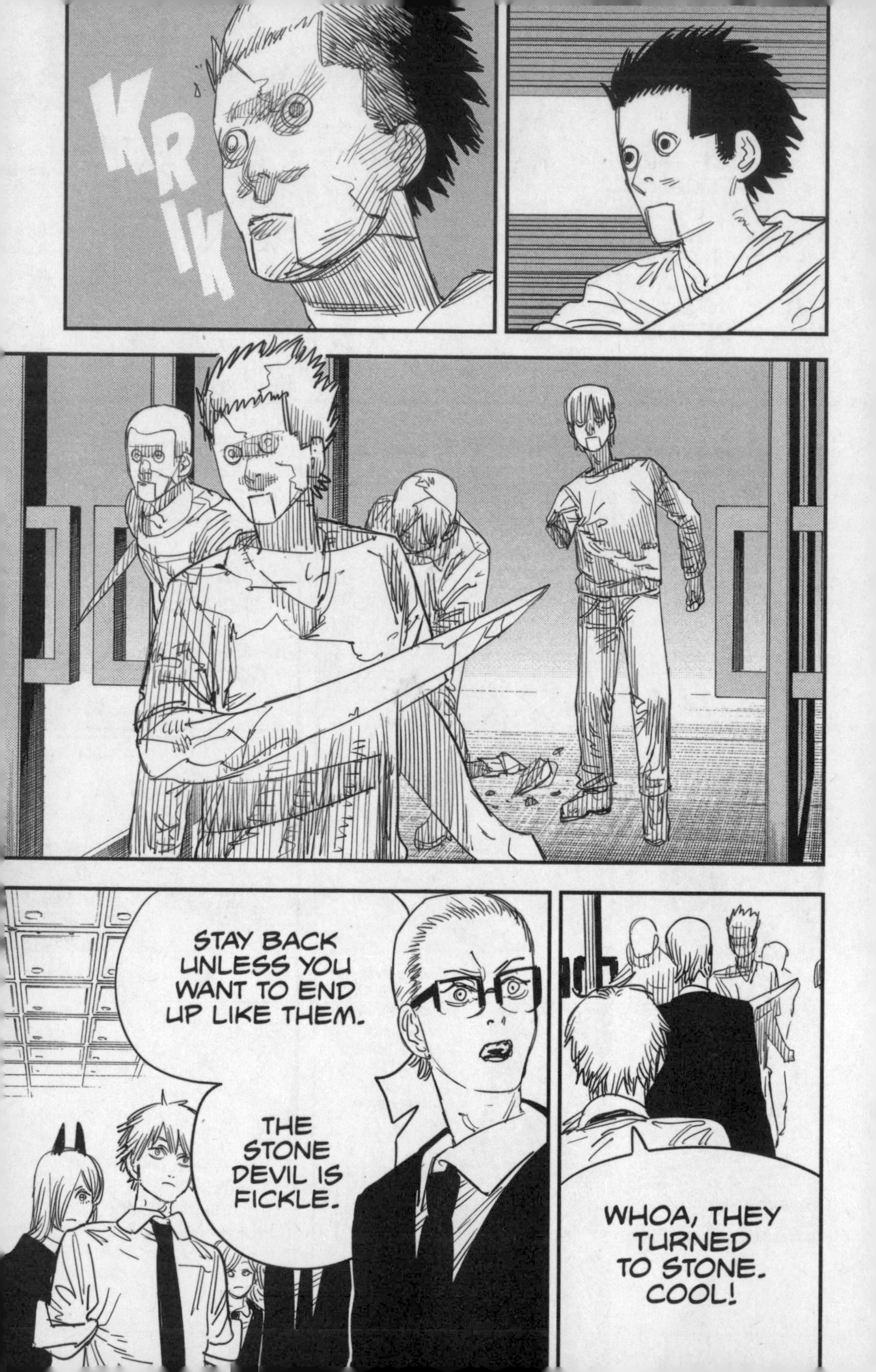
KRIK
WHOA, THEY TURNED TO STONE. COOL!
STAY BACK UNLESS YOU WANT TO END UP LIKE THEM.
THE STONE DEVIL IS FICKLE.

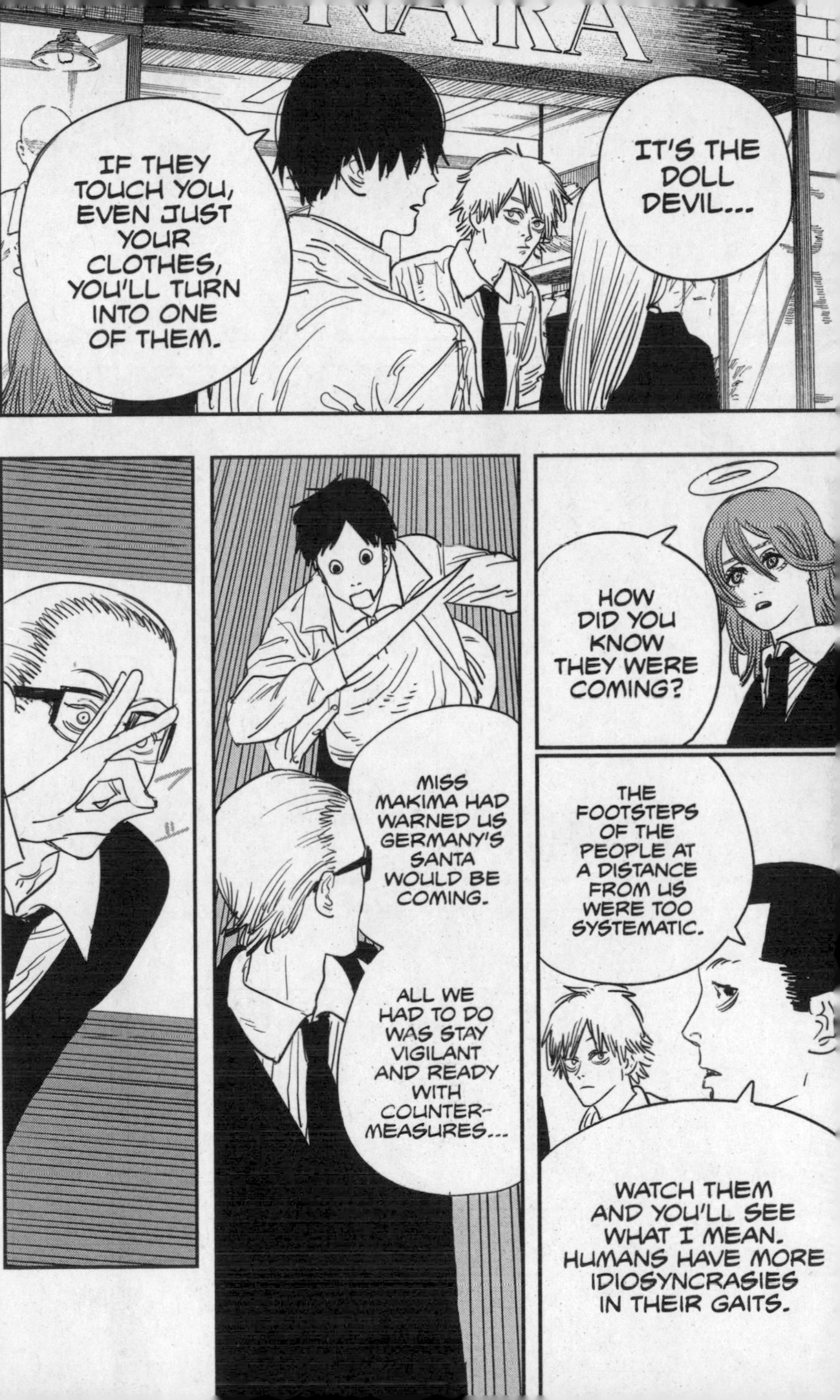
IT'S THE DOLL DEVIL...
IF THEY TOUCH YOU, EVEN JUST YOUR CLOTHES, YOU'LL TURN INTO ONE OF THEM.
HOW DID YOU KNOW THEY WERE COMING?
THE FOOTSTEPS OF THE PEOPLE AT A DISTANCE FROM US WERE TOO SYSTEMATIC.
WATCH THEM AND YOU'LL SEE WHAT I MEAN. HUMANS HAVE MORE IDIOSYNCRASIES IN THEIR GAITS.
MISS MAKIMA HAD WARNED US GERMANY'S SANTA WOULD BE COMING.
ALL WE HAD TO DO WAS STAY VIGILANT AND READY WITH COUNTER-MEASURES...

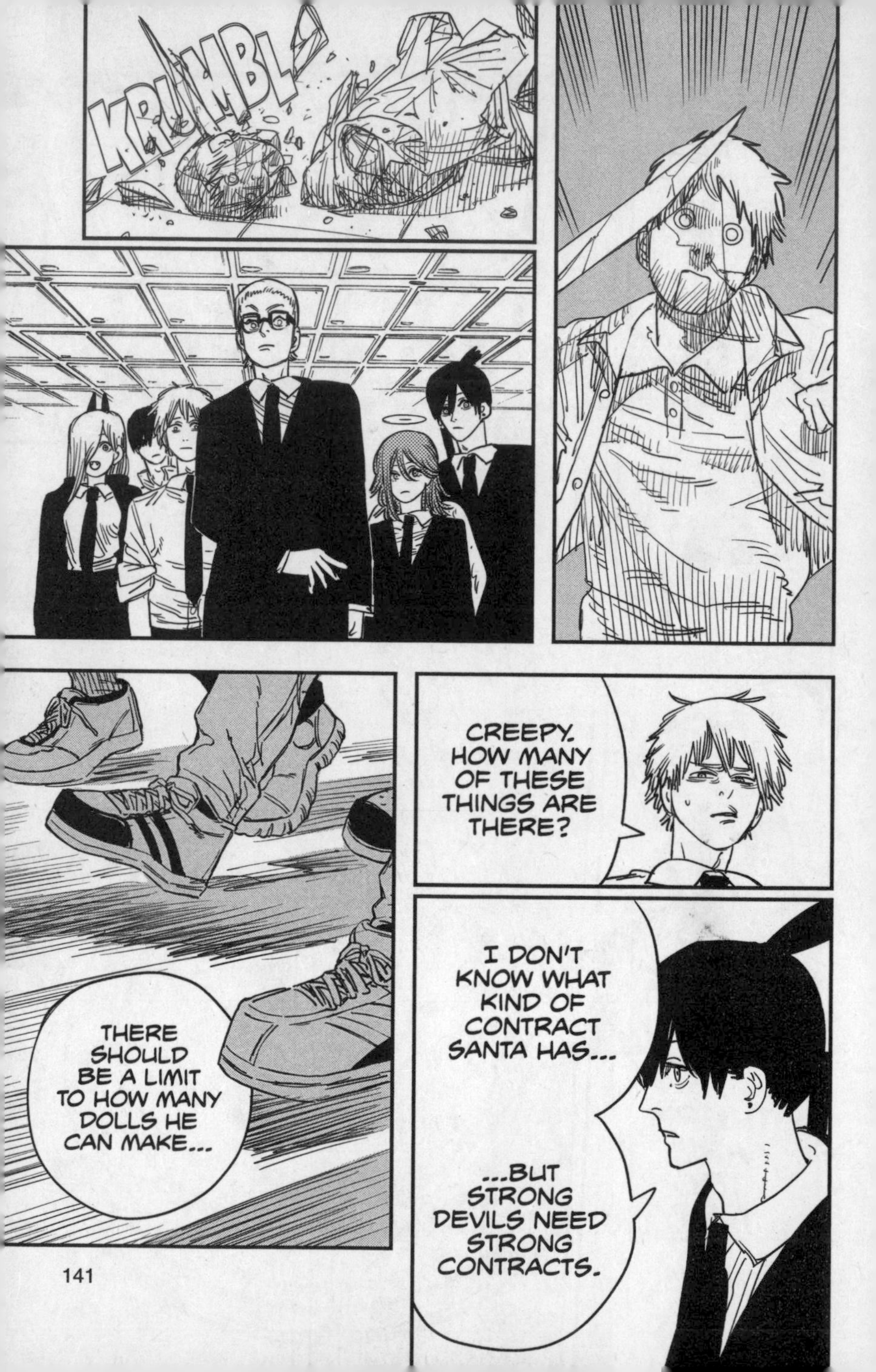
KRUMBL
CREEPY. HOW MANY OF THESE THINGS ARE THERE?
I DON'T KNOW WHAT KIND OF CONTRACT SANTA HAS...
...BUT STRONG DEVILS NEED STRONG CONTRACTS.
THERE SHOULD BE A LIMIT TO HOW MANY DOLLS HE CAN MAKE...

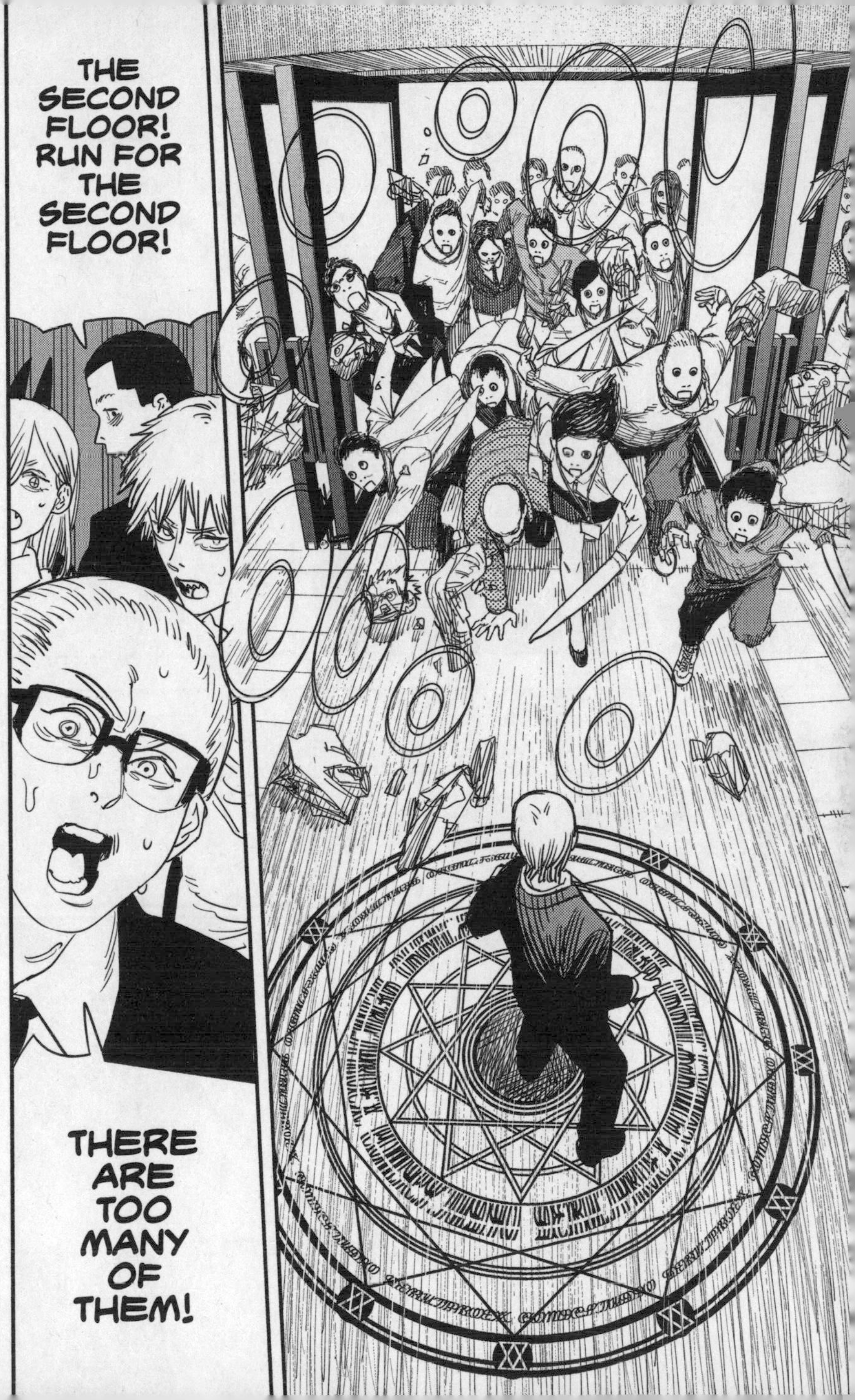
THE SECOND FLOOR! RUN FOR THE SECOND FLOOR!
THERE ARE TOO MANY OF THEM!

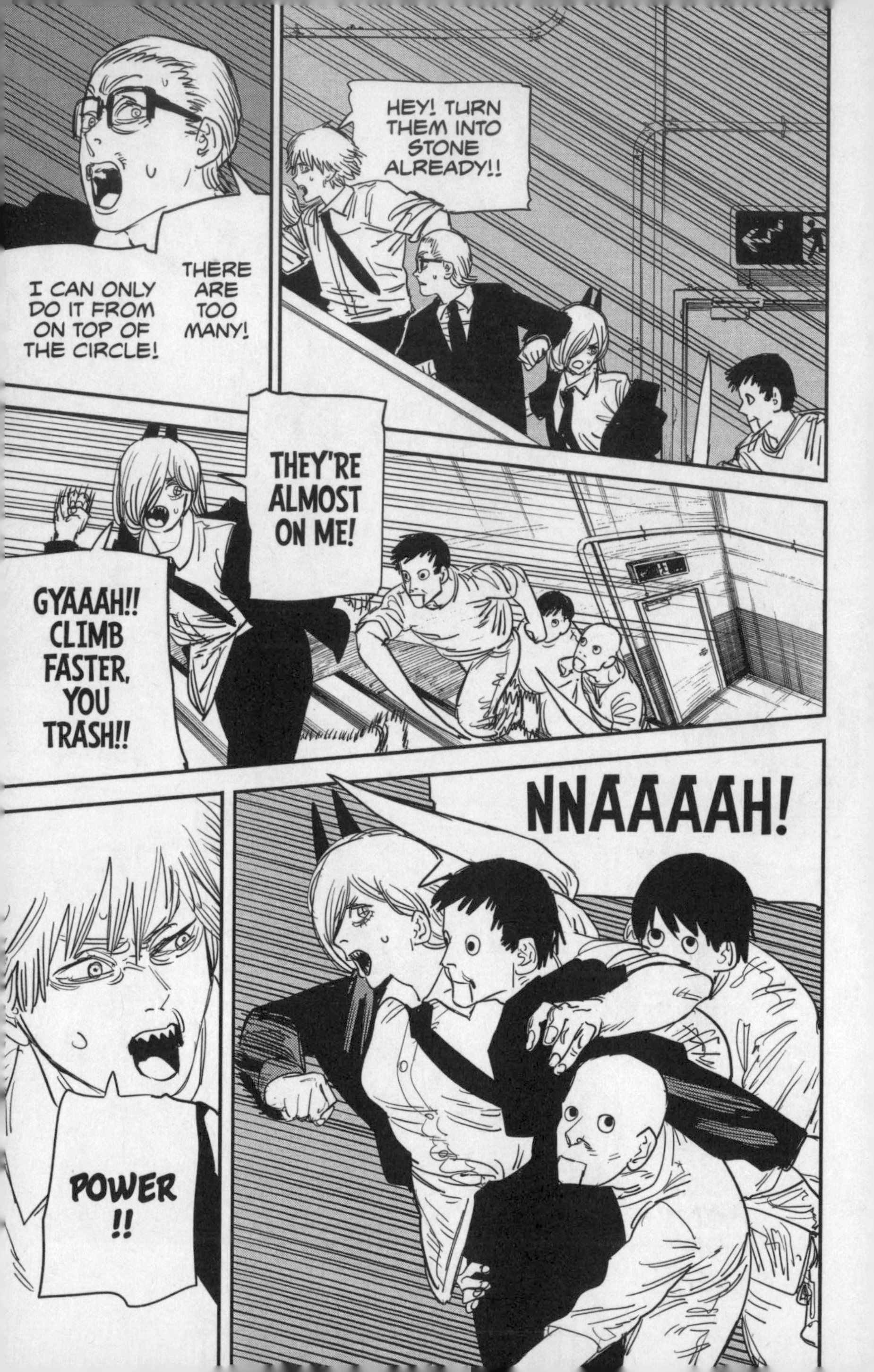
HEY! TURN THEM INTO STONE ALREADY!!
THERE ARE TOO MANY!
I CAN ONLY DO IT FROM ON TOP OF THE CIRCLE!
THEY'RE ALMOST ON ME!
GYAAAH!! CLIMB FASTER, YOU TRASH!!
NNAAAAH!
POWER !!

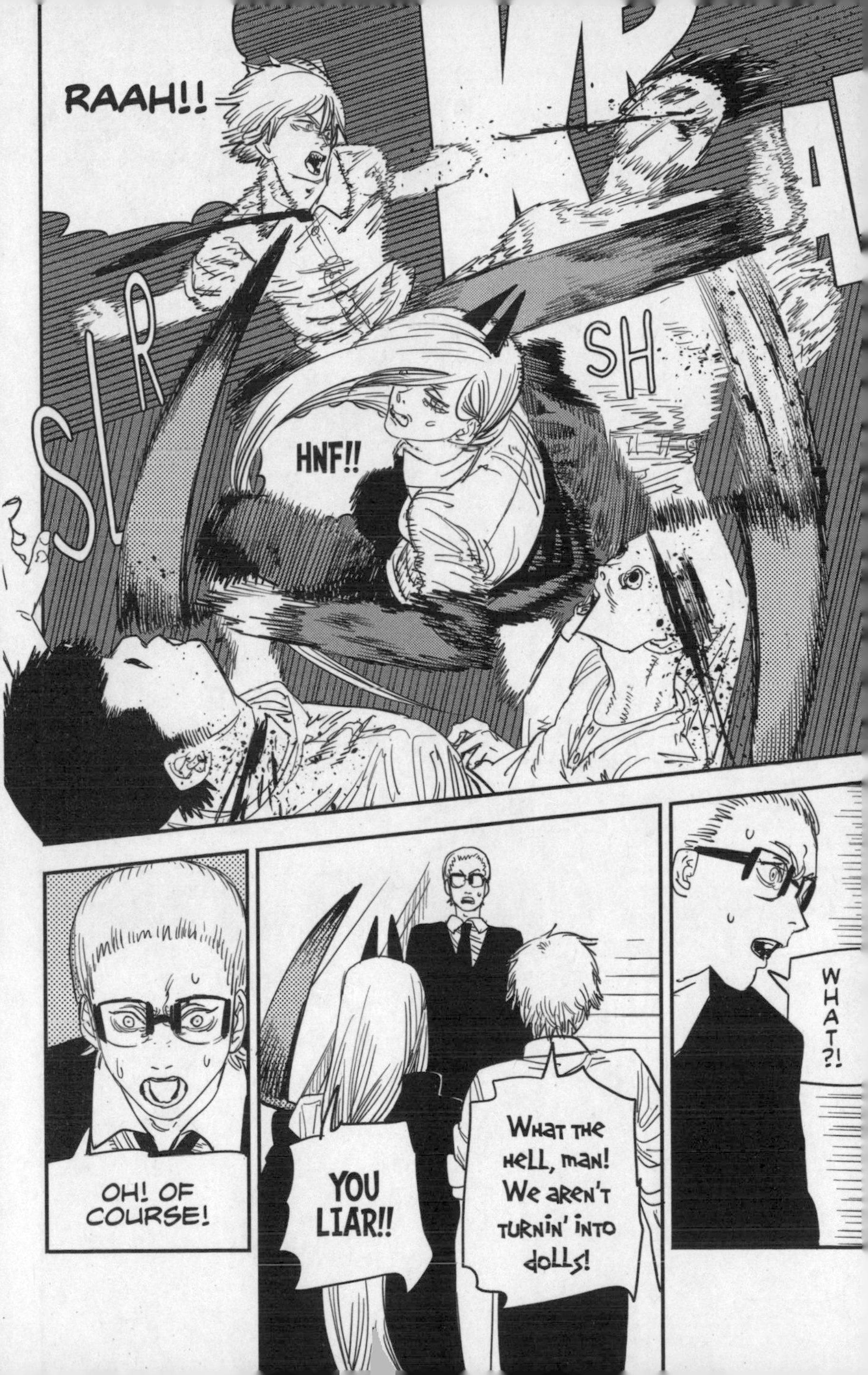
RAAH!!
SH
HNF!!
SLR
WHAT?!
What the hell, man! We aren't turnin' into dolls!
YOU LIAR!!
OH! OF COURSE!

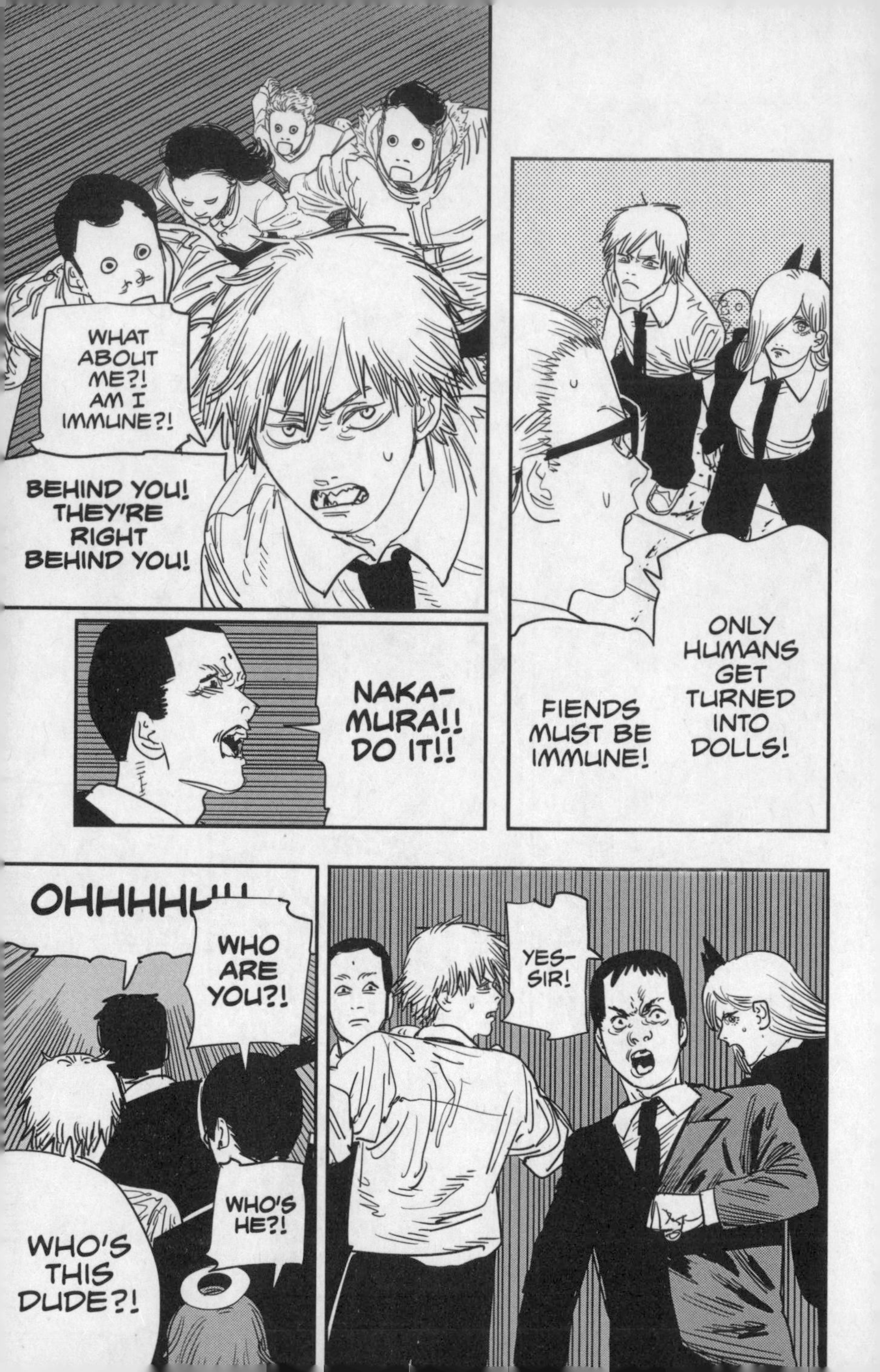
ONLY HUMANS GET TURNED INTO DOLLS!
FIENDS MUST BE IMMUNE!
WHAT ABOUT ME?! AM I IMMUNE?!
BEHIND YOU! THEY'RE RIGHT BEHIND YOU!
NAKA-MURA!! DO IT!!
YES-SIR!
OHHHHH
WHO ARE YOU?!
WHO'S HE?!
WHO'S THIS DUDE?!

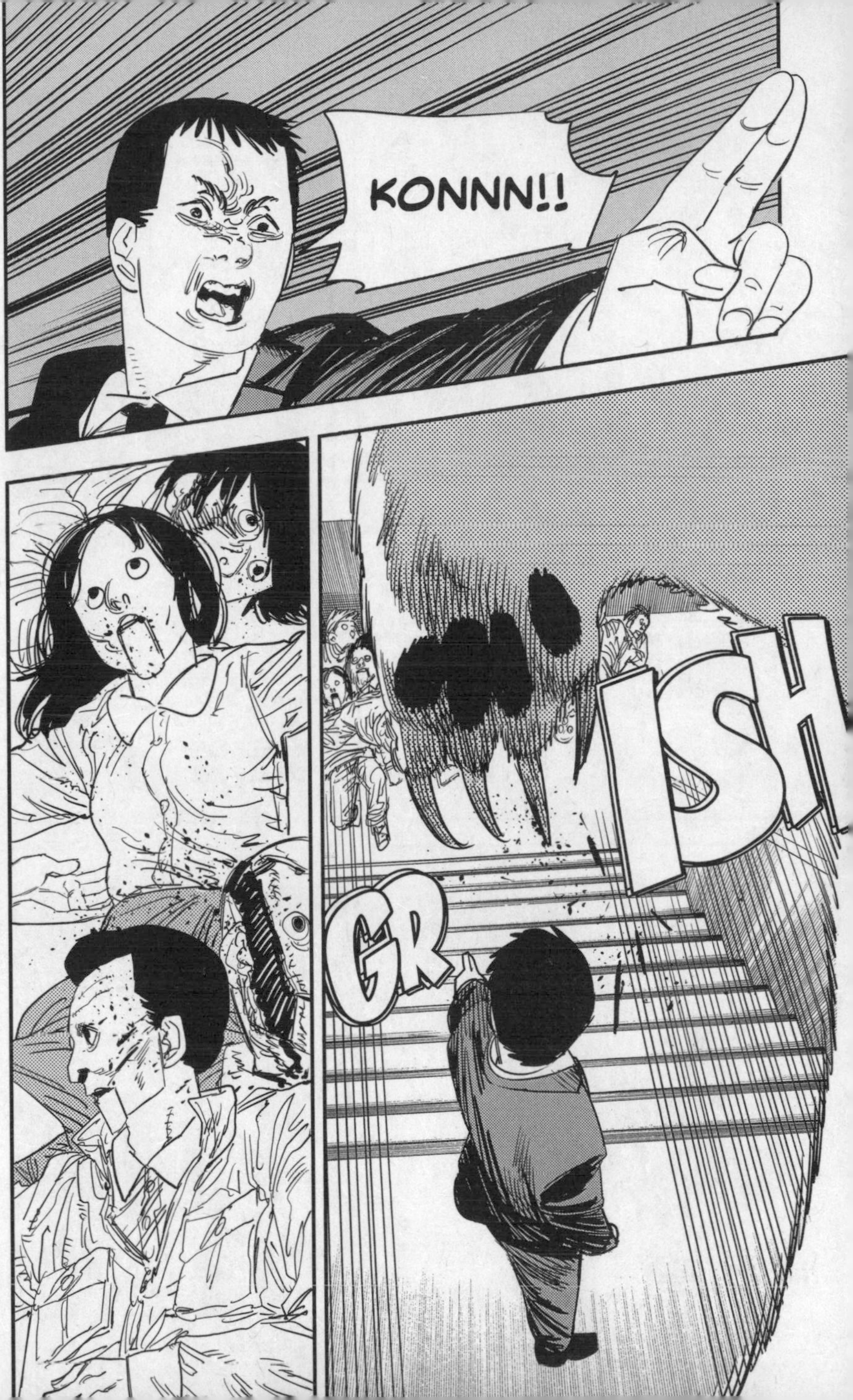
KONNN!!
GR
ISH

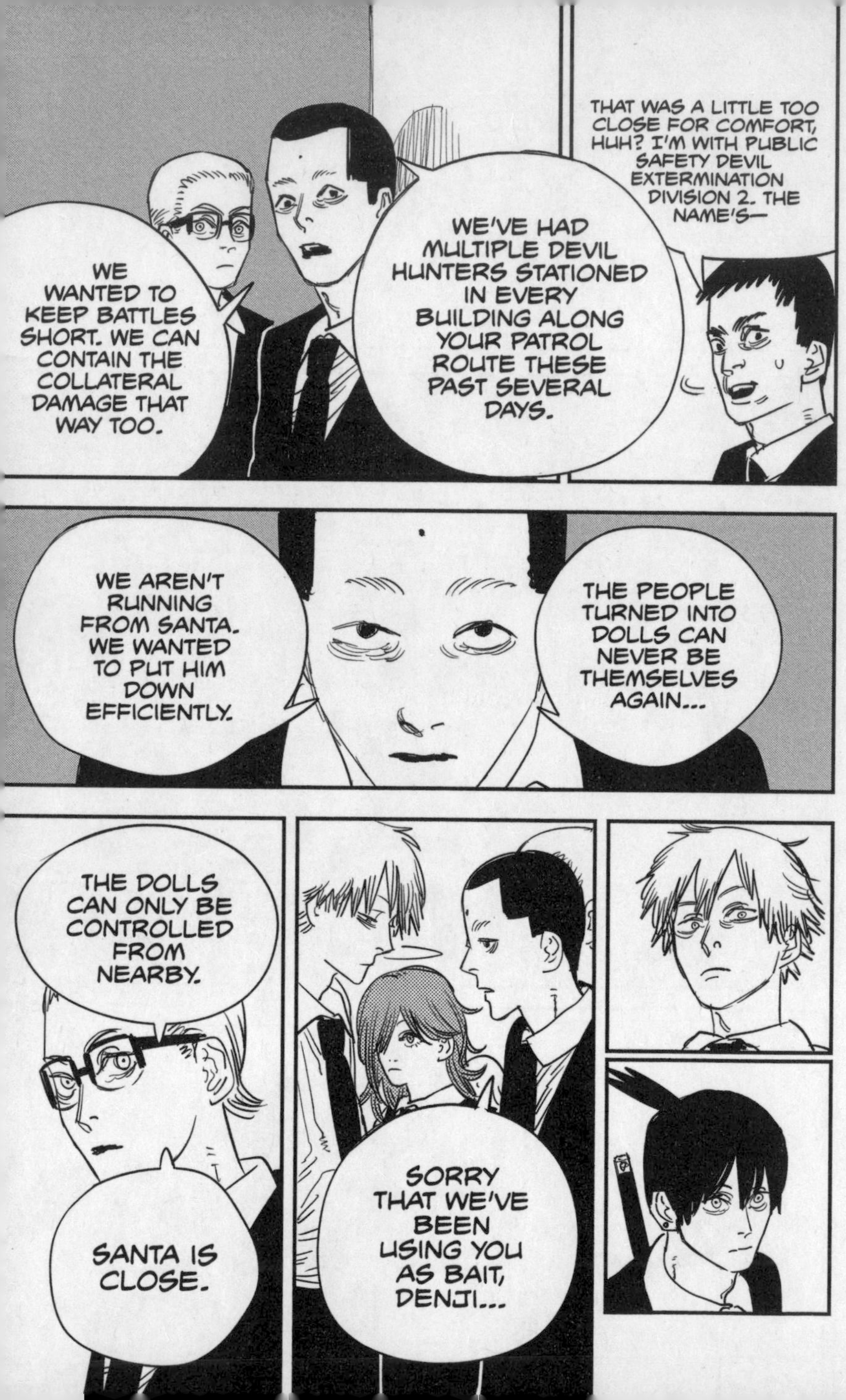
THAT WAS A LITTLE TOO CLOSE FOR COMFORT, HUH? I'M WITH PUBLIC SAFETY DEVIL EXTERMINATION DIVISION 2. THE NAME'S—
WE'VE HAD MULTIPLE DEVIL HUNTERS STATIONED IN EVERY BUILDING ALONG YOUR PATROL ROUTE THESE PAST SEVERAL DAYS.
WE WANTED TO KEEP BATTLES SHORT. WE CAN CONTAIN THE COLLATERAL DAMAGE THAT WAY TOO.
THE PEOPLE TURNED INTO DOLLS CAN NEVER BE THEMSELVES AGAIN...
WE AREN'T RUNNING FROM SANTA. WE WANTED TO PUT HIM DOWN EFFICIENTLY.
SORRY THAT WE'VE BEEN USING YOU AS BAIT, DENJI...
THE DOLLS CAN ONLY BE CONTROLLED FROM NEARBY.
SANTA IS CLOSE.

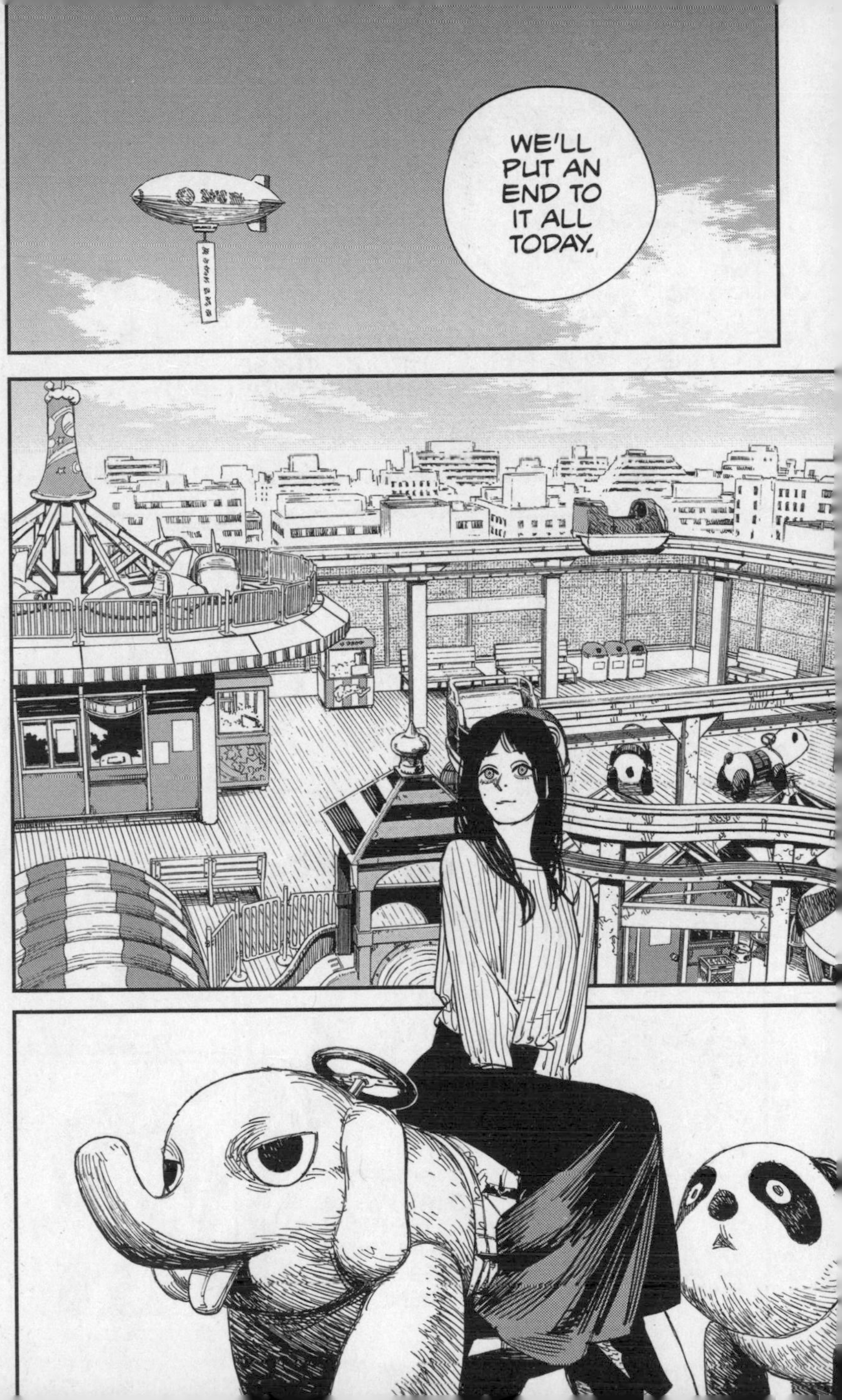
WE'LL PUT AN END TO IT ALL TODAY.

IT'S GOING TO GET NOISY SOON...
THIS DEPARTMENT STORE ISN'T SAFE! ALL CIVILIANS, PLEASE EVACUATE IMMEDIATELY VIA THE EMERGENCY EXITS!
I'M IMMORTAL. I'M IMMORTAL. I'M IMMORTAL...

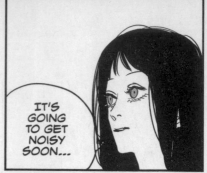

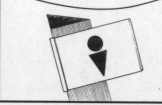

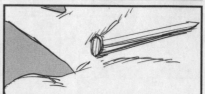

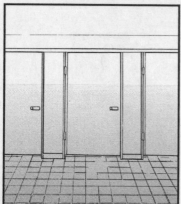

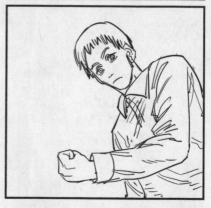

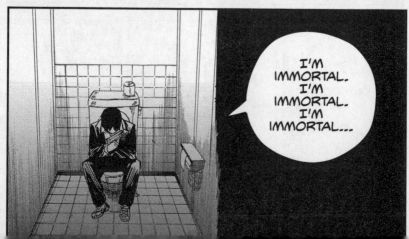

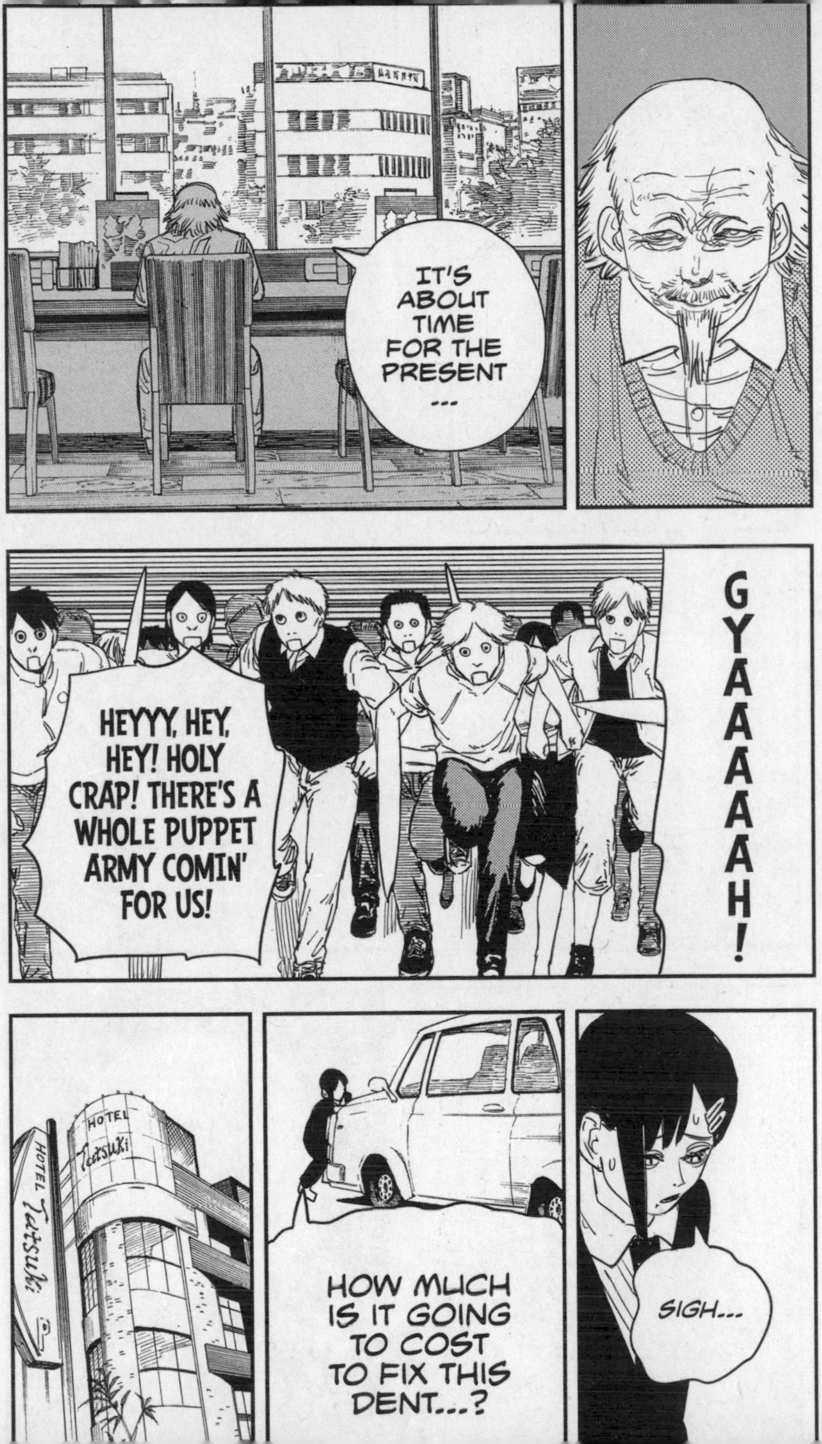
IT'S ABOUT TIME FOR THE PRESENT ...
GYAAAAAH!
HEYYY, HEY, HEY! HOLY CRAP! THERE'S A WHOLE PUPPET ARMY COMIN' FOR US!
SIGH...
HOW MUCH IS IT GOING TO COST TO FIX THIS DENT...?
HOTEL Tetsuki
HOTEL Tetsuki

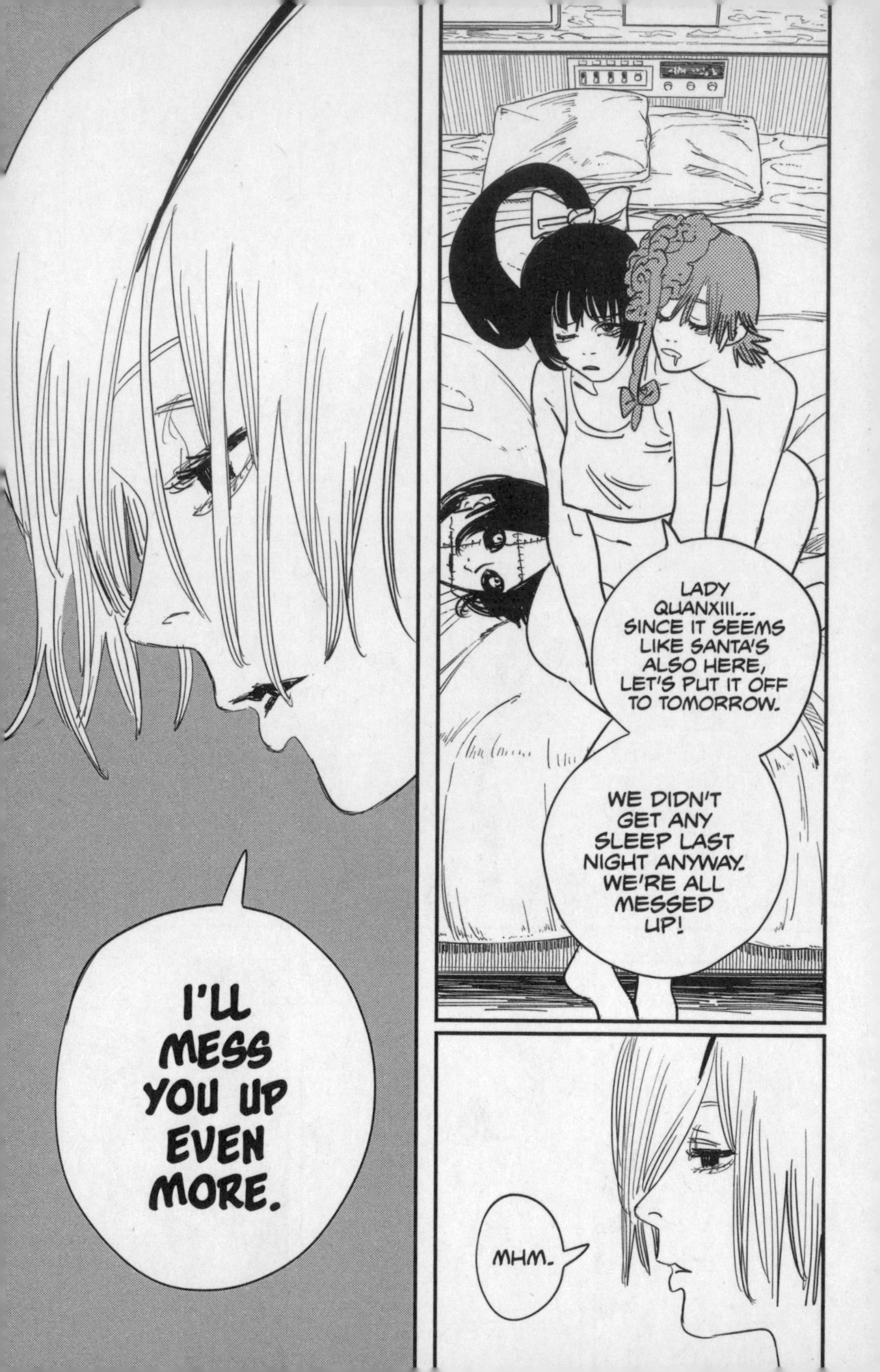
LADY QUANXIII... SINCE IT SEEMS LIKE SANTA'S ALSO HERE, LET'S PUT IT OFF TO TOMORROW.
WE DIDN'T GET ANY SLEEP LAST NIGHT ANYWAY. WE'RE ALL MESSED UP!
MHM.
I'LL MESS YOU UP EVEN MORE.

Chain saw man

# Chapter 60: Quanxi and the Fiends' 49-Person Massacre

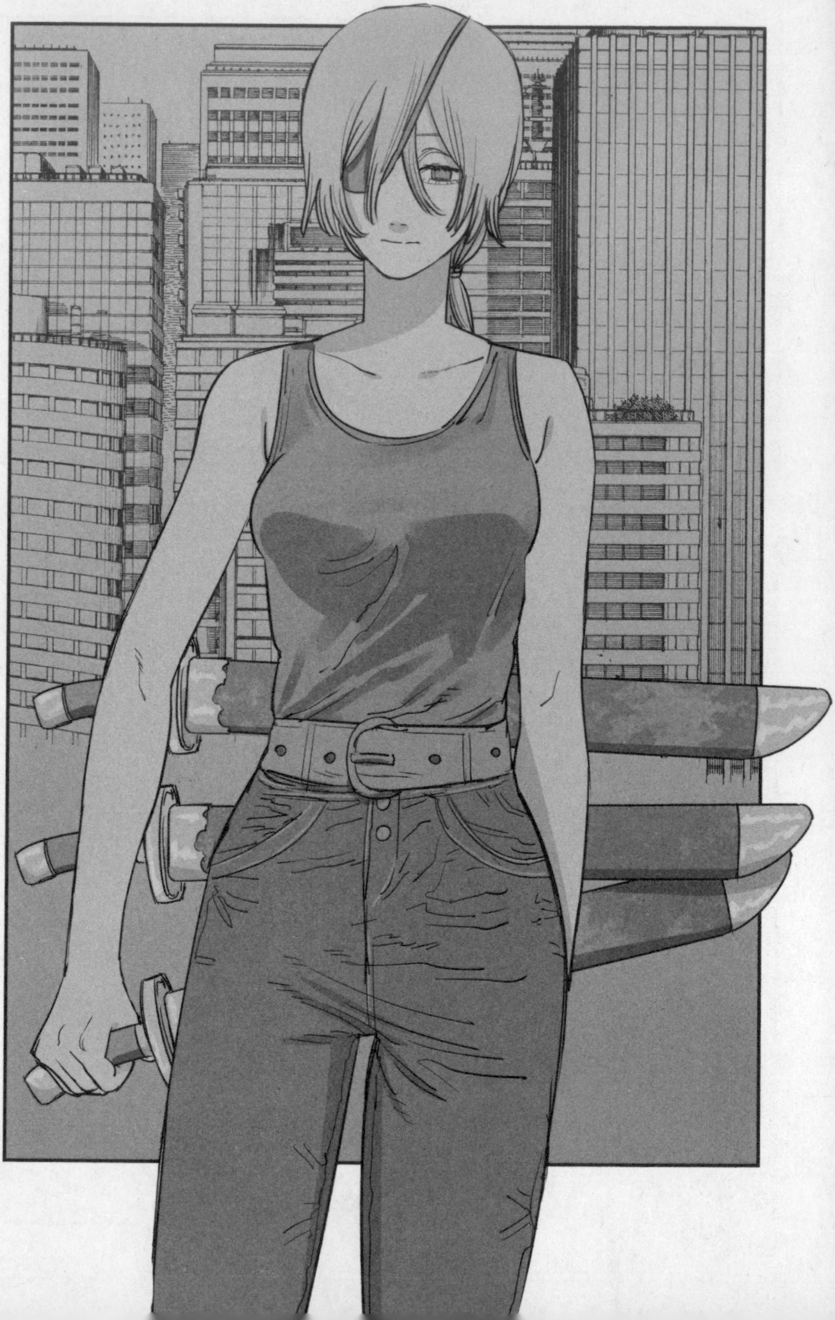

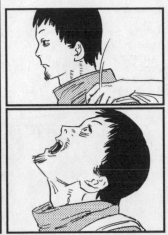

154

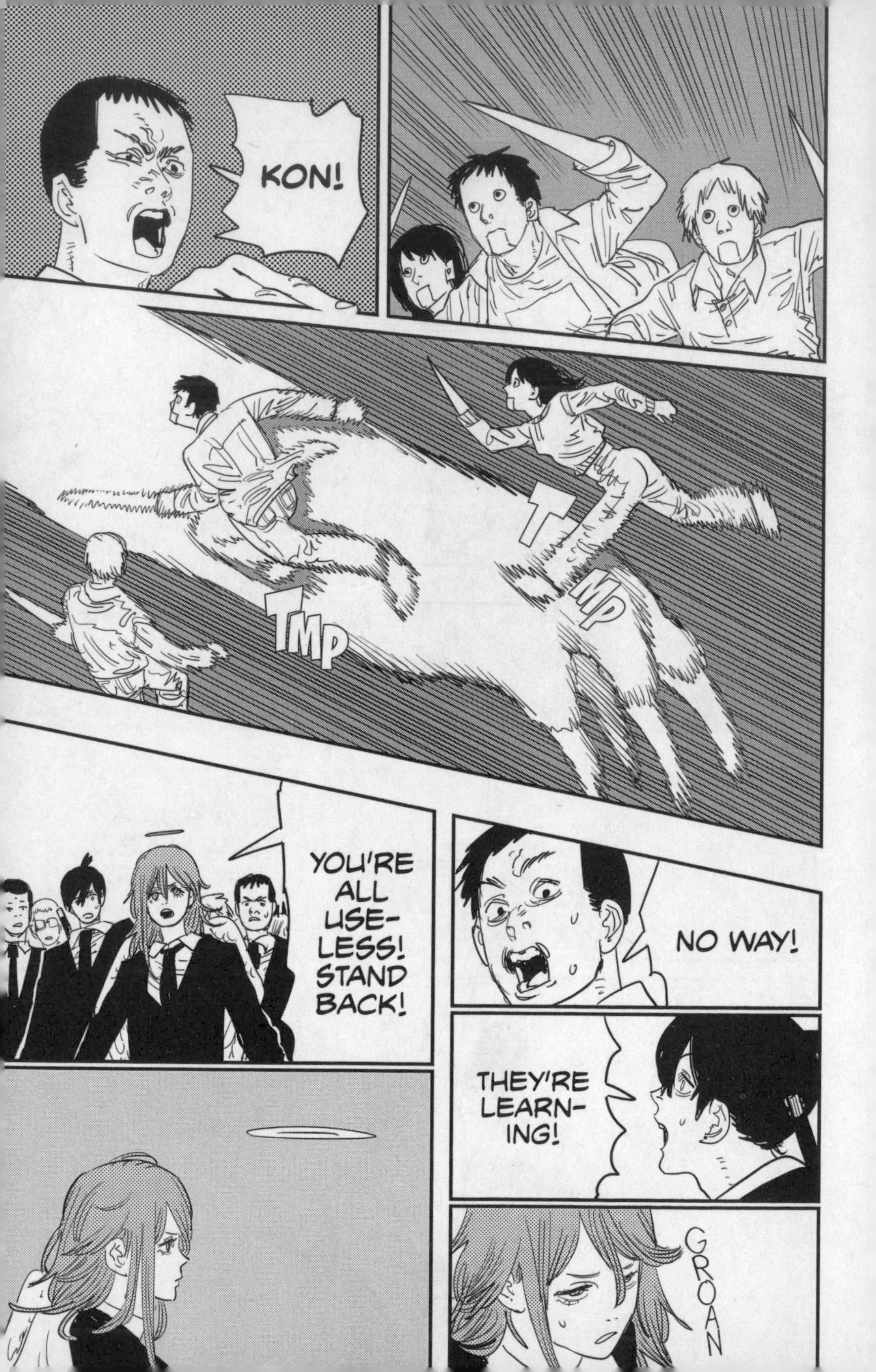
KON!
TMP
TMP
YOU'RE ALL USE-LESS! STAND BACK!
NO WAY!
THEY'RE LEARN-ING!
GROAN

USAGE: FIVE YEARS.

I'M SORRY, EVERYONE... I NEED TO USE YOU.

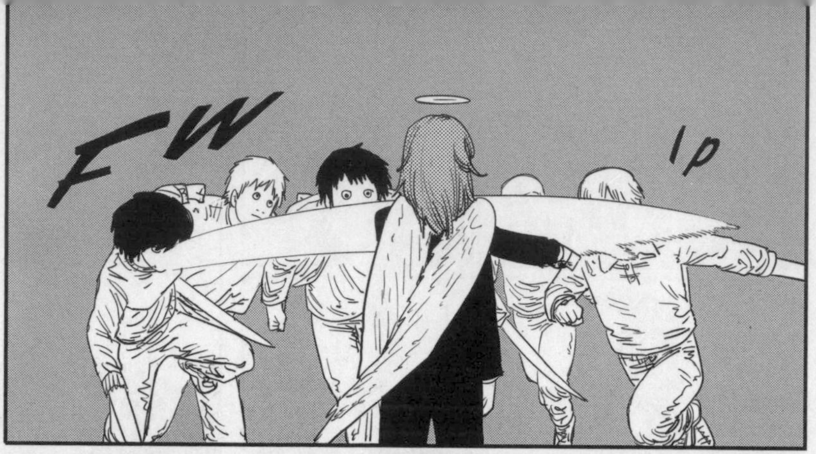
FW
ip

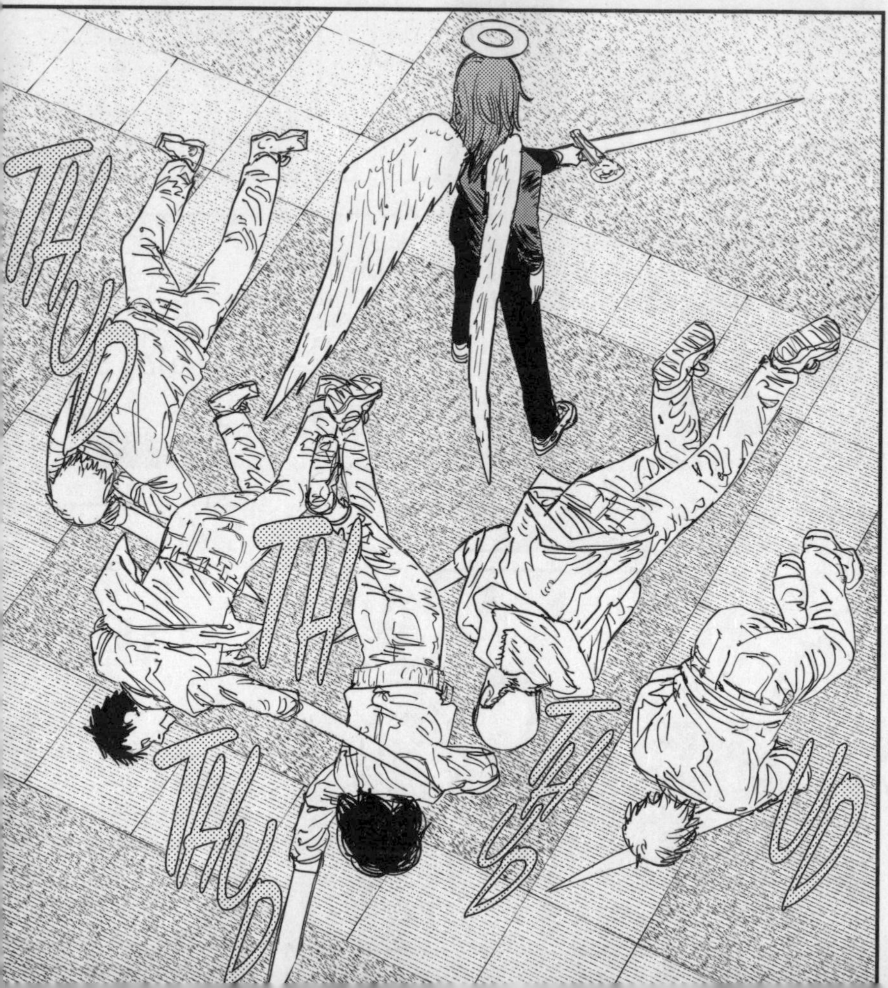
THUD
TH
THUD
THUD

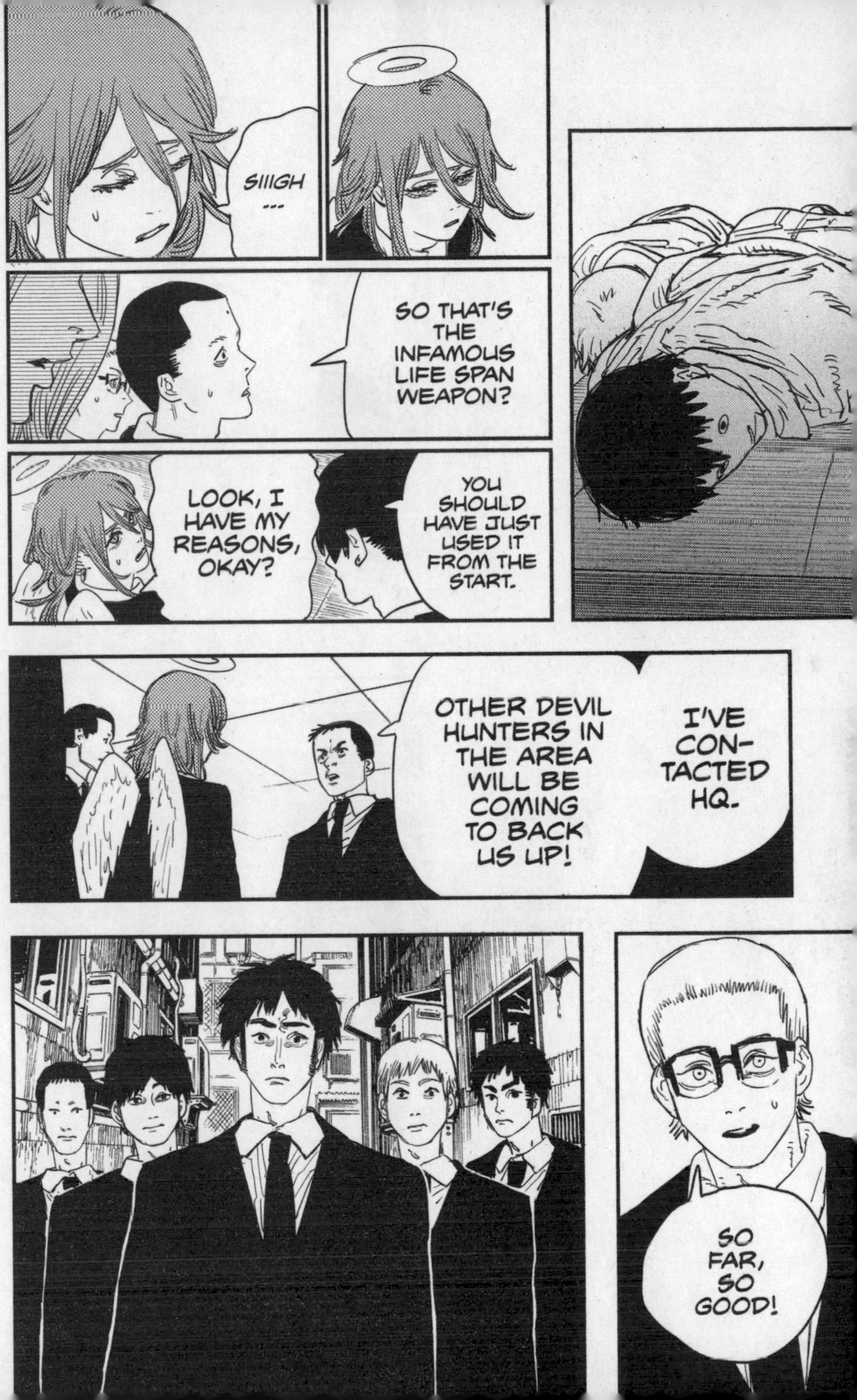
SIIIGH ...
SO THAT'S THE INFAMOUS LIFE SPAN WEAPON?
YOU SHOULD HAVE JUST USED IT FROM THE START.
LOOK, I HAVE MY REASONS, OKAY?
I'VE CON-TACTED HQ.
OTHER DEVIL HUNTERS IN THE AREA WILL BE COMING TO BACK US UP!
SO FAR, SO GOOD!

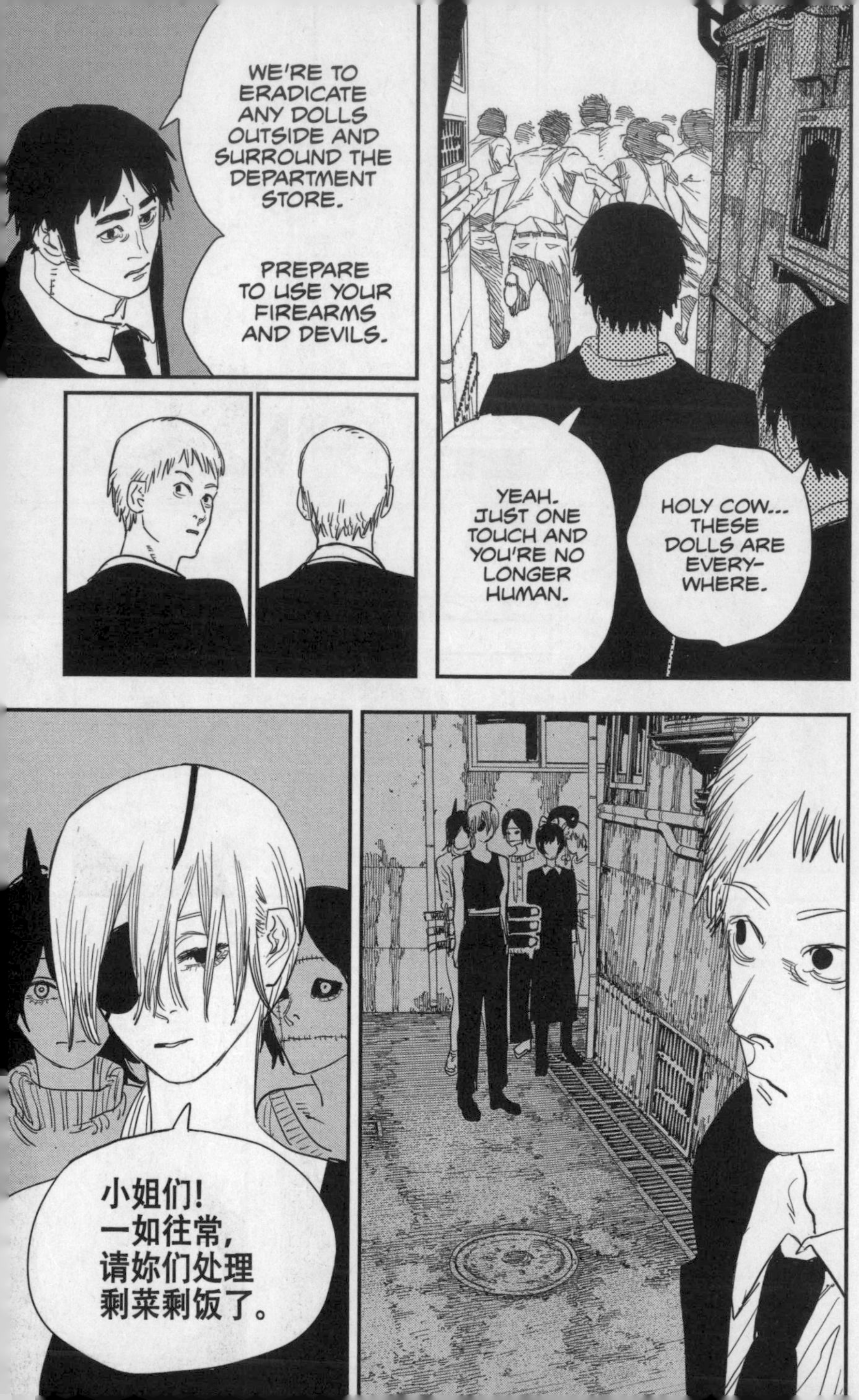
HOLY COW... THESE DOLLS ARE EVERY-WHERE.
YEAH. JUST ONE TOUCH AND YOU'RE NO LONGER HUMAN.
WE'RE TO ERADICATE ANY DOLLS OUTSIDE AND SURROUND THE DEPARTMENT STORE.
PREPARE TO USE YOUR FIREARMS AND DEVILS.
小姐们!一如往常,请妳们处理剩菜剩饭了。

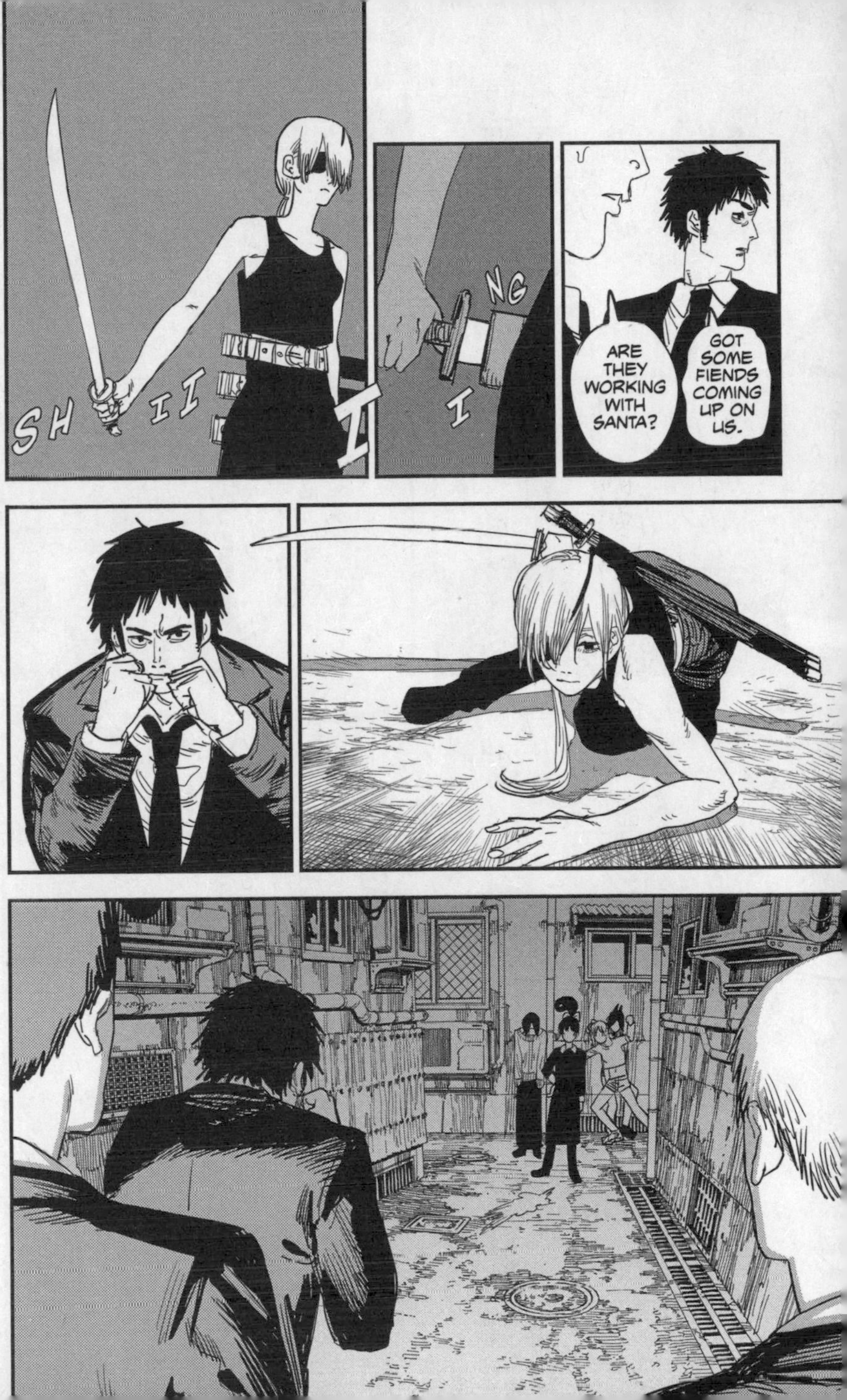
GOT SOME FIENDS COMING UP ON US.
ARE THEY WORKING WITH SANTA?
SHIIIING

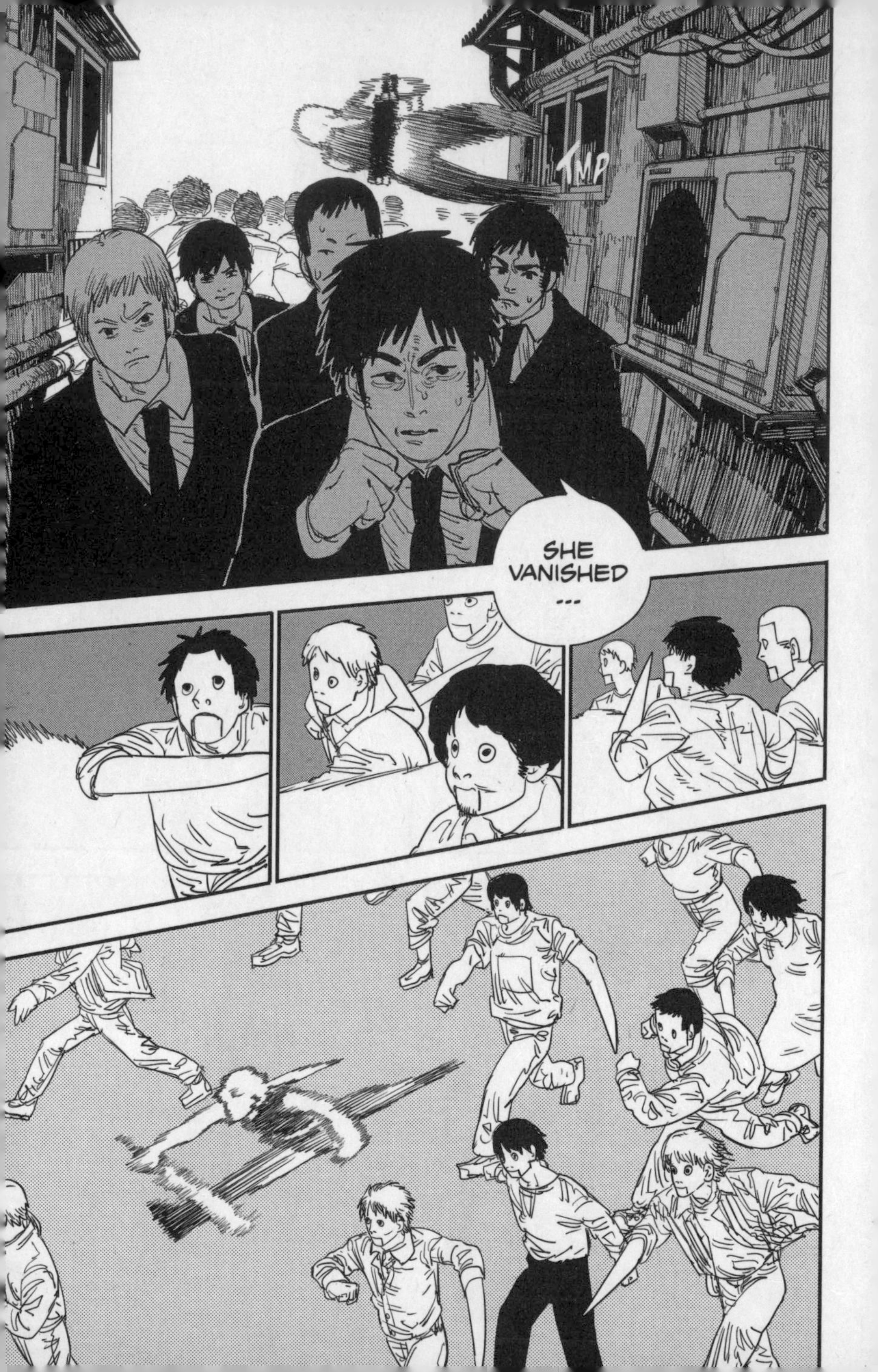
TMP
SHE VANISHED ---

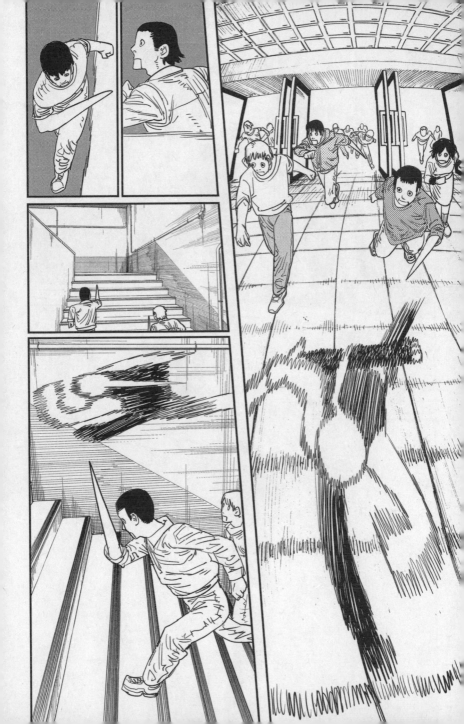

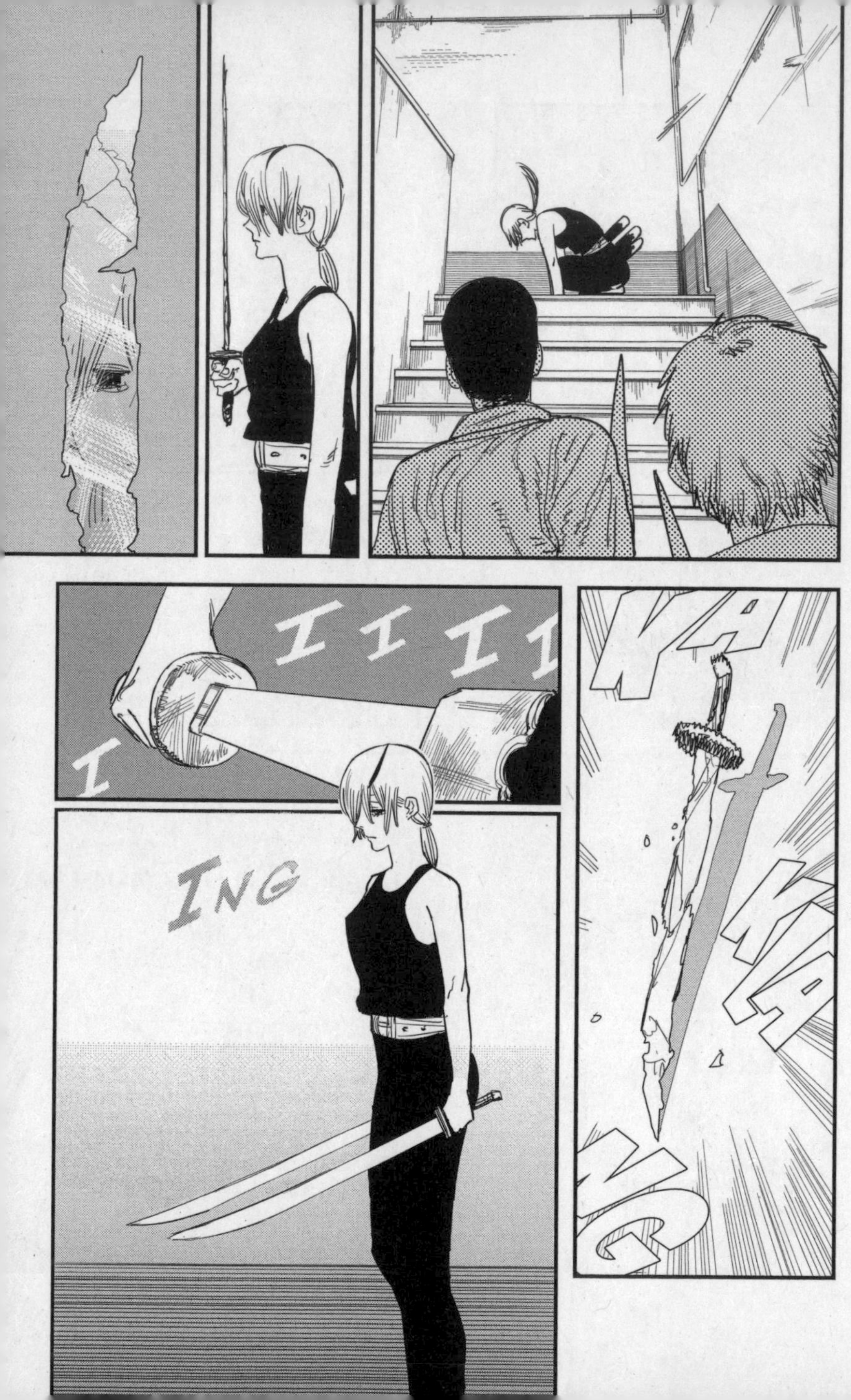
KA
KANG
IIIII
ING

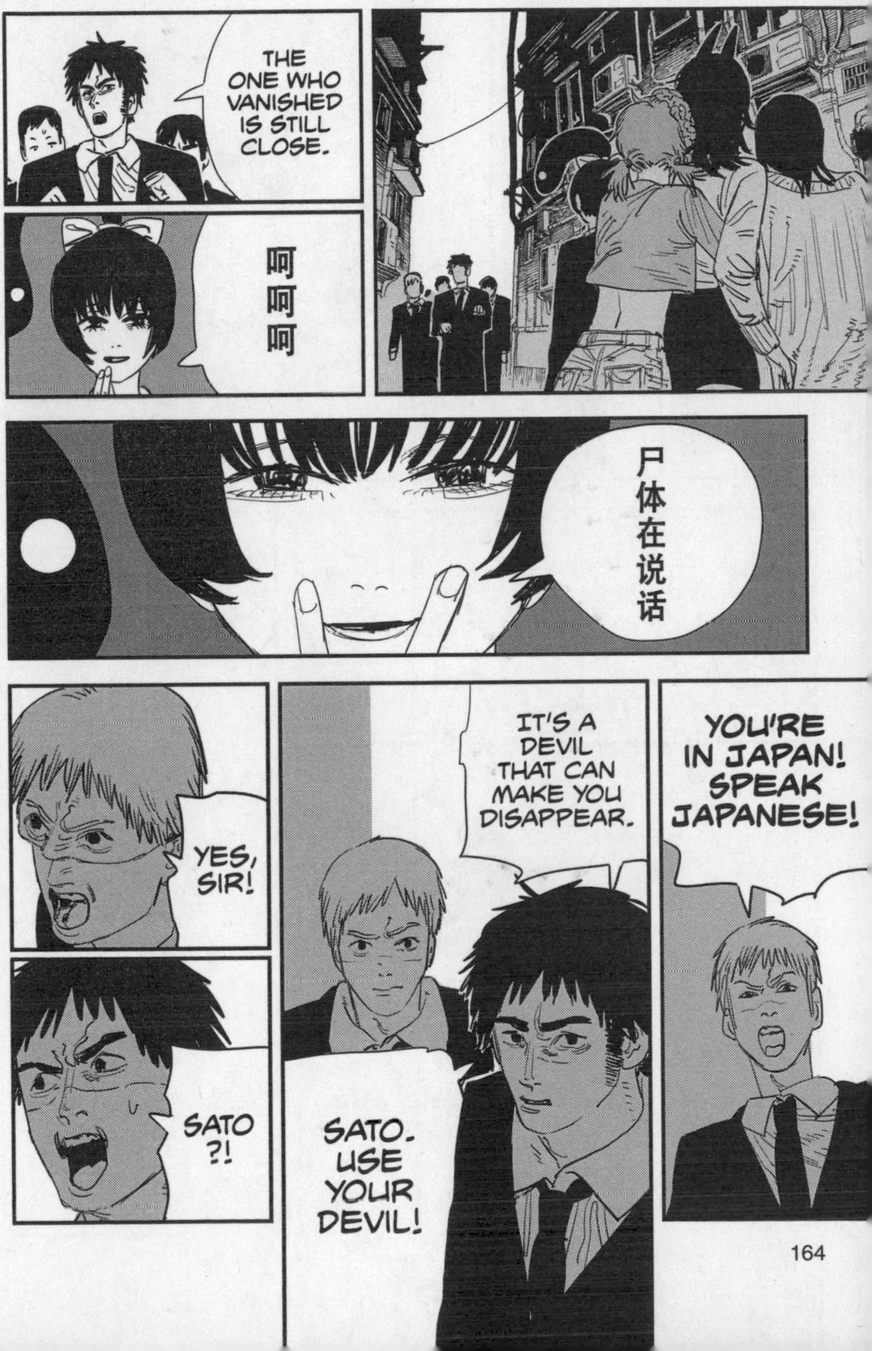
THE ONE WHO VANISHED IS STILL CLOSE.
呵呵呵
尸体在说话
YOU'RE IN JAPAN! SPEAK JAPANESE!
IT'S A DEVIL THAT CAN MAKE YOU DISAPPEAR.
SATO. USE YOUR DEVIL!
YES, SIR!
SATO ?!

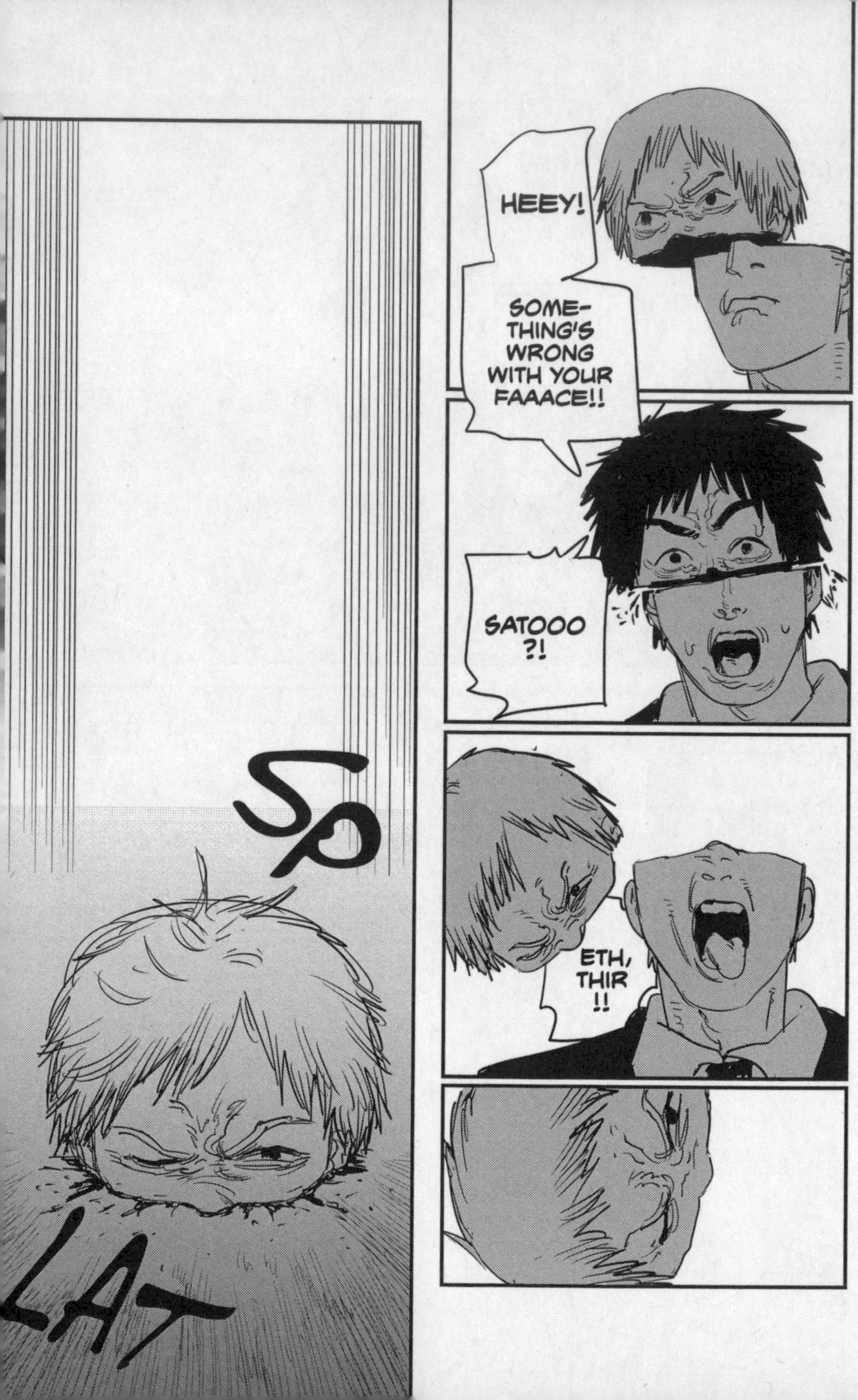
HEEY!
SOME-THING'S WRONG WITH YOUR FAAACE!!
SATOOO?!
ETH, THIR!!
Sp
LAT

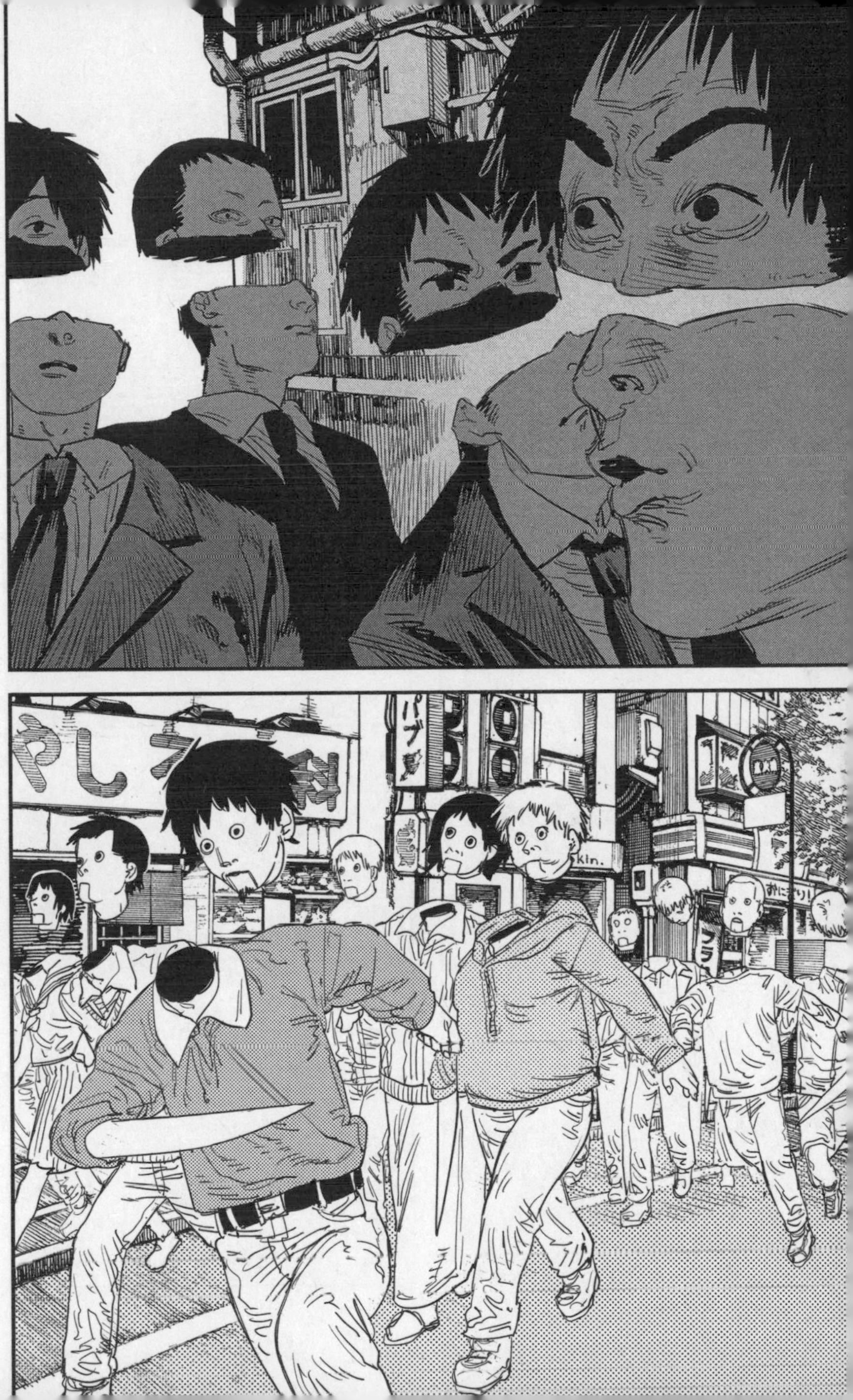
skin.

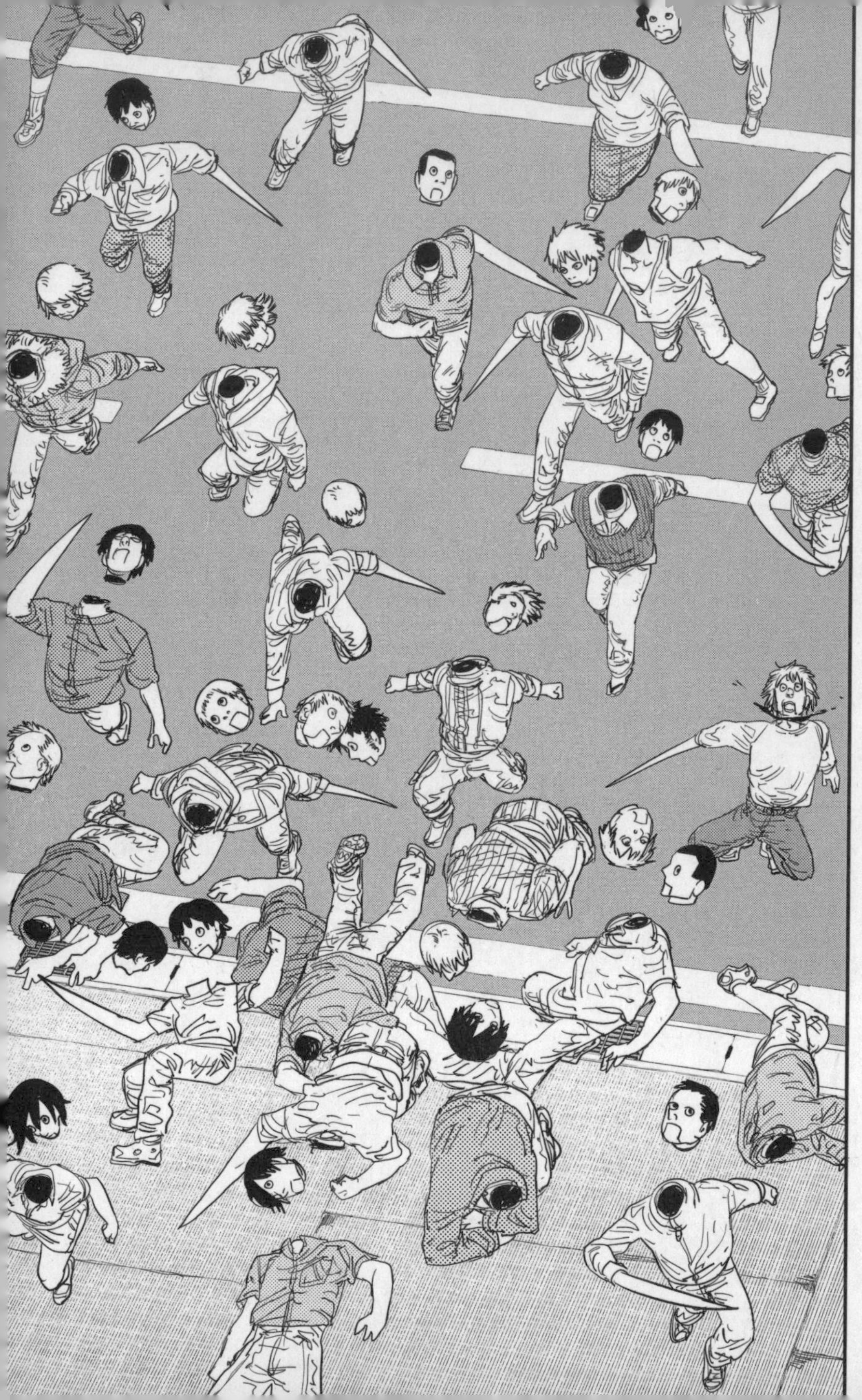

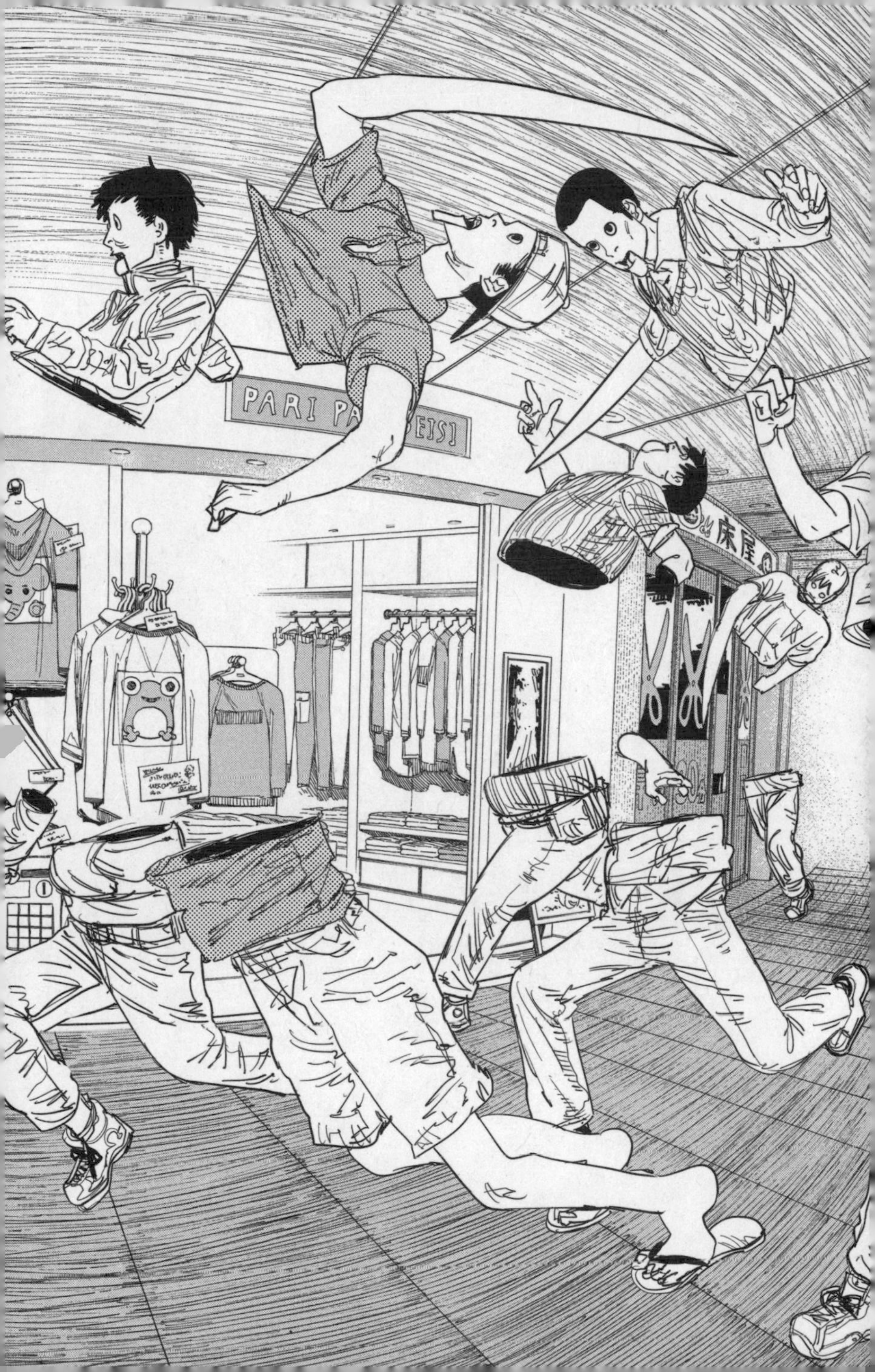
床屋

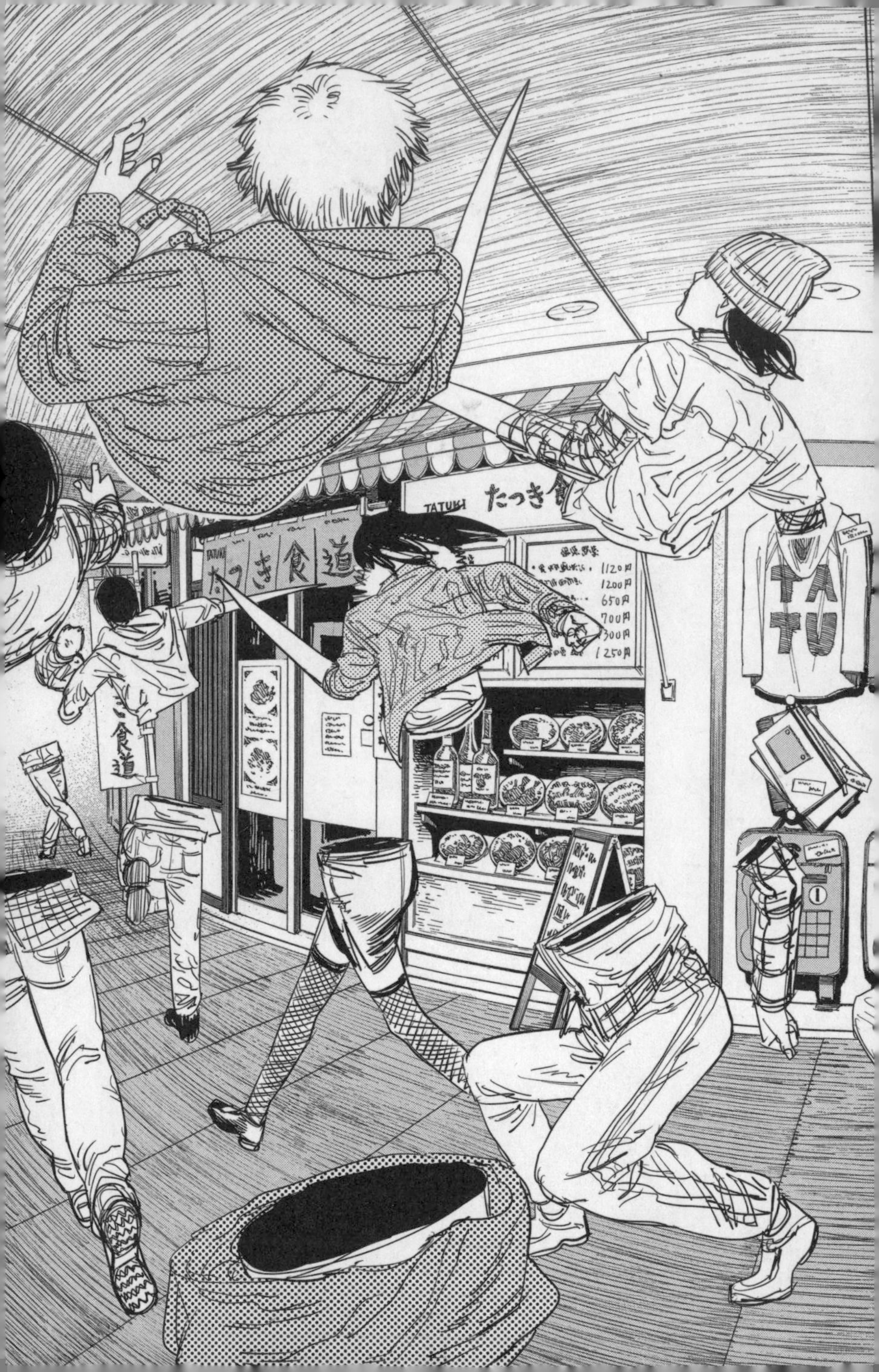
TA
TU
TATUKI たつき食
1120円
1200円
650円
700円
1250円
TATUKI
たつき食道
食道

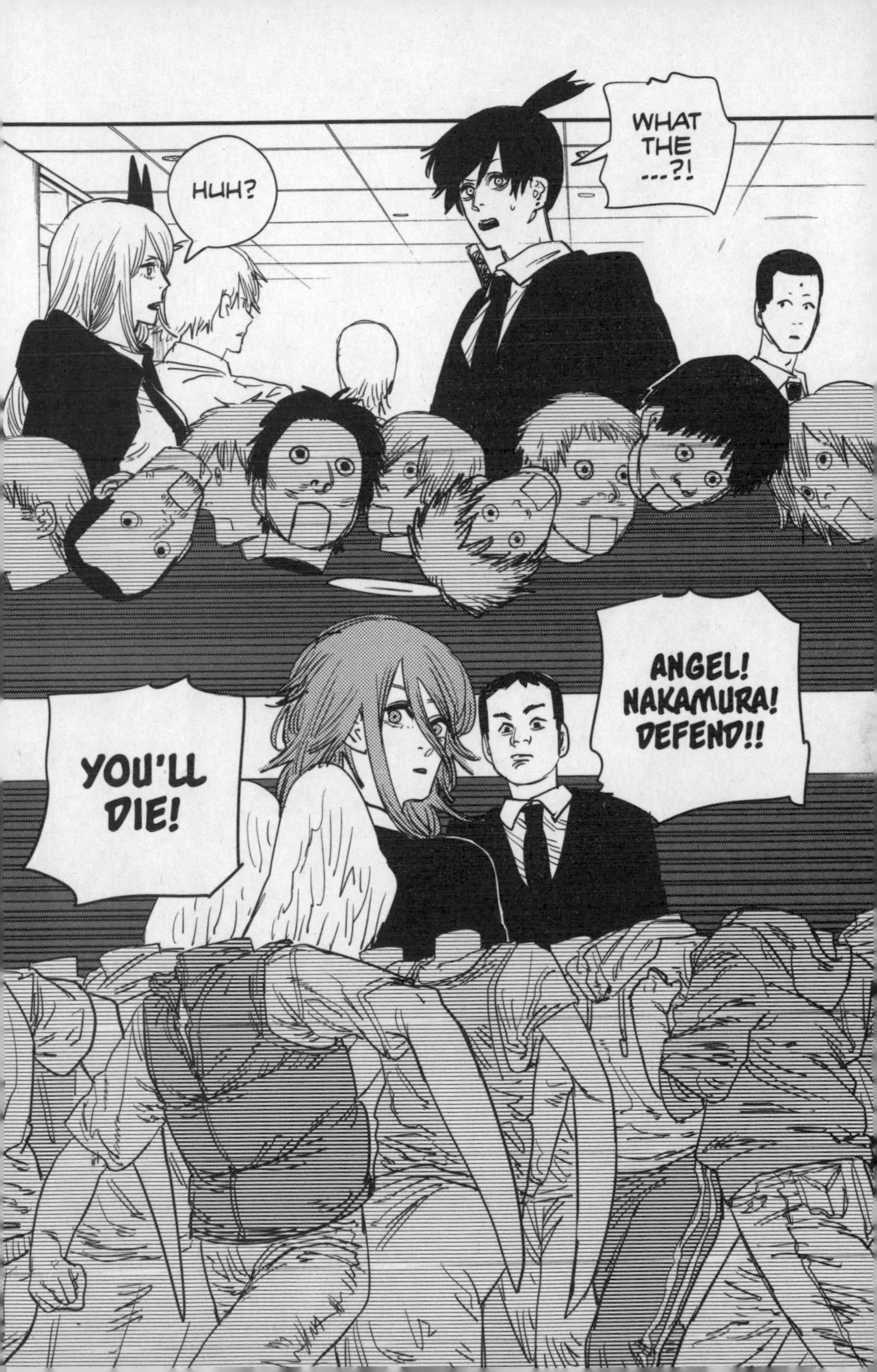
WHAT THE ...?!
HUH?
ANGEL! NAKAMURA! DEFEND!!
YOU'LL DIE!

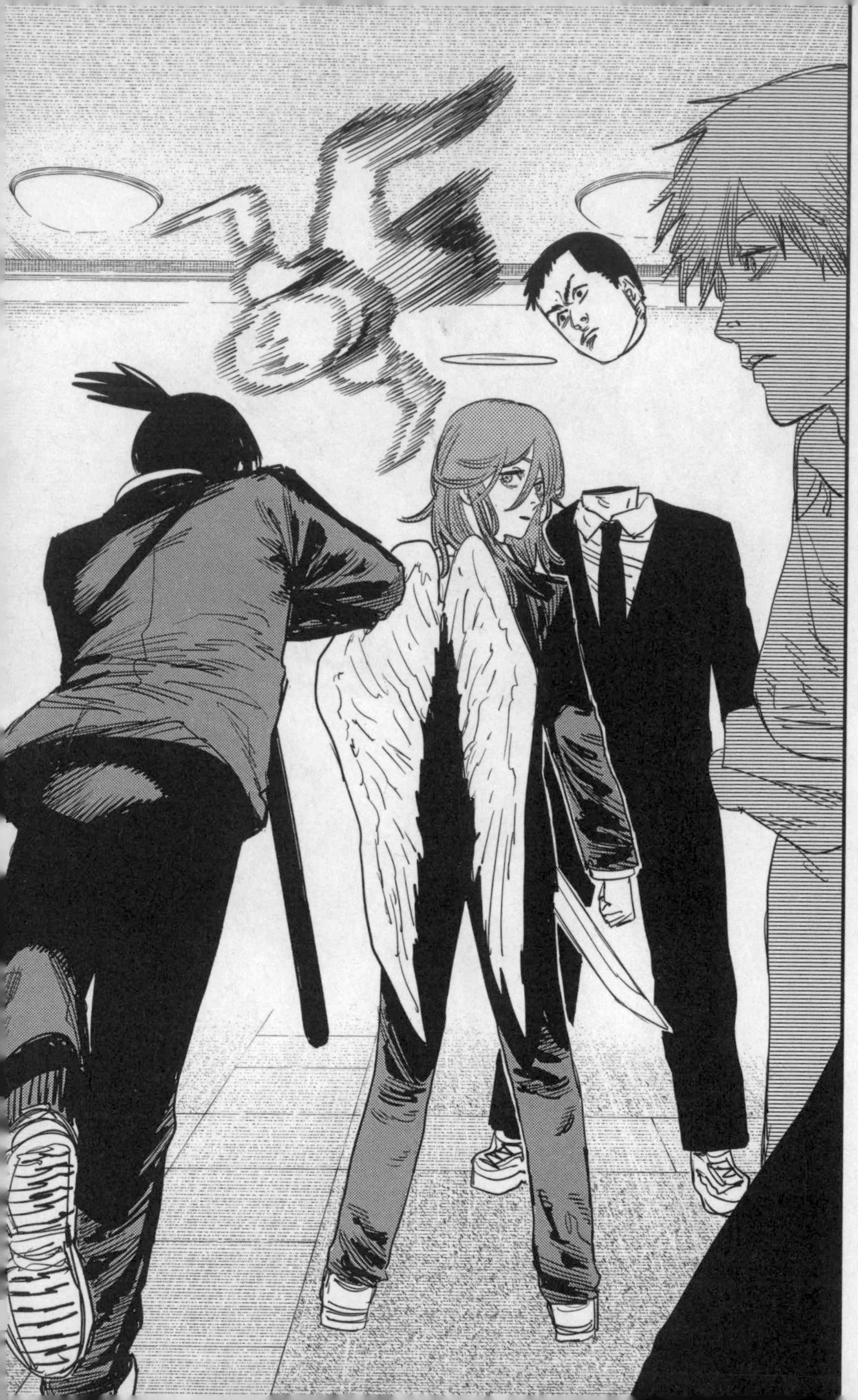

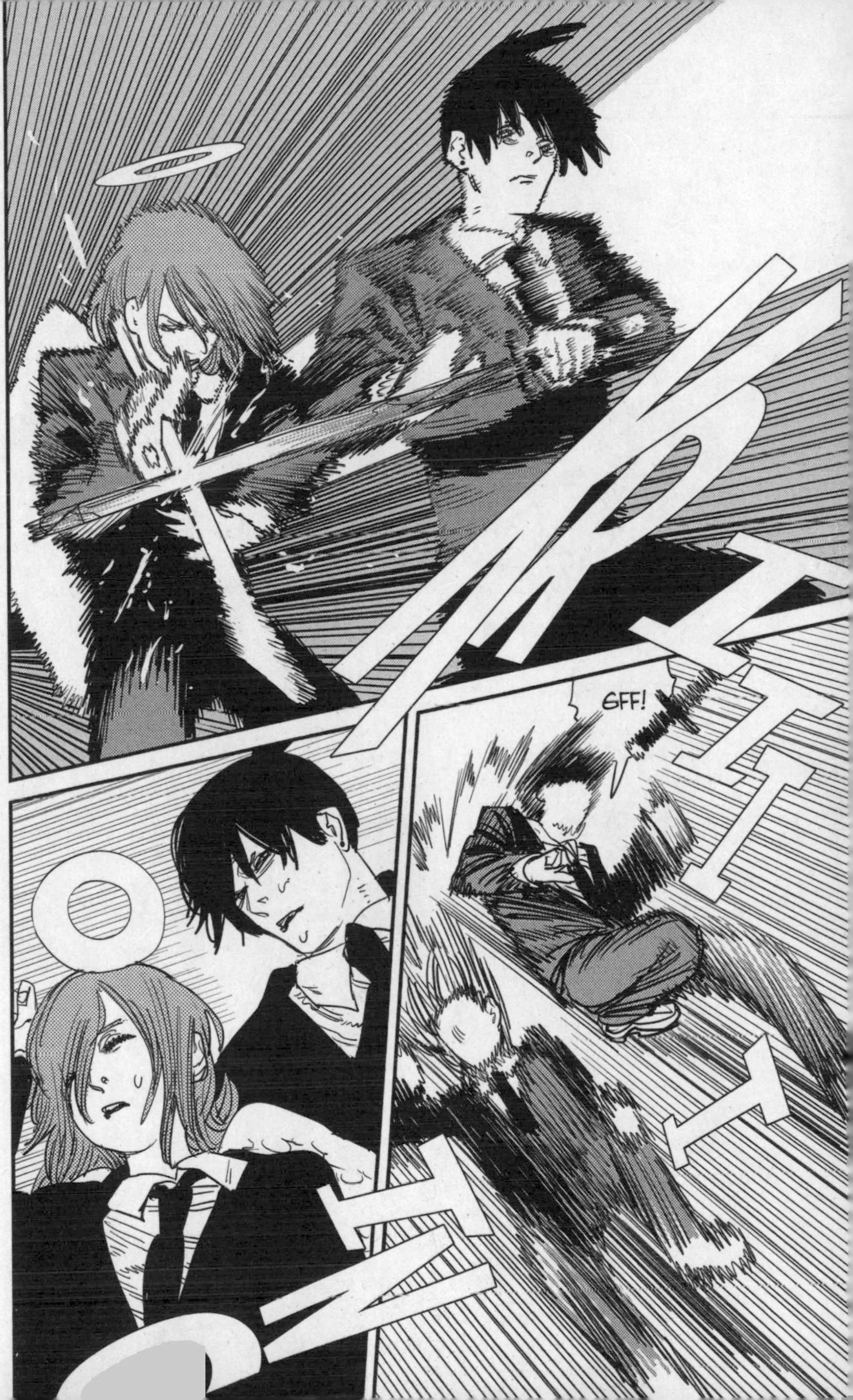
GFF!

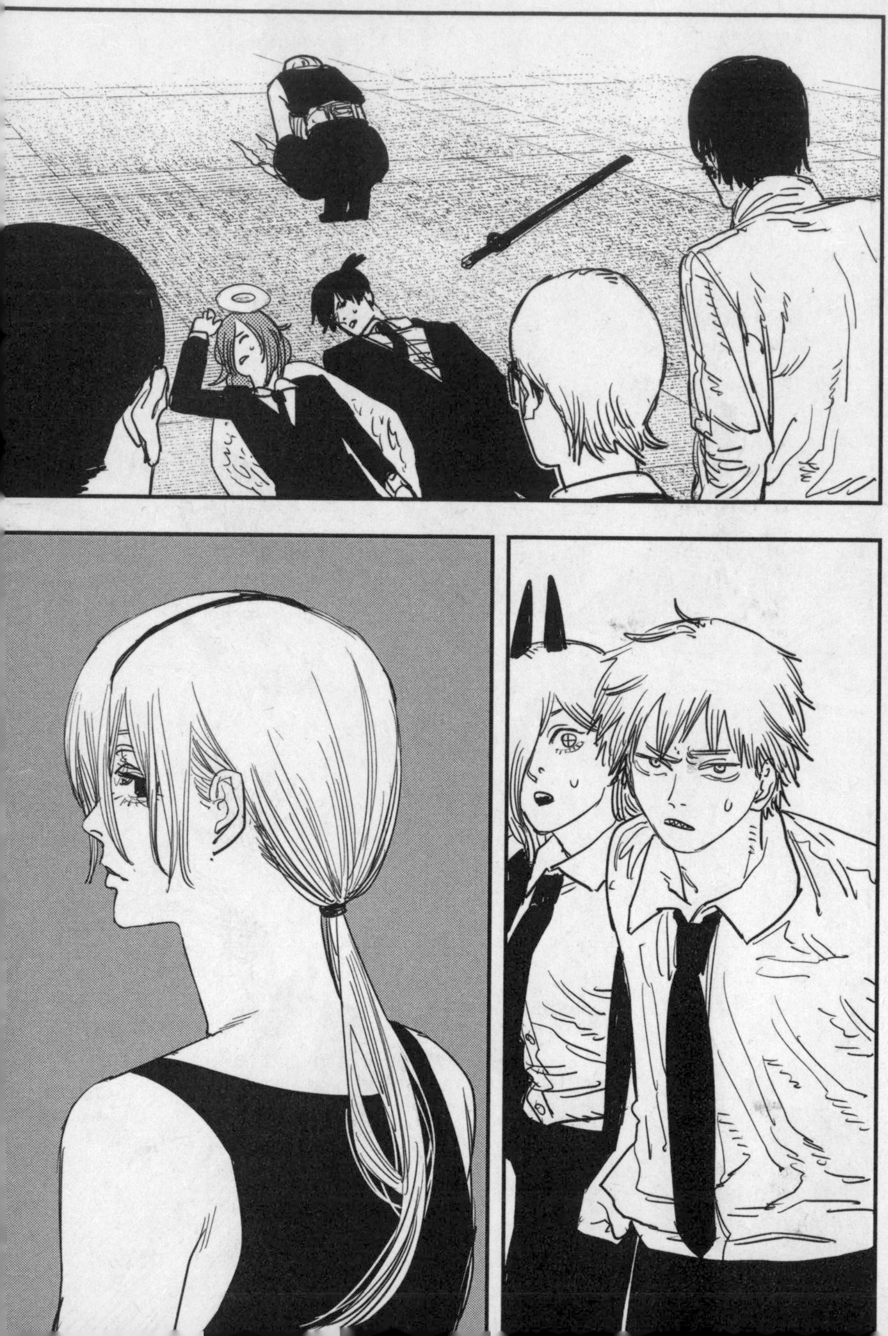

Chain saw man

# Chapter 61: News Reporter

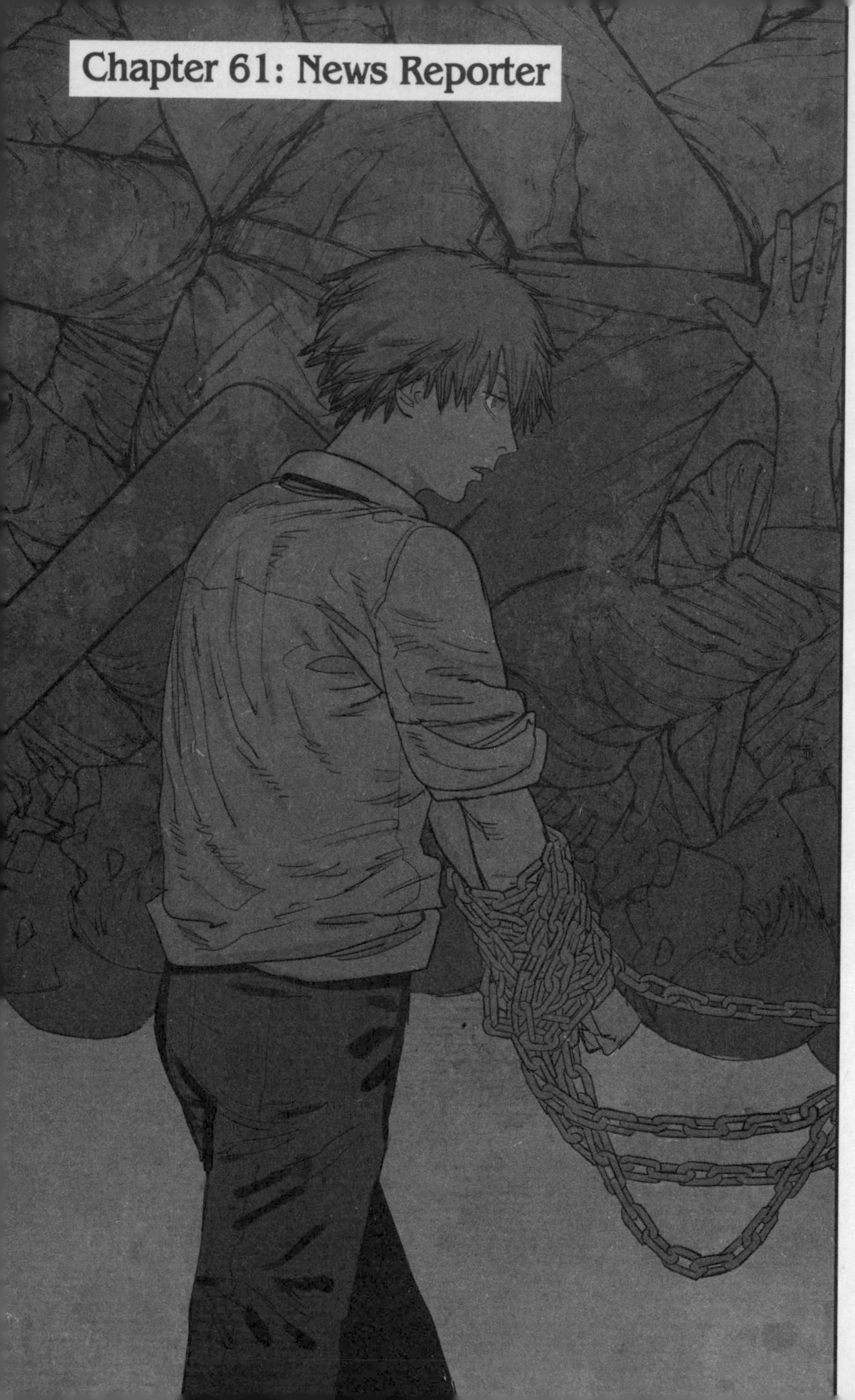

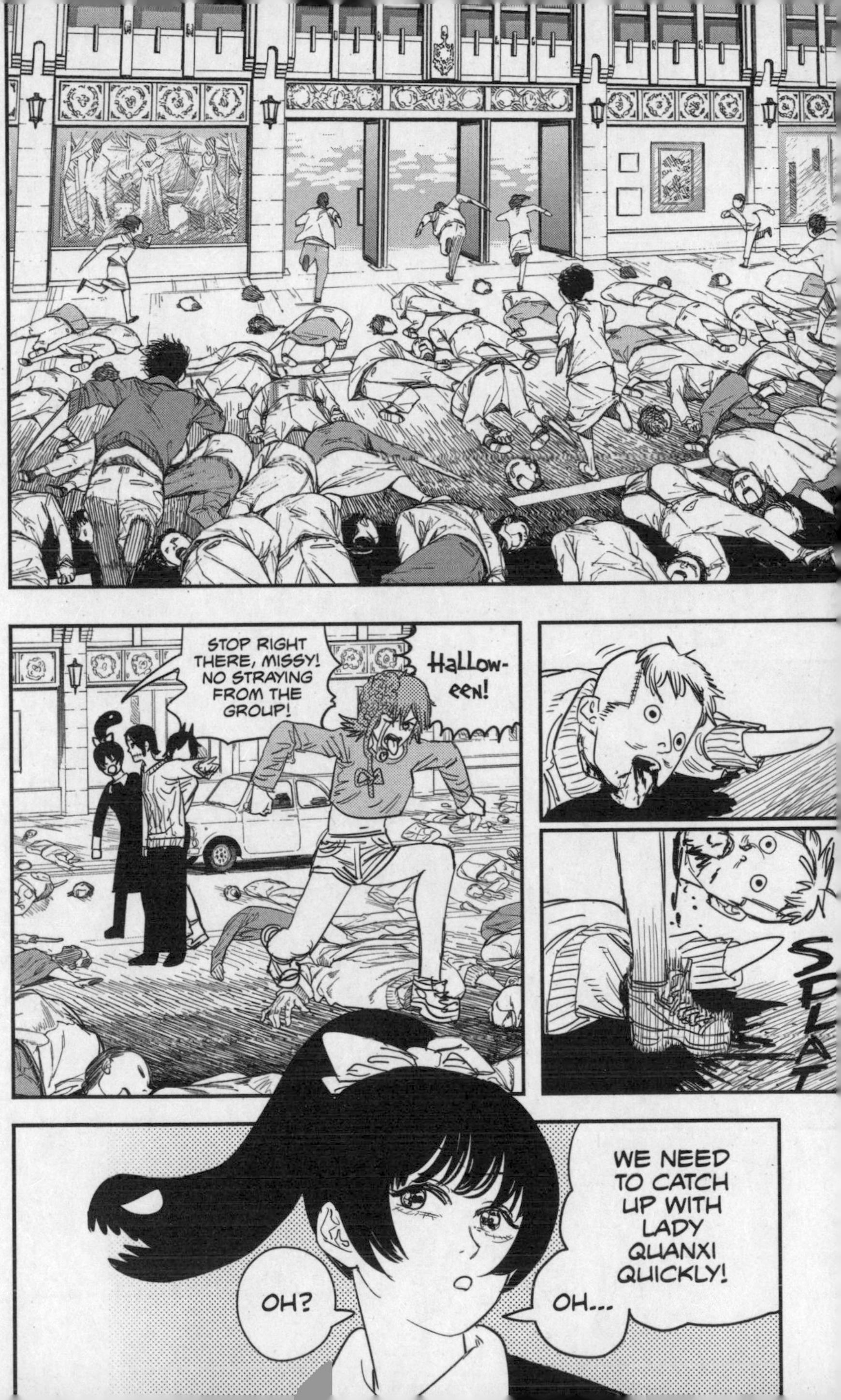
SPLAT
Hallow-een!
STOP RIGHT THERE, MISSY! NO STRAYING FROM THE GROUP!
WE NEED TO CATCH UP WITH LADY QUANXI QUICKLY!
OH...
OH?

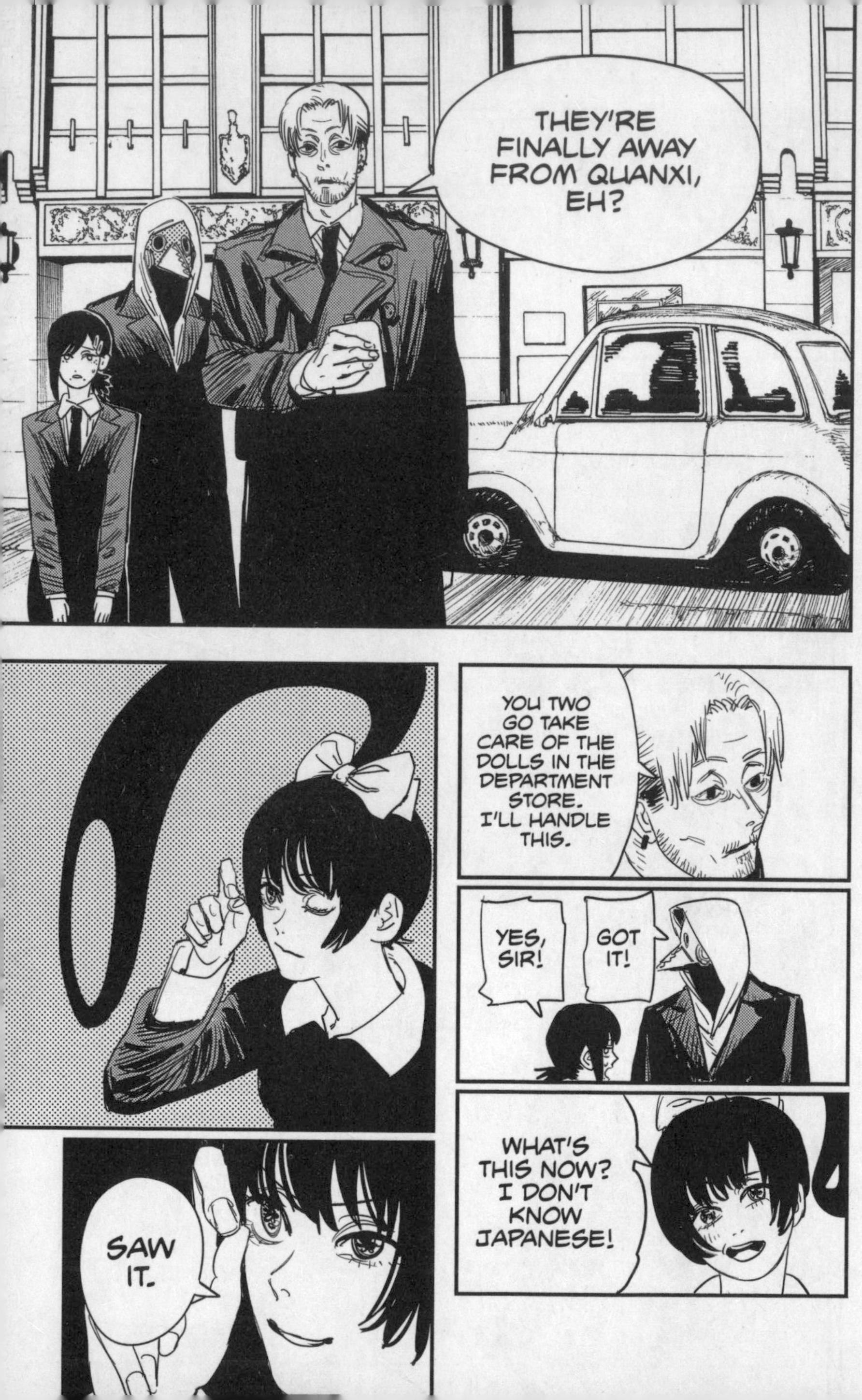
THEY'RE FINALLY AWAY FROM QUANXI, EH?
YOU TWO GO TAKE CARE OF THE DOLLS IN THE DEPARTMENT STORE. I'LL HANDLE THIS.
GOT IT!
YES, SIR!
WHAT'S THIS NOW? I DON'T KNOW JAPANESE!
SAW IT.

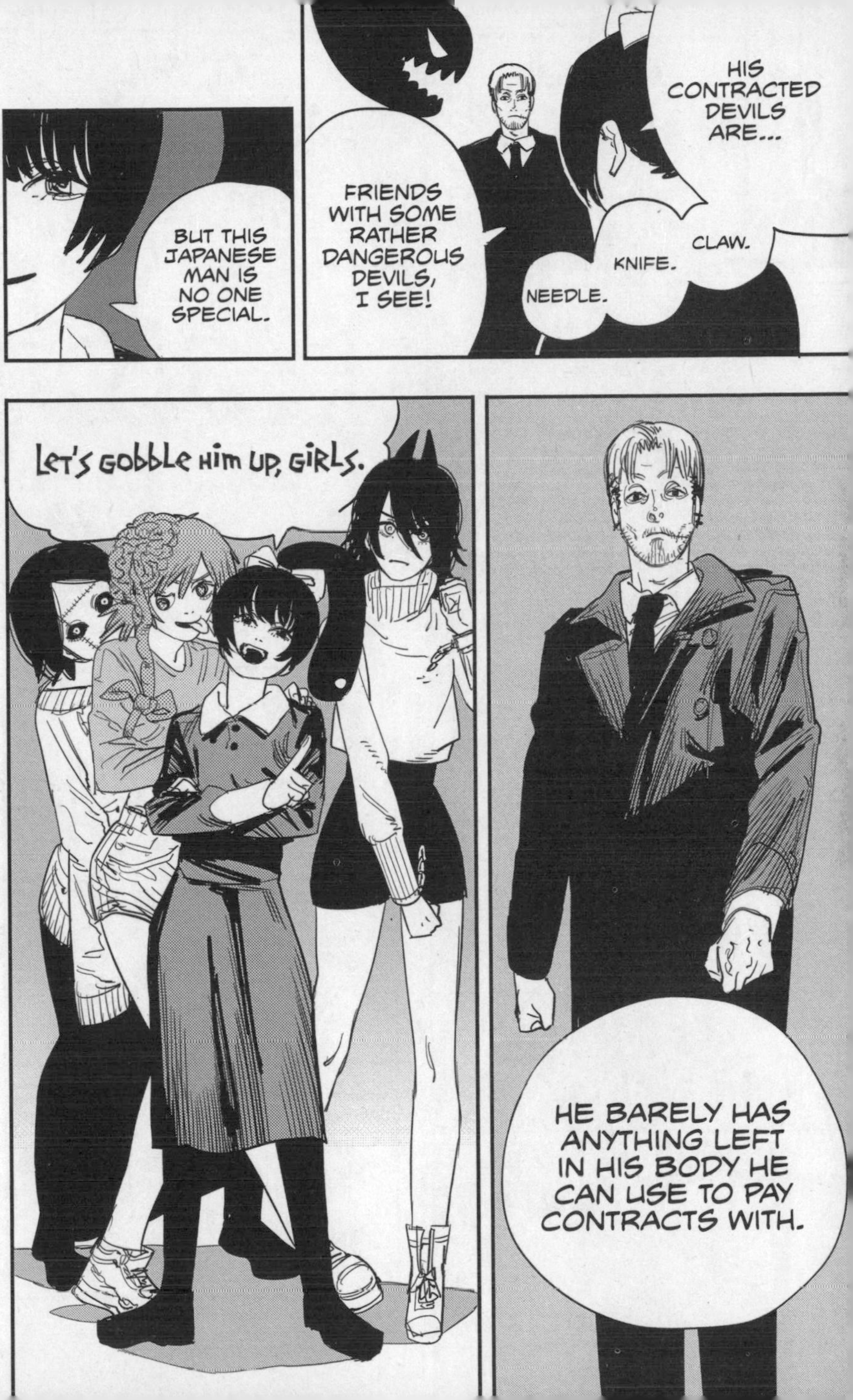
HIS CONTRACTED DEVILS ARE...
CLAW.
KNIFE.
NEEDLE.
FRIENDS WITH SOME RATHER DANGEROUS DEVILS, I SEE!
BUT THIS JAPANESE MAN IS NO ONE SPECIAL.
HE BARELY HAS ANYTHING LEFT IN HIS BODY HE CAN USE TO PAY CONTRACTS WITH.
Let's gobble him up, girls.

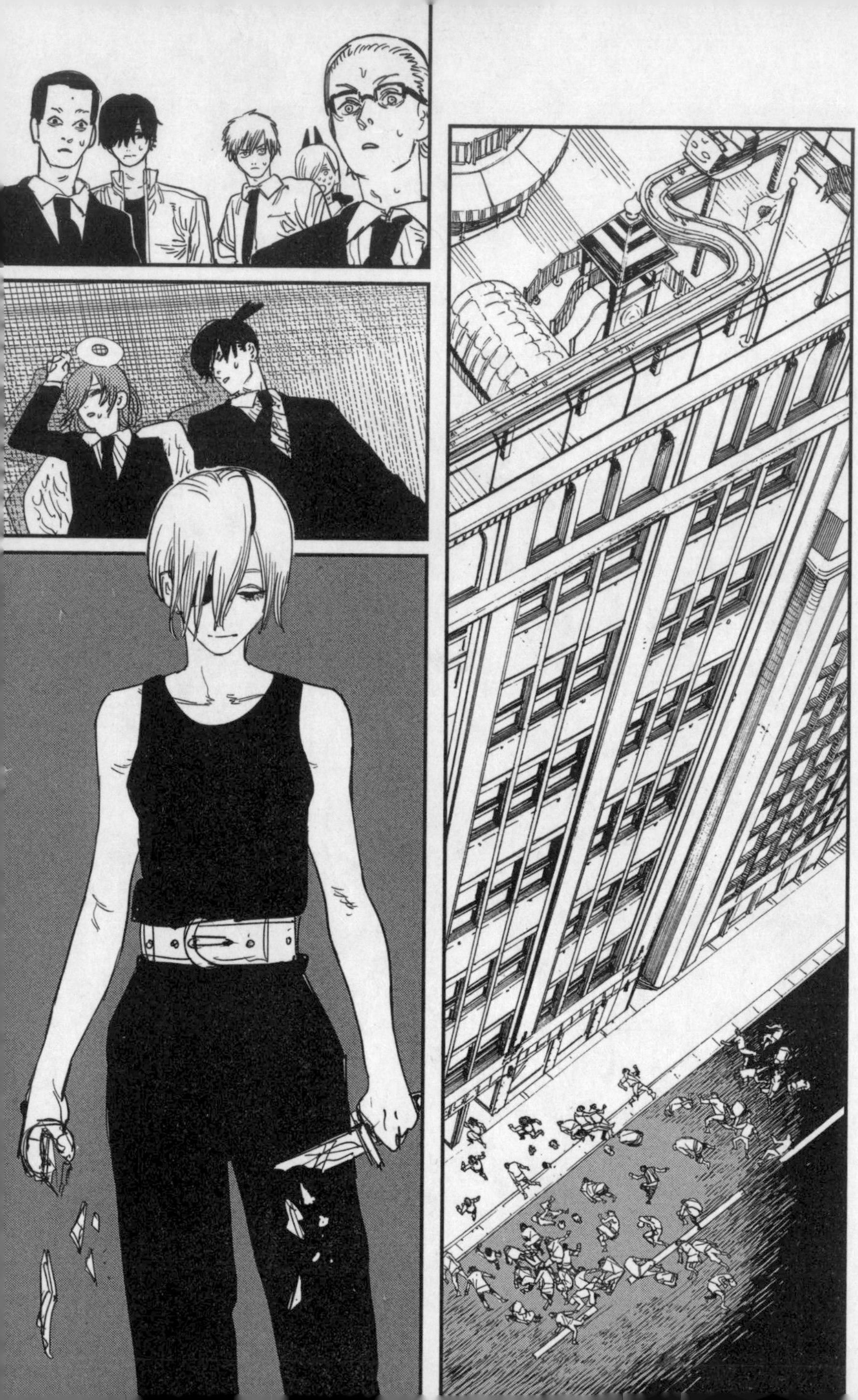

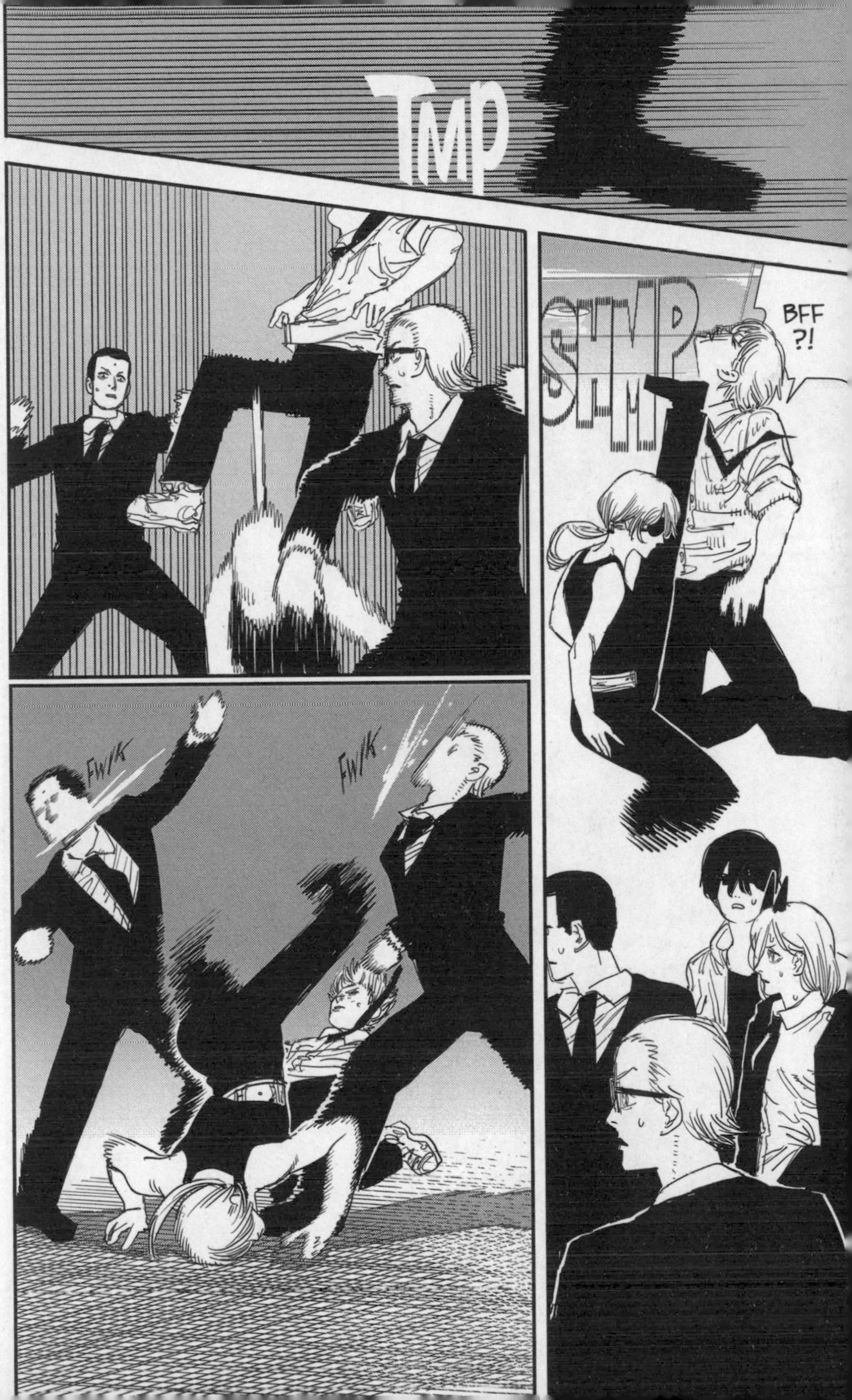
TMP
SHMP
BFF ?!
FWIK
FWIK

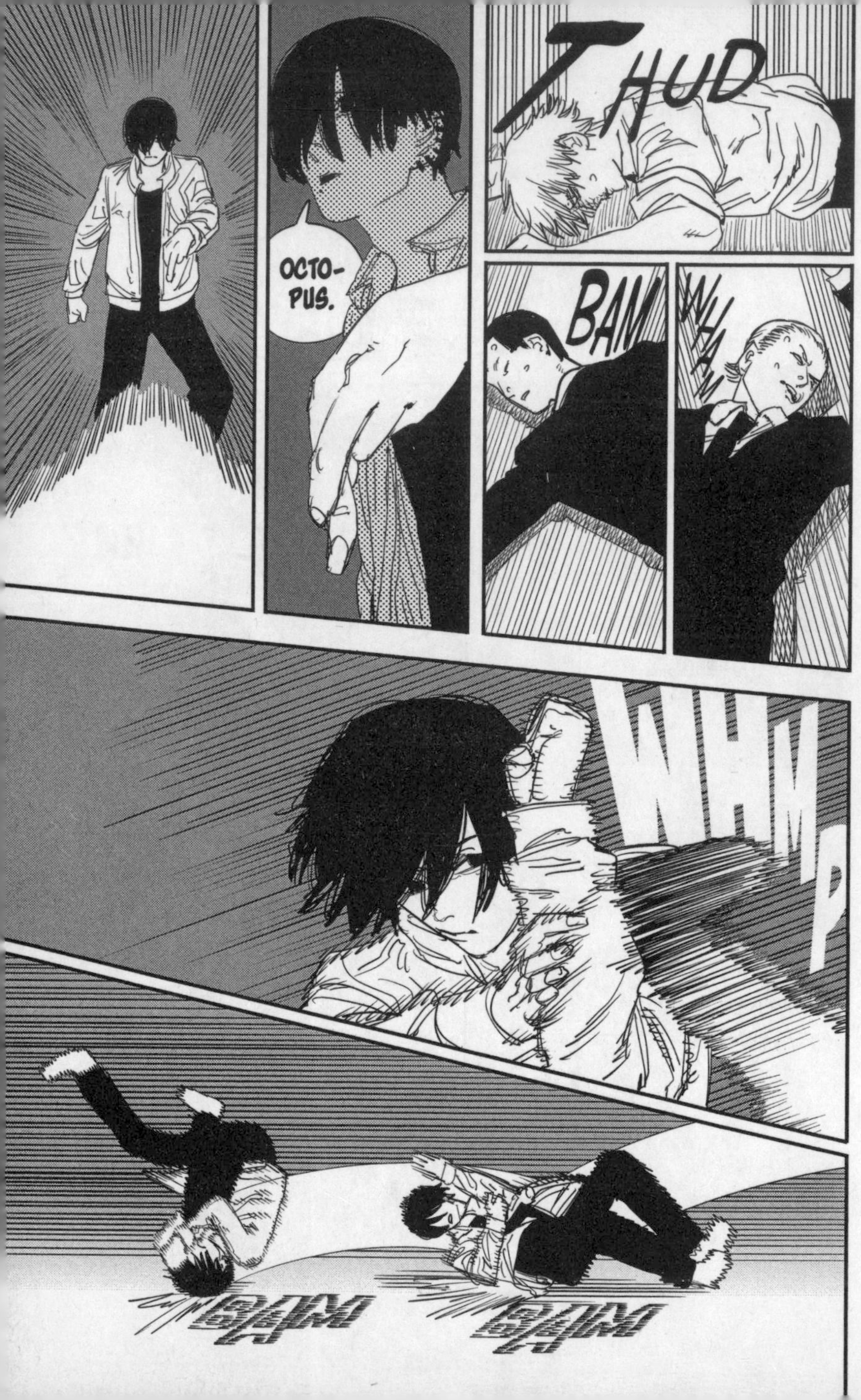
THUD
WHAM
BAM
OCTO-
PUS.
WHMP

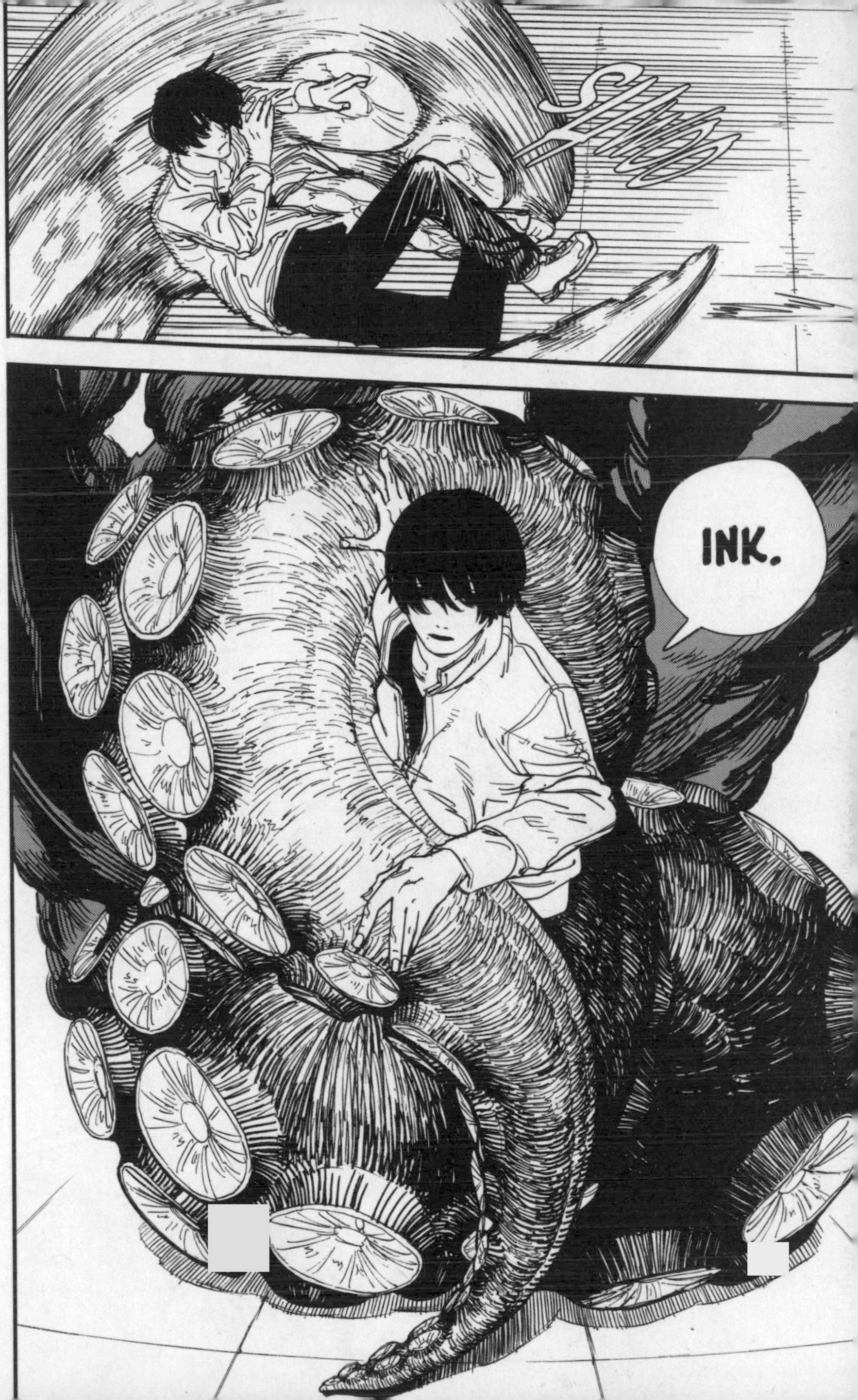
INK.

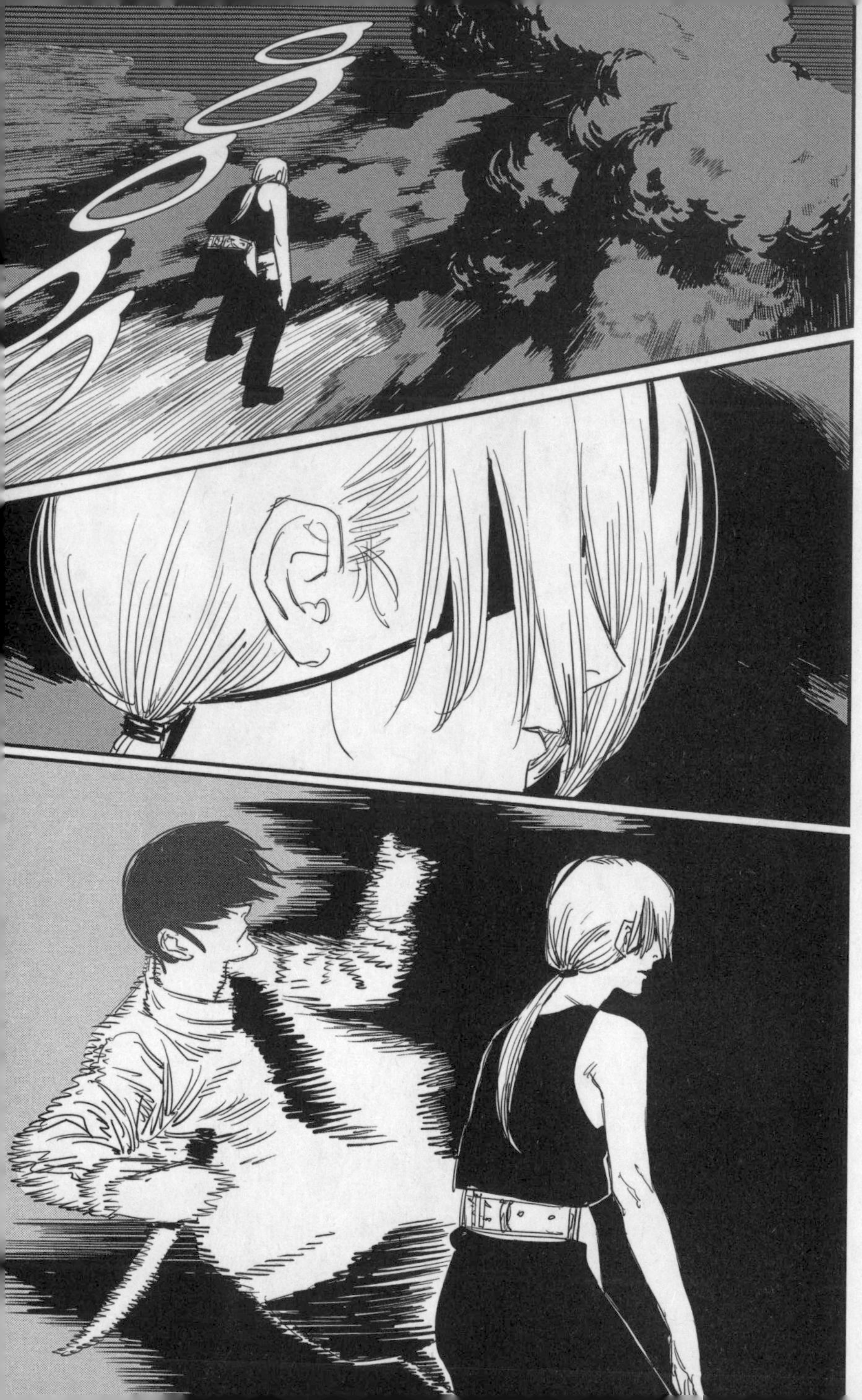

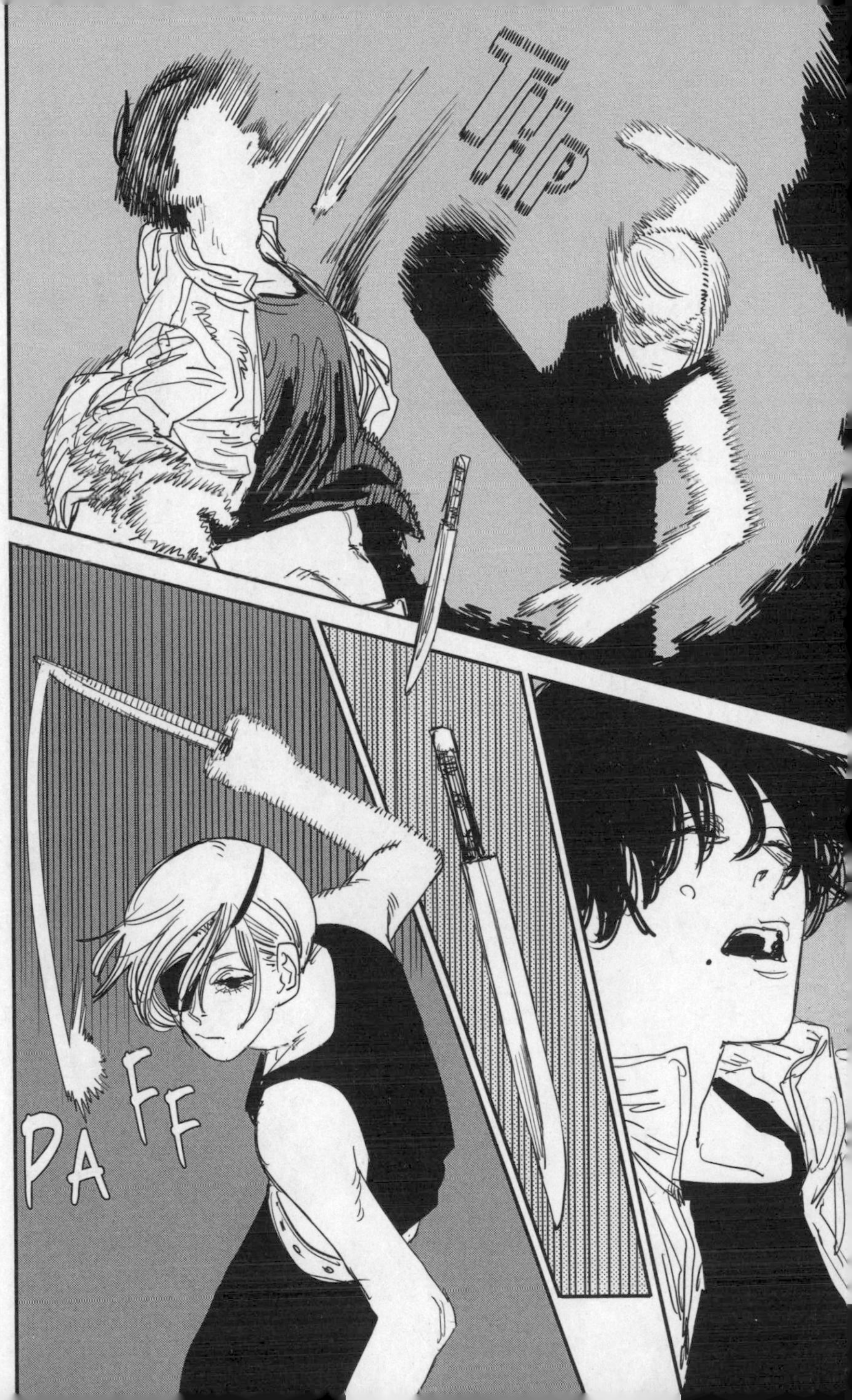
THP
PAFF

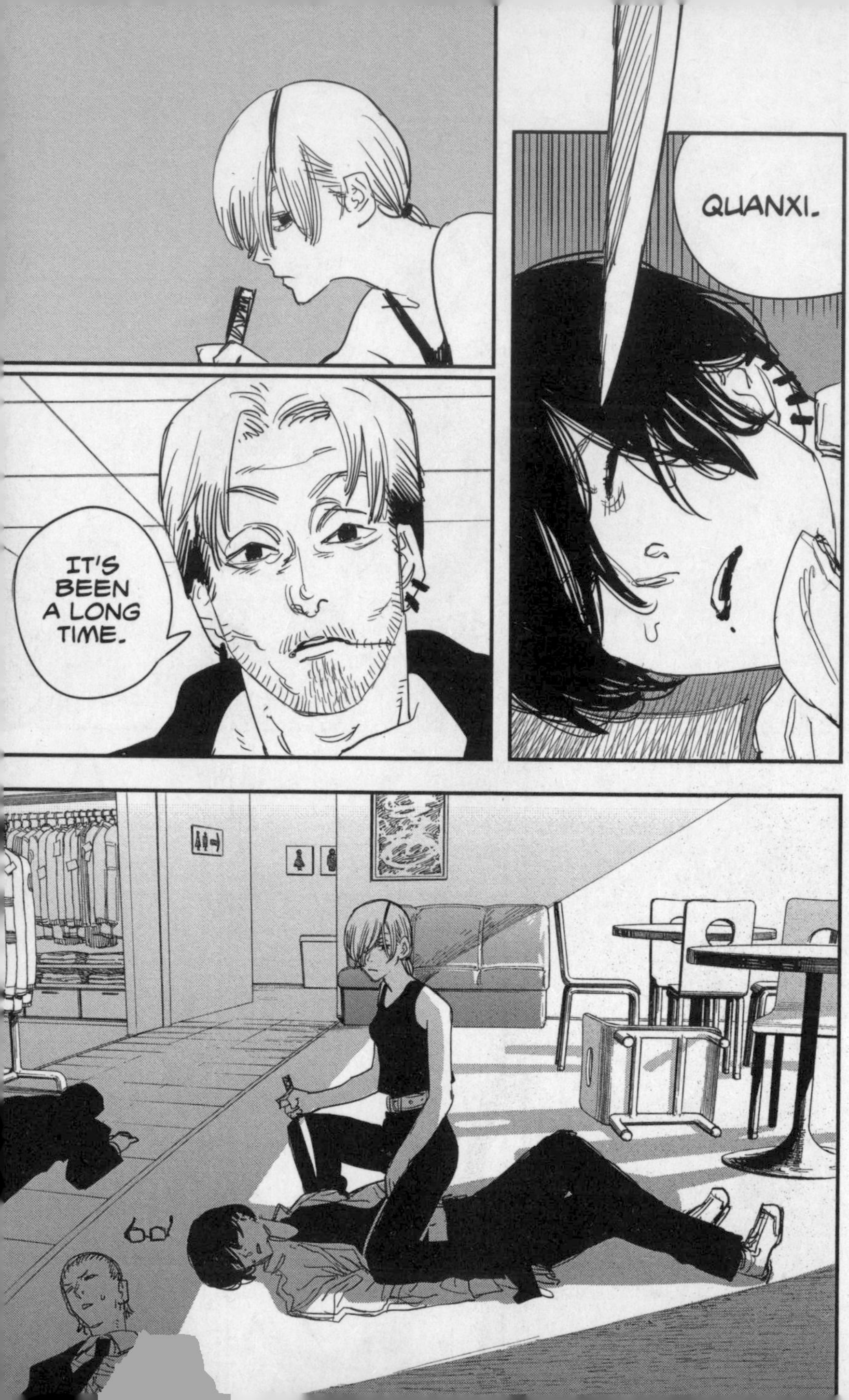
QUANXI.
IT'S BEEN A LONG TIME.

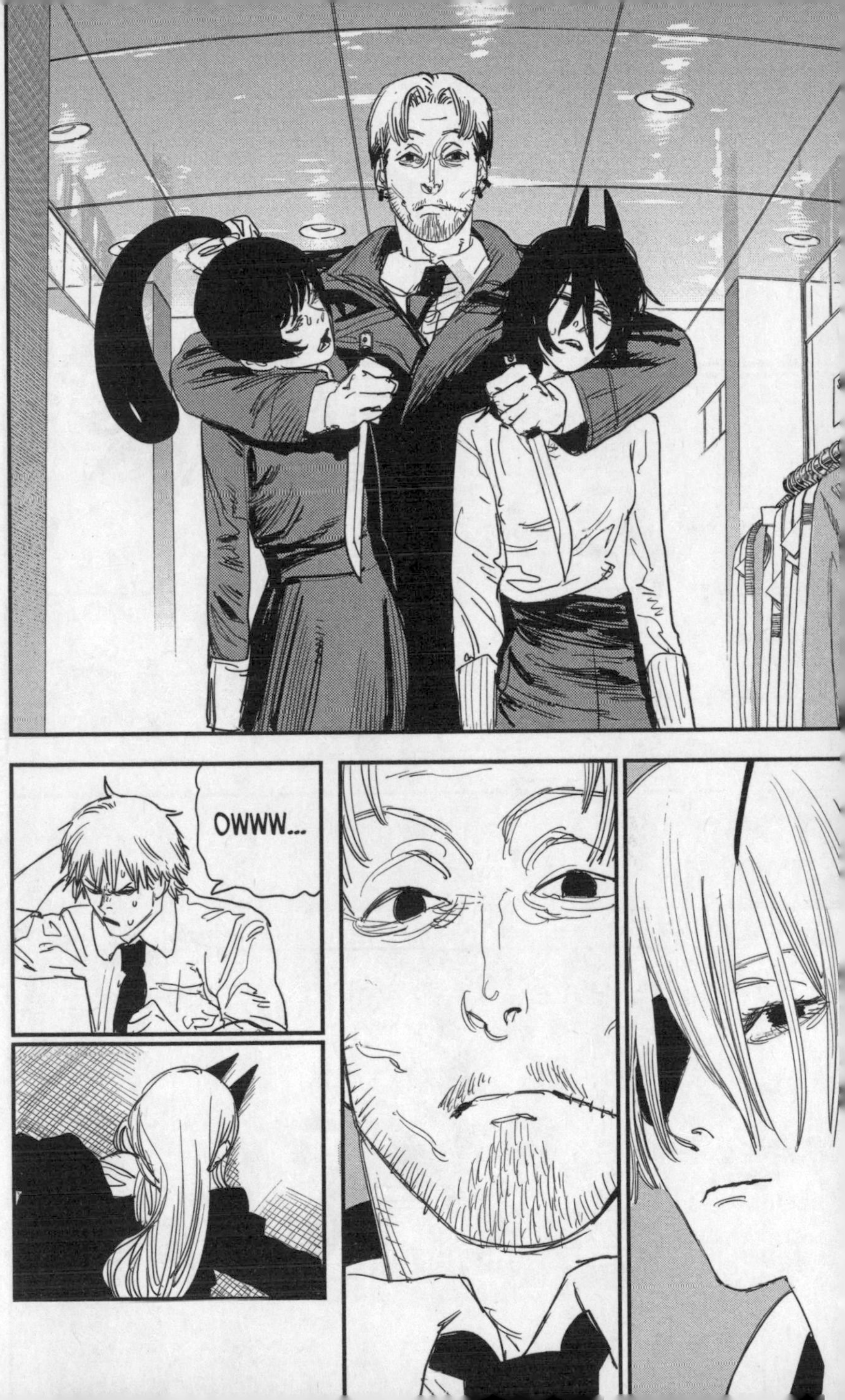
OWWW...

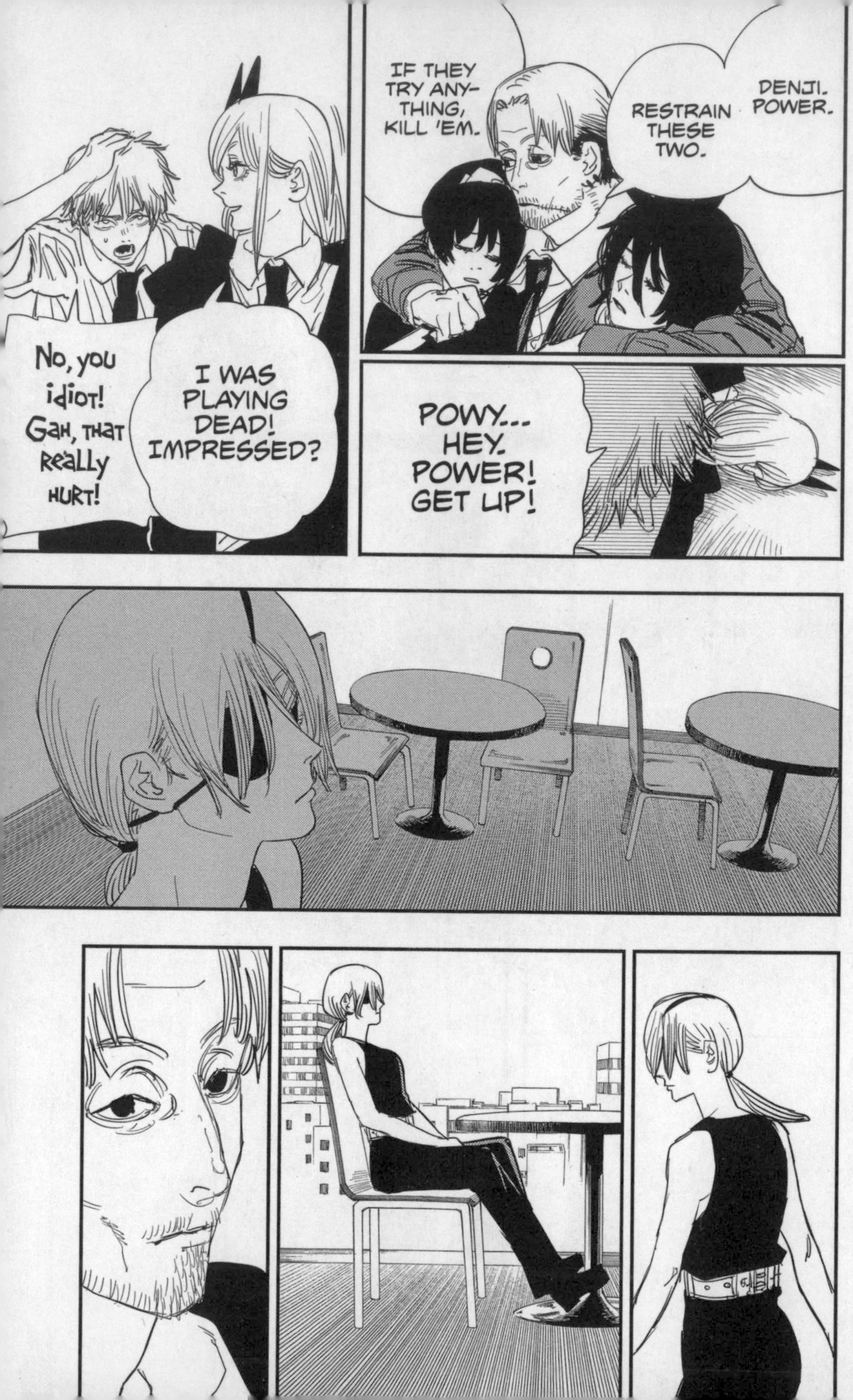
DENJI. POWER.
RESTRAIN THESE TWO.
IF THEY TRY ANYTHING, KILL 'EM.
POWY... HEY. POWER! GET UP!
I WAS PLAYING DEAD! IMPRESSED?
No, you idiot! Gah, that really hurt!

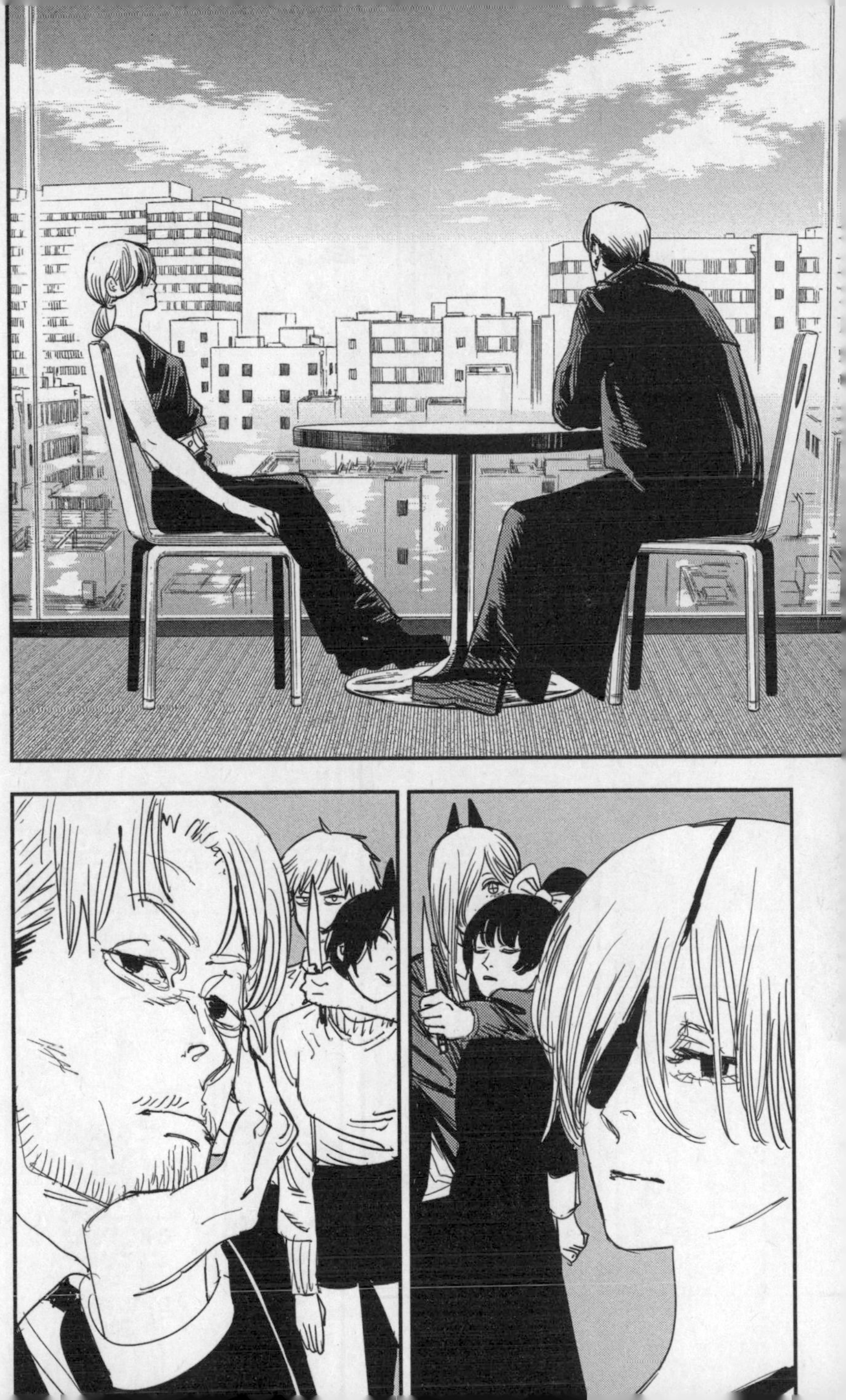

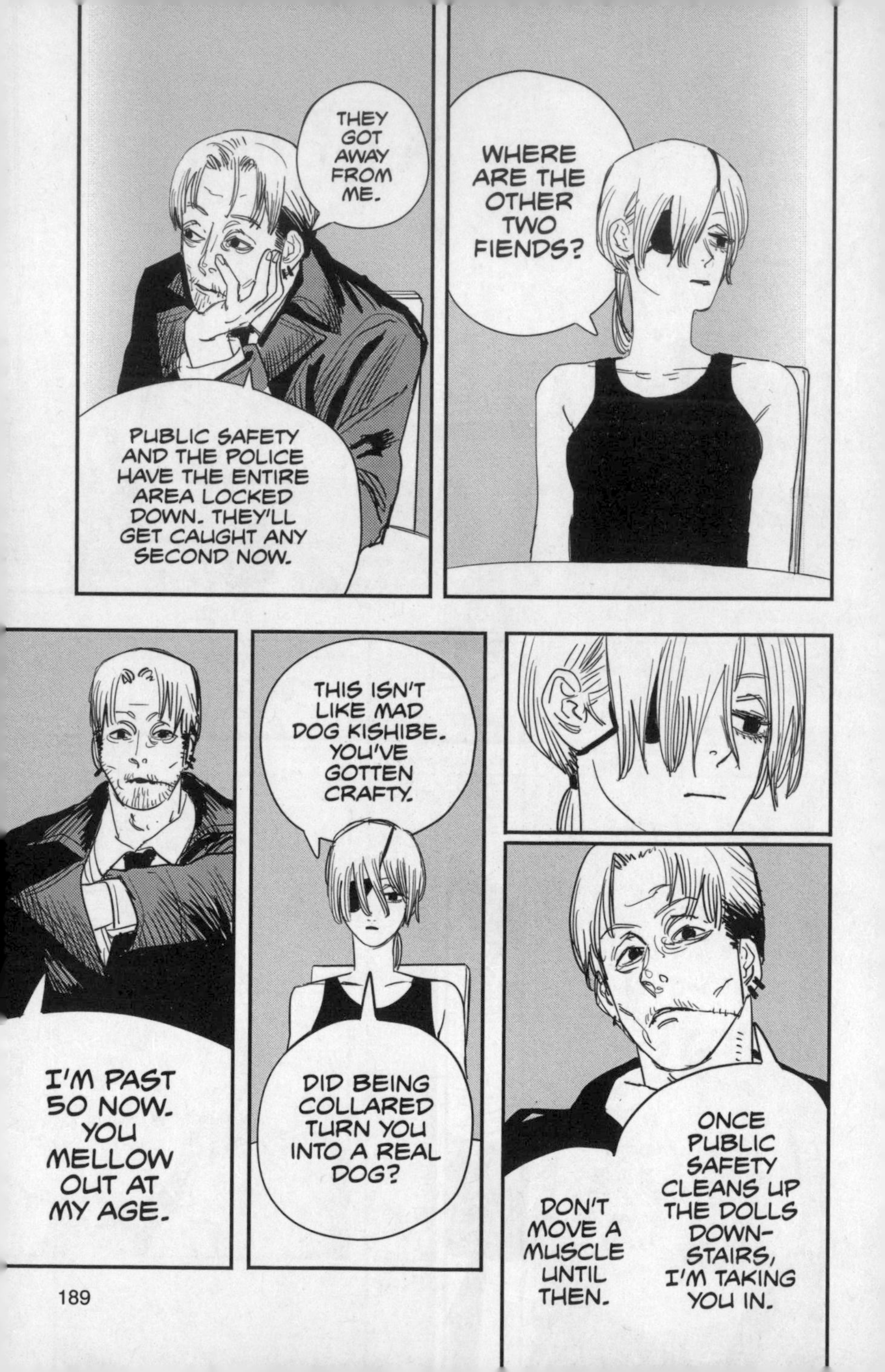
WHERE ARE THE OTHER TWO FIENDS?
THEY GOT AWAY FROM ME.
PUBLIC SAFETY AND THE POLICE HAVE THE ENTIRE AREA LOCKED DOWN. THEY'LL GET CAUGHT ANY SECOND NOW.
ONCE PUBLIC SAFETY CLEANS UP THE DOLLS DOWN-STAIRS, I'M TAKING YOU IN.
DON'T MOVE A MUSCLE UNTIL THEN.
THIS ISN'T LIKE MAD DOG KISHIBE. YOU'VE GOTTEN CRAFTY.
DID BEING COLLARED TURN YOU INTO A REAL DOG?
I'M PAST 50 NOW. YOU MELLOW OUT AT MY AGE.

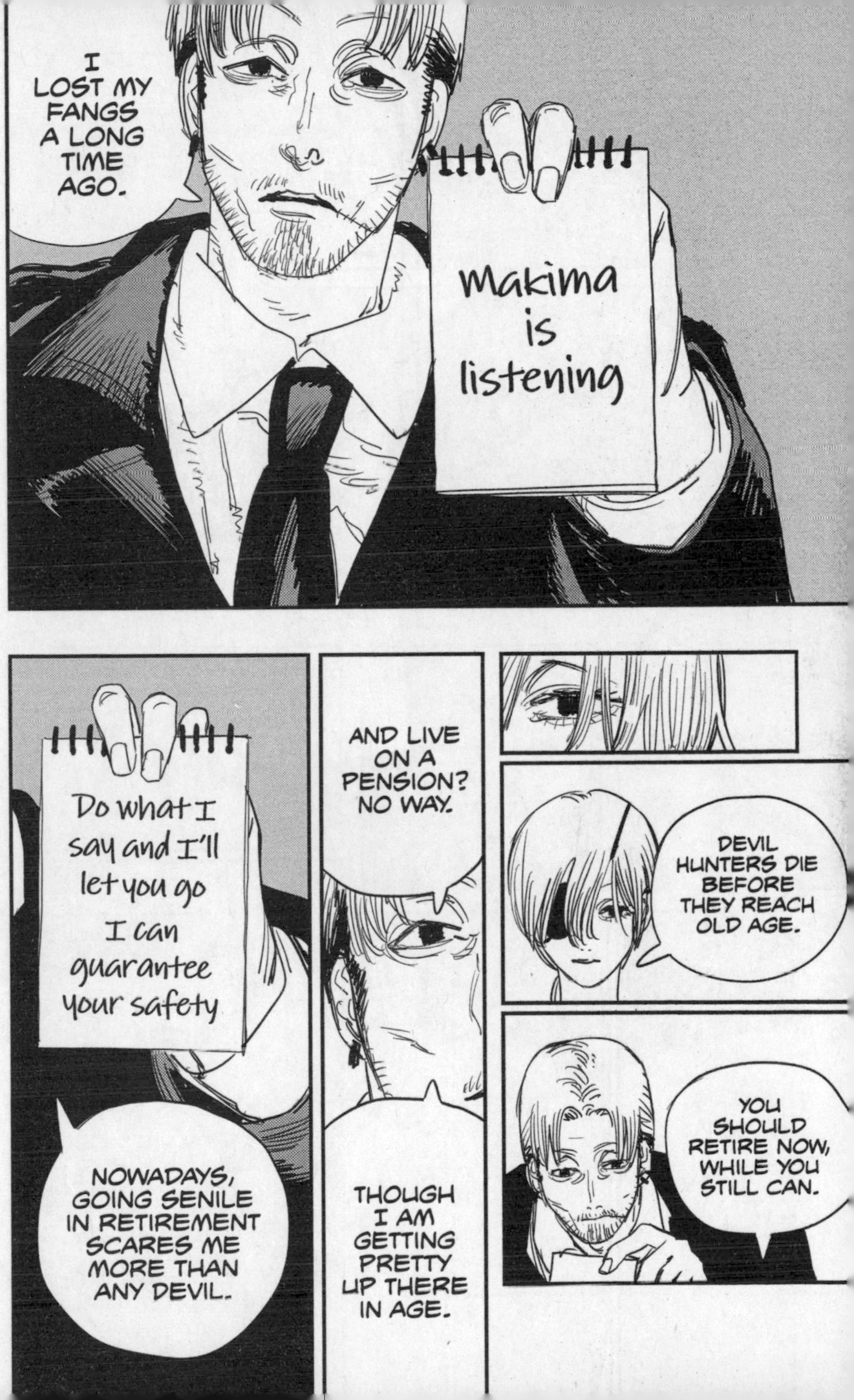
I LOST MY FANGS A LONG TIME AGO.
Makima is listening
DEVIL HUNTERS DIE BEFORE THEY REACH OLD AGE.
YOU SHOULD RETIRE NOW, WHILE YOU STILL CAN.
AND LIVE ON A PENSION? NO WAY.
THOUGH I AM GETTING PRETTY UP THERE IN AGE.
Do what I say and I'll let you go I can guarantee your safety
NOWADAYS, GOING SENILE IN RETIREMENT SCARES ME MORE THAN ANY DEVIL.

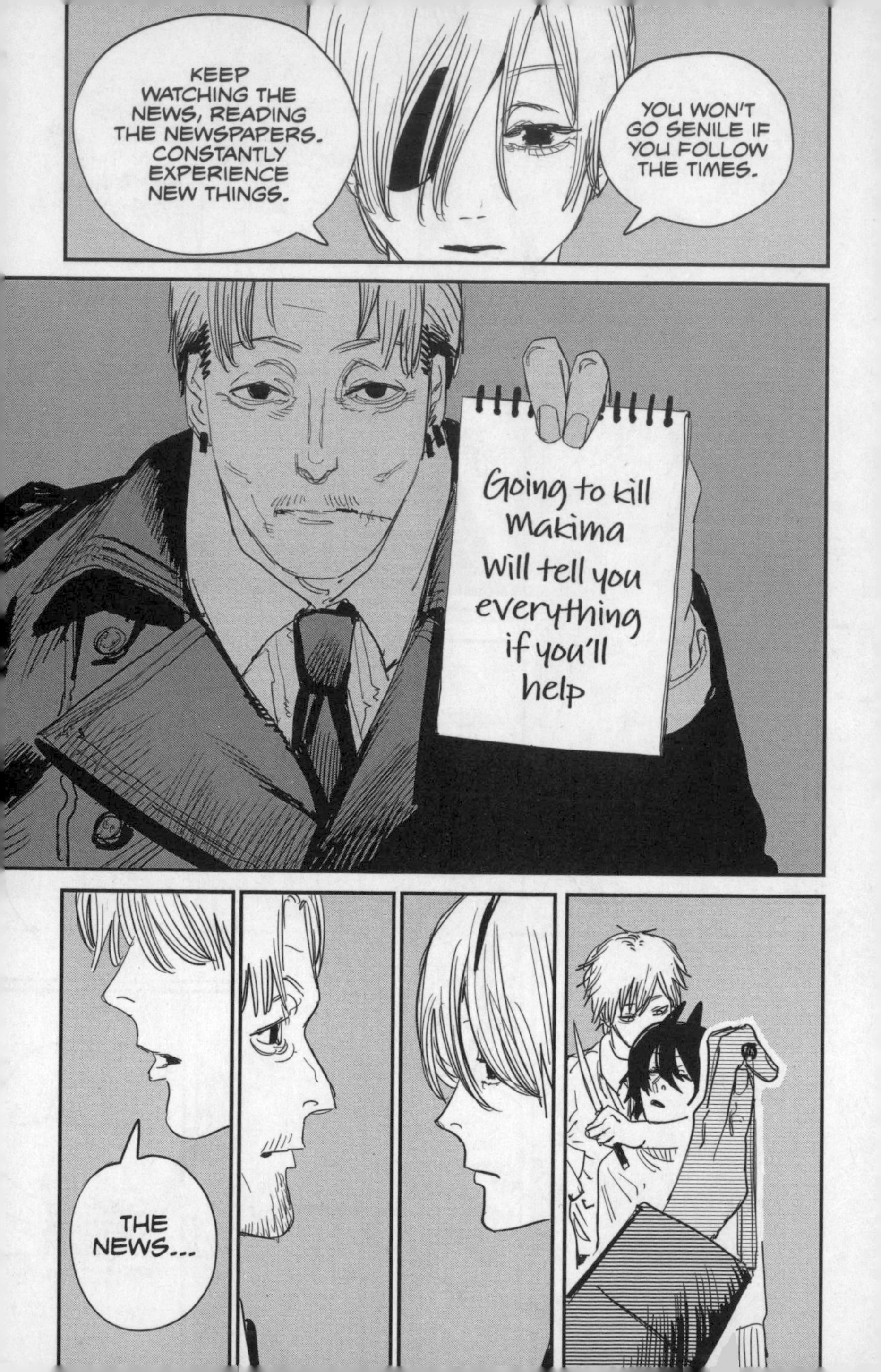
YOU WON'T GO SENILE IF YOU FOLLOW THE TIMES.
KEEP WATCHING THE NEWS, READING THE NEWSPAPERS. CONSTANTLY EXPERIENCE NEW THINGS.
Going to kill Makima
Will tell you everything if you'll help
THE NEWS...

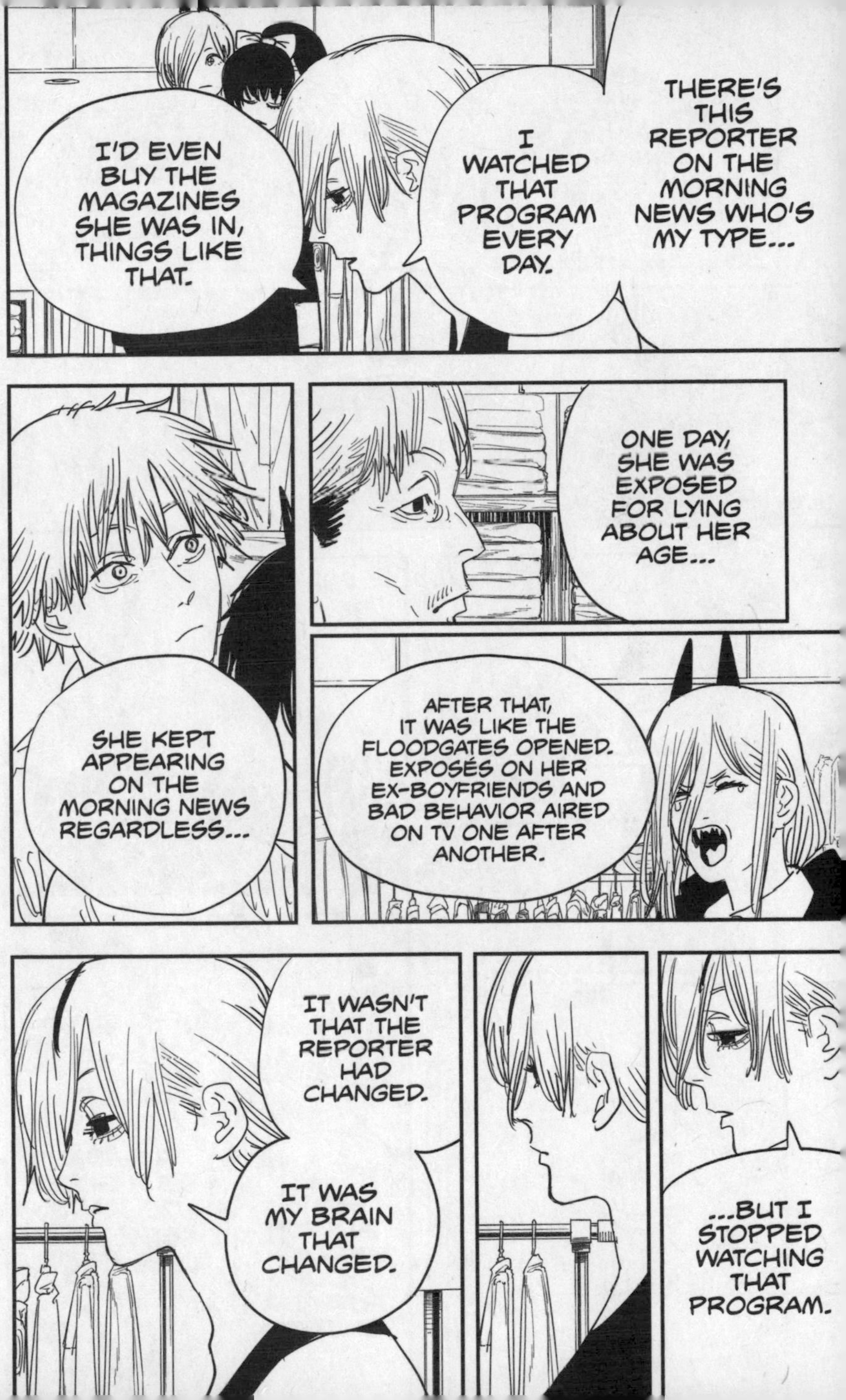
THERE'S THIS REPORTER ON THE MORNING NEWS WHO'S MY TYPE...
I WATCHED THAT PROGRAM EVERY DAY.
I'D EVEN BUY THE MAGAZINES SHE WAS IN, THINGS LIKE THAT.
ONE DAY, SHE WAS EXPOSED FOR LYING ABOUT HER AGE...
AFTER THAT, IT WAS LIKE THE FLOODGATES OPENED. EXPOSÉS ON HER EX-BOYFRIENDS AND BAD BEHAVIOR AIRED ON TV ONE AFTER ANOTHER.
SHE KEPT APPEARING ON THE MORNING NEWS REGARDLESS...
...BUT I STOPPED WATCHING THAT PROGRAM.
IT WASN'T THAT THE REPORTER HAD CHANGED.
IT WAS MY BRAIN THAT CHANGED.

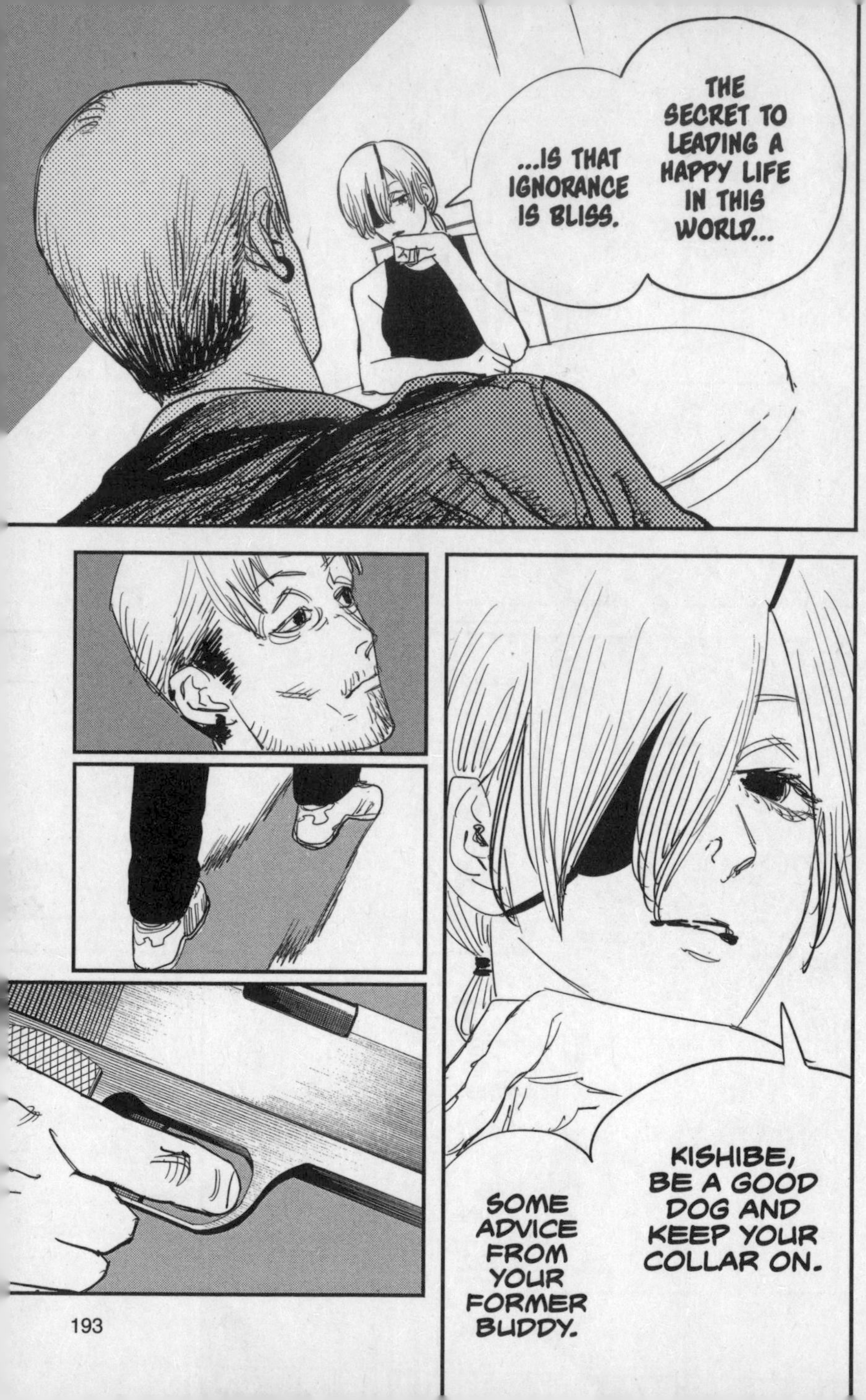
THE SECRET TO LEADING A HAPPY LIFE IN THIS WORLD...
...IS THAT IGNORANCE IS BLISS.
KISHIBE, BE A GOOD DOG AND KEEP YOUR COLLAR ON.
SOME ADVICE FROM YOUR FORMER BUDDY.

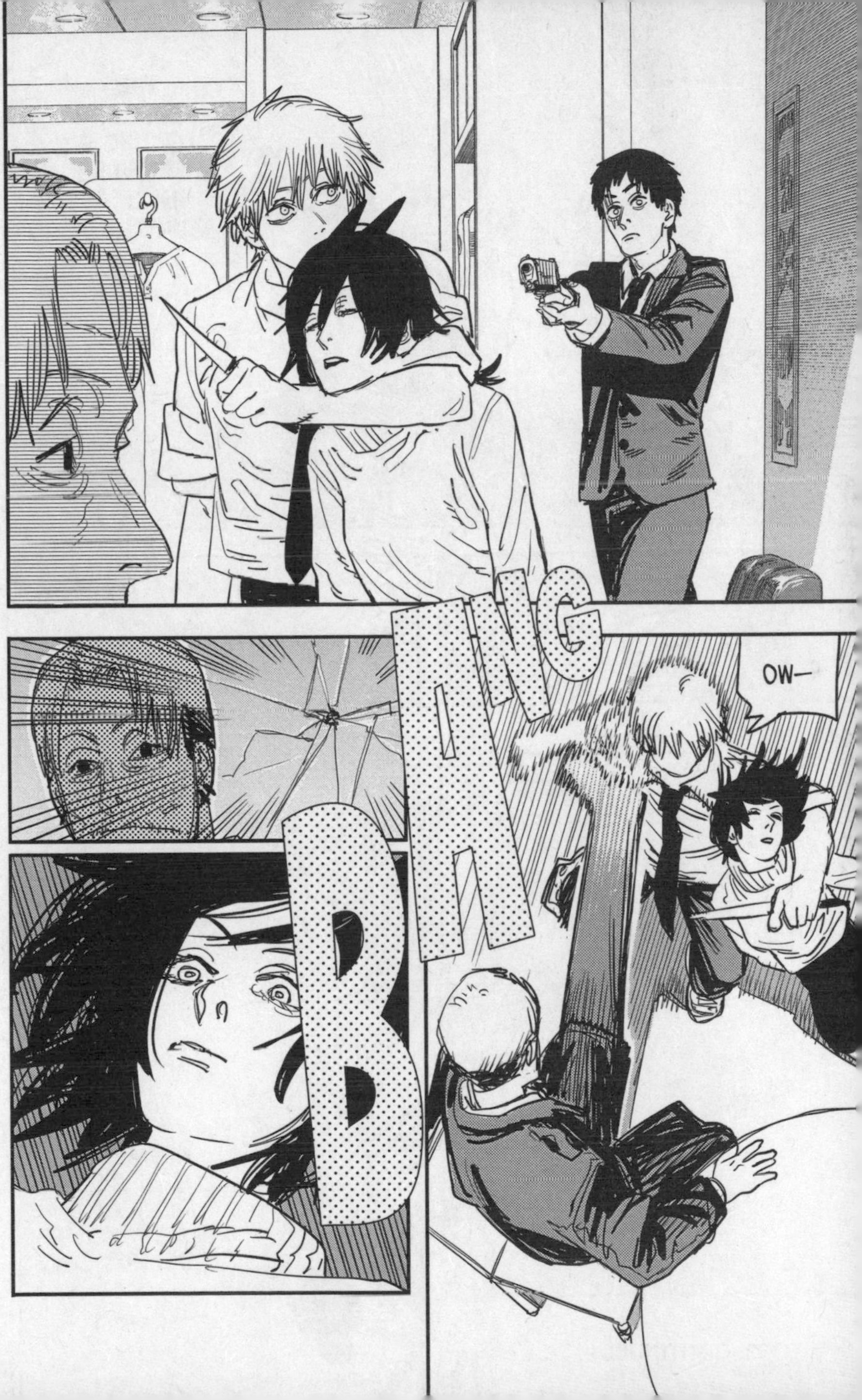
BANG
OW—

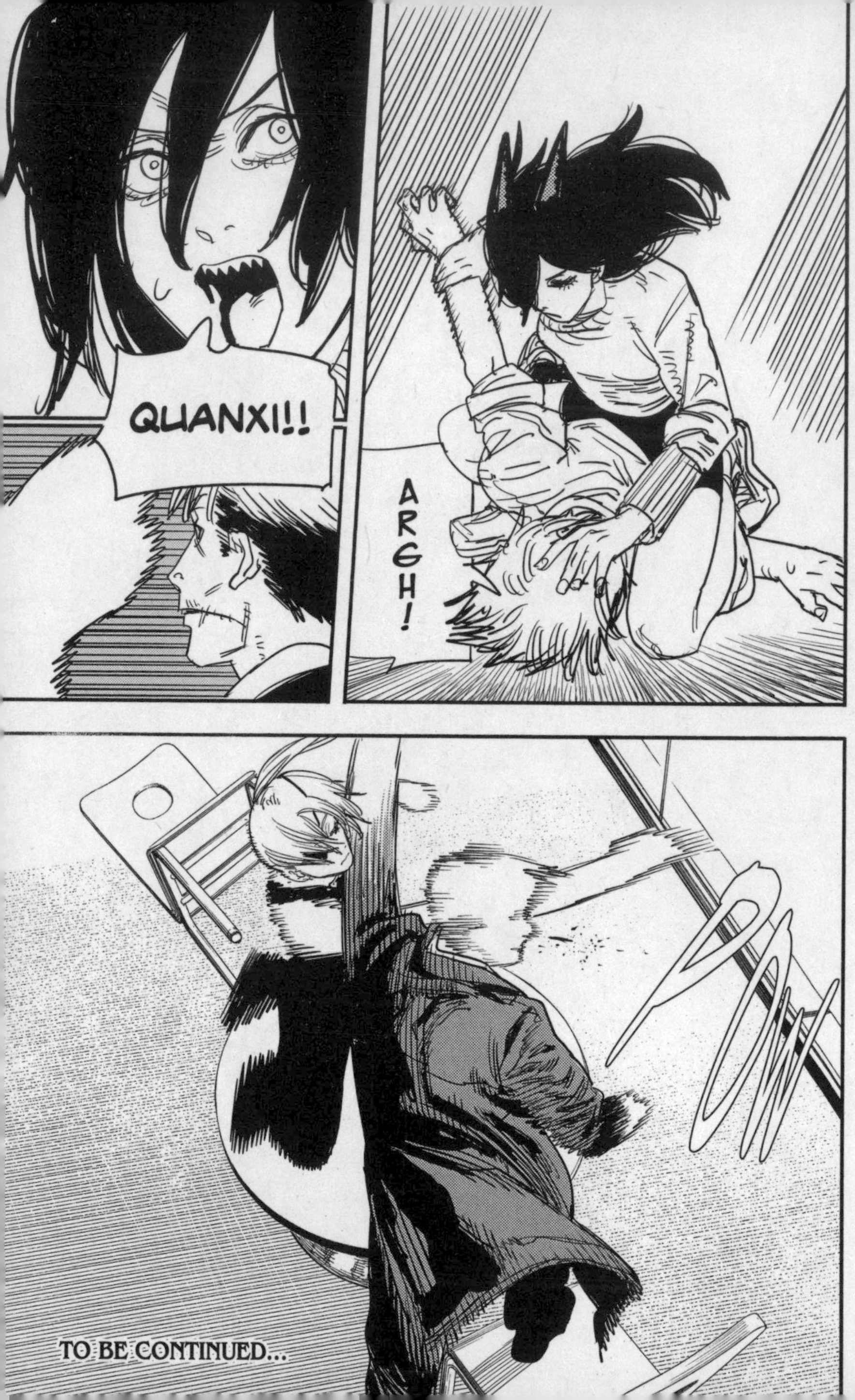
ARGH!
QUANXI!!
TO BE CONTINUED...

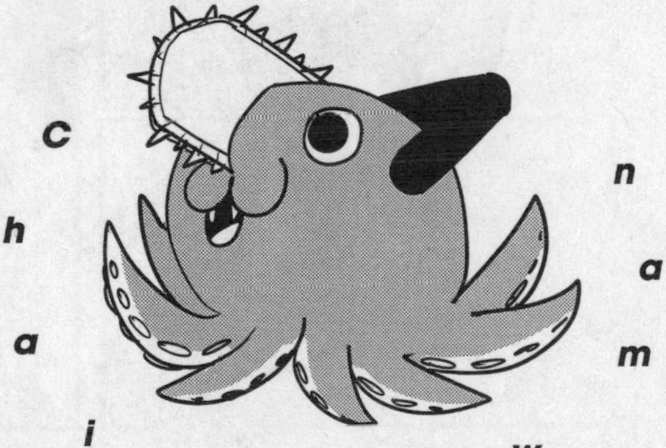
Chainsawman

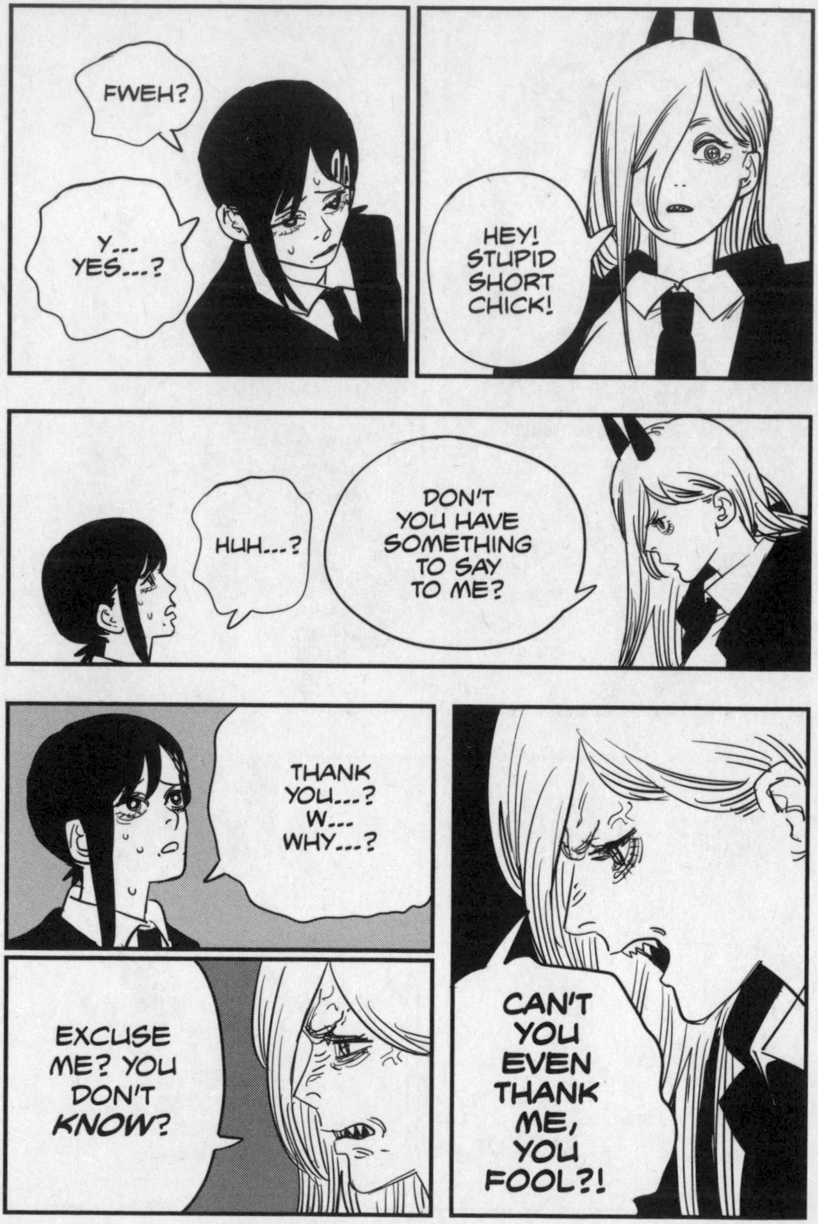
HEY! STUPID SHORT CHICK!
FWEH?
Y... YES...?
DON'T YOU HAVE SOMETHING TO SAY TO ME?
HUH...?
CAN'T YOU EVEN THANK ME, YOU FOOL?!
THANK YOU...? W... WHY...?
EXCUSE ME? YOU DON'T *KNOW*?

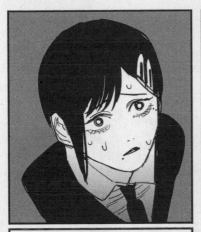

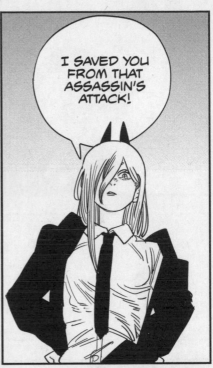

I SAVED YOU FROM THAT ASSASSIN'S ATTACK!
DON'T LISTEN TO THE THINGS POWER SAYS.
SHE'S CONVINCED HERSELF THAT SHE ACTUALLY SAVED YOU. SHE ALTERS THE MEMORIES IN HER BRAIN.
WHAT ARE YOU TALKING ABOUT...?
*THIS* IS WHAT JUST HAPPENED!

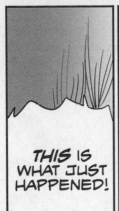

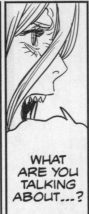

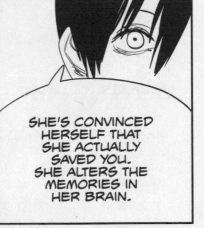

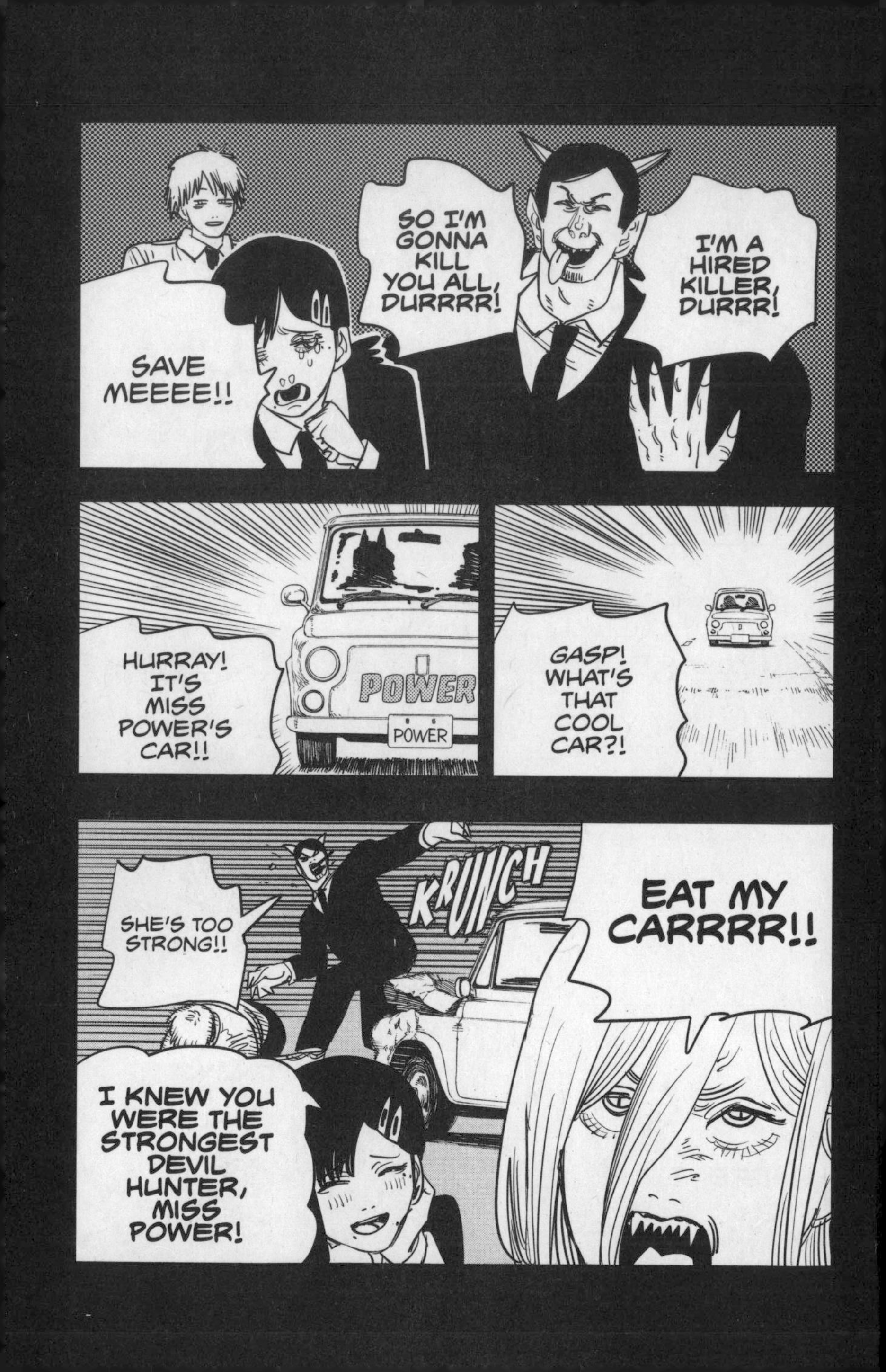
I'M A HIRED KILLER, DURRR!
SO I'M GONNA KILL YOU ALL, DURRRR!
SAVE MEEEEE!!
GASP! WHAT'S THAT COOL CAR?!
POWER
POWER
HURRAY! IT'S MISS POWER'S CAR!!
EAT MY CARRRR!!
KRUNCH
SHE'S TOO STRONG!!
I KNEW YOU WERE THE STRONGEST DEVIL HUNTER, MISS POWER!

# YOU'RE READING THE WRONG WAY!

# CHAINSAW MAN

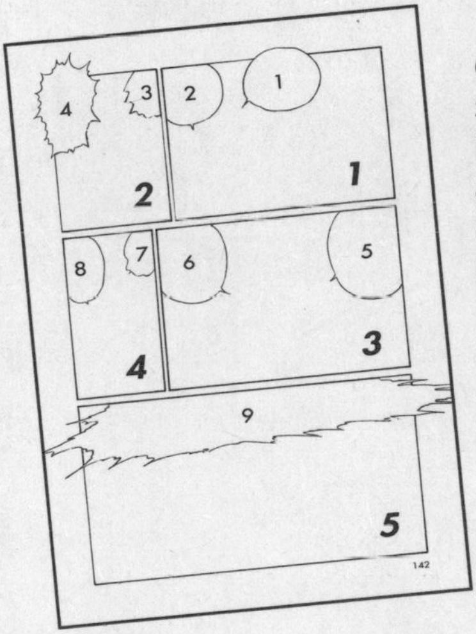

1
2
3
4
5
6
7
8
9
142


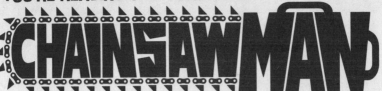

*Chainsaw Man* reads from right to left, starting in the upper-right corner. Japanese is read from right to left, meaning that action, sound effects and word-balloon order are completely reversed from English order.



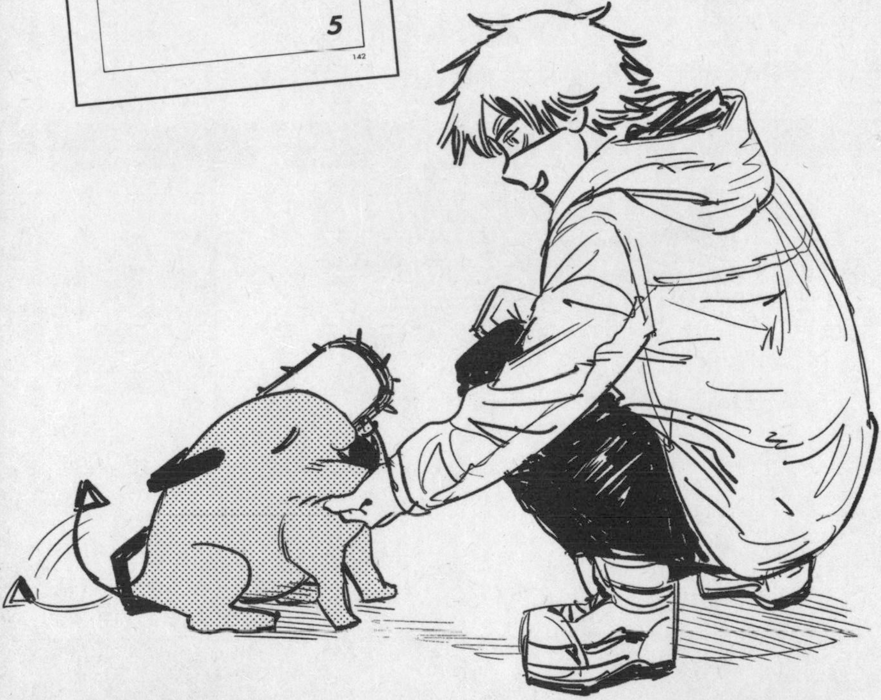